.NET Enterprise Development with VB.NET: From Design to Deployment

Matthew Reynolds

Karli Watson

with

Bill Forgey

Brian Patterson

Wrox Press Ltd. ®

.NET Enterprise Development with VB.NET: From Design to Deployment

Published by Wrox Press Ltd,
Arden House, 1102 Warwick Road, Acocks Green,
Birmingham, B27 6BH, UK
Printed in the USA
ISBN 1-861006-17-9

Trademark Acknowledgements

Credits

Authors
Matthew Reynolds
Karli Watson

Additional Material
Bill Forgey
Brian Patterson

Technical Architect
David Mercer

Lead Technical Editor
Matt Cumberlidge

Technical Editor
Richard Deeson

Managing Editor
Louay Fatoohi

Author Agent
Charlotte Smith

Project Administrators
Cathy Succamore
Beth Sacks

Cover
Chris Morris

Index
John Collin
Adrian Axinte
Bill Johncocks

Project Manager
Claire Robinson

Technical Reviewers
Maxime Bombardier
Andreas Christiansen
Susan Connery
Mitch Denny
Slavomir Furman
John Godfrey
Mark Horner
Don Lee
Johan Normén
Phil Powers-DeGeorge
Matthew Rabinowitz
Ranga Raghunathan
Larry Schoeneman
Keyur Shah
Marc H. Simkin
Chris Thibodeaux

Production Coordinator
Natalie O'Donnell

Illustrations
Abbie Forletta

Proof Readers
Chris Smith
Fiona Berryman

About the Authors

Matthew Reynolds

After working with Wrox Press on a number of projects since 1999, Matthew is now an in-house author for Wrox writing about and working with just about every aspect of the Microsoft .NET Framework. He's also a regular contributor to Wrox's *ASPToday*, *C#Today*, and Web Services Architect sites. He lives and works in North London and can be reached on matthewr@wrox.com.

> *For Fanjeev Sarin.*
>
> *Thanks very much to the following for their support and assistance in writing this book: Len, Edward, Darren, Alex, Jo, Tim, Clare, Martin, Niamh, Tom, Ollie, Amir, Gretchen, Ben, Brandon, Denise, Rob, Waggy, Mark, Elaine, James, Zoe, Faye, and Sarah. Thanks also go to my new friends at Wrox, including Charlotte, Laura, Karli, Dom S, Dom L, Ian, Kate, Joy, Pete, Helen, Vickie, John, Dave, Adam, Craig, Jake, Julian, and Paul.*

Karli Watson

Karli Watson is an in-house author for Wrox Press with a penchant for multicolored clothing. He started out with the intention of becoming a world famous nanotechnologist, so perhaps one day you might recognize his name as he receives a Nobel Prize. For now, though, Karli's computing interests include all things mobile, and upcoming technologies such as C#. He can often be found preaching about these technologies at conferences, as well as after hours in drinking establishments. Karli is also a snowboarding enthusiast, and wishes he had a cat.

> *Thanks go to the Wrox team, both for helping me get into writing, and then dealing with the results when I started. Finally, and most importantly, thanks to my wife, Donna, for continuing to put up with me.*

Bill Forgey

Bill is the Technical Lead in his current position, introducing project methodology, new technologies, standards, and training to development teams. He has spent some time consulting and has been exposed to technologies such as ASP, Delphi, Pascal, COM, C/C++, SQL, Java, ADO, Visual Basic, and now .NET. He also co-authored Professional VB.NET (Wrox Press) and Beginning Visual Basic .NET Databases (Wrox Press). Bill currently lives in Sacramento, California, and can be contacted via e-mail at bforgey@vbcentral.net.

Brian Patterson

Brian currently works for Affina, Inc. as a Technical Team Leader, where he is generally working with C++ on HP-UX or Windows development with any number of the Visual Studio languages. Brian wrote his first programming article at the age of 19 (1994) and has been writing for various programming publications ever since. Brian has co-authored several .NET related books including *Migrating to Visual Basic .NET* and *C# Bible*. You can generally find him posting in the MSDN newsgroups or by e-mail at BrianDPatterson@msn.com.

.NET Enterprise Development in VB .NET

Table of Contents

Table of Contents

Table of Contents

Table of Contents

.NET Enterprise Development in VB .NET

Prologue

The .NET Framework is Microsoft's great new programming world. It is designed to revolutionize the way in which businesses use the Internet by changing the way that services, devices, and users interact. The next generation of applications will be built with it allowing for much richer, broader, and all round better interaction with machines, and between machines.

As well as enabling a new way of interacting with our devices, .NET also provides a fast and efficient means of creating them. Using industry standards like XML, developers will be able to create applications that can traverse device and domain boundaries with ease. Naturally, none of this is much good unless businesses can be certain that their information can be kept secure. Microsoft has kept this in mind while developing .NET technologies, and has provided a secure means of keeping data on the Internet, allowing applications to deliver functionality tailored to the user.

This is a solution-focused book which uses an extended case study to give the reader a clear understanding of all the issues involved in the design and development of a complete enterprise application. It gives a broad based look at how to create a .NET enterprise application and how we can connect to it with various devices, in various ways, in a secure manner. So, whatever size application you need to create, reading this book will help you to understand how to go about it, and how to define more clearly the scope and breadth of any part of an enterprise application.

What Does This Book Cover?

Chapter 1 introduces us to the topics covered in this book and gives an outline of the application we develop throughout the rest of the book. Specifically, we look at distributed programming and N-tier apps in a generic way in order to set the background for our sample development.

Chapter 2 talks about the application design. We run through the Wrox Enterprise Objects or "WEO", which is a rich object layer built by the Builder tool (covered in Appendix A). Following on from this, we also look at how to use the tool, as well as how we can create and use stored procedures.

Once we have the basic application up and running, **Chapter 3** looks at building an application browser. We begin with a brief discussion on the various methods available to make the browser available for general use, and then we show how to build it, touching briefly on topics like authentication, adding menu options and running sub-applications.

Chapter 4 shows how we can build and hook up a desktop application to our business objects. We present a relatively simple example to demonstrate the principle of desktop apps. In this example we show, amongst other things, how we can edit customer information and use our application to search for customers on our database.

Chapter 5 discusses automated processes. We look at capturing, shipping, processing and reporting orders, and show how to build an order processor. While we discuss this topic we will also have a look at architectural issues and ways of making life easier when developing this sort of functionality.

Chapter 6 talks about Web Services. It shows how we can use Web Services to expose the functionality of the business objects. Initially, we use the Web Services with a desktop application, but in **Chapter 7** we show how to use our Web Services with ASP.NET. We also present our examples in a secure manner, using SSL to transfer user information to an authenticator service in IIS.

Since it is now possible to view data from many different clients, including wireless ones, **Chapter 8** takes a look at how we can use mobile clients to connect to our application. Specifically, we begin by talking about the Microsoft Mobile Internet Toolkit, and move on to demonstrate a small application, which makes use of our enterprise business objects.

Chapter 9 talks about services, and we begin by looking at the token-based authentication system we use to authenticate the users of remote objects. From here we look at building a service, connecting to it (while being authenticated), and finally how to install and run the service.

Chapter 10 discusses security and automated deployment. First we talk about code access security in depth, covering topics like obtaining evidence and evaluating permissions. After this we discuss application security and securing customer edits.

Chapter 11 delves into the topic of administration. In this chapter, we build an administration tool and show, amongst other things, some basic principles like stopping and starting the service. We also end with a brief discussion of the Microsoft Management Console.

The final chapter in the book, **Chapter 12**, deals with managing our enterprise application, and includes discussions on topics like performance counters, exception reporting, debugging, and load balancing. To round off, we have a brief discussion of Microsoft Application Center 2000.

Appendix A shows us the inner workings of the Builder tool used throughout the book to give the reader a better idea of what goes on behind the scenes.

Who Is This Book For?

People interested in this book will be those developing and selling off-the-shelf software products for use as line-of-business (or to an extent productivity) applications. People who customize either their own organization's off-the-shelf products or another organization's off-the-shelf products for deployment as a line-of-business application, and those developing line-of-business applications internally will also find this book an invaluable source of information.

Naturally, anyone who wishes to have a good look at the internals of an enterprise application in order to better appreciate what goes on "under the hood" would also benefit from reading this book. Of special interest is the Object Builder tool developed for this book by the author, which allows us to create objects for accessing data tables.

Intermediate in level, this book will help beginners and advanced developers alike to appreciate the scope and requirements inherent in building enterprise applications.

What You Need to Use This Book

To run the samples in this book you need to have the following:

- ❑   Windows 2000 or Windows XP
- ❑   Visual Studio .NET

Conventions

We've used a number of different styles of text and layout in this book to help differentiate between the different kinds of information. Here are examples of the styles we used and an explanation of what they mean.

Code has several fonts. If it's a word that we're talking about in the text – for example, when discussing a For...Next loop, it's in this font. If it's a block of code that can be typed as a program and run, then it's also in a gray box:

```
<?xml version 1.0?>
```

Sometimes we'll see code in a mixture of styles, like this:

```
<?xml version 1.0?>
<Invoice>
    <part>
        <name>Widget</name>
        <price>$10.00</price>
    </part>
</invoice>
```

In cases like this, the code with a white background is code we are already familiar with; the line highlighted in gray is a new addition to the code since we last looked at it.

Advice, hints, and background information comes in this type of font.

> **Important pieces of information come in boxes like this.**

Bullets appear indented, with each new bullet marked as follows:

- ❑ **Important Words** are in a bold type font.
- ❑ Words that appear on the screen, or in menus like Open or Close, are in a San Serif font similar to the one you see on the Windows desktop.
- ❑ Keys that you press on the keyboard, like *Ctrl* and *Enter*, are in italics.

Customer Support

We always value hearing from our readers, and we want to know what you think about this book: what you liked, what you didn't like, and what you think we can do better next time. You can send us your comments, either by returning the reply card in the back of the book, or by e-mail to feedback@wrox.com. Please be sure to mention the book title in your message.

How to Download the Sample Code for the Book

When you visit the Wrox site, http://www.wrox.com/, simply locate the title through our Search facility or by using one of the title lists. Click on Download in the Code column, or on Download Code on the book's detail page.

The files that are available for download from our site have been archived using WinZip. When you have saved the attachments to a folder on your hard-drive, you need to extract the files using a de-compression program such as WinZip or PKUnzip. When you extract the files, the code is usually extracted into chapter folders. When you start the extraction process, ensure your software (WinZip, PKUnzip, etc.) is set to use folder names.

Errata

We've made every effort to make sure that there are no errors in the text or in the code. However, no one is perfect and mistakes do occur. If you find an error in one of our books, like a spelling mistake or a faulty piece of code, we would be very grateful for feedback. By sending in errata you may save another reader hours of frustration, and of course, you will be helping us provide even higher quality information. Simply e-mail the information to support@wrox.com, your information will be checked and if correct, posted to the errata page for that title, or used in subsequent editions of the book.

To find errata on the web site, go to http://www.wrox.com/, and simply locate the title through our Advanced Search or title list. Click on the Book Errata link, which is below the cover graphic on the book's detail page.

E-mail Support

If you wish to directly query a problem in the book with an expert who knows the book in detail then e-mail support@wrox.com, with the title of the book and the last four numbers of the ISBN in the subject field of the e-mail. A typical e-mail should include the following things:

- ❑ The **title of the book**, **last four digits of the ISBN**, and **page number** of the problem in the Subject field.

- ❑ Your **name**, **contact information**, and the **problem** in the body of the message.

We *won't* send you junk mail. We need the details to save your time and ours. When you send an e-mail message, it will go through the following chain of support:

- ❑ Customer Support – Your message is delivered to our customer support staff, who are the first people to read it. They have files on most frequently asked questions and will answer anything general about the book or the web site immediately.

- ❑ Editorial – Deeper queries are forwarded to the technical editor responsible for that book. They have experience with the programming language or particular product, and are able to answer detailed technical questions on the subject.

- ❑ The Authors – Finally, in the unlikely event that the editor cannot answer your problem, he or she will forward the request to the author. We do try to protect the author from any distractions to their writing; however, we are quite happy to forward specific requests to them. All Wrox authors help with the support on their books. They will e-mail the customer and the editor with their response, and again all readers should benefit.

The Wrox Support process can only offer support to issues that are directly pertinent to the content of our published title. Support for questions that fall outside the scope of normal book support, is provided via the community lists of our http://p2p.wrox.com/ forum.

p2p.wrox.com

For author and peer discussion join the P2P mailing lists. Our unique system provides **programmer to programmer™** contact on mailing lists, forums, and newsgroups, all in addition to our one-to-one e-mail support system. If you post a query to P2P, you can be confident that it is being examined by the many Wrox authors and other industry experts who are present on our mailing lists. At p2p.wrox.com you will find a number of different lists that will help you, not only while you read this book, but also as you develop your own applications. Particularly appropriate to this book are the pro_windows_forms and the vs_dotnet lists.

To subscribe to a mailing list just follow these steps:

1. Go to http://p2p.wrox.com/.

2. Choose the appropriate category from the left menu bar.

3. Click on the mailing list you wish to join.

4. Follow the instructions to subscribe and fill in your e-mail address and password.

5. Reply to the confirmation e-mail you receive.

6. Use the subscription manager to join more lists and set your e-mail preferences.

Why this System Offers the Best Support

You can choose to join the mailing lists or you can receive them as a weekly digest. If you don't have the time, or facility, to receive the mailing list, then you can search our online archives. Junk and spam mails are deleted, and your own e-mail address is protected by the unique Lyris system. Queries about joining or leaving lists, and any other general queries about lists, should be sent to `listsupport@p2p.wrox.com`.

.NET Enterprise Development in VB .NET

1

Introduction

Throughout the course of this book, we shall build up a complete working enterprise application, as might be used by a book retailer. As we do so, we hope to demonstrate the scope of what such applications can achieve for a business, and how to address such fundamental issues as data concurrency, versioning, and security. We will also be introducing the Object Builder set of tools that we have developed which will aid in the development of software applications. The techniques we see here illustrate a basic example of one way to build software applications for the enterprise. The book is designed to allow you to leverage the lessons you learn throughout the book in your own applications and to give you some idea of how to design and construct solutions specific to your own business. It's unlikely that you'll be able to simply take the code samples from this book and use them instantly. Rather, they are blocks for building the foundation of your own applications.

Lately, we have seen a move away from standalone applications towards a more distributed model using Internet technologies – particularly web browsers and web servers. However, it's likely that over the course of the next couple of years we will see a resurgence in the desktop for several reasons that are discussed later. A significant part of this book therefore focuses on the development of desktop applications as well as intranet/extranet-based solutions. However, we will of course cover non-desktop applications, particularly web and Web Service applications in this book.

Some of the key topics of building an application for the enterprise that we shall be examining include:

- ❏ N-tier architecture with rich, usable business objects
- ❏ Desktop ("Windows Forms") development
- ❏ Web development (intranet/extranet and Internet)
- ❏ Access for mobile devices
- ❏ Web Services

❑   Deployment

❑   Centralized management and administration

❑   Security

Before we get started on our application itself, let's summarize a little of the background of enterprise applications in general.

The Changing Face of Enterprise

The business landscape in which modern companies now find themselves has undergone radical change over the last few decades. As national and global markets have opened up, so competition has become fiercer, and in order to survive, companies have to make greater and better use of the tools at their disposal. Recent advances in technology promise greater efficiency, and offer cheap and accessible new ways for customers to obtain the products or services they want.

In the early days of IT in the workplace, applications were confined to single machines, greatly limiting the problem domain that they could operate in. Many early desktop solutions relied on local copies of the company's databases being stored on each machine, where they would be accessed and manipulated independently. This simplistic model brings with it a raft of maintenance problems, as the changes in every local copy must be collated at some suitable time, often at the end of the business day, and the updated database must then be redistributed to each workstation. As technology improved, and applications became more sophisticated, solutions to this arrangement started to appear based on an online central database accessed over a network. Often, the workload of performing the tasks requested by users is shared between the desktop machines and the server: a model known as **distributed computing**.

Distributed Applications

Many modern enterprise solutions comprise several distributed applications, where the workload is shared between client and server according to the nature of the task and the power of the client machine.

These applications, running on fast local networks, are crying out to be extended to provide access through the wider Internet. Such intranet/extranet applications as we shall call them are appealing because the deployment problems are relatively non-existent. All you need to make an intranet-based application available externally is a suitable user interface for a web browser, and a means of connecting to the server. (There are wrinkles related to capabilities of different web browsers, but we won't go into this here.) This ease of deployment makes intranet/extranet applications very appealing, and explains the trend we've seen lately towards this kind of application in the enterprise.

The downside of such applications is that compromises must often be made to cater for the capabilities of the web browser and the limitations of the connection to the server, which can restrict the functionality and the usability of the application. Another point to consider is that this approach largely ignores the full capability of modern desktop computers, which are extremely powerful, but that power cannot be readily drawn on because virtually all application processing takes place on the server.

This has led to the development of what is known as the **rich client**, where the client application is more sophisticated and, depending on the capability of the client machine itself, can perform a number of tasks autonomously.

❏ Thin client – the client doesn't do much more than present the data issued by the server, take input from the user, and pass it back to the server.

❏ Rich client – the client is capable of doing much more with the data. For example, the server could return a set of raw values, which the client can then turn into a graph. It could validate user input before sending it to the server, and so on.

In practice, things are rarely this clear cut, and there are many graduations between thin and rich clients, but the underlying principle holds true nevertheless. Perhaps the most persuasive argument in favor of the rich client is that by performing a greater share of the processing locally, demand on the server is reduced, therefore allowing the server to support more simultaneous users.

The client-server term is a little simplistic for the networked setups found in today's world of commerce, but the underlying concept of a separation between client and server is still valid. Many such applications can still be thought of as client-server, although their underlying model is more sophisticated, such as the n-tier arrangement that we look at next.

The N-Tier Model

Microsoft did not invent the concept of "n-tier", but it's been such a big part of software development for Microsoft for so long that many now think of it as "theirs" and they market it as such. In fact, n-tier is simply a way of dividing up an application into a number of parts ("tiers" or "layers"), where each part does a specific job.

N-tier is an extension of client/server technology. In this paradigm, a single server provides data to a number of clients. (Although I say "single server", this may be more than one physical unit, and in some cases an application may use multiple servers. It's helpful however to think of client/server as "one server, many clients".)

Client-server techniques were originally developed as a natural extension to the way that software worked in mainframe environments – a large, powerful central processor of some kind (the mainframe itself) would perform the processing activities required by the application, and smaller, less powerful computers interacted with the user. As mainframes started to become less attractive to customers, due mainly to the "bang-for-buck" factor of smaller computers increasing (lower price, more power), a shift occurred. In effect, the user-end (or "client") computers became more powerful and cheaper, meaning that the central computers had to do less work.

What happened then was that the client-side code got "fatter", while in theory the server-side code got "thinner". Unfortunately, as the client-side software got more complex, deployment of this client-side software often became more problematic. Around about this point, Internet technologies (specifically web servers and web clients) got more sophisticated meaning that we started to come full circle back to a very powerful central server and much less sophisticated ("dumb") clients, which is highly similar to the mainframe approach.

Now with .NET we can start to see a shift away from this approach back again to "thickening" up the client-side code, meaning that more processing happens on the client. This shift will most likely happen because of the work that Microsoft has done in regard to various technology improvements to make deployment far easier. We look at these topics in Chapter 10.

Today, most distributed applications are modeled on the basis of three tiers: **Data**, **Business** and **Presentation**. If we look at it from a client/server standpoint, the Data and Business tiers can together be considered to be the server and the Presentation tier can be considered to be the client. (Although in web development the Presentation task is shared between the server and the client – but we're getting ahead of ourselves.)

❑ Data – this tier is responsible for extracting the data from the database and providing it to the Business tier and vice versa.

❑ Business – this tier is responsible for doing the actual processing for the application. For example, it's responsible for making sure that new orders are properly stored in the database, that users can search for customer information, and so on.

❑ Presentation – this tier is responsible for marshaling data between the business tier and the user.

This classic 3-tier design is useful from two standpoints – it makes building the initial application easier, and makes extending the application easier as well. Let's have a closer look at each of these tiers now.

The Data Tier

If we think about each of the tiers in turn, the Data tier is often just SQL Server or whatever DBMS you choose to base your application on. In enterprise environments, you may well find that the choice of DBMS solution has already been decided for you. In fact, in enterprise environments you may well find that you'll be tasked with using Oracle for your application. (Oracle is, after all the world's biggest database software development company, whereas Microsoft is the biggest software development company, period.) In this book, we're going to be using Microsoft SQL Server 2000.

In designing the application, you'll determine what data needs to be stored and the best way to store it. This will involve building the database schema and loading data into it. (We'll assume that you have some data, or at the very least have a set of test data that you want to build your application with.) Designing the Data tier is a task usually shared between qualified database administrators and developers working in a technical architect role.

The actual definition of the data tier in our application is somewhat gray. SQL Server itself definitely makes up the data tier, but the various objects that are used to communicate with SQL Server exist in part in the data tier and in part in the business tier. For example, the ADO.NET classes that physically communicate with SQL Server can be thought of "data tier" code, even though they run in the same process as the business tier code. The classes that we derive most of our business tier classes from (the Enterprise Objects as we are going to call them) could be thought of as either data tier or business tier depending on your perspective, although they too run inside of the business tier code.

The Business Tier

It's at the Business tier where the software design process starts to get really interesting. What you're trying to do at the business tier is build software that matches the formalized procedures and processes the business itself follows that are handed down from various parts of the management team. Building the Business tier is a combination of modeling those business processes while at the same time keeping an eye on object-oriented techniques and component based design to build a rich object model that developers can leverage in their applications.

Thinking about business processes for a moment, we might be looking at:

❏ When a delivery is received, the goods must be checked and loaded into the relevant bays in the warehouse.

❏ When a customer returns an item, they can have a full refund up to 30 days after the initial order, or a credit note after that date.

❏ When an employee wants to book vacation time, no other employee in their department is allowed to have that same time off.

In short, anything that the business does will be modeled as a process or procedure. If you want to automate or computerize that process, the Business tier for the application has to follow that procedure exactly.

The major reason why this model is so popular is that (assuming we're talking about a well managed company) business procedures change rarely. A company of any decent size is not going to change their returns policy every other day. Instead that policy will only change in consultation with various managers and decision makers within the organization.

Imagine we have an application for managing customer returns. That application uses objects in the Business tier to process the return. Because the objects in the Business tier have to follow the procedures of the company, we effectively ensure that the user using the application must also follow the procedures of the company by virtue of the fact that anything "illegal" will be disallowed. In addition, should those procedures change, the code in the Business tier is changed to come into alignment with the new rules. Once these code changes have been made live, the application will "feel" the effects of the new rules and again, the application user will be protected from doing anything that's not in accordance with the new rules.

In this application, we're going to be modeling a number of business processes. A lot of these processes will be fairly basic – due to the nature of the book medium we're limited on the complexity of what we can do – but they will demonstrate the logical steps involved.

The Presentation Tier

Another significant motivation for using n-tier is that the Presentation tier can comprise multiple applications, each tailored for a different platform or purpose, and yet still receive the benefit of the same Business tier code base. For example, we can build a desktop application for handling customer returns and build an additional ASP.NET web application for doing the same thing that uses the *same business objects*. This is the ultimate in code reuse – we've spent time building a single business object tier that can be reused by multiple applications throughout the organization, irrespective of their delivery mechanism. Although we'll talk about it in more detail in later sections, we can expect desktop applications, intranet/extranet applications, Internet applications, mobile applications and Web Services to all use the same, common Business tier.

> In our particular application, the classes that make up the Business tier are inherited from a set of core objects called "Wrox Enterprise Objects", or WEO. We'll see this in more detail in the next chapter.

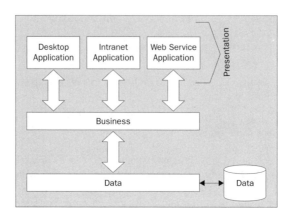

Another advantage to working with the n-tier model is that specialization of developers is quite feasible and even desirable. Developers tend to specialize by nature – and this model allows an ASP.NET developer to work on ASP.NET projects while steering clear of Windows Forms applications. Likewise, Windows Forms developers can leave the Web Services components to developers with more experience of them, and so on.

In addition to this, the more experienced developers can be assigned to work on the crucial Business tier, which underpins most of the activities of the other applications and the teams building those applications. It requires more skill and experience to understand the issues with scalability, extensibility, and so on that this tier throws up, and so teams can be structured so that junior developers can cut their teeth on the Presentation tier before being "mentored" up to working on the Business tier.

In our particular application, we'll first of all be seeing how to put some objects in the business tier. These objects will be inherited from objects defined in the Wrox Enterprise Objects (WEO) library. We'll use a utility called "Object Builder" to automatically generate a lot of the code for these objects based on the structure of the database. We'll then be able to customize these automatically generated classes to suit our exact needs.

Web Development

The Internet has risen in a very short space of time to become a hugely popular avenue for a whole range of activity, and few enterprises can afford to ignore it. Even if you supply bespoke desktop applications for your customers to use for online dealings with your company, some organizations may be unwilling to set up and maintain such applications, and would prefer a standard web interface. .NET has several features, such as automatic deployment and Remoting (which we'll see in Chapter 10 and Chapter 9 respectively), which make it relatively easy to deploy desktop applications at a business partner's location. However, it is quite likely that the partner may still prefer a web-based approach (again, it makes their desktop management easier), or indeed, perhaps your company is uncomfortable from a security standpoint.

Besides, desktop application development is largely inappropriate for private users who are generally more comfortable using traditional Internet sites. Your average user would be put off if, say, they had to download an application from http://www.amazon.com/, install it, and use that application to buy a book or a CD. Sure, Amazon would be able to build a far richer user interface that is easier to use once up and running, but getting to that stage requires a larger investment of time on the part of the user, and is quite likely to require more support services from Amazon.

Web Services

Web Services have been touted as one of the most significant advances in Internet development since the invention of HTML. In principle, a Web Service allows applications to access remote objects over the standard web infrastructure, that is, a combination of TCP and HTTP. To run a method on a remote object (a **Web Method**), all an application has to do is provide a URL, a method name, and the parameters that the method requires. If appropriate, the Web Service can then return a result for the calling application to make use of, just as if the web method were available locally.

> **Web Services are now starting to be called "application-to-application", or A2A in line with the classic B2C and B2B monikers of yore.**

When thinking about Web Services, it's tempting to think in terms of a physical problem. For example, imagine the physical distance if I have an application running on a computer in London that has to access an object running on a server in Bonn. Nevertheless, A2A doesn't *have* to relate to physical boundaries and it makes a great platform interoperability solution. Imagine I have a Java application and a VB6 application running on the same machine. If I need both applications to talk to each other, I can use Web Services to act as a "go-between" for the two applications. There's no need to think in terms of physical separation. Although Web Services are superb at dealing with either, think logical separation, not physical.

There are also a number of approaches being touted for Web Services:

❑ A library of functionality available to an application. These are sometimes referred to as "Internet Linked Libraries", which can be compared with "Dynamic Link Libraries". ("ILL" compared with "DLL".) The owner of the service can charge for access in much the same way as a COM or .NET component developer can charge for his libraries.

❑ A data server of some description. Classic examples of this would be providing access to a mainframe through a Web Service, or access to enterprise application functionality.

❑ A coordination server. In this example, a Web Service is used to control the activity of an application distributed across a number of computers.

Introducing .NET

There are two significant features of .NET that make deployment of desktop ("Windows Forms") applications in .NET far easier than their COM- or MFC-based equivalents.

With a COM- or MFC-based desktop application, developers often run up against problems because the DLL files that encapsulate the functionality are difficult to install (either in the form of components, or as statically-linked API functions). Problems like these constitute the phenomenon often referred to as "DLL Hell", which is in itself an involved topic that we won't delve into in much detail. Most of the problems stem from the fact that you can only have one version of a DLL installed on a computer at a given moment.

Developers tend to be very bad at engineering DLLs so that, when a new version is released, applications that are dependent on the old version do not break. What happens is that after installing Application B that uses version 2.0 of a given DLL, Application A that uses version 1.0 ceases to work properly. This causes massive problems in deployment because you may write an application for a set of users that breaks another application, or a user will install an application that breaks yours and so on.

Fortunately, .NET makes a real effort to purge the problems of DLL Hell that have plagued developers in recent years. The Framework is quite happy for you to have version 1.0 and version 2.0 of a given assembly both installed on one machine together. Moreover, an additional technology of .NET called "automated deployment" makes the distribution of the assemblies themselves far, far easier, but again that's something we won't go into until Chapter 10.

The upshot? Developers like desktop applications because they allow the user to have a richer interface. In addition, they would like to have the processing power required by the application to be distributed to computers on the LAN. However, what's stopped them pre-.NET is the deployment problems. With the deployment problems greatly reduced, we're likely to see this shift back to desktop development that we mentioned right at the beginning of this section.

The technology we use to deliver web applications in .NET is "ASP.NET", the successor to the popular Active Server Pages.

ASP.NET is essentially an attempt to combine the development model of Windows Forms with the flexibility of web applications – and by flexibility I mean the ability to be able to point a web browser at a URL and be given the opportunity to use that application. In ASP.NET, you draw controls onto a web page in much the same way that you draw controls onto a form with Windows Forms development. (Also, of course, this was how we did it in Visual Basic and to a degree with Visual C++ before Windows Forms.)

What's exciting about ASP.NET from a developer perspective is that we can now build reusable controls for web applications in a similar fashion to how we build reusable controls for Windows Forms applications. We cover this in more detail in Chapter 4.

The Sample Application

We've now covered enough background to have a closer look at the sample application that we will be building as we progress through this book. It will be a comprehensive application that encompasses many features required by enterprise applications, no matter what area of business they are concerned with. Our aim is to concentrate on the key aspects of developing such applications so that you will be able to apply the lessons to whatever application you may be working on. For this reason, many extra details that could be added to the application to make it more user-friendly and so on have been left out to focus on creating a fully-functioning distributed architecture that will be of general use. The following figure provides a bird's eye view of the finished application:

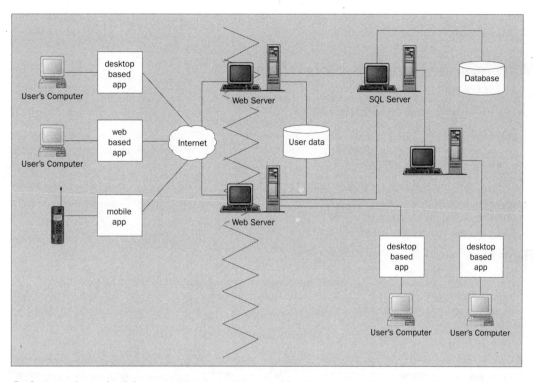

Let's now take each of these components in turn, and briefly examine their role in the overall picture.

The Application Browser

One of the most important features of our application is the desktop-based "Application Browser". This is a small application installed on users' computers, but that originally contains very little functionality. As the user chooses menu options that run different parts of the application, the assemblies that support the new functionality required are automatically downloaded and installed using .NET's automatic deployment.

How the browser is actually installed doesn't really matter, and is down to your organization's particular policies in that regard. Some organizations are sufficiently small for users to download and install their own software from a central server, and in such cases the application browser would perhaps be installed manually from a network share. Other (perhaps larger) organizations implement "standardized desktops" where the software installed on each desktop is identical and is published from a central location. (Norton Ghost is a common tool used to achieve this.) As part of the application deployment, the browser itself can be included in the image so the next time the desktop is updated, the application browser is automatically made available.

Web Services

In this book we're going to be looking at two sorts of Web Services: one that acts as a data server, and the other a coordination server. The first time we'll meet Web Services will be to build a "coordination" server that will allow the Application Browser to authenticate the user, to learn about the functionality available to that user, and to discover where the sub-applications running in the browser can find the code. (Chapter 3.)

The second time we meet Web Services will be exposing the functionality of the object model to business partners in a secure manner.

Management and Administration

In this book we're also going to be looking at a number of the management and administration topics that are important to enterprise applications.

In Chapter 10 we're going to look at the deployment of the application. Specifically we'll look at how the application browser can automatically download and run functionality downloaded from assemblies on a web server.

In Chapter 11, we're going to look at how we can build an application to help us administer the application. And in Chapter 12, we'll look at how we can instrument our application to help us get a better idea of how it's running once it's been deployed.

Security

Security in an enterprise application is a huge topic and has implications for most individual components of the application. For this reason, there isn't a "security" chapter in this book – we cover security as an ongoing topic in most of the chapters.

We look at security from two standpoints: authentication and authorization.

Authentication covers the activity of determining the identity of a user when he or she attempts to access the system. Ideally authentication in Windows applications should be done in cooperation with Windows itself. System administrators will create a definitive list of users that are able to log onto a workstation and are given specific capabilities through the application of roles. We attempt to tap into this functionality by hooking into the authentication capabilities built into Web Services. We cover this topic in Chapter 6 and again in Chapter 10.

Authorization is a little more complex than this and involves determining the capability of a user once they have identified themselves. With .NET, there are two aspects to authorization: resource access controlled through Code Access Security and application access controlled through whatever scheme we elect to build.

Code Access Security ("CAS") is built into .NET and is Microsoft's approach to trying to solve the horrendous security problems we run into daily in modern times with things like SirCam, Nimda and other Trojans, viruses, and worms that will no doubt be released after this book is printed. With pre-.NET technologies, objects are able to abuse system functionality because all code is granted the same level of permission on a computer. You may want to send an e-mail using Outlook, but should a virus be able to use the same code to send questionable images to all of the contents of your address book?

CAS promises to solve this problem by granting different levels of permission depending on a number of factors including code origin. A component downloaded from the Internet may not be able to access printers on your network, whereas a component downloaded from your *intranet* may be given access to do so.

Application access is a different story and you're largely free to develop whatever scheme most appeals to you. What you're trying to do irrespective of the scheme is to be able to say to one user, "You can access that application feature" whereas saying to another, "You, on the other hand, cannot access that same application feature." We detail such a scheme in Chapter 10.

The Mobile Interface

Accessing web applications from agents other than a desktop web browser has had a very poor start. A lot of this is related to the fact that WAP was hyped by the media to be a huge deal but actually fell flat on its face due to a combination of factors.

Despite the fact that mobile hasn't happened *yet*, the arguments that were being bandied around before the hype hit still apply. Allowing employees, business partners and customers access to web applications from a mobile device is a good idea. Take these examples:

- ❏ A shopper walking around a bookstore can check prices and availability with an online retailer to make sure he's getting the best deal
- ❏ A salesperson visiting a client site can check her next appointment in the parking lot
- ❏ A system administrator can be alerted to a problem with an application when at home

In Chapter 8 we take a look at making some of the functionality we build in the web application chapter available over mobile devices.

Summary

These are very exciting times for developers who are willing to expend the time and energy to acquire the skills to make use of the tools at our disposal. With the pace of technology's evolution showing no signs of relenting, these tools become ever more sophisticated. The business applications we can now create are increasingly powerful, and increasingly crucial to a business's success – so too are those able to develop and maintain such applications. This book gives an overview of the whole process of creating a modern enterprise application, including its data access components, desktop clients, and even a mobile interface. By following the book through this development process, you will acquire many skills that will give you an essential foundation for your future career in this complex field.

.NET Enterprise Development in VB .NET

2

Application Design

Throughout the course of this book we're going to be building a line-of-business application for a fictional book publisher. We're going to design this application as a reference implementation that you can use in your own line-of-business applications in your own organization, and we'll be presenting tools that will help you speed the development of your applications.

First of all, what's the difference between a "line-of-business" application and a "productivity" application? Well, a productivity application can best be described as an application that supports the business process, but one that isn't heavily tailored to the needs of an organization. Microsoft Office is a classic example – most modern businesses use MS Office for e-mail, letter writing and so on, but there's very little variation between the way in which this application is used between one business and the next.

Line-of-business applications are ones that are used in a very specific way to meet the unique business processes of an organization. Examples include Customer Relationship Management software like Siebel, accounting software like Great Plains or software for controlling printing presses, logistics, and so on. In modern businesses it's often the case that the quality and capability of these line-of-business applications sets one company aside from its competitors.

If you're reading this book, you're going to fall into one of three camps:

- ❑ You develop and sell off-the-shelf software products for use as line-of-business (or to an extent productivity) applications in an organization

- ❑ You are a consultant who customizes either your own organization's off-the-shelf products or another organization's off-the-shelf products for deployment as a line-of-business application at your client's site

- ❑ You develop line-of-business applications internally for your organization

This book is going to be of equal interest to you irrespective of which kind of developer you are.

Wrox Enterprise Objects

We're going to build the application described in this book using something called "Wrox Enterprise Objects", or "WEO" (pronounced "wee-oh"). WEO is designed to do two things – firstly it enables a rich, object-oriented layer that eases communication with business objects. Secondly, it provides a set of tools for creating that rich, object-oriented layer.

I don't have to tell any reader of this book that relational databases are based on the concept of rows and columns. Although we haven't built it yet, our database is going to contain a number of tables. The data in these tables describes a model of the organization at a given point in time. For example, the Authors table will contain a list of all of the authors that are working for or have ever worked for the publisher. Books will contain a list of all of the books that have been published or are currently being developed.

Depending on how we look at and interpret the data in this table, we can understand the state of the organization. We can see what books are being written at the moment, which authors are working on those books, the e-mail addresses of the authors working on the books and so on. The way this data is extracted and presented is a function of the line-of-business application software that we build to support the activities of the business.

In this book we're going to assume some rules about the organization:

❑   Entities exist in the business. These describe things or people involved in the day-to-day activity that we're trying to support. An Author is an example of an entity, as is Book, as is Invoice and so on.

❑   Certain activities change the state of an entity. We can Publish a book or we can Pay an author.

We're also going to make these assumptions about the database:

❑   A business process must be modeled in software, and we'll regard the set of business processes encapsulated in our application as definitive. (By that we mean we're not going to talk about functions outside of the model. We may choose not to develop the code that transfers money into an author's bank account, or pays a supplier. These are parts of the holistic business process of the organization – it's just that we're not going to worry about them.)

❑   Like entities are modeled in the database in one or more tables. (Most of the time this will be a table.) The Authors table will model Author entities. The Books table will model Book entities, and so on.

❑   Every entity has a unique, 32-bit integer identifier. We're not going to worry about complex primary keys where multiple or non-integer columns are used.

❑   We're going to use SQL Server – either the full version or SQL Server 2000 Desktop Engine, originally called MSDE – to store the model. (The reason why we advocate the Desktop Edition in this book is for self-learners to get up to speed without needing a license for SQL Server.)

❑   In terms of naming conventions, tables are named in plural form and entities are named in the singular. For example, we have a table called Books but an entity called Book.

❑   As a further convention, we'll stipulate that identifiers in the database will be expressed in Pascal Casing, for example AuthorId not AuthorID and BookXml not BookXML.

The principle behind 3-tier design, as used in this book is that the business tier is developed once to a very high standard and that the business tier models the exact business processes of the organization as determined by management. The business tier should only ever change whenever the business procedures themselves change and, in most organizations, it is likely that core business procedures change rarely.

This tier should be available to developers wishing to build applications of all kinds. These can be applications used by telephone operators performing customer service or sales activities, applications used by Internet companies for B2C or B2B e-commerce, reporting, and data warehousing applications. Because the business tier has so many possible "customers" (and I use "customers" here to include groups working within the organization or customers in a traditional sense), it should be very easy to use.

Imagine you're building an intranet page that needs to display a list of authors, together with a report of the current books the author is working on. Here are a number of possible steps involved.

1. We'll assume that a database exists on the LAN containing a list of authors. That database server has to be identified and a database connection string determined. A `System.Data.SqlClient.SqlConnection` object has to be configured to connect to the database.

2. Once a connection is possible, a stored procedure in the database has to be located that is capable of returning a list of the authors. This stored procedure has to be referenced from a `System.Data.SqlClient.SqlCommand` object.

3. The command is executed. A `System.Data.SqlClient.SqlDataAdapter` object is configured and used to populate a `System.Data.DataSet` object.

4. For each `Author` entity represented in the DataSet, another stored procedure has to be located that can return the books for that author. This has to be loaded into another DataSet in much the same way.

5. With the `Author` entity known and a list of `Book` entities (each represented by a `System.Data.DataRow` object), the developer can render the details to the screen. The author needs to know the names and types of the columns in order to render the information properly.

The problems in the approach we've just seen all lie in the fact that the business object developer has to understand how the entities are modeled in the database, specifically:

❑   The developer needs to know the database connection string.

❑   The developer needs to know the names of the stored procedures used to retrieve the information they need, and they also need to know the details of the parameters to call the stored procedures.

❑   Once the data has been loaded into the relevant DataSets, the developer needs to know how the tables are structured and which column to extract information from. This problem can be exaggerated in situations where the data held in a table cannot be intuited, for example what does a status code of "27" mean?

❑   In some cases the information may not be found in a single table.

What's needed is a rich object model. Compare this:

```
Console.WriteLine(row("email"))
```

...with this:

```
Console.WriteLine(author.Email)
```

Although there's conceptually no difference between the two lines, we've encapsulated the concept of the e-mail column into a property.

We can build upon this by adding more functionality to the class. Consider:

```
Console.WriteLine(row("firstname") + " " + row("lastname"))
```

...with this:

```
Console.WriteLine(author.Name)
```

Someone with an understanding of how the database is constructed will know that if you want to access the author's complete name, for example "Darren Clarke", you combine the values of the `firstname` and `lastname` columns putting a space in-between. However, in an ideal world we don't want the developer to have to know this – it's easier and more reliable to get them to use a property that has a specifically defined function.

How we deal with data once we have it is just one part of the problem. Extracting the data from the database is fraught with similar problems.

Here's a sample of code typical of that used to call a stored procedure from SQL Server using .NET:

```
' create a command...
Dim command As SqlCommand = New SqlCommand("GetAuthorById", connection)
command.CommandType = CommandType.StoredProcedure

' add params...
Dim idParam As SqlParameter = command.Parameters.Add("AuthorId", _
                                                     SqlDbType.Int)
idParam.Value = someValueSuppliedThroughAParameter

' fill a dataset...
Dim myDataset As DataSet = New DataSet()
Dim adapter As SqlDataAdapter = New SqlDataAdapter(command)
adapter.Fill(dataset)
```

Not only is that code extremely verbose, it relies on the developer both knowing what the stored procedure is called, and also the structure of the parameters that go into it. Compare that with this code:

```
Dim authors As DataSet = Author.GetAuthorById(27)
```

In this case, what we have is a class called `Author` that's used to model authors. This class has an understanding built-in as to how authors are actually stored in the database. In this case, we're accessing a shared method called `GetAuthorById`. This method is capable of connecting to the database, running the stored procedure and returning the results to the caller. Thanks to the IntelliSense features built into Visual Studio .NET, the developer only needs to know of the existence of the method – they don't need to worry about the specifics of the call, as IntelliSense will prompt them.

There's more. In an earlier code example we saw how we wanted to use properties defined on an entity to access information about it, for instance using `author.Email` rather than `row("email")`. What we need is a way of extracting objects that support the properties whenever we have a DataSet. We'll do this using an `EntitySet`, something we'll talk about in a moment.

The basis of WEO is to provide an easy method for creating an extremely rich, yet powerful object model for expressing business concepts and procedures. Let's look in more detail at how it works.

The WEO Object Model

The base currency of the WEO Object Model is the `Entity`. This class describes, basically, a row in a database table. Because we've made an assumption that a single row always represents a "thing" involved in the company's operations, we can say that an `Entity` represents a "thing". This can be either "very obvious" with entities like `Author`, `Book`, `Customer` or `Invoice`, or also quite granular such as `InvoiceDetailLine`.

In this book, we won't be building an object model from scratch. Instead we'll be using the **WEO Object Builder**. This utility can build 80% of the object model for us. Once we have the base 80%, it's down to us to build the other 20%. The Object Builder works by looking at the database structure and creating an object model capable of accessing it. For us, this means that the data access layer design process involves the following steps:

- ❑ Firstly, we have to decide what our application needs to do. This is a common first step in most software architecture processes.

- ❑ Secondly, build a database capable of storing the data that our application will need and that our application will generate and modify.

- ❑ Thirdly, we take the Object Builder, connect it to the database and get it to generate a set of `.vb` or `.cs` files. This is the "base model". These classes are then imported into a manually created VS.NET project.

- ❑ Finally, we build the project adding new functionality to the base model as required.

Although we'll take a look at the Object Builder in a moment, let's examine the core classes of WEO.

"Entity"

`EnterpriseObjects.Entity` is the base class from which all entity objects are inherited. It contains an array of `System.Object` objects populated from a `System.Data.DataRow` object and provides helper methods and properties from inherited objects to access columns from the **DataRow** and also provide access to the `Service` object (more on this later).

The way that the model is constructed is by inheriting from the classes defined in `EnterpriseObjects`. However, the wrinkle is that because the classes are closely tied to the database, if the database changes we want to change the structure of the classes as well.

If we say that our `Author` entity is based on the **Authors** table, each column in the table will have a matching property on the entity. **FirstName** will map to `FirstName`, **Email** will map to `Email` and so on. If we add a new column to the table, we need a new property. This means regenerating some of the code. As it's easier and safer to generate an entire new file rather than insert changes into an existing file, the Object Builder uses a model where there are two classes. Here's an example of the first one:

```
Public Class AuthorBase
   Inherits EnterpriseObjects.Entity
      ' properties...
      ...
End Class
```

This `AuthorBase` class contains automatically generated code that provides the functionality for the entity. It houses the properties that map to the columns and provides other services that we'll meet later. As a developer you *will not* be changing code in this class as each time the Object Builder is asked to synchronize the project this file will be scratched and rebuilt. The Object Builder creates another class, and here's an example:

```
Public Class Author
   Inherits AuthorBase
      ' your own customizations...
      ...
End Class
```

It's in this second class that you're free to add your own customizations, and we'll see how this works in a little while. This file is generated on the first synchronization but is never re-created when the project is synchronized, so anything you add here is safe and (touch wood) the Object Builder won't delete it.

"EntitySet"

`EnterpriseObjects.EntitySet` is derived from `System.Data.DataSet`, which means that it can do anything a DataSet can, but can also do some other things that a DataSet cannot. For the most part, this extra functionality will be to translate the `DataRow` objects contained within the DataTables within the DataSet to the appropriate type of entity.

Like the `Entity`, you get given two classes. The first one inherits from `EntitySet`, like this:

```
Public Class AuthorSetBase
   Inherits EnterpriseObjects.EntitySet

      ' Entities property and other functionality...
End Class
```

The second inherits from the base class:

```
Public Class AuthorSet
   Inherits AuthorSetBase
      ' your own customizations...
      ...
End Class
```

Usually, whenever a developer populates a `DataSet` object they just use a single table. I'm sure you're familiar with code like this:

```
Dim row As DataRow
For Each row In myDataSet.Tables(0).Rows
  ' do something...
  ...
Next
```

Although being able to hold multiple tables in a DataSet is sometimes very useful, when working with WEO the EntitySet is likely to contain only a single table. (The EntitySet does support multiple tables – it simply defaults to using the first table in the `Tables` collection unless you specifically request otherwise.)

Imagine you want to get hold of the e-mail column from row 3 of a DataSet. Here's what you'd need to do:

```
Console.WriteLine(myDataSet.Tables(0).Rows(3)("email"))
```

When working with an EntitySet you'll find that the `Entities` property returns an appropriate entity type. So, for an `AuthorSet` you'll get `Author` entities. For a `BookSet`, you'll get `Book` entities. Here's how we can do the same thing as before:

```
Console.WriteLine(myAuthorSet.Entities(2).Email)
```

Likewise, if we want to work with a list of entities, the EntitySet can provide us with strongly typed `Entity objects`, rather than `DataRow` objects, like this:

```
Dim theAuthor As Author
For Each theAuthor In myAuthorSet
  Console.WriteLine(theAuthor.Name)
Next
```

Another advantage to this method is that we get the opportunity to provide a new implementation of `ToString` for `Entity` objects. So, we might decide that the `ToString` method of `Author` should return the value returned by the `Name` property, like this:

```
Public Overrides Function ToString() As String
   Return Name
End Function
```

I'm sure you can see that this is far more straightforward and natural than the un-typed DataSet method that we're used to using.

"Service"

So we have a pretty consistent method for working with data once we have it, but how do we get it?

One thing that we have to deal with when working with data is that data can come from many different sources. In this application we're primarily interested in storing data centrally in SQL Server, but there are many ways we can access that data. We might be running the application on the same LAN as the server, in which case we can connect to it directly. Alternatively, we might be running the software on our home machine at the end of a DSL line or cable modem. We're still connecting to the same database, but we're using a different connection method to get to it. (In this case we're either talking about Web Services or Remoting, something we'll get to in a short while.)

As far as the application developer is concerned, the transport mechanism connecting the application to its data source is utterly irrelevant. For this reason, we need to build functionality into the object model so that when requested it can connect to and consume data from wherever the data is sourced.

To do this, we're going to split the object model in two. The side we've been looking at thus far is known as the "entity layer". The side we're about to look at is the "service layer". The service layer is the layer that provides data services to the entity. As before, we're going to have two classes to support the service layer: a base class and a class that we can customize.

Here's an example of a base class:

```
Public Class AuthorServiceBase
  Inherits EnterpriseObjects.Service
    ' GetAll...

    ...

    ' GetById...
    ...
End Class
```

And, as usual, we build another class inherited from this one that can be customized:

```
Public Class AuthorService
  Inherits AuthorServiceBase
    ' your own customizations...
    ...
End Class
```

It's in these classes that we'll implement the basic functionality for extracting data from the database. By default, the new service classes will support the shared GetAll and GetById methods. GetAll, obviously, retrieves all of the rows from the relevant table and returns them as an EntitySet object and GetById retrieves just a single row and returns it as an Entity object. Other methods, such as GetAllCustomersWhoseNameIsBob and GetAllBooksPublishedInYear, represent the 20% of the object model that Object Builder cannot build itself and you'll find this is where you spend the bulk of your time customizing.

The problem we have to be careful to avoid is we do not want to have two separate sets of objects that the developer needs to use whenever they build an application. In the scenario we've outlined so far, `GetAll` does return an `AuthorSet`, `BookSet` or whatever, but we need access to an `AuthorService` object in order to do this. A better approach is to configure the `Entity` object so that it can connect to and call methods on the relevant `AuthorService`. For example:

```
Public Class AuthorBase
   Inherits EnterpriseObjects.EntitySet
    ' GetAll...
    Public Shared Function GetAll() As AuthorSet
      Return ServiceObject.GetAll()
    End Function
    ' remainder of class implementation here...
    ...
End Class


Public Class AuthorServiceBase
   Inherits EnterpriseObjects.Service
    ' GetAll...
    Public Shared Function GetAll() As AuthorSet
      ' do the magic to get the data...
      ...
    End Function

    ' remainder of class implementation here...
    ...
End Class
```

In this way, to all intents and purposes to anyone using the object model the existence of the `AuthorService` and `AuthorServiceBase` objects are entirely transparent. This makes life far easier for the developer.

Some of you may be wondering why there's a split. Why have we split the methods into two separate objects? The reason is because when we're using Remoting to access the data, we don't want to have to have the assemblies containing the actual implementations of `AuthorService` and `AuthorServiceBase` on the computers running the code. We'll be relying on proxies to make the calls – again, this is something we'll cover in more detail later on.

"EnterpriseApplication"

The last aspect of WEO we have to discuss in this section is exactly how do the `Entity` objects find the service objects?

WEO provides a class called `EnterpriseApplication` that contains, among other things, a database connection string, proxy server settings and Remoting configuration information. A shared property of this class, `Application`, returns an instance that can be used to store information relevant to the current application, and that's any kind of application like a desktop application, an ASP.NET Web Service or some other type.

We'll learn more about `EnterpriseApplication` later.

Using the WEO Object Builder

You can find everything that you need to work through the examples in this book at this URL: http://www.wrox.com/Books/Book_Details.asp?ISBN=1861006179.

In this download package, you'll find the following:

- ❑   All the source code for the application that we build in this book.

- ❑   The EnterpriseObjects project. This contains the code that supports the WEO layer.

- ❑   The sample database.

- ❑   The Object Builder tool.

The first step is to install the database. Follow the instructions in the `Readme.txt` file in the Database folder to do this.

The second step is to install the EnterpriseObjects project on your computer. Do this by copying the entire `EnterpriseObjects` folder to a folder called `c:\BookManager` on your local computer. (You don't *have* to use `c:\BookManager` as the folder, but I *strongly* recommend it. You may have problems following along if you do not.)

The third step is to install the Object Builder. There isn't an install package for this as it's just a single `.exe` assembly. Extract the files to the `c:\BookManager` folder. The Object Builder tool will then be available at `c:\BookManager\Builder\bin\Builder.exe`.

Using the Object Builder Tool

The Object Builder works by generating new `.cs` or `.vb` files. These files can then be imported into any project. This generation process is known as "synchronization"; the database structure is "synchronized" with the project files. The Object Builder is not integrated with the Visual Studio .NET environment, so there is a manual process involved in getting things off-the-ground.

On your computer, use Visual Studio .NET to create a new Class Library project. I'm going to use the folder `c:\BookManager` and a project name of BookManagerObjects. To follow along with the chapter, it's probably best that you follow the same approach. Create the new project now.

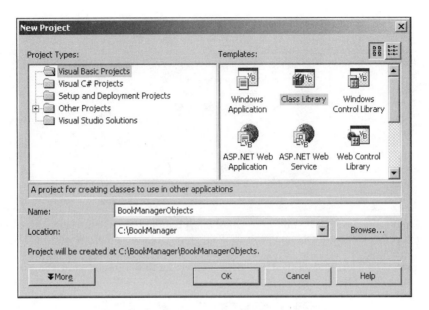

Once the project has loaded, you can delete the default `Class1` file.

Next you need to load the Enterprise Objects support classes into the solution. In a production environment, you'll probably want to include a reference to the finished assembly. However, in the exercises in the book it's typically going to be more useful for you to import the source files into your project. This will let you step through into the WEO layer to gain a better understanding of what's happening.

Using Solution Explorer, right click on the **BookManagerObjects** solution and select **Add | Existing Project** from the menu. Find the **EnterpriseObjects** project that you copied a moment ago into the `c:\BookManager` folder and add it.

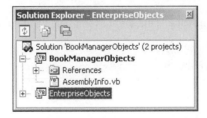

To make the classes in **EnterpriseObjects** visible to **BookManagerObjects**, you'll need to add a reference. Right click the **BookManagerObjects** project in Solution Explorer and select **Add Reference**. Change to the **Projects** tab and add a reference to the **EnterpriseObjects** project. If you're successful, you'll see this:

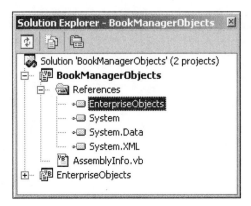

Once you've created the project you can use the Object Builder to create the new `.cs` or `.vb` files to import into the BookManagerObjects project. We'll go through these steps now.

When you run the Object Builder, you'll be presented with a splash screen. You want to create a new project, so click the Create a new project link.

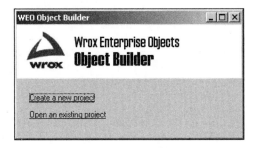

To create a new project, you need to provide three things:

❑ A database connection string. This should reference the database you created a moment ago.

❑ A path to create the new classes in. Use `c:\BookManager\BookManagerObjects`.

❑ A root namespace. Use `BookManagerObjects`.

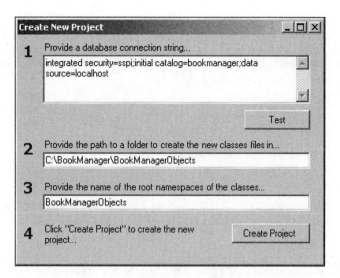

Make sure these three are configured properly and click Create Project.

When the project is loaded, you'll see an object tree reminiscent of the Server Explorer in Visual Studio .NET, SQL Server's Management Console and countless other Windows applications. The Object Builder has searched through the database for all of the tables and views that exist. Select the Authors table and you'll see the Include table in model check box.

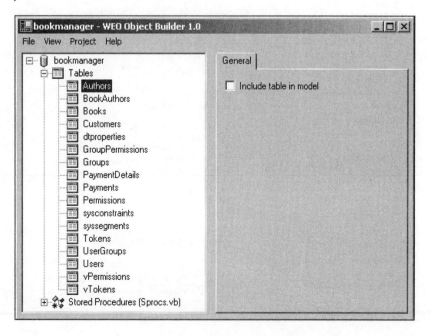

If you check on the Include table in model check box, a dialog will appear prompting you for the entity name. As a convention in our application, tables are named in the plural form, Authors, Books, Orders, etc. but entities are named in the singular. Make sure the recommended Authors entity name is Author. (The Builder will use the unsophisticated rule that if the name ends in "s" or "es", the name is a plural and will automatically suggest the singular form.)

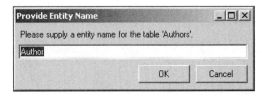

When you click OK, a bunch of new items will appear underneath the Authors table. Each of these represents a class that will be created by the builder. If you select one of the classes, you'll see the code that will be generated.

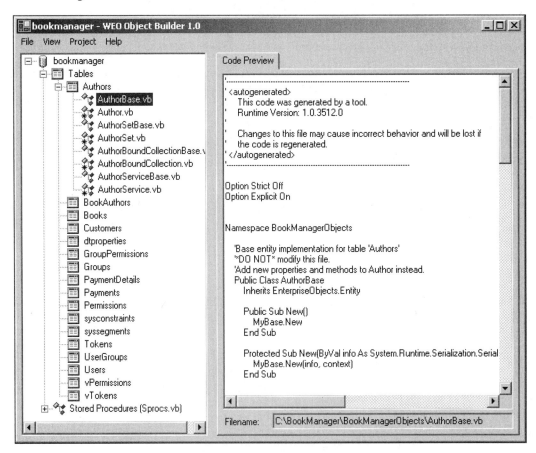

The small star to the left of the class icon indicates that the class will be regenerated when the project is synchronized. The first time you create a project, they'll all have stars because the project is new and none of the classes exist. After you synchronize the project, or when you open the Object Builder again, the classes that should not be regenerated, so the ones you'll add your customization code to, will not have stars, as in the above screenshot.

At the bottom of the tree, you'll notice an item marked Stored Procedures (Sprocs.vb). WEO makes heavy use of stored procedures in two ways. Firstly, it's able to create its own stored procedures to support the activity of the objects in the model. (We'll see this later in this chapter.) Secondly, it's able to use stored procedures that you yourself define to support your specific application. For the moment, you can ignore this.

To create the files, select Project | Synchronize from the menu. A window will pop up displaying the status of the synchronization.

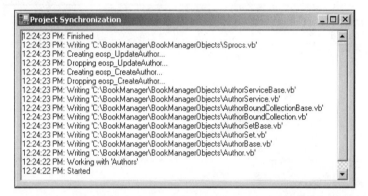

Using Windows Explorer, find the c:\BookManager\BookManagerObjects folder. You'll see a bunch of new files containing all of the classes we need to work with authors. As well as the files listed under the Authors table, you'll also find Sprocs.vb. This contains a class that can help the objects call stored procedures in the database, but we'll talk about this later.

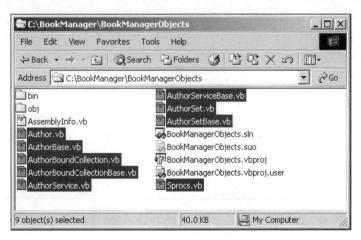

Close the Object Builder. You'll be prompted to save the project and I recommend saving the project to the same folder as the BookManagerObjects Visual Studio solution.

Now that we have a bunch of objects, let's see how we can use them in our application.

Consuming the Objects

Before getting started with the full-on implementation of our enterprise application, let's experiment a little with the capabilities of the WEO layer by building a basic application.

In order to use the object, we need to import the files that we just created into the BookManagerObjects project. Using Solution Explorer, right-click on the BookManagerObjects project and select Add | Add Existing Item. Select the newly created files, including Sprocs.vb and click Open.

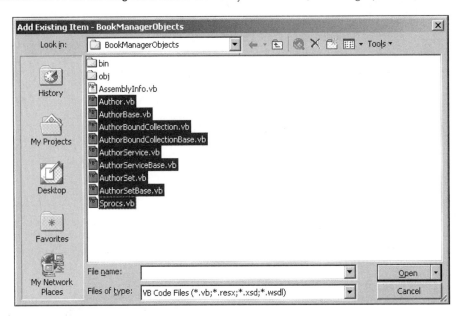

We can't just run a class library, so we'll need to create another project that we can use to present a user interface and consume the objects. Using Solution Explorer once more, right-click the BookManagerObjects solution and select Add | New Project. Create a new Windows Application project, call it TestApp and save it in c:\BookManager.

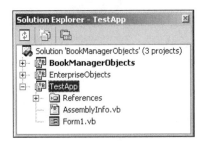

This project needs to be set as the "startup project", so right-click on TestApp and select **Set as StartUp Project**. This will cause Visual Studio .NET to run this application when we select **Debug | Start** from the menu.

For reasons that will become apparent in Chapter 3, rather than adding controls directly to `TestApp.Form1`, we'll create an additional Class Library project containing a user control. We'll draw controls onto the user control and put the user control on Form1.

Create a new Class Library project. Call it **CustomerEditor** and save it in `c:\BookManager`.

One last thing before we start designing the form and adding some event handler code: right-click on TestApp and select **Add Reference**. Change to the **Projects** tab and add references to BookManagerObjects, Customer Editor and EnterpriseObjects. Click **OK** and you'll see this:

Add a new user control to the **CustomerEditor** project called CustomerEditor.

Open the Designer for CustomerEditor and draw on a new ListBox control, like this:

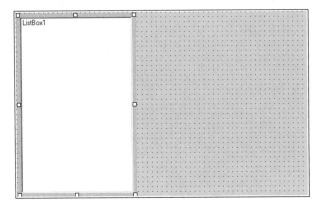

Add references to BookManagerObjects and EnterpriseObjects to the CustomerEditor project.

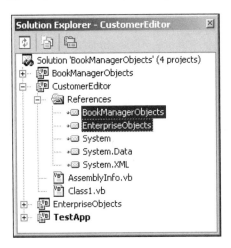

Open the code editor for the new class and add namespace import declarations for the two projects at the top of the code listing.

```
Imports EnterpriseObjects
Imports BookManagerObjects.BookManagerObjects
```

Change these properties on the ListBox:

❏   Name – change to listAuthors

❏   IntegralHeight – change to False

❏   Anchor – change to Top, Bottom, Left

The only configuration that the object model needs at this stage is a database connection string. This needs to be done in the constructor for Form1 of the TestApp, so add this code:

```
Public Class Form1()
    Inherits System.Windows.Forms.Form

    Private Sub New()

    ' This call is required by the Windows Form Designer
    InitializeComponent();

    ' Add any initialization after the InitializeComponent() call

        ' set the connection string...
        EnterpriseApplication.Application.ConnectionString = _
    "integrated security=sspi;initial catalog=bookmanager;data source=corrado"
    End Sub
```

Remember, you'll need to change that string to the specific string that you need for your configuration. You also need to add in an `Imports` statement for `EnterpriseObjects` to the top of `Form1`.

Let's try loading an `AuthorSet` containing all of the authors and looping through each one to populate the list box. In the Designer for **CustomerEditor**, double-click on the background of the user control and make these changes:

```
Private Sub CustomerEditor_Load(ByVal sender As System.Object, _
                        ByVal e As System.EventArgs) Handles MyBase.Load

    If Me.DesignMode = False Then
      ' get the authors...
      Dim authors As AuthorSet = Author.GetAll()

      ' loop them...
      Dim theAuthor As Author
      For Each theAuthor In authors
          ' add it...
            listAuthors.Items.Add(theAuthor.Email)
      Next
    End If

    End Sub
```

Obviously, Data Binding is an easier way of extracting data and populating a list box. However, in this instance, I want to illustrate how we can enumerate through an EntitySet.

Build the projects. This will make the CustomerEditor control available for use. Open the Designer for `Form1` and add a new CustomerEditor control to the form. Use the sizing handles to make the control as big as the form and set the `Anchor` property to `Top`, `Bottom`, `Left`, `Right`.

Even without running the code, you can see what we're trying to do there. Run the project and you'll see the results.

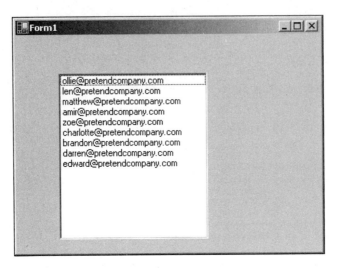

So let's look into the code that Object Builder put together for us to see what's actually happening.

The first thing we're doing there is using a shared method on the Author object called GetAll. In fact, this method is implemented in AuthorBase. If you open up AuthorBase, you'll be able to find this method:

```
Public Shared Function GetAll() As AuthorSet
   Dim service As AuthorService
   service = ServiceObject
   Return service.GetAllSvc()
End Function
```

This comes back to our earlier discussion as to how the client-side entity-related code has the intelligence to connect to the server-side service-related code in order to get data. The ServiceObject property returns an AuthorService object that supports a method called GetAllSvc.

So what exactly does the ServiceObject property do? In the AuthorBase class, look for the ServiceObject property implementation. You'll see that it calls a method called GetServiceObject. This method is implemented in the EnterpriseObjects.Entity class defined within the **EnterpriseObjects** project.

```
Public Shared ReadOnly Property ServiceObject As AuthorService
   Get
      Return
         CType(GetServiceObject(GetType(AuthorService)),AuthorService)
   End Get
End Property
```

The GetServiceObject method needs to determine where the service objects are located. The objects can either be installed on the local machine, or alternatively the objects may be installed on a remote machine. This is actually a relatively detailed topic that we'll go over in far more detail in Chapter 9. For now, we'll be connecting in "Direct" mode; in other words we are able to use the System.Data.SqlClient namespace to connect directly to SQL Server.

Service objects are cached in such a way that they are created the instant before they are first needed (just-in-time activation) and remain in memory for the entire life of the application. They are held in a Hashtable, stored as a shared member of `Entity`.

```
Public Class Entity
    ' members...
    Private _data As Object()
    Protected Shared _serviceObjects As HashTable
```

When we call `GetServiceObject`, we pass in the type of service object that we are looking to create. In our specific case here, we want to create `MyEnterpriseObjects.AuthorService`. When we receive the call, we'll look in the cache to see if we have an instance of it and, if not, we'll create one.

The wrinkle we have to deal with is that if we're connecting directly to the database (as we are here), we need to create the object in a different way than we do when connecting to the server using Remoting. I don't want to go into detail about this now, as this is covered in lots of detail in Chapter 9. However, I can tell you that we use "service object factories" to do this. The Direct factory, implemented in `EnterpriseObjects.DirectServiceObjectFactory` just creates an instance of the object that we request. First of all, here's how `GetServiceObject` works. It uses a property of `EnterpriseApplication` to find the service object factory that we're supposed to use. Once we have that, we can call `Create` on the applicable service object factory.

```
' ServiceObject - return our service object...
Protected Shared Function GetServiceObject(ByVal serviceObjectType _
                                           As Type) As Service

    ' Do we have the cache?
    If _serviceObjects Is Nothing Then
        _serviceObjects = New HashTable()
    End If

    ' Get it out of the cache...
    Dim serviceObject As Service = serviceObjects(serviceObjectType)
    If serviceObject Is Nothing Then

        ' Where do we get the object from?
        Dim factory As ServiceObjectFactory = _
                EnterpriseApplication.Application.ServiceObjectFactory
        serviceObject = factory.Create(serviceObjectType)

        ' add it...
        _serviceObjects.Add(serviceObjectType, serviceObject)
    End If
    Return serviceObject
End Function
```

The `DirectServiceObjectFactory`, the one that we'll use in this case, creates an instance of the specified type.

```
Public Overrides Function Create(ByVal serviceObjectType As _
                                 System.Type)As EnterpriseObjects.Service
    Return System.Activator.CreateInstance(serviceObjectType)
End Function
```

The upshot of all this is that we have an extensible system for creating separate different factories that know how to create either direct or remote objects that actually provide the data to the application. We cover this in far more detail in Chapter 9.

The "Email" Property

We also used the `Email` property in our code example. This relies on us having an instance of an `Author` object around and somehow the `Email` property is able to map onto the appropriate column in the **Authors** table and return data.

If you look at the code that iterates through the `AuthorSet`, you'll notice we're using a conventional `For Each` loop.

```
' get the authors...

Dim authors As AuthorSet = Author.GetAll()
Dim theAuthor As Author
For Each theAuthor In authors
   ' loop them...
    listAuthors.Items.Add(theAuthor.Email)
Next
```

`For Each` relies on the object that's being "`For Each`-ed" to be able to return a list of items back. `EntitySet` supports `System.Collections.IEnumerable`, which is the best way of signaling that a class contains a list of items and provides a method called `GetEnumerator` that can be used to move through that list.

Here's the implementation for `GetEnumerator` inside `EntitySet`. You'll notice that there are two options – the first returns an enumerator bound to the default "zeroth" table, whereas the second allows binding to any table. The second, in fact, creates a new `EntitySetEnumerator` object that's capable of enumerating through any entity set.

```
' GetEnumerator - create an enumerator for a table...
Public Overridable Function GetEnumerator() As IEnumerator _
                             Implements Ienumerable.GetEnumerator
   Return GetEnumerator(0)
End Function

Public Function GetEnumerator(ByVal tableIndex As Integer)
                                          As IEnumerator
   Return New EntitySetEnumerator(tableIndex, Me)
End Function
```

If we look at `EntitySetEnumerator`, the important property is `Current`. This returns the entity at the current position of the enumerator. In fact, what this does is call the `GetEntity` method on the `EntitySet` passing in the table index that we're interested in and the position in the set.

```
Public ReadOnly Property Current() As Object _
                   Implements System.Collections.IEnumerator.Current
   Get
      Return EntitySet.GetEntity(TableIndex, Position)
   End Get
End Property
```

GetEntity from EntitySet.vb is a really important function. It's effectively a factory for creating new Entity objects on demand and it's used in a variety of places in the WEO layer.

The EntitySet can be set to cache entities retrieved by setting the UseCaching property to True. By default this is off meaning that each call to GetEntity results in a new Entity object being created.

If we look at GetEntity, if you ignore the caching code you'll notice that the important parts of this method are related to creating the entity object and populating it.

```vb
Public Function GetEntity(ByVal index As Integer) As Entity
  Return GetEntity(0, index)
End Function

Public Function GetEntity(ByVal tableIndex As Integer, _
                          ByVal index As Integer ) As Entity

  ' do we have it in the cache?
  Dim newEntity As Entity

  ' caching?
  If UseCaching = True AndAlso tableIndex = 0 Then
    ' create it...
    If _entityCache Is Nothing Then
      _entityCache = New Hashtable()
    End If

    ' find it...
    If _entityCache.Contains(index) Then
      Return _entityCache(index)
    End if
  End If

  If newEntity Is Nothing Then
    ' create it...
    newEntity = System.Activator.CreateInstance(EntityType)
    newEntity.Populate(Tables(tableIndex).Rows(index))

    ' add it...
    If UseCaching = True AndAlso tableIndex = 0 Then
      _entityCache.Add(index, newEntity)
    End If

  End If

  ' return...
  Return newEntity

End Function
```

The EntitySet holds a System.Type object that represents the required entity type in a property called EntityType. This property is usually set in the constructor of the bound object. For example, the AuthorSetBase constructor sets the EntityType property to represent the Author class.

```
Public Sub New()

    Me.EntityType = GetType(Author)

End Sub
```

So, whenever the `GetEntity` method is called, the `EntitySet` knows which class should be used to create the `Entity` object and uses `System.Activator` to create an instance of that class. Once it has that class, it calls the object's `Populate` method passing in the `System.Data.DataRow` object that matches the requisite table index and position.

The `Entity` class holds the data related to the entity in a private array called _data. We use `Populate` to create and populate that array:

```
' Populate - set the data for the entity...
Public Sub Populate(ByVal row As DataRow)

    ' store the data...
    ReDim _data(row.ItemArray.Length -1)
    row.ItemArray.CopyTo(_data, 0)

End Sub
```

Open up `AuthorBase` and find the `Email` property. You'll see this:

```
Public Property Email As String
  Get
      Return CType(Me(3),String)
  End Get
  Set
    Me(3) = value
  End Set
End Property
```

You'll notice there that in both the `Get` and `Set` cases, `Email` defers processing to an indexer on the class itself. It also passes in the value of 3 to the indexer. This is the ordinal in the Authors table of the Email column.

> If you change the position of the column in the table, you'll need to synchronize the project to regenerate the properties. Likewise, you'll have to do this whenever you add new tables, rename columns or change the database structure in any way.

The indexer is responsible for extracting the relevant value from the DataSet stored in the private _data member. Here's the code that powers the indexer from `Entity.vb`:

```
' Data property...

Default Property Data(ByVal index as Integer) As Object
  Get
     Return _data(index)
  End Get
```

```
        Set(ByVal Value As Object)
          _data(index) = Value
        End Set
      End Property
```

Nothing too complicated there – the indexer simply wraps access to the private _data member.

An EntitySet inherits from DataSet and simply provides some extra functionality. Entity does not inherit from DataRow, even though all it's doing is just adding extra functionality, just like EntitySet does for DataSet. This is because it's not possible to inherit from DataRow, so we have to create a separate class that wraps access to the row.

The "Name" Property

Now that you know how the WEO layer is able to retrieve data from a database, let's look at how we can customize the generated object model to give us some extra functionality.

Go back to the CustomerEditor_Load method. Change the line that adds the author to the list box so that it doesn't add the content of the Email property but instead adds the entire object:

```
Private Sub CustomerEditor_Load(ByVal sender As System.Object, _
                    ByVal e As System.EventArgs) Handles MyBase.Load
   If Me.DesignMode = False Then
        Dim authors As AuthorSet = Author.GetAll()
        Dim theAuthor As Author
        For Each theAuthor In authors
            listAuthors.Items.Add(theAuthor)
        Next
    End If
End Sub
```

If you run the project now, you'll see that what we see is the full name of the class, but that's not particularly helpful.

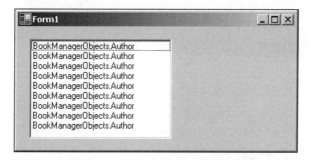

What the list box is doing here is calling the ToString method on the object it's given in order to get a string representation to add to the list. We can provide our own overloaded implementation of this method to return something more useful.

Close the application down if it's still running and open up the Author class. Add a new Name property and a new ToString method.

```
Public Class Author
  Inherits AuthorBase

  ' Name property...
  Public ReadOnly Property Name()As String
    Get
      Return FirstName & " " & LastName
    End Get
  End Property

  ' ToString...
  Public Overrides Function ToString() As String
    Return Name
  End Function
End Class
```

Now run the project and you'll get something more useful.

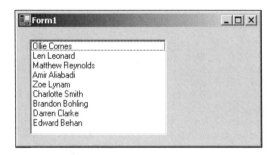

The Author class is yours to customize with your own methods and properties – anything that makes the object model easier to use. The Object Builder will never re-create these "final" classes if they already exist. However, they will re-create the base classes like AuthorBase or AuthorSetBase, so you should *not* add your own customization code to these classes. We'll be looking at this in more detail as we work through the book.

Relating Entities

The "relational" in "relational database" should tell us something about how data is built up in a database management system like SQL Server. In fact, it specifically tells us that data is somehow related, or linked together.

In fact, this definition of "relation" is a contemporary view. In one of the most famous articles on relational databases published in 1970, Dr E.F. Codd wrote that one of the base principles of a relational database system is that "all data is conceptually represented as an orderly arrangement of data into rows and columns, called a RELATION". So "relational" in the original meaning is what we now know as a "table".

Here's an example of one relational link in our database:

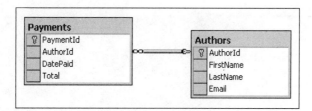

What this diagram tells us is that the Authors table is somehow linked to the Payments table. In our application, the Payments table is used to hold a record of all the royalty payments that an author has received.

Although we can't see it specifically on the diagram, I can tell you that this diagram represents a link from Payments.AuthorId to the master Authors.AuthorId table. There is a "primary key/foreign key relationship" between Payments and Authors.

It stands to reason, then, that:

❑   If we have an Author object, we should be able to get a list of related payments as a PaymentSet.

❑   If we have a Payment object, we should be able to get hold of the related Author object.

The Object Builder and WEO are able to understand this kind of relationship and can build properties and methods to satisfy them. In this section, we'll take a quick look at how we can see a list of payments whenever we select an author in the list – the classic master/details view.

Linking Payments

To access the Payments table in the database, we have to include the table in the Object Builder model. To do this, open up Object Builder again and load in the project you previously saved. Find the Payments table and check on the Include in Model option.

Select Project | Synchronize from the menu. This will create a bunch of files, and you'll need to import these files into the BookManagerObjects project.

Now, open the Designer for CustomerEditor.CustomerEditor. Add a new DataGrid control, like this:

Set the Name property of the DataGrid control to gridPayments. Set the Anchor property to Top, Bottom, Left, Right.

Whenever we change the selected author, we want to update the DataGrid. Double-click on the list box to create a new SelectedIndexChanged event handler and add this code. We'll go through this code in a moment, so don't worry about it too much for the time being.

```
Private Sub listAuthors_SelectedIndexChanged(ByVal sender As _
            System.Object, ByVal e As System.EventArgs) _
            Handles listAuthors.SelectedIndexChanged
    ' do we have a selection?
    gridPayments.DataSource = Nothing
    If listAuthors.SelectedIndex <> -1 Then
        ' get the author...
        Dim theAuthor As Author = _
                        listAuthors.Items(listAuthors.SelectedIndex)

        ' get the payments...
        Dim payments As PaymentSet = theAuthor.GetRelatedPayments()

        ' show them...
        gridPayments.DataSource = payments
    End If
End Sub
```

Run the project and select one of the authors. If you select **Len Leonard** and expand out the tree that appears in the DataGrid, you'll see this:

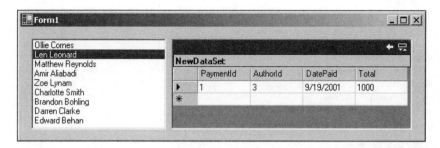

The trick here lies in the call to `GetRelatedPayments`. Object Builder created this method because it understands that a relationship exists between the **AuthorId** column in **Payments** and the **AuthorId** column in **Authors**. (You can learn more about the way the Object Builder works in Appendix A.)

```
Private Sub listAuthors_SelectedIndexChanged(ByVal sender As _
          System.Object, ByVal e As System.EventArgs) _
          Handles listAuthors.SelectedIndexChanged
    ' do we have a selection?
    gridPayments.DataSource = Nothing
    If listAuthors.SelectedIndex <> -1 Then
      ' get the author...
      Dim theAuthor As Author = _
                  listAuthors.Items(listAuthors.SelectedIndex)

      ' get the payments...
      Dim payments As PaymentSet = theAuthor.GetRelatedPayments()

      ' show them...
      gridPayments.DataSource = payments
    End If
End Sub
```

Open the code editor for `AuthorBase.vb` and you'll find this method:

```
Public Function GetRelatedPayments() As PaymentSet
    Return Payment.GetForAuthor(Me.Id)
End Function
```

You can see there that this method defers processing to a shared method on the `Payment` object itself. In fact, `GetForAuthor` is implemented in `PaymentBase.vb`, so open the code editor for this class.

```
Public Shared Function GetForAuthor(ByVal authorId As Integer) _
                                                As PaymentSet
    Dim service As PaymentService
    service = ServiceObject
    Return service.GetForAuthor(authorId)
End Function
```

No real surprises there, `PaymentBase.GetForAuthor` defers payment to a method with the same name on the service object, or rather `PaymentService`. Again, the method is implemented on `PaymentServiceBase` so open the editor for this class and find the `GetForAuthor` method.

```
' GetForAuthor - links to the Authors table...
Public Function GetForAuthor(ByVal authorId As Integer)As PaymentSet

  Dim sql As String
  sql = "Select * from Payments where AuthorId=" & authorId
  Return Ctype(Me.GetEntitySet(sql, GetType(PaymentSet)),PaymentSet)
End Function
```

Inserting Data

Object Builder creates methods that can make inserting rows in the bound tables far easier. On the entity classes you'll find a method called Insert. This method can be used to create a new row.

Some of the columns on each table will be marked as unable to hold null values. When building the Insert method, the Object Builder looks for these columns and for each one it finds, it adds a parameter to the method. The upshot of this is that if you want to call the method, you have to provide values for each of the "not nullable" columns. The method also assumes that the return value from the stored procedure is an integer returned with the return keyword.

Here's the definition for the Authors table. Notice how Email is the only column that can accept a null value:

Now, if you look in AuthorBase, you'll find the Insert method:

```
Public Shared Function Insert(ByVal firstName As String, _
                      ByVal lastName As String) As Author

  Return Author.ServiceObject.Insert(firstName, lastName)
End Function
```

You can see there that the method takes two parameters – firstName and lastName. With the exclusion of AuthorId, which is a special case because it's the ID column, these two columns are the non-null columns defined on the table.

If you want a version of this method that will insert the e-mail, you'll need to create your own stored procedure and method for accessing it. We cover this activity in the next section and again in Chapter 4.

Of course, `Insert` defers processing to a matching method on `AuthorService`, or specifically on `AuthorServiceBase`. Open `AuthorServiceBase` and you'll find the `Insert` method:

```
Public Function Insert(ByVal firstName As String, _
                       ByVal lastName As String) As Author

  Return Me.GetById(Sprocs.eosp_CreateAuthor(firstName, lastName))
End Function
```

This method calls into the shared `eosp_CreateAuthor` method on `Sprocs`. This method in turn runs the stored procedure that actually performs the insert. You can see that this method takes the same parameters, in other words the same set of non-null columns, as the `Insert` method itself. `eosp_CreateAuthor` will return the ID of the new author, and this is passed to `GetById` whose job it is to build an `Author` entity object from the ID. This is then returned back to the caller.

Your Own Stored Procedures

As you've probably gathered by now, the Object Builder is fairly limited in what it can do, but it provides a very powerful way to work with typed sets of items in applications.

Those of you who have experience at building large, database-centric applications will know that stored procedures are a staple that we cannot do without. However, consuming stored procedures in .NET can be a chore because the code used to consume them is so verbose.

To illustrate this, here's the code that calls the `eosp_CreateAuthor` stored procedure:

```
Public Shared Function eosp_CreateAuthor(ByVal firstName As String , _
                                ByVal lastName As String)As Integer

   ' create a connection...
   Dim connection As System.Data.SqlClient.SqlConnection = _
                     New System.Data.SqlClient.SqlConnection(_
   EnterpriseObjects.EnterpriseApplication.Application.ConnectionString)
   connection.Open()

   ' create a command...
   Dim command As System.Data.SqlClient.SqlCommand  = _
        New System.Data.SqlClient.SqlCommand("eosp_CreateAuthor", _
                                             connection)
   command.CommandType = System.Data.CommandType.StoredProcedure

   ' parameters...
   Dim firstNameParam As System.Data.SqlClient.SqlParameter  = _
                command.Parameters.Add("@firstName", _
                                       System.Data.SqlDbType.VarChar, _
                                       32)
   firstNameParam.Value = firstName
   Dim lastNameParam As System.Data.SqlClient.SqlParameter  = _
                command.Parameters.Add("@lastName", _
                                       System.Data.SqlDbType.VarChar, _
```

```
                                              32)
   lastNameParam.Value = lastName
   Dim returnValueParam As System.Data.SqlClient.SqlParameter  = _
                   command.Parameters.Add("@returnValueParam", _
                                          System.Data.SqlDbType.Int)
   returnValueParam.Direction = System.Data.ParameterDirection.ReturnValue

   ' execute...
   command.ExecuteNonQuery()

   ' cleanup...
   command.Dispose()
   connection.Close()

   ' return...
   Return CType(returnValueParam.Value,Integer)
End Function
```

That's quite verbose! However, because Object Builder has wrapped this stored procedure in a method, calling it is just a matter of calling a single method and providing a few parameters. Here's the `Insert` method from `AuthorBase`:

```
Public Function Insert(ByVal firstName As String , _
                   ByVal lastName As String)As Author

   Return Me.GetById(Sprocs.eosp_CreateAuthor(firstName, lastName))
End Function
```

So far we've only seen how we can use stored procedures automatically generated by Object Builder. However, Object Builder works equally well with stored procedures that we create ourselves.

Creating a Stored Procedure

Imagine we needed a stored procedure that could return all of the PaymentDetails rows for a given Author. Here's the relationship:

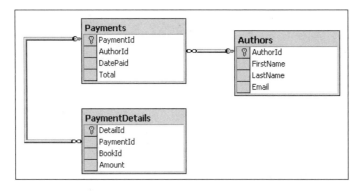

We can see that there's no direct relationship between PaymentDetails and Authors. If we want all the PaymentDetails rows for a given author, we have to find all the Payments rows for an author and then find all the PaymentDetails rows for each payment.

We can express that in SQL with this statement:

```
SELECT * FROM payments
    INNER JOIN paymentdetails ON
        payments.paymentid=paymentdetails.paymentid
```

> I've used **SELECT** * for brevity here. **SELECT** * is convenient, but bad practice!
> Whenever you need to return columns, always specify them explicitly. When we come
> to build the stored procedure, you'll see this in action.

To try this, using Server Explorer show all of the rows in the PaymentDetails table. On the toolbar, click the SQL button. Replace the SQL code that VS.NET has created with the SQL code above. Click the red exclamation mark to run the command and you'll see something like this:

Each row in the results represents a PaymentDetails row that's also been bound to the Payments table. You can see that we have an AuthorId column. By selecting rows that have a given author ID, we can return all the payment details for an author.

Create a new stored procedure with this code:

```
CREATE PROCEDURE GetPaymentDetailsForAuthor
(
  @authorId int
)
AS
  SELECT Payments.PaymentId, DetailId, DatePaid, Amount, BookId FROM
  payments
    INNER JOIN paymentdetails ON
      payments.paymentid=paymentdetails.paymentid
    WHERE authorid=@authorid
```

Creating the stored procedure is easy, but you need to select the tool of choice.

For those of you with a full copy of SQL Server installed, you *cannot* create stored procedures from within VS.NET's Server Explorer, and you'll have to use the Enterprise Manager.

For those of you using SQL Server 2000 Desktop Edition (née MSDE), you *can* create stored procedures from within VS.NET's Server Explorer.

Whichever tool you use, the principle is the same. Take the stored procedure code I've presented above and create a new procedure.

Calling the Procedure

Now that you've created the stored procedure, we can call it from within our own code. If you open up the Object Builder, you'll find the new `GetPaymentDetailsForAuthor` stored procedure has been detected. (If it's not in the list, select **View | Refresh** from the menu or press **F5**.)

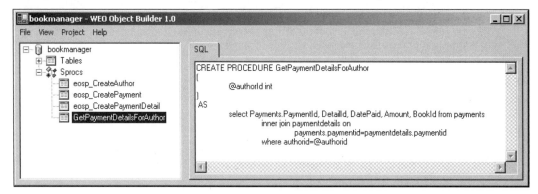

Because the Object Builder has detected the existence of the stored procedure, we know that it created a shared method on the `Sprocs` class called `GetPaymentDetailsForAuthor`. All we have to do is call it, but before we can call it we need to synchronize the project so select **Project | Synchronize** from the menu.

Remember, this will recreate the base classes (`AuthorServiceBase`, `AuthorBase` and so on) but will leave the non-base classes (`AuthorService`, `Author`, etc.) intact. This is why we do not add customizations to the base classes.

When we finally run these business objects on a separate server accessed through Remoting (we cover this in Chapter 9), the model we work on is that we have to call the method from a service object, or specifically in this case we should call it from `AuthorService`. As we need to be careful to abstract the service layer away from the developer, we'll need to add a method to `Author` that defers processing over to `AuthorService`.

Remembering that we shouldn't add code to the "base" classes, open the code editor for `AuthorService`, add a directive at the top of the listing to include `System.Data` and add this code:

```
Public Class AuthorService
   Inherits AuthorServiceBase

   ' GetPaymentDetails...
   Public Function GetRelatedPaymentDetails(ByVal authorId As _
                                  Integer)As DataSet

      ' run it...
      Return Sprocs.GetPaymentDetailsForAuthor(authorId, GetType(DataSet))
```

```
    End Function
End Class
```

The line of interest there is obviously the call to the shared `Sprocs.GetPaymentDetailsForAuthor` method. The `authorId` parameter is obviously required otherwise we cannot specify which author we need, but why do we need to pass a reference to the `System.Data.DataSet` type?

Well, the method is responsible for creating the DataSet that needs to be returned. In our case, we're going to keep this as a DataSet, but in others it could be that we want to create an `AuthorSet` or some other kind of strongly typed EntitySet. If you look at the `GetPaymentDetailsForAuthor` method in `Sprocs`, you'll find a call to `System.Activator.CreateInstance` that creates the DataSet that the `SqlDataAdapter` needs to squirt the data into.

```
Public Shared Function GetPaymentDetailsForAuthor(ByVal authorId _
                     As Integer, ByVal useDatasetType As _
                     System.Type)As DataSet

   ' create a connection...
   Dim connection As System.Data.SqlClient.SqlConnection  = _
                 New System.Data.SqlClient.SqlConnection(_
EnterpriseObjects.EnterpriseApplication.Application.ConnectionString)
   connection.Open()

   ' create a command...
   Dim command As System.Data.SqlClient.SqlCommand  = _
                           new System.Data.SqlClient.SqlCommand(_
                           "GetPaymentDetailsForAuthor", _
                           connection)
   command.CommandType = System.Data.CommandType.StoredProcedure

   ' parameters...
   Dim authorIdParam As System.Data.SqlClient.SqlParameter  = _
                 command.Parameters.Add("@authorId", _
                                     System.Data.SqlDbType.Int)
   authorIdParam.Value = authorId

   ' extract the dataset...
   Dim adapter As System.Data.SqlClient.SqlDataAdapter  = _
                     New System.Data.SqlClient.SqlDataAdapter(command)
   Dim myDataset As System.Data.DataSet  = _
                 CType(System.Activator.CreateInstance(useDatasetType), _
                 System.Data.DataSet)
   adapter.Fill(myDataset)
   adapter.Dispose()

   ' cleanup...
   command.Dispose()
   connection.Close()

   ' return dataset...
   Return myDataset
End Function
```

On `AuthorBase`, we already have a method called `GetRelatedPayments`. In order to keep the naming consistent, the method we use to get the service object to run the stored procedure should be named similarly, for example `GetRelatedPaymentDetails`.

Add this method to `Author`, remembering to first add a namespace import declaration for `System.Data` so that we can properly access DataSet:

```
Public Function GetRelatedPaymentDetails()As DataSet

   ' service...
   Return ServiceObject.GetRelatedPaymentDetails(Id)
End Function
```

Again, there's nothing amazing there. All we're doing is deferring processing over to `AuthorService` and providing the current author ID.

Finally, to test this we need to tweak the `SelectedIndexChanged` event handler for the list in `CustomerEditor`. Find the handler and change the `GetRelatedPayments` call to a `GetRelatedPaymentDetails` call.

```
Private Sub listAuthors_SelectedIndexChanged(ByVal sender As _
                        System.Object, ByVal e As System.EventArgs) _
                        Handles listAuthors.SelectedIndexChanged

   ' do we have a selection?
   gridPayments.DataSource = Nothing
   If listAuthors.SelectedIndex <> -1 Then

      ' get the author...
      Dim theAuthor As Author = _
            listAuthors.Items(listAuthors.SelectedIndex)

      ' get the payments...
      Dim payments As DataSet = theAuthor.GetRelatedPaymentDetails()

      ' show them...
      gridPayments.DataSource = payments
   End If
End Function
```

Run the project and you'll find that the new stored procedure is called and the results shown in the DataGrid.

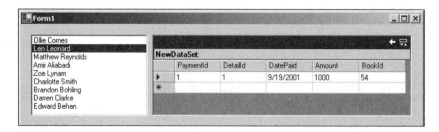

Although the stored procedures automatically created by Object Builder are useful, throughout this book we'll be spending a lot of time creating stored procedures for use in our application. The process we've been through in this section is one that you'll repeat a lot, so here's a recap:

❑ Design and create a new stored procedure in SQL Server's Enterprise Manager or in VS.NET's Server Explorer.

❑ Open the Object Builder project. Find the stored procedure to make sure it exists.

❑ Synchronize the project.

❑ Add a method to the relevant service class (*not* the service *base* class) that can call the method in `Sprocs`.

❑ Add a method to the relevant entity class (*not* the entity *base* class) that defers processing to the service class.

Naming Your Stored Procedures

You can give your stored procedure virtually any name you like. However, the object builder will treat any stored procedure prefixed with `eosp_` ("Enterprise Object Stored Procedure") as its own, so try to avoid prefixing your own stored procedure with this otherwise it could be deleted or modified by the Object Builder.

Summary

In this chapter we took our first practical look at how the Enterprise Objects and the application we discussed in the introductory chapter actually work.

In the first instance we downloaded the various bits and bobs that we need to get the application working. We then took a look at how to create a project using the Object Builder tool and asked it to generate code that we could use in a project.

After this, we built a simple application that would allow us to use the WEO objects and the new objects derived from these so that we could step through into the code and see what was actually happening under the hood. We also saw what in theory would happen when inserting new rows into the database.

Finally, we took a look at building our own stored procedures and using them from inside our applications.

.NET Enterprise Development in VB .NET

3

The Application Browser

One of the key precepts for the application we build in this book is the Application Browser. In essence, an Application Browser is similar to a web browser – you connect a web browser to a web server in order to access that web server's functionality. With an Application Browser, you connect to an Application Server in order to use that Application Server's functionality.

Conceptually, the desktop application browser offers similar functionality to that offered by an equivalent desktop application. What is special about the browser is that, like a web browser, the functionality available to the user is not fixed when the browser was compiled. For instance, if you go to Amazon's web site, your web browser is now effectively running an application that allows you to browse and buy books, yet you don't have to install anything special on your computer to do so. The application browser is similar – it allows developers and system administrators to roll new functionality out to users without their having to follow certain steps for installation.

Before We Begin

It's very important that you follow these instructions carefully before beginning this chapter!

In the last chapter, we built a small executable containing a user control that showed a list of authors. Clicking on one of the authors updated a DataGrid to show their details. We want to now take that user control and plug it into the application browser that we're going to build.

To have the best chance of following this chapter, I recommend setting the properties of the CustomerEditor project so that the CustomerEditor.dll assembly is written to c:\BookManager\CustomerEditor\bin .

Using Solution Explorer, right-click on the CustomerEditor project and select Properties. In the list on the left, choose Configuration Properties, and then click on Build. Find the Output Path property and change it to:

```
C:\BookManager\CustomerEditor\bin
```

That's more or less shown here:

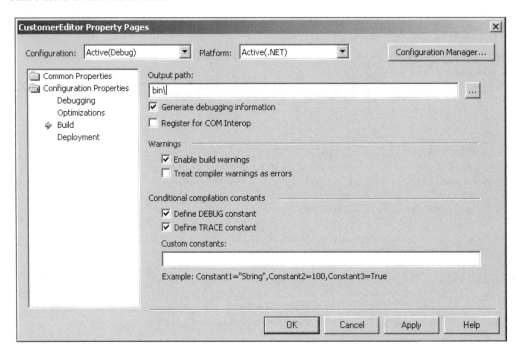

Click OK. Build the project and the CustomerEditor.dll assembly should appear in the c:\BookManager\CustomerEdtior\bin folder. *Check this now*, because if it's not there you're going to have horrendous difficulties following along.

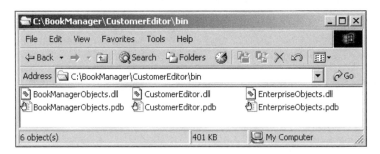

Browser Distribution

Traditionally, software distribution has been done in a number of ways. Perhaps the most obvious is for software to be produced, burnt onto CD, and sold. Nowadays, increasing amounts of software is made available for electronic download, either as part of a "buy and download" scheme as operated by a number of online retailers, or as a "shareware" (the "try it and buy it if you like it" approach). Of course, I'm just talking about legitimate software distribution here. Pirated software can be – and is – distributed either through physical or online channels.

Thinking about our application for a moment, what we're trying to do is free it from the confines of the private company network. This is something that's been happening for a number of years now, either using the intranet/extranet model, or by utilizing web applications. There's an argument that an e-commerce retailer's web site, such as Amazon, can in actuality be seen as just an extension of their own private systems. When you buy something from Amazon, you don't talk to a telephone sales operator as you may have done in the past with such an outfit, but rather you use the web-based equivalent of the application that would have been used by the now-redundant operator on the company network. It's a cruel world, but I can't deny that I'd rather use an application myself than have to deal with some buffoon on a telephone more interested in hitting on their colleagues than helping me buy the book I want!

That's all very well for relatively simple customer-facing applications of that nature. In the traditional line-of-business application environment however, employee's applications have remained firmly stuck to the company LAN. With our approach, we shall use the power of .NET to take the software off the LAN, and make it accessible to the private computers of employees working from home, hotel rooms, as well as their offices. In the same swoop, we'll also take the application right into the offices of suppliers, customers, and our business partners. You might be thinking that there's nothing very new about all this, and indeed we could accomplish these aims with a traditional Visual Basic or MFC application, but it would be a bit of a handful. What this book will illustrate is how *easy* it is to do now that we have the tools of the .NET Framework.

Creating remotely accessible applications such as this elicits two significant problems. Firstly, we'll throw up some horrendous security issues. What if our trusted business partner gives a copy of the client application to a competitor, unwittingly or otherwise? That competitor may then be able to access our hard-won customer database in its entirety, and could easily undercut or outmaneuver us to win their business.

Secondly, the client application starts to go "out of bounds" with regards to the control that the various administrative staff have over its deployment. In large enterprise installations, you often find that the administrative team is fairly strict regarding what they will or will not allow to be installed on employee workstations, in terms of both hardware and software. It's quite common practice for administrators to put together a few key desktop configurations. Applications required by certain users are somehow installed into one of these configurations. When a new machine is required, or the configuration has been updated, the workstation is instructed to obtain the new configuration. As the configuration contains the application, once the desktop has updated itself, the new application is automatically available.

.NET offers a different model of software distribution. Imagine that a given application is made up of a number of different assemblies, each assembly performing a specific task. For instance, one assembly might allow the user to modify customer information while another allows them to review orders before they are processed. Each of these assemblies makes up a "sub-application". (We're simplifying a little here by saying that a single sub-application is implemented in a single assembly, whereas it's likely that a sub-application would in fact constitute several different assemblies.) With a .NET application, we can automatically download assemblies as required from a web server, as a background process without the user ever knowing what's going on.

As far as enterprise deployment is concerned, this is very significant and, in this author's opinion, quite brilliant! Here's a step-by-step overview:

1. For the initial deployment of the application browser, the system administrators install it as part of their standard desktop configurations. These configurations are then rolled out as normal. The browser does *not* contain any application-specific functionality at this point, a bit like a web browser without any cached pages.

2. The different assemblies that make functionality for various tasks available to users are put onto a web server accessible over the network or the Internet as appropriate.

3. The browser somehow "knows" what assemblies are available from the web server, and constructs menu options that users can select to access the functionality that they represent.

4. When the user requests some of this functionality by clicking a menu option, the browser automatically downloads the assembly from the web server, installs it, and runs the code.

In this chapter, we're going to concentrate on how the browser can "know" what assemblies are available for download, and also what functionality each encapsulates. We'll do this by using a Web Service that firstly authenticates the user, and secondly publishes a list of the functionality that that user is permitted to access.

For example, imagine one of our supplier companies has an application browser installed on a workstation on their network. The user opens the browser, enters their username and password, and is given back a list of things that they can do. Along with this list are the instructions that tell the browser which options to add to the menus. Each option also contains a reference to an assembly, together with a URL from which the assembly can be downloaded. Once we're at this point, we have a browser client application that we can roll into our enterprise configurations for the private company network and also make freely downloadable for clients, suppliers, and other business partners. The distribution of the client itself isn't important – what is important is that the authentication works in a secure, efficient manner, and that users are only given access to what they're supposed to have access to.

In this chapter, we're going to be looking at putting together the basic elements of the application browser and designing a pluggable architecture that allows us to build sub-applications for our users. We're also going to put together a basic Web Service for the authentication and "functionality publishing" processes.

What we're *not* going to do at this stage is worry about the authentication process itself – in fact, any username and password will yield the same user identity and the same set of application functionality. We'll cover this in Chapter 10. We're also not going to worry about controlling which users can access what functionality. This will also be covered in Chapter 10.

Getting Going

As good a place to start as any is with the Web Service. As mentioned before, this will be responsible for authenticating the user and providing a catalog of the user's available functionality.

The authentication process works by using a "token". The Web Service exposes a method called `Authenticate` that takes the details given by the user, and determines whether they are allowed basic access to the application. This authentication is performed against whatever backend system we like (in this chapter, there isn't a process for doing this as such – everyone is just authenticated – but we'll put this system into place in Chapter 10) and a token is returned. The token is simply a string of about 40 bytes in length. This token is retained by the browser, and used in subsequent requests to the application.

So, if authentication is successful, the Web Service will return a token. If authentication is not successful, it will throw an exception that the client will be able to intercept and act upon accordingly. Again, this is something that we'll talk about more in Chapter 10.

Assuming we have a token, we can then call `GetFunctionalityCatalog`. This Web Method will return an object to the client, that is, the application browser. This returned object will in fact be a collection of objects built from a class that we're going to call `AppFunctionality`. This class will contain descriptive information for display and, perhaps more importantly, information that we need to get hold of and then execute the assembly when its functionality is requested.

Building the Web Service

Without any further ado, let's get stuck into coding the Web Service. Create a new Visual Basic | ASP.NET Web Service project and call it BookCoordinator. (I chose this name because the service "coordinates" the activity of all of the browsers.) It's best to create the service in a blank VS.NET solution. During the book, we'll be adding a ton of projects to the separate application browser solution.

> I'm going to assume you're using the web server installed on your local computer, so throughout this chapter we'll use the hostname **"localhost"** to access the Web Service. If you want or need to build the Web Service on another computer on your network, remember to change **localhost** to the hostname that works for you.

By default, Visual Studio .NET will create a new `.asmx` (for "Active Service Methods") file called `Service1.asmx`. As this is a fairly useless name, delete the file in Solution Explorer, and create a new Web Service page called `Coordinator.asmx`. To do this, right-click BookCoordinator and select Add | Add Web Service and enter the new name in the dialog:

To debug the service, we'll need to run it from within Visual Studio, so right-click **Coordinator.asmx** and select **Set As Start Page**.

We'll build and test the `Authenticate` method first. Right-click **Coordinator.asmx** in Solution Explorer, select **View Code**, and add this method to the `Coordinator` class:

```
<WebMethod()> _
Public Function Authenticate(ByVal username As String, _
                             ByVal password As String) _
                             As String

   Return Guid.NewGuid().ToString()
End Function
```

What we're doing there is using the `System.Guid` class to create a new GUID ("globally unique identifier") that we'll use as the token. Those of you who've done any COM development will be very familiar with GUIDs, but for those of you who have not, they are essentially a 128-bit (read as "very long") random number that's guaranteed to be globally unique. As we don't have an authentication system to speak of, it doesn't matter to us what token we get back just so long as we get something back.

Debugging Web Services

For those of you who haven't seen Web Services before, I'll briefly run through the debugging interface that the Framework provides. If you want to dig into Web Services further then take a look at *Professional ASP.NET Web Services, ISBN 1861005458*, also by Wrox Press.

If you run the project now, Visual Studio will fire up Internet Explorer to display the debugging interface for the `Coordinator.asmx` page. In this screenshot, you can see that the URL is shown as **http://localhost/BookCoordinator/Coordinator.asmx**. This is the URL that will be later used to access the Web Service:

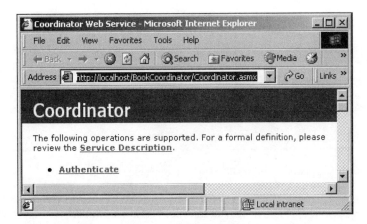

You'll also notice that IE displays a link with the name of our `Authenticate` method. If you click on this, it will take you to a page that lets us invoke this method:

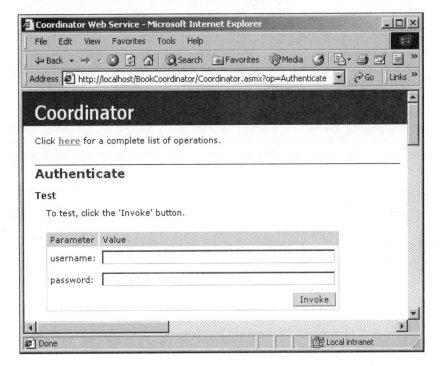

Now enter values for username and password into the form. Click the Invoke button and a new window will appear:

The new window that appears contains the **SOAP response** that is constructed by the `Coordinator` class in response to the call to `Authenticate`. More properly, what actually happens is that the `System.Web.Services.WebService` class that the `Coordinator` class is derived from is told that a call to `Authenticate` needs to be made and the class is also told which parameters will be passed into the call. The class then makes the call to the method and is given back a string, in this case **29328a4c-a093-4e81-82e4-99d3a76dc1b6**, (remember, this is the random GUID, so you'll get an entirely different string), and this string is wrapped up in what's called a **SOAP envelope**.

Web Services are built on the protocol called Simple Object Access Protocol, or SOAP. This is simply a way of expressing calls into methods and the responses from those methods using XML. The actual way SOAP works is not of particular interest to us here – what is important is that we can put together an object that sits on a web server somewhere and is capable of listening to requests from clients, running methods and returning the responses. This is almost the last time we'll talk about SOAP in this book because .NET does such a fabulous job of abstracting the "SOAP plumbing" away from us that there's no need to care *how* it works, just that it *does*.

Although in our case our Web Service is on our local computer, it could be accessible to the Internet at large. Say we have a copy of our application browser running on an employee's home computer. That browser could authenticate itself through the Web Service in much the same way as that computer could request a regular web page.

This is a rather academic discussion, so let's press on and see what else we can do with the Web Service.

Adding a Namespace

Before we press on, if you look at the Web Service's initial page (with the link to the `Authenticate` method), you'll see a block of text that starts like this:

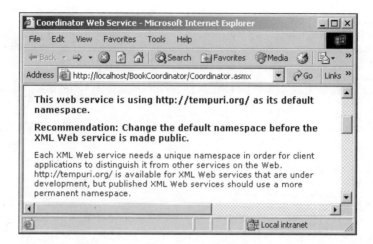

This message is telling us that we need to come up with a new namespace for our Web Service before it's made public. The namespace is the mechanism that ensures that the names we use in our Web Service are distinct to names used by other Web Services. Suppose one of our methods returns an object of class `Customer`. How do we distinguish our `Customer` from another developer's `Customer` class? It is by adding a namespace that we provide this distinction.

Close down Internet Explorer now to stop debugging. Open the code editor for `Coordinator.asmx.vb` and add the `WebService` attribute before the class definition:

```
<WebService(Namespace := "http://www.wrox.com/bookmanager/")> _
Public Class Coordinator
    Inherits System.Web.Services.WebService
```

We're using the `System.Web.Services.WebService` attribute here to supply a namespace of `http://www.wrox.com/bookmanager/` for the `Coordinator` class. This namespace can be used to prefix the names in our service to make them unique.

What's odd about this is that although namespaces look like URLs, in fact they have virtually nothing to do with URLs. The URL we've used as the namespace here isn't even a valid page, although there's no reason why it couldn't be. The crucial point of a namespace is that it is a unique identifier, and company URLs work well because they're under your own control as a developer. If you own the domain pretendcompany.com, for example, you could build a namespace URL around that domain. As the domain is yours, no one else is going to use it in their namespaces, hence you won't ever run into the problem of your namespace clashing with someone else's.

The "GetFunctionalityCatalog" Method

The last thing we need to do before building the client is to put together the `GetFunctionalityCatalog` method. This method will return an array of `AppFunctionality` objects, each one of these representing a piece of functionality that our application is capable of performing.

In the first instance, our application is only going to have one piece of functionality – the customer viewer application that we built in the last chapter. If you remember, rather than building the interface for this application as a form, we built it as a user control. This was because the ultimate intention was to use that same application from within our application browser. When we create our instance of `AppFunctionality`, we'll give it the path to the assembly that contains the user control and the name of the user control. From that we should be able to create an instance of the control and show it in the application browser.

We have yet to build the `AppFunctionality` class, so let's do that now. Using Solution Explorer, create a new class in `BookCoordinator` called `AppFunctionality`. Add this code:

```
Public Class AppFunctionality
    ' members...
    Public Name As String
    Public MenuText As String
    Public ToolbarIconUrl As String
    Public TooltipText As String
    Public AssemblyUrl As String
    Public TypeName As String
End Class
```

Now, open the code editor for `Coordinator.asmx.vb` and add this method:

```
<WebMethod()> _
Public Function GetFunctionalityCatalog(ByVal token As String) _
                                        As AppFunctionality()
    ' create a 1 element array...
    Dim functionality(0) As AppFunctionality

    ' create it...
    functionality(0) = New AppFunctionality()
    functionality(0).Name = "Customer Editor"
    functionality(0).MenuText = "Customer Editor"
    functionality(0).ToolbarIconUrl = ""
    functionality(0).TooltipText = "Allows you to edit customer information"
    functionality(0).AssemblyUrl = _
          "c:\BookManager\CustomerEditor\bin\CustomerEditor.dll"
    functionality(0).TypeName = "CustomerEditor.CustomerEditor"

    ' return it...
    Return functionality
End Function
```

What we're doing here is creating a new `AppFunctionality` object and storing it in an array. We've provided the name of the sub-application, together with other necessary information. You'll notice that I've provided the explicit path to the `CustomerEditor` application that we put together in the last chapter – you might have to change this if the path to the `.dll` on your own computer is different. Last of all, we've provided the name of the `CustomerEditor.CustomerEditor` class.

If you now test this method using the Internet Explorer interface we used for `Authenticate` earlier (it doesn't matter what value you provide for the `token` parameter), you'll get a block of XML back that contains the information given in the code above. The trick now is for our client application to read that information:

```xml
<?xml version="1.0" encoding="utf-8" ?>
<ArrayOfAppFunctionality xmlns:xsi="http://www.w3.org/2001/XMLSchema-instance"
                         xmlns:xsd="http://www.w3.org/2001/XMLSchema"
                         xmlns="http://www.wrox.com/bookmanager/">
  <AppFunctionality>
  <Name>Customer Editor</Name>
  <MenuText>Customer Editor</MenuText>
  <ToolbarIconUrl />
  <TooltipText>Allows you to edit customer information</TooltipText>
  <AssemblyUrl>c:\BookManager\CustomerEditor\bin\CustomerEditor.dll
    </AssemblyUrl>
  <TypeName>CustomerEditor.CustomerEditor</TypeName>
  </AppFunctionality>
</ArrayOfAppFunctionality>
```

Building the Client

Let's now look at the basics of our application browser. What we need to do is:

❑   Connect to the Web Service to authenticate the client

❑   Assuming the client can be authenticated, we need to get the functionality catalog

❑   The catalog needs to be read and new menu items created

❑   When the user selects one of these menu items, we load up the assembly containing that sub-application's main user control and execute it

The first thing we'll do is build the basic application, so we'll put together a form with a menu bar, a status bar, and a frame which will hold the sub-application's main user control.

Create a new **Visual Basic | Windows Application** project in the BookManager folder, and call it ApplicationBrowser. Make sure you do this in a new solution, as it would make life quite complicated if you tried to use the same solution as the Web Service. Delete the default Form1 form and create a new form called Browser, as this is easier than renaming the file and then modifying the code.

Add new MainMenu and StatusBar controls to the form. Set the **Name** property of the MainMenu control to **menuMain** and the **Name** property of the StatusBar control to **statusBar**.

Using the menu editor, add new top-level menu items to **menuMain**. Call them **menuFile**, **menuView** and **menuHelp**, and set their Text properties to **&File**, **&View** and **&Help** respectively. In Windows, the ampersand indicates that the following menu letter should be underlined.

Next, add a Panel control and size it so that it occupies most of the space on the form. Set its name to **panelApp** and its Anchor property to **Top, Bottom, Left, Right**.

Before we see a screenshot of the form, open the Collection Editor for the **Panels** property of **statusBar** using the **Properties** window. Add three panels with the properties below:

Panel Name	Property	Value
panelStatus	Text	Ready
	AutoSize	Spring
panelUser	Text	*Clear this property*
	AutoSize	Contents
panelConnection	Text	*Clear this property*
	Autosize	Contents

Click OK. You won't be able to see the panels until you set the ShowPanels property to True.

You should have something that looks like this:

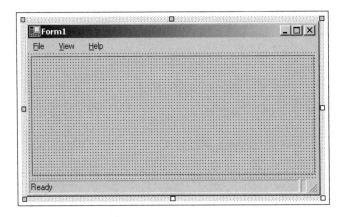

Authentication

Now that we have the basic elements of the form in place, let's turn our attention to authentication.

When we start the browser, the first thing we want to do is pop-up a login form that asks for a username and password. This form will have the intelligence to connect to the Web Service and get the token (or deal with the lack of token if there was a problem with authentication). If we are given a token, the login form will get the functionality catalog back. Both the retrieved token and the functionality catalog will be stored as shared members on the login form for use by other forms in the browser, most notably the Browser form.

Still in the ApplicationBrowser project, create a new Windows Form called Login using Solution Explorer. Add two label controls, two text box controls, and two button controls, like this:

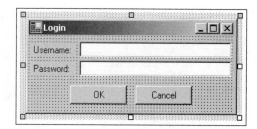

You can deduce the properties for the labels on this form, but you must also:

❑   Change the Name property of the first text box to textUsername

❑   Change the Name property of the second text box to textPassword

❑   Change the Name property of the OK button to buttonOk

❑   Change the Name property of the Cancel button to buttonCancel

In addition, we need the form to not be resizable, so change the FormBorderStyle to FixedDialog, and set the MinimizeBox and MaximizeBox buttons to False. Finally, set the StartPosition property to CenterScreen.

If the user clicks the Cancel button, we want to close the application down. Double-click on the Cancel button to create a new Click event handler, and add this code:

```
Private Sub buttonCancel_Click(ByVal sender As System.Object, _
                               ByVal e As System.EventArgs) _
                               Handles buttonCancel.Click

    Application.Exit()
End Sub
```

Of course, if the user clicks the OK button, we want to attempt to authenticate using the Web Service, so we have to add a reference to the Web Service to our project. There are a number of ways that we can do this, but I'm going to use a method that will work even if your Web Service is on another computer.

Flip over to your BookCoordinator project. Run it and click on the Service Description link. This will open the WSDL document for the Web Service. WSDL stands for "Web Services Description Language" and in essence contains a list of the methods that the Web Service supports. You can learn a lot more about WSDL beyond adding project references to Web Services in the book *Professional ASP.NET Web Services, ISBN 1861005458*, also from Wrox Press. We need to give that WSDL document to our ApplicationBrowser project so that ApplicationBrowser clients can talk to the BookCoordinator Web Service.

Select the URL from the Address bar, right-click it and select Copy. The URL should look like this:

```
http://localhost/BookCoordinator/Coordinator.asmx?WSDL
```

Flip-back to the ApplicationBrowser project. In Solution Explorer, right-click the project name, and select Add Web Reference.

When the dialog appears, paste the URL into the **Address** bar and click the green arrow button to the right (or hit *Enter*):

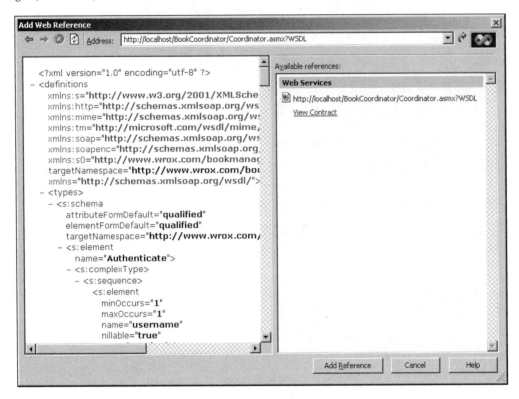

You can see the WSDL document in the left-hand pane. We don't need to worry too much about this, as it's a little like SOAP in that it's a well-abstracted enabling technology that Visual Studio .NET manages so well that we don't really need to worry about it.

Click the **Add Reference** button to add the reference. It will appear in Solution Explorer as localhost, or as the hostname in the URL of the WSDL file if this was different:

As localhost isn't a very meaningful name, right-click on the reference, select **Rename** and change the name to **Coordination**.

This process of adding the web reference creates a class that can communicate with the Web Service (known as the **Web Service proxy class**). The class itself shares the same name as the .asmx file – so in our case it's called Coordinator. The name that appears in Solution Explorer is actually the name of the namespace that contains the proxy class. We've changed this to Coordination, so if our root namespace is ApplicationBrowser, the full name of this class is ApplicationBrowser.Coordination.Coordinator. To call methods on the Web Service, all we have to do is instantiate the proxy class and call the methods just as if they were normal, local methods. .NET handles all the SOAP magic that passes the call over the wire.

Now we need to hook up the **OK** button. Open the Designer for Login, and double-click on the **OK** button to create a new click event handler. Add this code:

```
Private Sub buttonOk_Click(ByVal sender As System.Object, _
                            ByVal e As System.EventArgs) _
                            Handles buttonOk.Click

    ' get the service...
    Dim service As Coordination.Coordinator  = _
                                        New Coordination.Coordinator()

    ' authenticate...
    Try

        _token = service.Authenticate(textUsername.Text, textPassword.Text)

        ' now we have a token, get the functionality catalog...
        _functionality = service.GetFunctionalityCatalog(Token)

        ' store the username...
        _username = textUsername.Text

        ' create the browser...
        Dim myBrowser As Browser = New Browser()
        myBrowser.Show()
        Me.Hide()
    Catch ex As Exception
        MessageBox.Show("You could not be authenticated: " & ex.Message)
    End Try
End Sub
```

You can see from this code that calling remote Web Service methods is no different to how we're used to calling methods on local objects.

What we're assuming here is that if Authenticate cannot get a token, it will throw an exception. This exception is reported to the user – although it's perhaps preferable to catch the exception, and act accordingly depending on what is the cause. Typically, we would differentiate between exceptions caused by communication issues (a classic problem with Web Services) and exceptions that arise due to security issues.

We're going to store the token, username, and the functionality catalog as private members of the form. After we've stored that information, we create a new `Browser` instance, and show it. We also hide the login dialog, but we don't close it. (If we were to close it, the application would close, which wouldn't be what we needed!)

Add this code to the top of the class definition. Notice how we've created these as shared members because we will need to access them from `Browser` later on:

```
Public Class Login
   Inherits System.Windows.Forms.Form

   ' members...
   Private Shared _currentLogin As Login
   Private _token As String
   Private _username As String
   Private _functionality As Coordination.AppFunctionality()
```

On a few occasions, we'll need to access an instance of the `Login` class without having a physical reference to it. The best approach is to store a reference to it, using the self-referential VB keyword `Me`, in a shared member the first time a `Login` object is created. We'll use the `_currentLogin` member here. We'll also create a shared property called `CurrentLogin` that will return that reference to the caller. The upshot is that wherever we are in the application, we can access an instance of `Login` containing the application functionality catalog and the current user's details.

Add this code to the constructor for `Login`:

```
        Public Sub New()
          MyBase.New()

          ' This call is required by the Windows Form Designer
          InitializeComponent()

          ' save an instance of us as the current login...
          _currentLogin = Me
        End Sub
```

Also add this property:

```
        ' CurrentLogin property...
        Public Shared ReadOnly Property CurrentLogin() As Login
          Get
            Return _currentLogin
          End Get
        End Property
```

Finally, add these properties to provide access to the members:

```
        ' Token property...
        Public ReadOnly Property Token() As String
          Get
            Return _token
          End Get
        End Property
```

```
    ' Functionality property...
    Public ReadOnly Property Functionality() As Coordination.AppFunctionality()
      Get
        Return _functionality
      End Get
    End Property

    ' Username property...
    Public ReadOnly Property Username() As String
      Get
        Return _username
      End Get
    End Property
```

When the application runs, we want the Login form to be displayed first, and not the Browser form. Open the project properties and set the Startup object to Login – this is located under **Common Properties | General**.

If you run the project now, nothing much will happen, although the user will be authenticated and we will get a token and a functionality catalog returned.

Closing the Application

You'll notice that if you close the browser window, the application will keep running. For now we need to use the **Debug | Stop Debugging** option in Visual Studio, but we'll see how to get the application to close properly in this section.

What we need to do is "listen" for when the browser windows close, and once they have all closed, then close the Login dialog, terminating the application. We can monitor window closing by hooking into the Closed event of the Browser form, but monitoring window opening is a little trickier. To do this, we'll add a shared method to Login called BrowserOpened that we'll call from within the constructor on Browser.

First of all, add this member to Login:

```
Public Class Login
  Inherits System.Windows.Forms.Form

  ' members...
  Private Shared _currentLogin As Login
  Private _token As String
  Private _username As String
  Private _functionality As Coordination.AppFunctionality()
  Private _numBrowsers As Integer = 0
```

Then add this method. When a new Browser class is created, we'll call this method from the constructor in Browser. It will increment the browser count, but also wire in a handler to listen for the Closed event:

```
    ' BrowserOpened method...
    Public Sub BrowserOpened(ByVal theBrowser As Browser)

      ' increment...
```

```
        _numBrowsers += 1

        ' listen for a close...
        AddHandler theBrowser.Closed, New EventHandler(AddressOf Me.BrowserClosed)
    End Sub
```

We'll call this method from within the constructor for `Browser`. In that way, `_numBrowsers` will be incremented each time a window is created.

First though, add this method:

```
    ' BrowserClosed method...
    Private Sub BrowserClosed(ByVal sender As System.Object, _
                              ByVal e As System.EventArgs)

        ' decrement...
        _numBrowsers -= 1

        ' do we need to close?
        If _numBrowsers = 0 Then
            Me.Close()
        End If
    End Sub
```

You'll notice that this method is not shared. That's because we need access to a `Login` class that we can close with the `Close` method. In a moment, we'll tie that method into the `Closed` event of the browser window. When this event fires, the method will be called, we'll decrement the shared `_numBrowsers` member and, if it's zero, we know all the browsers have been closed and we can close the `Login` window. This will shut down the application correctly.

Finally, open the code editor for `Browser` and add this code to the constructor:

```
    Public Sub New()
        MyBase.New()

        ' This call is required by the Windows Form Designer
        InitializeComponent()

        ' tell the login window that we have opened...
        Login.CurrentLogin.BrowserOpened(Me)
    End Sub
```

If you run the project now, you should find that when you close the browser window, the application will close properly.

Adding Menu Options

The next important step is to test that we can load up our **Customer Editor** sub-application. To do this, we need to have a menu option. The user clicks on the option and the sub-application is loaded. Simple!

My preferred method for working with menu options in Windows Forms applications is to derive new classes from `System.Windows.Forms.MenuItem` and overload the `OnClick` method. This tends to be the easiest way to react to a menu click. For example, in this case we'll create new classes called `SubApplicationMenuItem` and whenever any of these are clicked, we'll call a public method in the `Browser` class that we'll also build, called `RunSubApplication`.

Create a new class in the **ApplicationBrowser** project called `SubApplicationMenuItem`. When the code editor appears, add these namespace import declarations:

```
Imports System.Windows.Forms
Imports ApplicationBrowser.Coordination
```

Set the class to inherit from `MenuItem` and add these two members – one to store the instance of the browser to which the menu item belongs, and the other to store the functionality that it relates to:

```
Public Class SubApplicationMenuItem
    Inherits MenuItem

' members...
Public myBrowser As Browser
Public Functionality As AppFunctionality
```

The constructor for this class will require a parameter for each of these, so we need an instance of `Browser` and an instance of `AppFunctionality`. As well as storing the values, we'll also update our `Text` property. Add a constructor to the `SubApplicationMenuItem` class:

```
Public Sub New(ByVal theBrowser As Browser, _
               ByVal functionality As AppFunctionality)

    ' save...
    Me.myBrowser = theBrowser
    Me.Functionality = functionality

    ' set the text...
    Me.Text = Me.Functionality.MenuText
End Sub
```

As mentioned before, we can respond to the user clicking the menu item by overloading the `OnClick` method. At this point, we need to call back into the `Browser` that we're associated with, and pass in an `AppFunctionality` object. Add this method to `SubApplicationMenuItem`:

```
' OnClick...
Protected Overrides Sub OnClick(ByVal e As System.EventArgs)
    ' run it...
    myBrowser.RunSubApplication(Functionality)
End Sub
```

What we'll do is test that all works properly and then look at how we can actually load up the application.

Open the code editor for `Browser` and add this method:

```
' RunSubApplication...
Public Sub RunSubApplication(ByVal functionality As _
                             Coordination.AppFunctionality)
  ' display a message box for now...
  MessageBox.Show(functionality.AssemblyUrl)
End Sub
```

As you can see, all this does is display a message box when `RunSubApplication` is called.

Of course, none of this will work unless we actually create and add the `SubApplicationMenuItem` objects to the menu. We'll do this by responding to the `Load` event of the form and asking `Login` to return the collection of `AppFunctionality` objects that the user is allowed to have. We'll iterate through the collection and add new items. Add this method to `Browser.vb`:

```
Protected Overrides Sub OnLoad(ByVal e As System.EventArgs)
  ' update the menu...
  Dim functionality As Coordination.AppFunctionality
  For Each functionality In Login.CurrentLogin.Functionality
    ' create a new menu item...
    Dim item As SubApplicationMenuItem = New SubApplicationMenuItem(Me, _
                                               functionality)

    ' add it to the view menu...
    menuView.MenuItems.Add(item)
  Next
End Sub
```

Run the application now and you'll find that we do indeed get given a menu option. The details for this menu option have come from the Web Service in the form of the functionality catalog. If the Web Service returned different `AppFunctionality` objects from the catalog (because the user had different privileges), we'd be presented with different options in this menu:

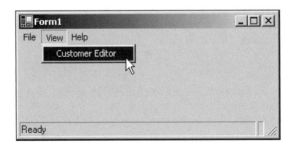

If you click on the menu option, you'll see a message box reporting the URL (or rather, the path) of the assembly containing the customer editor.

Updating the Caption

At the moment, our browser's caption is Form1, which is both useless and messy! We'll now add a property, called Caption, to Browser that accesses this label. The sub-applications will then be able to set the caption through this property.

First off, open the code editor for Browser and add this constant and private member:

```
Public Class Browser
    Inherits System.Windows.Forms.Form

    ' const...
    Private Const BaseCaption As String = "Application Browser"

    ' members...
    Private _caption As String
```

Then, add this property:

```
    ' Caption property...
    Public Property Caption() As String
      Get
        Return _caption
      End Set
      Set(ByVal Value As String)
        ' save it...
        _caption = Value

        ' set the text...
        If _caption <> "" Then
          Text = _caption & " - " & BaseCaption
        Else
          Text = BaseCaption
        End If
      End Set
    End Property
```

Next, find the OnLoad method and add this code:

```
    Protected Overrides Sub OnLoad(ByVal e As System.EventArgs)

      ' set the caption...
      Caption = ""

      ' update the menu...
      Dim functionality As Coordination.AppFunctionality
      For Each functionality In Login.CurrentLogin.Functionality

        ' create a new menu item...
        Dim item As SubApplicationMenuItem = _
                       New SubApplicationMenuItem(Me, functionality)

        ' add it to the view menu...
```

```
            menuView.MenuItems.Add(item)
        Next
    End Sub
```

Now if you run the application, the Browser will have a more appropriate caption than **Form1**.

We now have a mechanism for sub-applications to add their own caption. However, they won't supply the complete caption, and we'll take what they supply ("Customer Editor", "Current Orders", and so on) and tack "Application Browser" onto the end of it, separated with a dash. We'll implement this later on.

Running Sub-Applications

We're now at a point where we can run the sub-application. However, because we haven't got the Remoting code up at this point, we need to provide a database connection string that the sub-application can use. If you recall, we did this in the last chapter by using this code in the constructor of **Form1**:

```
Public Sub New()
    MyBase.New()

    ' This call is required by the Windows Form Designer
    InitializeComponent();

      ' set the connection string...
      EnterpriseApplication.Application.ConnectionString = _
    "integrated security=sspi;initial catalog=bookmanager;data source=localhost"
    End Sub
```

We need to do the same thing again, but this time we'll do it from within the constructor of **Login**. The first step is to add a reference to the **EnterpriseObjects** assembly, so do this in the way described in Chapter 2.

Open the code editor for **Login** and add a namespace import for **EnterpriseObjects**:

```
    Imports EnterpriseObjects
```

Next, add this code to the constructor:

```
    Public Sub New()
        MyBase.new()

        ' This call is required by the Windows Form Designer
        InitializeComponent()

          save an instance of us as the current login...
        _currentLogin = Me

        ' set a database connection...
        EnterpriseApplication.Application.ConnectionString = _
        "integrated security=sspi;initial catalog=bookmanager;data source=corrado"
    End Sub
```

> **Don't forget to adapt this connection string to suit your particular system configuration.**

Now when the Browser is started, any sub-application that runs will be able to access that connection string through `EnterpriseApplication.Application` in the usual way.

We can now build the body of `RunSubApplication`. All this code needs to do is:

- ❑ Load the assembly. In our case, that's `c:\BookManager\CustomerEditor\bin\CustomerEditor.dll`.

- ❑ Create an instance of the required type, this being the user control that provides the main UI for the sub-application. In our case, that's `CustomerEditor.CustomerEditor`.

- ❑ Display the control by adding it to the `Controls` collection of `panelApp`, which is the panel control that takes up most of the space on the `Browser` form.

During this procedure, an expected exception is `System.IO.FileNotFoundException`. This will be thrown if the assembly cannot be found. We'll treat any other exception as "unexpected" and we'll pass it over to a generic exception handler.

Unexpected exceptions will be handed over to a method called `HandleException`. To begin with, this can simply display a message box. Later, we'll enhance this to display more comprehensive debugging information and even use the Coordination Web Service as a reporting mechanism.

The sub-application control itself will be held in a private member called `_subApp`. We'll be able to set and get this member through a property called `SubApp`, which we'll add in a short while. When we set `SubApp`, quite a lot of things need to happen, but we'll explain these as we go.

Before we start, add a private member to `Browser`:

```
Public Class Browser
  Inherits System.Windows.Forms.Form

  ' const...
  Private Const BaseCaption As String = "Application Browser"

  ' members...
  Private _caption As String
  Private _subApp As Control
```

Here's the code for `RunSubApplication`, replacing our previous code used for testing purposes:

```
' RunSubApplication...
Public Sub RunSubApplication(ByVal functionality As _
                            Coordination.AppFunctionality)

    ' load the assembly...
    Try
      Dim subAppAssembly As System.Reflection.Assembly = _
            System.Reflection.Assembly.LoadFrom(functionality.AssemblyUrl)
```

```
        ' load the type...
        Dim newSubApp As Object = _
                        subAppAssembly.CreateInstance(functionality.TypeName)
        If Not newSubApp Is Nothing Then
          ' add it...
          SubApp = CType(newSubApp, Control)
        Else
          Alert("The sub-application '" & _
                functionality.TypeName & _
                "' could not be found in '" & _
                functionality.AssemblyUrl)
        End If
      Catch ex As System.IO.FileNotFoundException
        Alert("The assembly '" & functionality.AssemblyUrl & _
              "' could not be found.")
      Catch ex As Exception
        HandleException(ex)
      End Try
    End Sub
```

The `System.Reflection.Assembly` has a shared method called `LoadFrom` that can be used to load any assembly into the current application domain. We use this in the first instance to load up the assembly containing the `CustomerEditor.CustomerEditor` control. It will return a new `System.Reflection.Assembly` object that references the loaded assembly.

The `CreateInstance` method can then be used to create an instance of the required type, which we express as a string. Interestingly, if the type doesn't exist in the assembly, this method does *not* throw an exception. Instead, it just returns null. Once we have that, we try to cast the object to a `System.Windows.Forms.Control` (which *will* throw an exception if it cannot be done) and set the `SubApp` property. This property does most of the magic, and here it is:

```
    ' SubApp property...
    Public Property SubApp() As Control
      Get
        return _subApp
      End Get
      Set(ByVal Value As Control)
        ' reset...
        Me.panelApp.Controls.Clear()

        ' do we have one?
        If Not Value Is Nothing Then
          ' cast it to a control...
          _subApp = CType(Value, Control)

          ' show it...
          _subApp.Dock = DockStyle.Fill
          Me.panelApp.Controls.Add(_subApp)
        Else
          _subApp = Nothing
        End If
      End Set
    End Property
```

All we want to do is make the new control the sole item in the `Controls` collection of the `panelApp` panel that takes up the entire form area. We can get the automatic layout functionality of Windows Forms to make the control occupy all of the available space by setting the `Dock` property to `Fill`, which is what we do. If we don't get given a control (we want to clear the view), we remove all of the controls and set `_subApp` to `null`.

You'll notice there that we're using our own `Alert` method rather than the more usual `MessageBox.Show` method. `MessageBox.Show` requires a lot of parameters in order to present a decent looking box (one with a caption and an icon), and our `Alert` method adds a default caption and icon making life a bit easier. There are two versions of the method – the second of which allows us to control which buttons and icon are used. Add this code to `Browser`:

```
' Alert - quick message box...
Public Function Alert(ByVal message As String) As DialogResult
  Return Alert(message, MessageBoxButtons.OK, _
            MessageBoxIcon.Exclamation)
End Function

Public Function Alert(ByVal message As String, _
                ByVal buttons As MessageBoxButtons, _
                ByVal icon As MessageBoxIcon)As DialogResult

  Return MessageBox.Show(Me, message, BaseCaption, buttons, _
                   icon)
End Function
```

As we said before, `HandleException` isn't going to do anything amazing at this point. It will simply take the exception and use `Alert` to open a message box:

```
' HandleException...
Public Sub HandleException(ByVal ex As System.Exception)

  ' do something quick for now...
  Alert(ex.GetType().ToString() & ":" & ex.Message & "\r\n" & _
      ex.StackTrace)
End Sub
```

So does it work? Run the application and select **View | Customer Editor** from the menu to find out!

Communicating with the Browser

OK, so we've proven the principle that we can run the same sub-application from within the browser. However, what happens if the sub-application needs to add menu options, change the caption, and so on?

We need a mechanism for the browser and sub-application to communicate. The most appropriate way to do this is to add two interfaces – `EnterpriseObjects.IBrowser` and `EnterpriseObjects.ISubApplication` – to each side.

The `Browser` class will implement `IBrowser`. The interface contains properties for setting the caption and status bar, and also contains prototypes for `HandleException` and `Alert`. There are also a number of other methods that we haven't met yet, and we'll need to add stub implementations for each of these and come back to them at a more appropriate time.

If you look in the `EnterpriseObjects` code, you'll find `IBrowser`. Open it and take a look at the code:

```
Imports System.Windows.Forms

Namespace EnterpriseObjects

   Public Interface IBrowser

      ' Properties
      Property Caption() As String
      Property Status() As String

      ' Methods
      Public Sub HandleException(ByVal ex As Exception)
      Public Function Alert(ByVal message As String) As DialogResult
      Public Function Alert(ByVal message As String, _
                            ByVal icon As MessageBoxIcon) As DialogResult
      Public Function Alert(ByVal message As String, _
                            ByVal buttons As MessageBoxButtons, _
                            ByVal icon As MessageBoxIcon) As DialogResult
      Public Sub AddMenuItem(ByVal subApp As ISubApplication, _
                            ByVal path As String, ByVal item As MenuItem)
   End Interface
End Namespace
```

Open the code editor for `Browser`. At the top of the code listing, add a reference to `EnterpriseObjects` and also make `Browser` implement `IBrowser`:

```
Imports ApplicationBrowser.Coordination
Imports EnterpriseObjects

   Public Class Browser
      Inherits System.Windows.Forms.Form
      Implements IBrowser
```

The first property that's missing is the `Status` property. This property will update the status bar text, and we can create this now:

```
' Status property
Public Property Status() As String Implements IBrowser.Status
  Get
    Return panelStatus.Text
  End Get
  Set(ByVal Value As string)
    If Value <> "" Then
      panelStatus.Text = Value
    Else
      panelStatus.Text = "Ready"
    End If
  End Set
End Property
```

Make the `Alert` implementations we added previously implement `IBrowser.Alert`. Now add stub implementations for the remaining members. We'll come back to these in a short while:

```
' AddMenuItem - add an item to the menu
Public Sub AddMenuItem(ByVal subApp As ISubApplication, _
                       ByVal path As String, ByVal item As MenuItem) _
                       Implements IBrowser.AddMenuItem

End Sub

Public Function Alert(ByVal message As String, _
                      ByVal icon As MessageBoxIcon) As DialogResult _
                      Implements IBrowser.Alert
  Return Alert(message, MessageBoxButtons.OK, icon)
End Function
```

You will also need to make the `Caption` property we created earlier implement `IBrowser.Caption`, and the `HandleException` method will need to implement `IBrowser.HandleException`. You should find that the project now compiles, as we have implementations for everything defined by the interface.

"ISubApplication"

The other side of this puzzle is `ISubApplication`. The purpose of this interface is to enable the `Browser`, or rather "the class that implements `IBrowser`" to pass over a reference to itself so that the sub-application can add menu items, set the caption, use the exception handler and so on. In fact, it only contains one member:

```
Public Interface ISubApplication

  ' Members
  Sub SetBrowser(ByVal browser As IBrowser)

End Interface
```

Start a new instance of Visual Studio .NET and open the **CustomerEditor** project. Open the code editor for the `CustomerEditor` class and make it implement `ISubApplication`. In addition, add a member called _browser:

```
Public Class CustomerEditor
   Inherits System.Windows.Forms.UserControl
   Implements ISubApplication

   ' Members
   Private _browser As IBrowser
```

Next, add this property and method to abstract access to _browser:

```
Public ReadOnly Property Browser() As IBrowser
   Get
      Return _browser
   End Get
End Property

Public Function IsInBrowser() As Boolean
   If Not Browser Is Nothing Then
      Return True
   Else
      Return false
   End If
End Function
```

As we might not actually be hosted inside the browser, we want to make sure that we have a mechanism to test that we are in a browser. The rule is simple – if `Browser` is not `Nothing`, we are, otherwise we're not.

Now, add this implementation of the `SetBrowser` method:

```
Public Sub SetBrowser(ByVal browser As IBrowser) _
                     Implements ISubApplication.SetBrowser
   _browser = browser
End Sub
```

To test that this works, we'll try calling a method on `Browser`. `SetBrowser` will be called *immediately after* the class is created, which means that _browser will not be set inside the constructor for `CustomerEditor`. By the time we get to the `Load` event though, it will be set and we can use it. Add this code to `CustomerEditor_Load`:

```
Private Sub CustomerEditor_Load(ByVal sender As System.Object, _
                                ByVal e As System.EventArgs) _
                                Handles MyBase.Load

    If Me.DesignMode = False Then
    ' Get the authors
    Dim authors As AuthorSet = Author.GetAll()

    ' Loop them
    Dim theAuthor As Author
    For Each theAuthor In authors
       ' Add it
       listAuthors.Items.Add(theAuthor)
    Next

       ' Update the browser
       If IsInBrowser() = True Then
          Browser.Caption = "Customer Editor"
       End If
    End If
End Sub
```

Build the project, but remember you can't run it from this instance of Visual Studio as we have to run it from the other Visual Studio project. Also, we need to make a few changes to the RunSubApplication method of Browser.

Flip over to the other Visual Studio project and find the SubApp property. Add this code:

```
' SubApp property
Public Property SubApp() As Control
   Get
      Return _subApp
   End Get
   Set(ByVal Value As Control)
      ' Reset
      Me.panelApp.Controls.Clear()

      ' Do we have one?
      If Not Value is Nothing Then
         ' Cast it to a control
         _subApp = CType(Value, Control)
         If TypeOf(_subApp) Is ISubApplication Then
            _iSubApp = CType(_subApp, ISubApplication)
            _iSubApp.SetBrowser(Me)
         Else
            _iSubApp = Nothing
         End If

         ' Show it
         _subApp.Dock = DockStyle.Fill
         Me.panelApp.Controls.Add(_subApp)
      Else
         _subApp = Nothing
```

```
          _iSubApp = Nothing
      End if
    End Set
  End Property
```

Of course, we also need to define _iSubApp, so add this member to Browser:

```
Public Class Browser
    Inherits System.Windows.Forms.Form
    Implements IBrowser

    ' Constant
    Private Const BaseCaption As String = "Application Browser"

    ' Members
    Private _caption As String
    Private _subApp As Control
    Private _iSubApp As ISubApplication
```

The VB.NET "Is" keyword is great for checking whether an object implements a given interface. In this case, if the object we have does implement EnterpriseObjects.ISubApplication, we call SetBrowser passing over ourselves, or rather the IBrowser that we implement.

Run the project now and select **View | Customer Editor** from the menu. Notice how the caption is set to **Customer Editor**, which proves that the sub-application is able to communicate back to the browser through IBrowser:

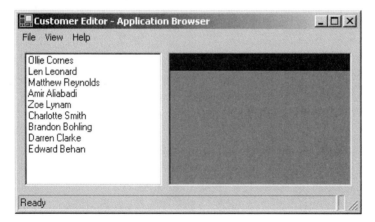

Opening New Browsers and Other UI Tidbits

The main reason that we've gone through a bit of a rigmarole to separate the application functionality into the `Login` class is that we want our application to support many open browsers at once. Just as Microsoft Word and Excel allow you to open multiple documents simultaneously (the Multiple Document Interface, or MDI), users need the ability to open several instances of the application at once. This means that the user could have the Customer Editor open in one browser, and, at the same time, have another instance of the browser open accessing another application or even another view of the Customer Editor.

Open the Designer for `Browser` and add a new menu item beneath the top level **File** menu item. Set its **Name** property to `menuFileNewBrowser`, and the **Shortcut** property to **F8**:

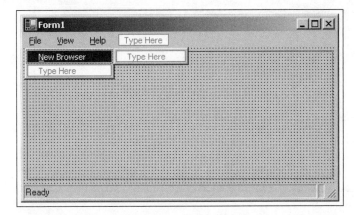

> Note that here we have used the editor for this method, rather than creating a new class like we did before. This is because the editor is best when menu items are static, and creating a new class derived from **System.Windows.Forms.MenuItem** works best for dynamic menu items.

Double-click on the **New Browser** option. This will create a click event handler. Add this code:

```
Private Sub menuFileNewsBrowser_Click(ByVal sender As System.Object _
                            ByVal e As System.EventArgs) _
                            Handles menuFileNewsBrowser.Click

    CreateNewBrowser()
End Sub
```

Then, add this method:

```
' CreateNewBrowser
Public Function CreateNewBrowser() As Browser
  ' Create and show
  Dim newBrowser As Browser = New Browser()
```

89

```
        newBrowser.Show()

        ' Return
        Return newBrowser
    End Function
```

Run the application and you'll be able to create as many new browsers as you like. The application will only close if you close them all.

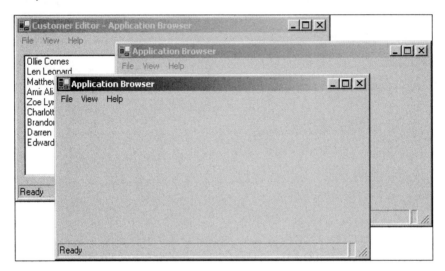

Sub-Application Menu Items

Sub-applications need to be able to add menu options to the browser menu when they start running. These sub-application menu items need to be "merged" into the existing Browser menu. Although .NET menus (implemented in System.Windows.Forms.Menu and its derivatives) support merging, the support doesn't exactly suit our needs.

.NET's menu-merging functionality assumes that you have two MainMenu controls that need to be merged together. In our situation, because a UserControl object cannot have a MainMenu control bound to it, our only option is to use a ContextMenu. However, ContextMenu controls do not support top-level items, so we would have to do a lot of kludging and messing around. It's easier, in my opinion, to create new MenuItem objects and pass them over to IBrowser telling it where to put them.

Open another instance of Visual Studio and open the code editor for CustomerEditor. Find the SetBrowser method and add this code:

```
        Public Sub SetBrowser(ByVal browser As IBrowser) _
                        Implements ISubApplication.SetBrowser

            ' Set the browser
            _browser = browser

            ' Add the options
```

```
            Dim item As MenuItem = New MenuItem("Create New Customer")
            AddHandler item.Click, New EventHandler(AddressOf CreateNewCustomerClicked)
            browser.AddMenuItem(Me, "Customer", item)
        End Sub
```

What we're doing is creating a new menu item containing the text **Create New Customer**. This item is wired up to the `CreateNewCustomerClicked` method that we'll build in a little while. To display the menu item, we pass it over to `Browser` and give it the name of the top-level item we want it to appear under, namely **Customer**.

Next, add this method to respond to the menu click:

```
        ' CreateNewCustomerClicked
        Public Sub CreateNewCustomerClicked(ByVal sender As System.Object, _
                                            ByVal e As EventArgs)

            If IsInBrowser() = True Then
               Browser.Alert("Create new customer clicked!")
            End If
        End Sub
```

Add an `Imports` statement for `System.Windows.Forms` to the top of the class. Build the project, and flip back to the **ApplicationBrowser** project.

When `AddMenuItem` is called, we have to find the top-level menu item that we want to add the option to. If the item does not exist, we create one and add it to the menu. The one wrinkle we must deal with is to ignore any ampersands ("&") that appear in the `Text` property of the menu item, and indicate that the subsequent character should appear underlined. As far as Windows is concerned, it's no longer fashionable to always display these underscores (some applications do, however). If you want to see them, tap the **Alt** key to enter keyboard navigation mode and you'll see what I mean.

Here's the method:

```
        ' AddMenuItem - add an item to the menu
        Public Sub AddMenuItem(ByVal subApp As ISubApplication, _
                               ByVal path As String, ByVal item As MenuItem) _
                               Implements IBrowser.AddMenuItem

           ' What are we looking for?
           Dim lookForPath As String = path.Replace("&", "")

           ' Find a top-level item
           Dim addTo As MenuItem = Nothing
           Dim topLevel As MenuItem
           For Each topLevel In menuMain.MenuItems

              ' Ignore & characters in the string when comparing
              If String.Compare(topLevel.Text.Replace("&", ""), _
                                lookForPath, True) = 0 Then
                 addTo = topLevel
                 Exit For
              End If
```

```
    Next

    ' Did we get a top-level item?
    If addTo Is Nothing Then
      ' Create one if not
      addTo = New MenuItem(path)
      menuMain.MenuItems.Add(addTo)
    End If

    ' Add the new item
    addTo.MenuItems.Add(item)
End Sub
```

If you run the program and select View | Customer Editor, the new Customer menu option will appear. You can click on the option to show the message box:

Adding the Item to the Proper Location

So we can now add new menu items, but not in the correct place! The last menu item on a menu bar should always be Help, and if there's a Window option, that should always precede Help. In addition, we want the first option to be File, followed by Edit then View, so our new Customer menu items are ordered: File, Edit, View, Customer, Window and Help.

At the moment of course, we don't have Edit or Window options, so our first move is to add those. Call them menuEdit and menuWindow.

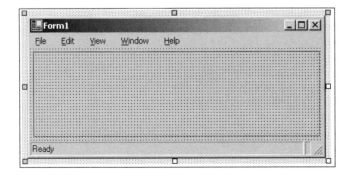

`MenuItem` has a property called `Index` that records the item's location in the menu. If, when we create the new item, we give our new item the same `Index` as the **Window** menu (held in `menuWindow`), the new menu will appear in the correct location and **Window** will be bumped along to the next location. Oddly enough, this can all be done in a single line of code:

```
' AddMenuItem - add an item to the menu
Public Sub AddMenuItem(ByVal subApp As ISubApplication, _
                       ByVal path As String, _
                       ByVal item As MenuItem) _
                       Implements IBrowser.AddMenuItem

    ' What are we looking for?
    Dim lookForPath As String = path.Replace("&", "")

    ' Find a top-level item
    Dim addTo As MenuItem = Nothing
    Dim topLevel As MenuItem
    For Each topLevel In menuMain.MenuItems
      ' Ignore & characters in the string when comparing
      If string.Compare(topLevel.Text.Replace("&", ""), _
                        lookForPath, True) = 0 Then
        addTo = topLevel
        Exit For
      End If
    Next

    ' Did we get a top-level item?
    If addTo Is Nothing Then
      ' Create one if not
      addTo = new MenuItem(path)
      menuMain.MenuItems.Add(addTo)
      addTo.Index = menuWindow.Index
    End If

    ' Add the new item
    addTo.MenuItems.Add(item)
End Sub
```

Now if you run the application and select **View | Customer Editor**, the option will now appear in the correct location:

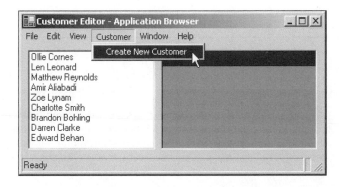

Removing Items

If we use the **View** menu to select a new sub-application, we have to remove the menu items that the old sub-application was using; otherwise the user could get confused. To do this, we need to store the items when they are first added. The ideal candidate for this task is a `System.Collections.ArrayList`. When the `SubApp` property is set, as well as clearing the `Controls` collection of `panelApp`, we need to iterate through all of the menus, removing any items that also appear in the `ArrayList` that we populated as menu items were added.

First, add a new member to `Browser`:

```
Public Class Browser
    Inherits System.Windows.Forms.Form, IBrowser

    ' Constant
    Private Const BaseCaption As String = "Application Browser"

    ' Members
    Private _caption As String
    Private Control _subApp
    Private _iSubApp As ISubApplication
    Private _subAppMenuItems As ArrayList = New ArrayList()
```

Then, add this code to the bottom of `AddMenuItem`. (Some code is omitted for brevity.)

```
    ' AddMenuItem - add an item to the menu
    Public Sub AddMenuItem(ByVal subApp ISubApplication, _
                           ByVal path As String, _
                           ByVal item As MenuItem) _
                           Implements IBrowser.AddMenuItem

        ...

        ' Did we get a top level item?
        If addTo Is Nothing Then
          ' Create one if not
          addTo = New MenuItem(path)
          menuMain.MenuItems.Add(addTo)
          _subAppMenuItems.Add(addTo)
          addTo.Index = menuWindow.Index
        End if

        ' Add the new item
        addTo.MenuItems.Add(item)
        _subAppMenuItems.Add(item)
    End Sub
```

These two will work together to populate the list when items are added by the sub-application.

The next step is to clear the sub-application menu items. We'll break this out into a separate method. Remember, all we need to do is loop through each of the top-level menu items in the main menu, and then loop through all of the items that were added by the sub-application removing each one. In addition, if a top-level menu item that we added has no items, we want to delete that too. Here's the code:

```
' RemoveSubAppMenuItems
Protected Sub RemoveSubAppMenuItems()

   ' Loop through each top-level item
   Dim item As MenuItem
   For Each item In menuMain.MenuItems
      ' Remove all items that also figure in our array
      Dim subItem As MenuItem
      For Each subItem In _subAppMenuItems
         item.MenuItems.Remove(subItem)
      Next
   Next

   ' Remove any orphaned top-level items
   Dim subAppItem As MenuItem
   For Each subAppItem In _subAppMenuItems
      ' Remove
      menuMain.MenuItems.Remove(subAppItem)
   Next

   ' Clear the array
   _subAppMenuItems.Clear()
End Sub
```

This approach may seem a little counterintuitive because we call Remove even though we don't know if the item actually exists within the menu or not. The outermost loop goes through each of the top-level menu items, and the inner loop iterates the array in _subAppMenuItems. We then remove items from the MenuItems collection of the top-level menu itself – in other words the actual options. After we've done this, we go through the sub-application's items again and remove any that appear from the top-level as well.

To get this to work, we need to add a call to ResetSubAppMenuItems to the SubApp property:

```
' SubApp property
Public Property SubApp() As Control
   Get
      Return _subApp
   End Get
   Set(ByVal Value As Control)
      ' Reset
      Me.panelApp.Controls.Clear()
      RemoveSubAppMenuItems()

      ...

   End Set
End Property
```

To test this, run the application and select View | Customer Editor from the menu a few times. If it's working properly, you should only ever see one Customer | Create New Customer option.

Adding Menu Separators

If we add options to an existing menu, we ideally want a separator between the options defined by the browser itself and those defined by sub-applications. The View menu is a classic example – if the sub-application defines an option called View | Options, we want to keep this separate from items in the View menu that we add to select sub-applications.

To test this, open up the CustomerEditor project once more and find the SetBrowser method. Change the call to AddMenuItem so that the menu is added to View rather than Customer:

```
Public Sub SetBrowser(ByVal browser As IBrowser) _
                Implements ISubApplication.SetBrowser

    ' Set the browser
    _browser = browser

    ' Add the options
    Dim item As MenuItem = New MenuItem("Create New Customer")
    AddHandler item.Click, New EventHandler(AddressOf CreateNewCustomerClicked)
    Browser.AddMenuItem(Me, "View", item)
End Sub
```

Build that project. Flip back to the Browser project, run it, select View | Customer Editor and you'll notice that the View menu now contains another option:

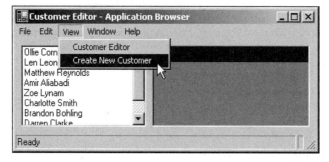

To deal with this, when we find a top-level menu item to add the option to, we need to look at the last option in the menu. If that option is *not* in the _subAppMenuItems array, then we *should* add the separator. Adding a separator to the menu is a little odd – you have to create a new MenuItem being careful to specify a Text property containing a single dash. This new item is also added to _subAppMenuItems so that the existing implementation for RemoveSubAppMenuItems can get rid of the separators too. Here's the code:

```
    ' AddMenuItem - add an item to the menu
    Public Sub AddMenuItem(ByVal subApp As ISubApplication, _
                    ByVal path As String, ByVal item As MenuItem)
                    Implements IBrowser.AddMenuItem

    ' What are we looking for?
    Dim lookForPath As String = path.Replace("&", "")
```

```
' Find a top-level item
Dim addTo As MenuItem = Nothing
Dim topLevel As MenuItem
For Each topLevel In menuMain.MenuItems
   ' Ignore & characters in the string when comparing
   If string.Compare(topLevel.Text.Replace("&", ""), _
                     lookForPath, True) = 0 Then

     addTo = topLevel
     break
   End If
Next

' Did we get a top-level item?
If addTo Is Nothing Then

   ' Create one if not
   addTo = new MenuItem(path)
   menuMain.MenuItems.Add(addTo)
   _subAppMenuItems.Add(addTo)
   addTo.Index = menuWindow.Index
Else
   ' Do we need a separator?
   Dim needSep As Boolean =Not(_subAppMenuItems.Contains(addTo.MenuItems _
                                       (addTo.MenuItems.Count - 1)))

   If needSep = True Then
     ' Create one and add
     Dim sep As MenuItem = New MenuItem("-")
     addTo.MenuItems.Add(sep)
     _subAppMenuItems.Add(sep)
   End If
End If

' Add the new item
addTo.MenuItems.Add(item)
_subAppMenuItems.Add(item)
End Sub
```

Now if you run the project, you should see a separator between options that the browser defines and options that the sub-application defines:

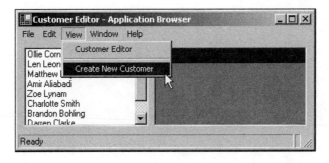

Summary

In this chapter, we built the basic application browser for our desktop applications. This browser provides a window that sub-applications can plug into. It also provides a common set of authentication features to the sub-applications and powers the automatic Internet deployment of sub-applications that we cover in Chapter 10.

When the browser starts, we ask for the username and password. This is then given to an authentication server that authenticates the user and returns a security token and the functionality catalog if the user is granted access. The functionality catalog is then used to create the View menu, with options for each sub-application that the user may access.

When one of these options is selected, the assembly is loaded using the shared LoadFrom method of System.Reflection.Assembly. The type that contains the main UI for the application is then created and displayed on the form.

.NET Enterprise Development in VB .NET

4

Developing for the Desktop

In this chapter, we're going to take a look at building a desktop application in earnest. Although we put together a basic application in Chapter 2 and used it again when developing our browser in Chapter 3, we haven't built anything really substantial.

We'll start off by building a full Customer Editor that demonstrates using data binding and some other basic Windows Forms UI that we'd expect to see in a desktop application. In Chapter 4 we will cover the following:

- ❑ Running a sub-application so that we can debug it
- ❑ Building a Windows Form application that will allow us to view and update our data
- ❑ Dealing with the issues involved in saving changes back to the database

Debugging

First off, we need to solve a problem that some of you may have spotted when we built the browser in the last chapter. If we build a sub-application, when we run it in the browser we can't step into it and debug it.

What we need to do is load the sub-application when the browser runs. OK, so this runs contrary to the basic principle of the browser – it's a lightweight application that loads, on demand, application modules. However, for debugging purposes it's perfectly reasonable to attach a payload to the browser in this way.

The trick is to make this as easy as possible. What we'll need to do is import the sub-application assembly into the solution in the usual way. To do this, right-click on the **ApplicationBrowser** solution and select **Add | Existing Project**. When prompted, find and import the `CustomerEditor.vbproj` file. As **CustomerEditor** is dependent on **BookManagerObjects** and **EnterpriseObjects**, you'll need to add these projects too.

You'll have four projects in Solution Explorer at this point. (I've collapsed them to save space.)

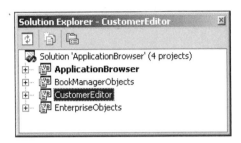

We now need to directly reference CustomerEditor from ApplicationBrowser. Right-click on the ApplicationBrowser project, select Add Reference and add a reference to the CustomerEditor project. You'll now have something like this:

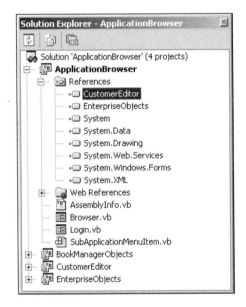

To enable us to load the CustomerEditor sub-application when the browser runs, we need a new menu item. As the SubApplicationMenuItem class that we built in Chapter 3 relies on having an AppFunctionality object, which we won't have as we're short-circuiting the coordination Web Service at this point, we'll need a new class. We'll call it SubApplicationDebugMenuItem. This will take a System.Type object that references the sub-application, or specifically CustomerEditor.CustomerEditor.

Create a new class called SubApplicationDebugMenuItem. Make it derive from MenuItem and also add members in which we can store a Browser object and a Type object.

```
Public Class SubApplicationDebugMenuItem
    Inherits System.Windows.Forms.MenuItem
```

```
' members...

Public _browser As Browser
Public _subAppType As Type
```

Then add this constructor that requires a Browser and a Type.

```
Public Sub New(ByVal theBrowser As Browser, ByVal subType As Type)

  ' save...
  Me._subAppType = subType
  Me._browser = theBrowser

  ' set the menu text...
  Me.Text = "Debug: " & subType.ToString()
End Sub
```

You'll notice that's very similar to the constructor for SubApplicationMenuItem.

When the menu item is clicked, we want to create a new instance of the sub-application class. We'll use the CreateInstance method of System.Activator to do this. Activator is the object we have to use if we want to create an object when all we have is a System.Type object that refers to the class.

Remember, this new class will be derived from System.Windows.Forms.MenuItem. We can take this new instance and set the Browser object's SubApp property. In doing so, we'll cause the browser to display the control and update the menu items.

```
' OnClick...
Protected Overrides Sub OnClick(ByVal e As System.EventArgs)
  ' run...
  _browser.SubApp = CType(System.Activator.CreateInstance(_subAppType), _
                      System.Windows.Forms.Control)

End Sub
```

That's all the code we need to write to power the menu item. Now we just have to add it. The optimum place to do this is after we've added the menu items that we created for each item in the functionality catalog. Open the code editor for Browser and add this code to OnLoad:

```
Protected Overrides Sub OnLoad(ByVal e As System.EventArgs)

  ' set the caption...
  Caption = ""

  ' update the menu...
  Dim  functionality As Coordination.AppFunctionality
  For Each functionality In Login.CurrentLogin.Functionality
    ' create a new menu item...
    Dim item As SubApplicationMenuItem = New SubApplicationMenuItem(Me, _
                                            functionality)
```

```
    ' add it to the view menu...
    menuView.MenuItems.Add(item)
Next

    ' add a sub-application...
    menuView.MenuItems.Add(New SubApplicationDebugMenuItem( _
                          Me, GetType(CustomerEditor.CustomerEditor)))
End Sub
```

Remember, because the **CustomerEditor** project is included in the solution, we can directly reference its types. It's this direct reference that will allow us to step into the sub-application and set breakpoints in a way that we couldn't do before.

Before you run the project, open the code editor for `CustomerEditor.vb`. Set a breakpoint on the first line of `CustomerEditor_Load`.

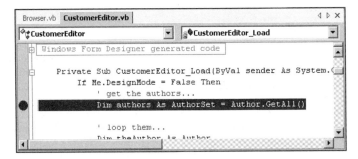

Run the project. You'll notice that the View menu has a **Debug: CustomerEditor.CustomerEditor** option.

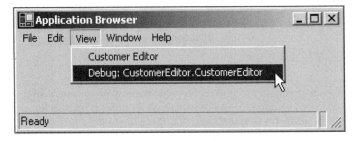

Click it and you'll find that the sub-application is loaded, but you'll also notice that the breakpoint "catches".

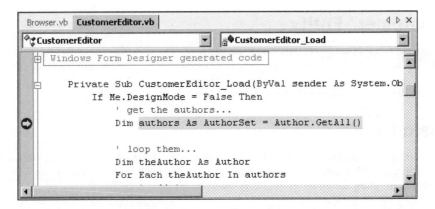

Remember that the original **Customer Editor** option will load the sub-application using the original technique discussed in Chapter 3. If you select View | Customer Editor, the breakpoint will not catch. However, reselect View | Debug: CustomerEditor.CustomerEditor once more and you'll notice that it does.

What About Deployment?

This is perfect for debugging, but obviously when it's time to roll the application into a production setting you don't want this functionality in place.

When you do need to do this, remove any lines that add `SubApplicationDebugMenuItem` objects from the `Load` event handler. (We'll talk about a technique for doing this in Chapter 12.) In addition, remove the sub-application project and its dependents (or at least, the dependents that it has that the browser doesn't need) from the solution. This will return the project to a state where it can be properly deployed.

Editing Customers

The first activity we'll look at for our customer editor is the classic forms editor. We'll return a complete set of customers in a `CustomerSet` and use data binding to present an edit form to the user. One thing that's missing from the common controls in .NET is a VCR-like control that allows us to page through records, like the one in Microsoft Access. We'll also build one of those, or one that looks very much like it.

Quite why this control is missing from .NET is a bit of a mystery. I suspect Microsoft had so much faith in control building being ridiculously easy that it decided to let developers do it themselves. I'm sure we'll see plenty of third-party controls like these eventually.

The "Customer" Entity

So far, when we've used the Object Builder, we haven't built objects for the `Customers` table. Open the Object Builder now and include the `Customers` table in the model. Give the entity a name of `Customer`.

Synchronize the project and add the new classes to `BookManagerObjects`.

The Basic Form

We'll kick off by building the basic form for customer editing. To do this, open the Designer for `CustomerEditor` and remove the existing ListBox and DataGrid controls. You'll also have to remove the code from `CustomerEditor.vb` that uses the controls.

When you've done that, add new controls like this:

You could probably guess the names of the TextBox controls, but in order they are: `textFirstName`, `textLastName`, `textEmail`, `textCompanyName`, `textAddress1`, `textAddress2`, `textCity`, `textRegion`, `textPostalCode`, `textCountry`, `textPhone`, and `textFax`.

When we want to edit customers, we'll set a property on `CustomerEditor` called `Customers`. This property will set up the data binding so that the values flow from the database to the user interface. However, we'll build this a little later on, once we have a mechanism through which we can get the customers from the database.

Building the Control Library

For this exercise, and the desktop application we build in the next section, we'll build a separate control library that all of the sub-applications can use. We'll build one aesthetic control that will help us improve the look of sub-applications and another control to implement the VCR buttons.

Using Solution Explorer, right-click on the ApplicationBrowser solution and select Add | New Project. Add a new Windows Control Library project to the solution called ApplicationBrowserControls.

The first control we'll build is a basic control that will allow us to put a small caption bar at the top of the form. This will help with the aesthetics of the form by delineating where the sub-application ends and the form begins. Create a new control called Caption by right-clicking on the ApplicationBrowserControls project in Solution Explorer and selecting Add | Add User Control. Using the Designer, set the BackColor property of the form to ControlDark. Then, add a Label control to the form. Set its Name property to labelCaption, its ForeColor to ControlLightLight. Then, set the Font property to Verdana, 9.75 point, style=Bold. Finally, set the Anchor property to Top, Left, Right and the Text property to Sub-application Caption. You'll have something like this.

Next, open the code editor and add this property to abstract access to the Text property of the Label control.

```
<Browsable(True), _
    DesignerSerializationVisibility(DesignerSerializationVisibility.Visible)> _
Public Property Overrides Text() As String
  Get
    Return labelCaption.Text
  End Get
  Set(ByVal value As String)
    labelCaption.Text = value
  End Set
End Property
```

You will also need to add an Imports statement for System.ComponentModel. Build the project to create the new control class.

Next, add a reference to the ApplicationBrowserControls project to the CustomerEditor project. Add a new Caption control to the CustomerEditor form. Set the Text property to Customer Editor.

Now that we have everything in place, we can turn our attention to editing data.

Retrieving Data

Working with data in a client application can be a relatively involved topic, mainly because we have to optimize our application so we get the maximum utilization of the least amount of data. It's important that we send the least amount of data possible across the network. This is usually a good way to improve the performance of distributed applications.

You're probably already aware that we can do most of this using a DataSet (or in our case, a CustomerSet) and data binding – so there's nothing particular tricky about doing this. However, in an enterprise application there are a few things to be careful of.

We're religious about data disconnection so, whenever we need data, we go to the server, ask for the data we want and process it. In order to make our application as scalable as possible it's essential that we get *exactly the right amount of data*. If we get too little, we incur the expense of having to go away to the server and request more data. If we get too much, we incur extra processing time at the database and extra transfer time on the network.

Imagine we have 100,000 customers. (We don't, our sample database is pretty small!) It's almost tempting to suggest that if we want to edit a customer we download the whole lot and let the user scroll through it. This is madness for two reasons. Firstly, we'll be transferring a huge amount of data over the network. Multiply this by 1,000 users and you'd better hope you have gigabit Ethernet to every desk. Secondly, it's totally unusable. If Alex Drew phones up, how is the operator going to find his record among 100,000 if all they have is a button to move from one record to the next? Yes it's possible, but it would take a very long time.

Broadly speaking, there are two types of data. With one type you need to see the entire set. For example, say we have five brands of books; if we build a sub-application to edit brands we can download the whole set. It's small enough to not cause a serious problem and the user should have no problems navigating a small set of data with VCR-like buttons.

The other type is where you have a great sea of data that the user needs to drill into. For example, if Alex Drew phones up, the user can type DREW into a search box and the sub-application will ask for a small set of results where the surname started with DREW. This reduces the amount of traffic passing over the network, and hopefully creates a small set of results that the user can work with.

What you actually search for is going to depend on what data you're working with. For a large set of customers, if you're looking for retail customers, a surname in combination with a postal code would be reasonable. For business customers, perhaps just the company name would suffice. To do the same job with a set of products, you might enter a product code, or the manufacturer name, some words from the description, and so on. However, whatever data we are looking at, if we're dealing with a large set of data some search functionality is likely to yield the most usable and scalable results.

Searching for Customers

In this part of the exercise we're going to create a separate user control in our ApplicationBrowserControls project called `EntitySetScroller`. This control will hold an EntitySet in a property called (not surprisingly) `EntitySet` and will manage a set of buttons to allow the user to move through the EntitySet. It will also deal with updating the data when the user changes the information.

This control will work in combination with the data binding features in Windows Forms. What this means is that we'll use the standard TextBox control to present the data, but bind the `Text` property of each control to the relevant column in whatever table the EntitySet happens to contain. We're going to construct `EntitySetScroller` in such a way that it will work with any EntitySet.

Before we build the control, we need to deal with searching. This involves a few steps:

- ❑ We need to add a search box and button to the form so that the user can enter their search query
- ❑ We need a stored procedure in the database that will do the searching
- ❑ We need to present the results to the user

We'll do these in order. Open the Designer for CustomerEditor and add Label, TextBox, and Button controls, like this:

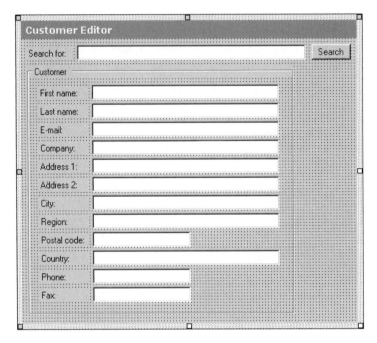

Set the Name property of the TextBox control to textSearchFor. Clear the Text property. Set the Anchor property to Top, Left, Right.

Then, set the Name property of the Button control to buttonSearch. Set the Anchor property to Top, Right.

The "FindCustomers" Stored Procedure

In this exercise, to search the customers, we're going to build a single stored procedure and access it through the Customer class. What data this stored procedure searches on is going to vary from application to application – as we suggested before, retail customers will most likely be uniquely identified by a last name and a postal code. Business customers by a company name, although again if you have a large number of customers with similar names you may want to combine this with a postal code. We're going to build a stored procedure that searches through the last name and the company name.

> Searching by ID could be a useful function for the user to have, although it's highly unlikely the customer will ever have their ID to hand should they phone up and need help. We're not going to implement this here, but it's easy to do based on the principles I'm going to introduce.

Searching textual data (`char`, `varchar` or `text` fields) on a database can be very expensive, so we have to be careful to construct the search in such a way that it's not too expensive. Of course, any text columns that we search through must be indexed, otherwise we have to scan the entire table to get the results we want, which is never good!

We'll be searching through the `LastName` column and the `CompanyName` column, and we'll assume that we have indexes on both of these. (If you downloaded the **BookManager** SQL Server database from the Wrox web site, it will indeed have the indexes in place.)

If we run this query to find all the customers with a `LastName` that is exactly equal to `Drew`:

```
SELECT * FROM Customers WHERE LastName='Drew'
```

…then SQL Server will indeed use the index to find the data, meaning that we've got a high-performance query.

If we run this query to find all the customers with a `LastName` that starts with `Drew`:

```
SELECT * FROM Customers WHERE LastName LIKE 'Drew%'
```

…then SQL Server will again use the index, so we still have a high-performance query.

However, if we run this query to find the customers with a `LastName` that contains `Drew`:

```
SELECT * FROM Customers WHERE LastName LIKE '%Drew%'
```

…then SQL Server *cannot* use the index. This query will result in a table seek; in other words every single row in the database will be read and examined in order to build the set of results to return to the server. This is horrendously expensive and is bound to cause problems!

As finding names that start with a given expression is index-based and therefore fast, we'll go for that even though it's a little more expensive than returning exact matches.

> I've used "**SELECT ***" here to save space. Obviously, "**SELECT ***" is bad practice – you should always name each column you require explicitly.

Using SQL Server Enterprise Manager, create a new stored procedure using this code:

```
CREATE PROCEDURE FindCustomers
(
  @searchFor varchar(64)
)
AS
  SELECT CustomerId, FirstName, LastName, Email, CompanyName, Address1,
    Address2, City, Region, PostalCode, Country, Phone, Fax, Timestamp
    FROM Customers WHERE
      LastName LIKE @searchFor + '%' OR
      CompanyName LIKE @searchFor + '%'
```

Now, open the Object Builder, load the project, and synchronize the changes. This will create a new method called FindCustomers in Sprocs.vb.

```
Public Shared Function FindCustomers(ByVal searchFor As String , _
                        ByVal useDatasetType As Type )As DataSet

    ' create a connection...
    Dim connection As System.Data.SqlClient.SqlConnection = _
             New System.Data.SqlClient.SqlConnection( _
      EnterpriseObjects.EnterpriseApplication.Application.ConnectionString)
    connection.Open()

    ' create a command...
    Dim command As System.Data.SqlClient.SqlCommand = _
            New System.Data.SqlClient.SqlCommand("FindCustomers", connection)
    command.CommandType = System.Data.CommandType.StoredProcedure

    ' parameters...
    Dim searchForParam As System.Data.SqlClient.SqlParameter = _
       command.Parameters.Add("@searchFor", System.Data.SqlDbType.VarChar, 64)
    searchForParam.Value = searchFor

    ' extract the dataset...
    Dim adapter As System.Data.SqlClient.SqlDataAdapter = _
                        New System.Data.SqlClient.SqlDataAdapter(command)
    Dim myDataset As System.Data.DataSet = _
      CType(System.Activator.CreateInstance(useDatasetType),System.Data.DataSet)

    adapter.Fill(myDataset)
    adapter.Dispose()

    ' cleanup...
    command.Dispose()
    connection.Close()

    ' return dataset...
    return myDataset
End Function
```

Wiring up "FindCustomers"

Now all we have to do is wire up this method into the Customer entity class. Open the code editor for Customer.vb and add this code:

```
' FindCustomers - search for customers...
Public Function FindCustomers(ByVal searchFor As String) As CustomerSet
    Return Customer.ServiceObject.FindCustomers(searchFor)
End Function
```

Now, open the code editor for `CustomerService.vb` and add this code:

```
' FindCustomers - search for customers...
Public Shared Function FindCustomers(ByVal searchFor As String) _
                                    As CustomerSet
    ' run the sproc and return...
    Return CType(Sprocs.FindCustomers(searchFor, GetType(CustomerSet)), _
                                    CustomerSet)

End Function
```

That's it! Now we can call the `FindCustomers` stored procedure through a shared method with the same name in `Customer`.

The "EntitySetScroller" Control

Now that we have a way of searching for customers, we can turn our attention to building our `EntitySetScroller` control. Add a new user control to the **ApplicationBrowserControls** project and call it `EntitySetScroller`.

To this new control, add some more controls, like this:

The control properties are:

❏ First Label control: set the `Text` property to `Pos:`

❏ First TextBox control: set the `Name` to `textPosition`, clear the `Text` property.

❏ Second Label control: you can't see this on the screenshot without looking for an absence of dots, but it's between the end of the textbox and the first button. Set the `Name` to `labelCount`. Clear the `Text` property.

❏ First Button control: set the `Name` property to `buttonFirst`.

❏ Second Button control: set the `Name` property to `buttonPrevious`.

❏ Third Button control: set the `Name` property to `buttonNext`.

❏ Fourth Button control: set the `Name` property to `buttonLast`.

Add a reference to the **EnterpriseObjects** project into the **ApplicationBrowserControls** project. Open the code editor for `EntitySetScroller`. Add a namespace import reference for `EnterpriseObjects`.

```
Imports EnterpriseObjects
```

Then, add two private members:

```
Public Class EntitySetScroller
    Inherits System.Windows.Forms.UserControl
```

```
' members...
Private _entitySet As EntitySet
Private _bindingTable As DataTable
```

To use the control, we'll give it an EntitySet through the `EntitySet` property. This will update the `_entitySet` private member. However, as a DataSet and therefore an EntitySet can contain multiple tables, to control which table we actually want to bind to we'll have another property called `BindingTable`. If we don't explicitly set this, the property will automatically return the zeroth DataTable in the `EntitySet` object's `Tables` collection. When we detect changes to the properties, we'll need to update the view, which we'll do through a method called `UpdateView`.

Add these properties to implement that logic:

```
' EntitySet property...
Public Property EntitySet() As EntitySet
  Get
    Return _entitySet
  End Get
  Set(ByVal value As EntitySet)
    ' set it...
    _entitySet = Value

    ' update the view...
    UpdateView()
  End Set
End Property

' BindingTable property...
Public Property BindingTable() As DataTable
  Get
    ' do we have anything explictly set?
    If _bindingTable Is Nothing Then
      Return EntitySet.Tables(0)
    Else
      Return _bindingTable
    End If
  End Get
  Set(ByVal value As DataTable)
    ' set it...
    _bindingTable = value
  End Set
End Property
```

Data binding in Windows Forms is heavily dependent on something called a Binding Manager. This is a class that keeps track of what property on what control is bound to what data.

Out-of-the-box, the Framework comes with two binding managers, both derived from `System.Windows.Forms.BindingManagerBase`. The first is called `System.Windows.Forms.PropertyManager` and the second is called `System.Windows.Forms.CurrencyManager`. `PropertyManager` is used for binding to properties on a single object, whereas `CurrencyManager` is used for binding to properties on a single object, where that object can be found in a list of some description. The word "currency" in "CurrencyManager" comes from "concurrency", rather than "money".

We can bind a property to an item of data with a call like this:

```
textFirstName.DataBindings.Add("Text", myDataTable, "FirstName")
```

In this case, we're adding a binding to the control `textFirstName`. We're binding that control's `Text` property to the `FirstName` property of the `myDataTable` object, which we'll assume is a `DataTable`.

This call prompts the parent of the control (in this case, the `Form`) to create a binding manager to handle all data binding to data contained within `myDataTable`. Now imagine another dozen controls all bind their `Text` properties to various properties on `myDataTable`. What happens is that the data binding process automatically looks at the current object in `myDataTable`. (This will automatically start at the first item, which in the case of a DataTable is always a DataRow.) The values from the properties on the DataRow are extracted and copied into the associated property on the control itself, in this case `Text`.

Likewise, if the `Text` property is changed, the related property on the DataRow also changes.

Now, imagine we want to display a different DataRow. Ideally, we want to be able to do this in a single call, like `MoveNext`, and have all of the controls automatically deal with updating all of their `Text` properties to reflect the new position in the list.

This is done through the binding manager. When the first data binding call occurs, the `Form` object creates a new `CurrencyManager` bound to `myDataTable` and adds it to the `BindingContext` collection. When the second, third, fourth, etc. data binding calls occur, the `Form` object looks to see if `myDataTable` already has a binding manager in the `BindingContext` collection.

As binding managers are added to the container's `BindingContext` collection, it's safe to assume that we can get hold of any binding manager we want. `BindingManagerBase` implements a property called `Position` that we can set to move the current item around. So, set it to `0` and we'll see the first item. Set it to `2` and we'll see the third item, and so on.

When we bind the controls, we'll use the `BindingTable` property of the `EntitySetScroller`. So, our binding call will actually look like this:

```
textFirstName.DataBindings.Add("Text", scroller.BindingTable, "FirstName")
```

To get hold of the `BindingManagerBase` object for `BindingTable`, we'll need a property that looks at the `Form` object's `BindingContext`. From inside of the control itself, we can access the `Form` through the `Parent` property. Add this property to `EntitySetScroller`:

```
' BindingManager property...
Public ReadOnly Property BindingManager() As BindingManagerBase
  Get
    Return Me.Parent.BindingContext(BindingTable)
  End Get
End Property
```

Before we can build the project, we need to build `UpdateView`. This method will control the enabled state of the buttons so that we can't move beyond the bounds of the list, and update the textbox and label controls. Add this method:

```
' UpdateView
Protected Sub UpdateView()
  ' are we enabled?
  If Not EntitySet Is Nothing Then
    ' enable...
    Enabled = True

    ' set the text...
    textPosition.Text = (BindingManager.Position + 1).ToString()
    labelCount.Text = "of " & BindingTable.Rows.Count.ToString()

    ' can we move back...
    Dim canMoveBack As Boolean  = True
    If BindingManager.Position = 0 Then
      canMoveBack = False
    End If
    Dim canMoveForward As Boolean = True
    If BindingManager.Position = BindingTable.Rows.Count - 1 Then
      canMoveForward = False
    End If

    ' enable...
    buttonFirst.Enabled = canMoveBack
    buttonPrevious.Enabled = canMoveBack
    buttonNext.Enabled = canMoveForward
    buttonLast.Enabled = canMoveForward
  Else
    Enabled = False
  End If
End Sub
```

This code makes up the basic functionality of `EntitySetScroller`. Build the project to make the new control available to `CustomerEditor` and we'll move on to actually binding the data.

Binding the Data

Open the Designer for `CustomerEditor` and if you look in the Toolbox you should find `EntitySetScroller`. Add one to the form and set the `Dock` property to `Bottom`. Also, make sure you change the `Name` property to `scrollerCustomers`.

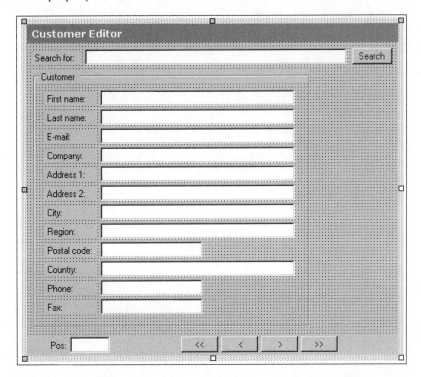

What we'll do is create a property on `CustomerEditor` called `Customers` that accepts a `CustomerSet`. When this is populated, we'll reset the data bindings and give the `CustomerSet` to the `EntitySetScroller`. Resetting the data bindings is important – if we're already bound to one `CustomerSet`, we want to clear the existing bindings so that we can replace them with our new ones. Here's the code:

```
Public Property Customers() As CustomerSet
  Get
    Dim Temp As Object = scrollerCustomers.EntitySet
    Return CType(Temp, BookManagerObjects.BookManagerObjects.CustomerSet)
  End Get
  Set(ByVal Value As CustomerSet)
    ' set it...
    Dim Temp As Object = Value
    scrollerCustomers.EntitySet = CType(Temp, EnterpriseObjects.EntitySet)

    ' clear our bindings...
    textFirstName.DataBindings.Clear()
```

```
          textLastName.DataBindings.Clear()
          textEmail.DataBindings.Clear()
          textCompanyName.DataBindings.Clear()
          textAddress1.DataBindings.Clear()
          textAddress2.DataBindings.Clear()
          textCity.DataBindings.Clear()
          textRegion.DataBindings.Clear()
          textPostalCode.DataBindings.Clear()
          textCountry.DataBindings.Clear()
          textPhone.DataBindings.Clear()
          textFax.DataBindings.Clear()

          ' do we have anything?
          If Not Value Is Nothing Then
              ' bind to...
              Dim bindTo As DataTable = scrollerCustomers.BindingTable

              ' create our bindings..
              textFirstName.DataBindings.Add("Text", bindTo, "FirstName")
              textLastName.DataBindings.Add("Text", bindTo, "LastName")
              textEmail.DataBindings.Add("Text", bindTo, "Email")
              textCompanyName.DataBindings.Add("Text", bindTo, "CompanyName")
              textAddress1.DataBindings.Add("Text", bindTo, "Address1")
              textAddress2.DataBindings.Add("Text", bindTo, "Address2")
              textCity.DataBindings.Add("Text", bindTo, "City")
              textRegion.DataBindings.Add("Text", bindTo, "Region")
              textPostalCode.DataBindings.Add("Text", bindTo, "PostalCode")
              textCountry.DataBindings.Add("Text", bindTo, "Country")
              textPhone.DataBindings.Add("Text", bindTo, "Phone")
              textFax.DataBindings.Add("Text", bindTo, "Fax")
          End If
      End Set
End Property
```

We'll populate the `Customers` property when the user clicks the **Search** button. When the user does this, we'll assert that the search term contains three or more characters. Again, this is a scalability issue. If the user enters a search term of "s" on a database containing 100,000 customers you may end up with several thousand customer records being returned.

Double-click on the **Search** button and add this code:

```
Private Sub buttonSearch_Click(ByVal sender As System.Object, _
                               ByVal e As System.EventArgs) _
                               Handles buttonSearch.Click

    ' get the term...
    Dim term As String = textSearchFor.Text
    If term.Length >= 3 Then
        ' get the Customers...
        Me.Cursor = Cursors.WaitCursor
        Dim found As CustomerSet = Customer.FindCustomers(term)
        Me.Cursor = Cursors.Default
```

```
     ' what happened...
     If found.Tables(0).Rows.Count > 0 Then
       ' show it...
       Customers = found
     Else
       Browser.Alert("No customers were found.", MessageBoxIcon.Information)
     End If
   Else
     Browser.Alert("You must enter three or more characters.")
   End If
End Sub
```

What this method will do is retrieve the search terms from the textbox. If they're valid, it will call the shared FindCustomers method on the Customer entity class, which in turn will defer processing over to the service object whereupon the stored procedure will be called.

If the stored procedure returns no rows, we display a message to that effect. Otherwise, we set the Customers property, and this will pass the EntitySet to the EntitySetScroller and set up the data binding.

Run the project and enter a search term of DREW. You'll see this:

Likewise, you'll get different results if you search for PHOENIX.

Moving Around

So far we've only returned a single record. Let's look at how we can move around the set of data that we've been given.

The `Position` property of `BindingManagerBase` lets us change the current item, so all we need to do is wire up the buttons so that when we click them, the position is changed. For completeness, we'll create methods called `MoveNext`, `MovePrevious`, `MoveFirst`, and `MoveLast` that manage the navigation and wire up the buttons to them.

Using the Designer for `EntitySetScroller`, double-click on each of the buttons in turn and add this code:

```
Private Sub buttonFirst_Click(ByVal sender As System.Object, _
                      ByVal e As System.EventArgs) _
                      Handles buttonFirst.Click

    MoveFirst()
End Sub

Private Sub buttonPrevious_Click(ByVal sender As System.Object, _
                      ByVal e As System.EventArgs) _
                      Handles buttonPrevious.Click

    MovePrevious()
End Sub

Private Sub buttonNext_Click(ByVal sender As System.Object, _
                      ByVal e As System.EventArgs) _
                      Handles buttonNext.Click

    MoveNext()
End Sub

Private Sub buttonLast_Click(ByVal sender As System.Object, _
                      ByVal e As System.EventArgs) _
                      Handles buttonLast.Click

    MoveLast()
End Sub
```

To manage the position, we'll create our own property called `Position`. This will defer processing to the `Position` property, but will come in very handy later. Add this property:

```
Public Property Position() As Integer
  Get
    If Not BindingManager Is Nothing Then
       Return BindingManager.Position
    Else
       Return -1
    End If
  End Get
  Set(ByVal Value As Integer)
    ' move it...
```

```
         If Not BindingManager Is Nothing Then
             BindingManager.Position = Value
         End If
      End Set
   End Property
```

Then, add these methods:

```
      Public Sub MoveFirst()
         Position = 0
      End Sub

      Public Sub MoveLast()
         Position = BindingTable.Rows.Count - 1
      End Sub

      Public Sub MovePrevious()
          ' remove one from the position...
         If Position <> 0 Then
            Position -= 1
         End If
      End Sub

      Public Sub MoveNext()
          ' add one to the position...
         If Position <> BindingTable.Rows.Count - 1 Then
            Position += 1
         End If
      End Sub
```

Whenever the position changes, we need to update the view. We do this for two reasons. Firstly, the value of textPosition needs to be updated. Secondly, we need to change the enabled states of the buttons to prevent the user from going outside of the bounds of the list.

One way to do this is to hook into the PositionChanged event of the BindingManagerBase returned by the BindingManager property. In response to this event, we'll call UpdateView. If we use this technique, and another control on the form unrelated to EntitySetScroller happens to change the position for the binding, our view will automatically update.

We need to hook up the events on two occasions: when the EntitySet property itself is set, and if we should explicitly set the BindingTable property. Make this change to EntitySet:

```
      ' EntitySet property...
      Public Property EntitySet() As EntitySet
         Get
            Return _entitySet
         End Get
         Set(ByVal Value As EntitySet)
            ' set it...
            _entitySet = Value

            ' update the events...
```

```
      UpdateEvents()

      ' update the view...
      UpdateView()
   End Set
End Property
```

Then, add this code to `BindingTable`:

```
' BindingTable property...
Public Property BindingTable() As DataTable
  Get
     ' do we have anything explictly set?
     If _bindingTable Is Nothing Then
        Return EntitySet.Tables(0)
     Else
        Return _bindingTable
     End If
  End Get
  Set(ByVal value As DataTable)
     ' set it...
     _bindingTable = value

     ' update the events...
     UpdateEvents()
  End Set
End Property
```

The `UpdateEvents` method itself is quite simple. We just add the event handler as discussed:

```
Public Sub UpdateEvents()
   ' ignore if we don't have an entity set...
   If EntitySet Is Nothing Then
     Exit Sub
   End If

   ' listen for changes to the binding manager...
   AddHandler BindingManager.PositionChanged, _
            New EventHandler(Addressof BindingManagerPositionChanged)
End Sub
```

Again, the `PositionChanged` method itself is pretty trivial.

```
Protected Sub BindingManagerPositionChanged(ByVal sender As System.Object, _
                                     ByVal e As System.EventArgs)
   ' update...
   UpdateView()
End Sub
```

Run the project and search for PRETEND. You'll be able to scroll through the results set.

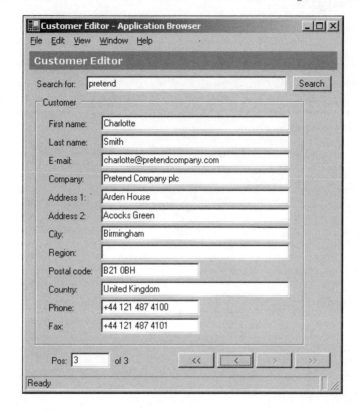

Changing Data

An "editor" isn't much of an "editor" if you can't change information. In this section, we'll take a look at how we can update the underlying database.

It won't come as much of a surprise if I tell you that the Entity class is capable of saving its own changes back to the database. The method to do this is called SaveChanges.

However, there's a little more to it than that, and in this section we'll take a look at:

❑   How we can tell the user that changes to the database need to be made

❑   How we can validate changes before they are committed

❑   How we can handle concurrency issues

Flagging Changes

When we edit data using the SQL Server Enterprise Manager, VS.NET Server Manager or Microsoft Access, we're shown a little pencil icon to tell us that we've changed some data and that changes need to be saved. We'll add the same functionality to `EntitySetScroller`.

To detect when changes need to be made, we'll hook into the `ColumnChanged` event of the DataTable returned by `BindingTable`. This will fire whenever the user makes changes to any of the data bound controls. When this happens, we'll update our own state to indicate that we are "dirty", in other words our changes need to be saved.

First off, we'll need a member to indicate if we are dirty or not. Add this code to `EntitySetScroller`:

```
Public Class EntitySetScroller
   Inherits System.Windows.Forms.UserControl


   ' members...
   Private _entitySet As EntitySet
   Private _bindingTable As DataTable
   Private _isDirty As Boolean
```

Next, we need to hook up an event handler to listen for when the data changes. Add this code to `UpdateEvents`:

```
Public Sub UpdateEvents()
   ' ignore if we don't have an entity set...
   If EntitySet Is Nothing Then
     Exit Sub
   End If

   ' listen for changes to the binding manager...
   AddHandler BindingManager.PositionChanged, _
              New EventHandler(Addressof BindingManagerPositionChanged)


   ' listen for changes to the data...
   AddHandler BindingTable.ColumnChanged, _
     New DataColumnChangeEventHandler(Addressof BindingTableColumnChanged)

End Sub
```

When the event fires, we need to update our dirty flag and update the view, providing that our `_isDirty` member has changed to `True`.

```
Protected Sub BindingTableColumnChanged(ByVal sender As System.Object, _
                          ByVal e As DataColumnChangeEventArgs)
   ' have we changed state?
   If _isDirty = True Then
     Exit Sub
   End If
```

```
        ' flag...
        _isDirty = True

        ' update...
        UpdateView()
    End Sub
```

To report the new state, we're going to display a small graphic. I've used a screen capture utility to take these from SQL Server Enterprise Manager. You'll find them in the download package for the book if you don't want to get them yourselves. You'll need two: one for "view" and one for "edit". The bitmaps should be 16 pixels wide and 16 pixels tall.

To make them available in the control, we'll use an ImageList. Using the Designer, add a new ImageList control to EntitySetScroller. Set its Name property to imagelistState. Use the Images collection and the Collection Editor to add the two bitmaps in the order of "View" then "Edit".

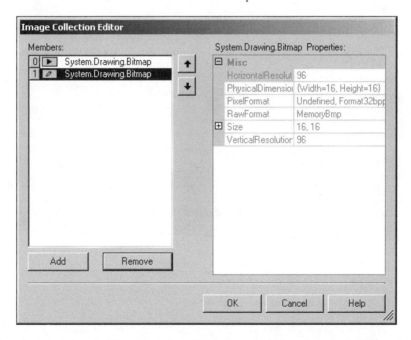

Click OK, and again using the Designer add a PictureBox control to the left of the Pos: label. Set its Size property to 16, 16. Set the Name property to imageState.

In addition, add a new button to the control. Set its Name property to buttonSave, and its Enabled property to False.

We need an enumeration to provide easier access to the images in the ImageList. Add this code to EntitySetScroller:

```
Public Class EntitySetScroller
    Inherits System.Windows.Forms.UserControl

    ' members...
    Private _entitySet As EntitySet
    Private _bindingTable As DataTable
    Private _isDirty As Boolean

    ' enum...
    Public Enum StateImage
        View = 0
        Edit = 1
    End Enum
```

Now we can turn our attention to UpdateView. When this method is called, if _isDirty is False we need to set the Image property of imageState to the image that corresponds to StateImage.View. If it's True, we need to use StateImage.Edit. Add this code:

```
' UpdateView
Protected Sub UpdateView()
    ' are we enabled?
    If Not EntitySet Is Nothing Then
        ' enable...
        Enabled = True

        ' set the text...
        textPosition.Text = (BindingManager.Position + 1).ToString()
        labelCount.Text = "of " & BindingTable.Rows.Count.ToString()

        ' can we move back...
        Dim canMoveBack As Boolean = True
        If BindingManager.Position = 0 Then
            canMoveBack = False
        End If
        Dim canMoveForward As Boolean = True
        If Position = BindingTable.Rows.Count - 1 Then
            canMoveForward = False
        End If

        ' enable...
        buttonFirst.Enabled = canMoveBack
        buttonPrevious.Enabled = canMoveBack
        buttonNext.Enabled = canMoveForward
        buttonLast.Enabled = canMoveForward
```

```
      ' update the image...
      If _isDirty = False Then
         imageState.Image = imagelistState.Images(CType(StateImage.View,Integer))
      Else
         imageState.Image = imagelistState.Images(CType(StateImage.Edit,Integer))
      End If
      buttonSave.Enabled = _isDirty
   Else
      Enabled = False
   End If
End Sub
```

Now run the project and load some data. Change one of the fields and click onto another field. The arrow icon will change to a pencil icon. (The changes will only be written to the bound data when the focus on the TextBox control is lost, which is why you have to click onto another control.) The image will be updated immediately after the ColumnChanged event has fired.

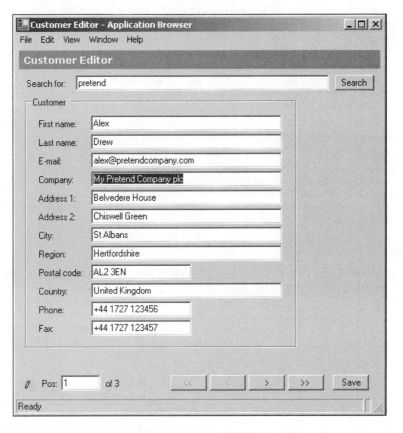

A Word About Concurrency

In multi-user applications, we have to deal with **concurrency**. With many users all using the same system at the same time, we have to be careful that any changes we make don't upset the changes another user has made or is trying to make.

Here's an example. Suppose Edward starts editing a customer record. As Edward is editing the record, Darren opens the same record, makes a single change, and saves the changes. A little while after this, Edward saves his changes. The upshot – Darren's changes are lost forever.

There are two basic types of concurrency:

❑ Optimistic concurrency. This is where you assume that you are going to be the only person changing the data. In other words you have retrieved the record and you believe you're the only person to be working on that record. When it comes to save, you check for and resolve any issues.

❑ Pessimistic concurrency. This is where you assume that someone else is going to want to change a particular record. When you retrieve it, you lock it preventing anyone else from being able to edit it. When you're done, your changes are saved and the lock is released.

With .NET, Microsoft has backed optimistic concurrency. It's done this because with ADO.NET it's very keen on the concept of disconnection – you get some data, work with it and send new data back if there is any. Because of the nature of disconnection, there is no continual connection between the client and the database server during the work period. The upshot of this is that firstly, the application can scale really well, but secondly, the database cannot manage any locking. This means that, without building some mechanism to manage pessimistic concurrency, we're left with just the option of optimistic concurrency.

Although we're not going to be looking at it in this book, if you wanted to implement pessimistic concurrency, one option would be to build a separate application that manages locks. The clients could connect to this service over Remoting or through a Web Service. However, you'd have to be very careful to get the optimum scalability out of such a system.

Timestamps

SQL Server has a data type called a "timestamp". If we add one of these columns to a table, whenever an update is issued against a given row, the timestamp is updated. Despite the name, the timestamp is actually implemented as a 64-bit integer number – in effect, it's a version number. We don't have to manage updating this value. SQL Server does it for us.

Our Customers table already has a timestamp column, and the WEO layer is able to work with the timestamp to manage optimistic concurrency.

Entity classes based on tables that have a timestamp column, like Customer, automatically implement the EnterpriseObjects.IConcurrentEntity interface. This interface defines three methods:

```
Public Interface IConcurrentEntity
   Public Function GetTimestamp() As System.Data.SqlTypes.SqlBinary
   Public Sub RefreshTimestamp()
   Public Function HasChanged() As Boolean
End Interface
```

The `IConcurrentEntity` interface, in combination with methods automatically added to the service objects by the Object Builder, automatically manages the concurrency. We discuss the Enterprise Objects, of which `IConcurrentEntity` is a member, further in Appendix A. Here's what they do:

- ❏ `GetTimestamp` – this method returns the timestamp of the entity, as it was when it was loaded from the database. This effectively abstracts whatever property returns the value of the timestamp column. (The name of this column may change from table to table as the database administrator is free to define whatever name they like for the timestamp column.)

- ❏ `RefreshTimestamp` – this method updates the timestamp of the entity with whatever timestamp is currently stored in the database. (We'll explain why we need this later.)

- ❏ `HasChanged` – this method returns a Boolean indicating whether or not the timestamp in the entity matches the timestamp in the database. If `True`, the entity is no longer the most up-to-date version.

If you open the code editor for `CustomerBase`, you'll find that this class does indeed implement `IConcurrentEntity`:

```
Public Class CustomerBase
    Inherits EnterpriseObjects.Entity
    Implements EnterpriseObjects.IConcurrentEntity
```

Again in `CustomerBase`, find the `Timestamp` property. As we cannot change the timestamp, this is a read-only property.

```
Public ReadOnly Property Timestamp() As System.Data.SqlTypes.SqlBinary
  Get
     Return New System.Data.SqlTypes.SqlBinary(CType(Me(13), System.Byte()))
  End Get
End Property
```

In our case, 13 happens to be the ordinal number of the timestamp column in the **Customers** table.

The implementation for `GetTimestamp` simply abstracts the `Timestamp` property:

```
Public Function GetTimestamp()As System.Data.SqlTypes.SqlBinary
  Return Me.Timestamp
End Function
```

The implementations for `HasChanged` and `GetLatestTimestamp` defer processing to `CustomerService`.

```
Public Function HasChanged()As Boolean
   Return Customer.ServiceObject.HasChanged(Me.Id, Me.GetTimestamp())
End Function

Public Sub RefreshTimestamp()
  Me(13) = Customer.ServiceObject.GetLatestTimestamp(Me.Id).Value
End Sub
```

HasChanged is a basic method that passes the ID of the entity and the current timestamp over to the service. If you look at CustomerServiceBase, once it gets there it defers processing to the EnterpriseObjects.Service base class, after it's retrieved the latest timestamp using GetLatestTimestamp:

```
Public Function HasChanged(ByVal id As Integer, _
            ByVal timestamp As System.Data.SqlTypes.SqlBinary ) As Boolean
   Return Me.HasChanged(timestamp, Me.GetLatestTimestamp(id))
End Function
```

Both CustomerBase.RefreshTimestamp and CustomerServiceBase.HasChanged use GetLatestTimestamp. This method again defers to the EnterpriseObjects.Service base class, whereupon a stored procedure is used to get the latest timestamp.

In the next section, we'll take a look at how we can use this information to properly manage optimistic concurrency.

Saving Changes

At this point, we have a subtle problem, although it's more "something to be aware of" than a problem. We're using the PositionChanged method of BindingManagerBase to listen for when the position has actually changed. However, there is no PositionChanging event, so we don't get told when the position is *about to change.*

This is actually quite important. Imagine this: if we have changed some data, and then the user attempts to move off the current record by clicking one of the VCR buttons, we need an opportunity to save the changes. Without PositionChanging, we don't have that.

There are two approaches we can take to solve this problem. One, is to inherit our own class from CurrencyManager and implement the new method. This means we somehow have to hook into the calls that the Form makes to set up the binding and replace the CurrencyManager that the DataTable wants to use. This is non-trivial.

The other approach is to come to an agreement that when we use the EntitySetScroller, we'll always change the position using the Position property, rather than getting the CurrencyManager from the BindingContext and changing it there. We're going to use this simpler, second approach just to keep things easy.

This is a perfectly acceptable approach on most forms, but it's worth bearing in mind that if you add any third-party controls to the form that can affect the position of the binding manager in a similar way to EntitySetScroller, you may run into problems.

To save the changes, we need to get hold of the current Entity. We can do this by building a new property and by hooking into the Current property of the binding manager. Add this property to EntitySetScroller:

```
Public ReadOnly Property Entity() As Entity
  Get
    Return _entitySet.GetEntity(Position)
  End Get
End Property
```

Saving the changes is simplicity itself. Add this code to the `Position` property. This will cause the entity to be saved whenever the user tries to navigate to another entity.

```
Public Property Position() As Integer
  Get
    If Not BindingManager Is Nothing Then
      Return BindingManager.Position
    Else
      Return -1
    End If
  End Get
  Set(ByVal value As Integer)
    ' do we need to save changes?
    CheckSave()

    ' move it...
    If Not BindingManager Is Nothing Then
      BindingManager.Position = value
    End If
  End Set
End Property
```

Flip-over to the Designer and double-click on the **Save** button. Add this code:

```
Private Sub buttonSave_Click(ByVal sender As System.Object, _
                    ByVal e As System.EventArgs) _
                    Handles buttonSave.Click
    CheckSave()
End Sub
```

The `CheckSave` method itself is relatively complex because it has to deal with the concurrency issues. The first thing we have to do is quit if the `_isDirty` flag returns `False`, because if it is `False`, there are no changes in memory that we need to save.

```
Public Sub CheckSave()
  ' are we dirty?
  If _isDirty = False Then
    Exit Sub
  End If
```

We can then retrieve the current entity. If we don't have one, we don't have to do anything.

```
    ' do we have an entity...
    Dim current As Entity = Entity
    If Not current Is Nothing Then
```

Next, we have to determine if the entity supports concurrency. (If it doesn't, we'll just save the changes and ignore any problems that might occur.) We can determine if it does support concurrency by calling the `SupportsConcurrency` method.

```
' concurrency...
Dim concurrent As IConcurrentEntity = Nothing

' does the entity support concurrency?
Dim saveOk As Boolean = False
If current.SupportsConcurrency() = True Then
```

If the entity does support concurrency, we store the reference to the `IConcurrentEntity` interface in a local variable. We then call the interface's `HasChanged` method. If the entity has not changed, we flag `saveOk` to True. Otherwise, we don't flag it and call the `UnderlyingDataChanged` event. (We'll build this in a moment.) On the other hand, if the entity does not support concurrency, we always flag `saveOk` to True.

```
' if it's changed, we need to just ditch the changes...
concurrent = CType(current, IConcurrentEntity)
If concurrent.HasChanged() = False Then
  saveOk = True
Else
  ' throw an event...
  RaiseEvent UnderlyingDataChanged(Me, New EventArgs())
End If
Else
  saveOk = True
End If
```

Should we be able to save, we call the `SaveChanges` method. We'll go through this in a moment.

```
' save...
If saveOk = True Then
  current.SaveChanges()
End If
```

The next part is important – if the entity does support concurrency, we have to load up the new timestamp into the entity. We do this because after we've saved the changes, the timestamp will be changed. If we try to make more changes to the entity, when we come to save the timestamp won't match because we'll have the old timestamp.

```
' get the latest timestamp, if we need it...
If Not concurrent Is Nothing Then
  concurrent.RefreshTimestamp()
End If
End If
```

Finally, we reset `_isDirty` and update the view.

```
' reset...
_isDirty = False
UpdateView()
End Sub
```

Before we can run the project, we need to wire up the UnderlyingDataChanged event, otherwise we won't be told when the data changes. First of all, add this delegate definition to the ApplicationBrowserControls namespace and this event to the EntitySetScroller class:

```
' events...
Public Delegate Sub UnderlyingDataChangedEventHandler( _
                                    ByVal sender As System.Object, _
                                    ByVal e As System.EventArgs)



Public Class EntitySetScroller
   Inherits System.Windows.Forms.UserControl

    ' events...
   Public Event UnderlyingDataChanged As UnderlyingDataChangedEventHandler


   ...
End Class
```

Now, open the code editor for CustomerEditor. Add this code to the constructor:

```
Public Sub New()
MyBase.New()

' This call is required by the Windows.Forms Form Designer.
InitializeComponent()

' events...
AddHandler scrollerCustomers.UnderlyingDataChanged, _
     New ApplicationBrowserControls.UnderlyingDataChangedEventHandler( _
     AddressOf ScrollerCustomersUnderlyingDataChanged)
End Sub
```

Finally, add this method to CustomerEditor:

```
Protected Sub ScrollerCustomersUnderlyingDataChanged( _
                                    ByVal sender As System.Object, _
                                    ByVal e As System.EventArgs)

   Browser.Alert("The customer record that you are trying to edit " _
           & "has been changed by another user. Your changes cannot " _
           & "be saved and you should use the 'Search' button again " _
           & "to reload the information.")
End Sub
```

Run the project now. Make a change to one of the fields in the usual way. Notice how the arrow icon changes to a pencil icon.

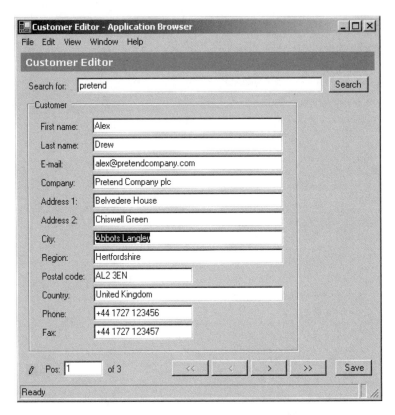

Click the Save button, or attempt to navigate to another entity and the changes will be saved to the database. Here's what the data looks like in SQL Server Enterprise Manager.

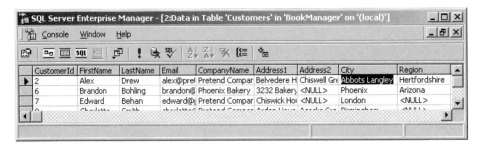

Testing the Concurrency

To test to see if the concurrency works, view the Customers table in SQL Server Enterprise Manager, as shown above. Change some of the data. In this case, I've changed the City field to Watford. (You can change any data you like, but obviously you need to edit the row in Customers that matches the Entity on the Customer Editor.)

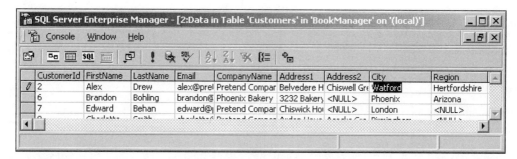

Flip back to the Customer Editor, change some data for the entity again. Now click the Save button, and you'll see this:

As the message states, you won't be able to edit this Entity until you click Search to reload the data. When you do this, the updated value will be shown in the editor.

What Happens in an Update

We need to take a look at what happens when the SaveChanges method is called on the Customer object.

For the most part, if you need to update information there are two ways you can go. You can either use a general-purpose method (the one we're using here), or you can use a custom-written one. Custom-written ones can be tuned to your exact requirements, so are likely to yield better performance. (For example, if you only need to update one column, you only need to send the data for a single column and SQL Server only has to process a single column. A general-purpose function has to work with all of the columns, so there's more to send and more data for SQL Server to chew through.) The advantage of a general-purpose method is that we can use it without having to do much work. That's precisely what we're doing here, in fact.

If you open the code editor for CustomerBase, you'll find the SaveChanges method. This is not a small method because it has to "line up" the data for the update. Handling null values causes all the issues here. For example, for the first two columns, we know that FirstName and LastName can never be null, so we can just store them in local variables. Compare this to Email, which can be null and so we have to check the value and set emailParam to be either the value in the column or DBNull.Value.

```
Public Overrides Sub SaveChanges()

    ' line up the update params... '
    Dim firstNameParam As String = Me.FirstName
    Dim lastNameParam As String = Me.LastName
    Dim emailParam As Object
```

```
      If (Me.IsEmailNull = False) Then
        emailParam = Me.Email
      Else
        emailParam = System.DBNull.Value
      End If
      ...
```

I'll omit the remainder of the code that builds up the parameters for brevity, but it looks very similar to this code. Of course, you can find it yourself in the code that the builder generates.

Once we have all of the parameters, we can call the Update method on the CustomerService object. This takes all of the columns except the timestamp columns.

```
    Customer.ServiceObject.Update(Me.Id, firstNameParam, lastNameParam, _
                    emailParam, companyNameParam, address1Param, _
                    address2Param, cityParam, regionParam, postalCodeParam, _
                    countryParam, phoneParam, faxParam)
    End Sub
```

If you look now in CustomerServiceBase, you'll find the Update method. This method simply defers to the eosp_UpdateCustomer stored procedure built by the Object Builder. Notice how the nullable columns take a System.Object as their type rather than a value type.

```
    Public Sub Update(ByVal id As Integer,ByVal firstName As String, _
                  ByVal lastName As String, ByVal email As Object, _
                  ByVal companyName As Object, ByVal address1 As String, _
                  ByVal address2 As Object, ByVal city As String, _
                  ByVal region As Object, ByVal postalCode As String, _
                  ByVal country As String, ByVal phone As Object, _
                  ByVal fax Object)

      Sprocs.eosp_UpdateCustomer(id, firstName, lastName, email, _
                  companyName, address1, address2, city, region, postalCode, _
                  country, phone, fax)
    End Sub
```

You can probably guess what the eosp_UpdateCustomer stored procedure looks like, but here it is anyway:

```
  CREATE PROCEDURE eosp_UpdateCustomer
  (
    @customerId Int,
    @firstName VarChar(32),
    @lastName VarChar(32),
    @email VarChar(48) = null,
    @companyName VarChar(48) = null,
    @address1 VarChar(32),
    @address2 VarChar(32) = null,
    @city VarChar(16),
    @region VarChar(16) = null,
    @postalCode VarChar(16),
    @country VarChar(32),
```

```
    @phone VarChar(16) = null,
    @fax VarChar(16) = null
)
AS
    UPDATE Customers SET FirstName=@firstName, LastName=@lastName, Email=@email,
        CompanyName=@companyName, Address1=@address1,
        Address2=@address2, City=@city, Region=@region,
        PostalCode=@postalCode, Country=@country, Phone=@phone, Fax=@fax
        WHERE CustomerId=@customerId
```

Adding New Customers

In this exercise, we haven't looked at how to add a new customer. I'm not going to take you through how to do this step by step now, as it's pretty trivial.

The `EntitySetScroller` control cannot handle the concept of adding records. This is because we've built the control in such a way that it can only work with a defined set of data (in other words a set that's been retrieved from the database). If we roll in the ability to work with data that doesn't already exist on the database, we start to complicate the simplicity of the control.

One solution to this is to rework the `CustomerEditor` so that when the View | Create Customer menu option is selected, the `EntitySetScroller` is hidden and replaced with OK and Cancel buttons. You'd have to create a new `Customer` entity and bind the fields on the control to properties on this entity. In other words, we need to short-circuit the functionality of the `EntitySetScroller` when adding data.

When it's time to save the new record, the `Customer` entity already supports methods for inserting new customers into the database. We can call the static `Insert` method and provide values for all of the fields. There is a version of `Insert` that takes all of the possible values, rather than the ones we met in Chapter 2, which just takes the non-null fields.

Summary

In this chapter, we took a look at how we could build a simple desktop application that would allow us to view and edit data in our database. We kicked off by looking at how we could run the sub-application in such a way that we could debug it, and then moved on to build the basic form.

To get the data that we need to work on, we've mandated that we're always expected to search for the data we want to edit. This means that if we have 100,000 customers in the database, we'll only be pulling back a handful of these from the server to work on.

We then built a custom control that would allow us to navigate through an entity set. This control had the intelligence to understand when data had been changed and provided a way for the user to save the data. We also illustrated how the optimistic concurrency features of WEO can prevent data from being lost.

.NET Enterprise Development in VB .NET

5

Automated Processes and Transactions

In this chapter, we're going to take a look at how to create automated processes within our application. In enterprise applications, it's often typical for system components to act autonomously, with no user interaction. Within the enterprise arena, we might have an application that runs unattended each night backing up our essential data, or we could have a system component that automatically produces and sends orders to suppliers by comparing our outstanding commitments with current stock levels.

Specifically, we're going to look at a pretty basic piece of system functionality which accepts and processes orders from customers. Along the way, we'll take a look at how to handle transactions, work with XML documents, and look at some architectural concepts that make building this kind of application straightforward.

Our Approach

Virtually all organizations are founded on the concept of a customer buying something. (Well, this might not have been strictly true of a great deal of dot coms before the bubble burst!) In our example, we would want to allow our distributors and wholesalers to place orders for books directly. Let's now break this problem down into its constituent parts.

Order Capture

We need a way of capturing orders into our application. In today's world, there are several ways of doing this, using a combination of physical and electronic channels:

❑ Our customer calls a telephone sales operator, who takes down their order, and enters it into the enterprise application using a desktop or Web-based "sub-application"

❑ Our customer faxes or sends their order, which is then retyped into the same "sub-application" by one of our employees

❑ One of the customer's employees makes orders using a web application (in a similar way to how you might use "Amazon.com")

❑ The customer's computer system connects directly to ours and enters the order straight into our system

Whichever combination of these four possible channels is used, we will of course still have to process the order in the same way once we've got it.

Order Processing

Once the order has been captured, we'll assume that the order is stored in the relational database that supports the application. We have to deal with the fact that we have a finite amount of goods available for sale, and that customers may have attempted to buy more goods than we currently have available. A customer could order 1000 of a certain title when we only have 500 ready to ship. Or, a customer could order all 500 and another order could be received for a further 50 from another customer. We really want to produce invoices for each order or part order.

We have to be able to put goods on "back order" – incomplete orders must be tracked until they are fulfilled entirely.

Order Shipping

When we process an order, or part thereof, we have to handle the logistics of physically getting the books to the customer. We may choose to do this by informing our warehousing and distribution partner that a certain set of books must be dispatched to a certain customer. Alternatively, if we handle our own distribution, we would inform our own warehouse.

Ideally we need to cater for logistical problems that could occur at this point. For example, say we receive an order for 500 of a given title, and our records show that we have 500 in the warehouse. It could later turn out that 100 of those are in fact in the process of being allocated to a previous order, or we may discover that an employee has "borrowed" one copy for his son. In such cases, we have to be able to readjust the order and the invoice so that the customer only pays for the actual quantity of the product that we were able to supply, and the rest are put on back order.

Order Reporting

As well as all of the above, we have to be able to report to the customer the status of their order as it is processed. In general, snail-mail is not really appropriate for this task, as status reports may not arrive until after the order itself! We really need to use one of the following:

❑ "Face mail" – we pick up a phone and talk to them, like we did in the old days!

❑ E-mail – we send a human-readable e-mail that someone must usually action manually at the other end. (In some cases of course, a computer could process messages intended for human recipients automatically.)

❑ Electronic – we send a message directly into the customer's computer system for it to process as appropriate.

In cases where problems occur (and in our case, they're likely to be related to delays in processing the order because of goods not being physically available), we need to be able to cancel the part of the unprocessed order, or the entire order, following the customer's request.

Scope of the Problem

The system we've outlined in the past four sections could quite easily become a pretty large and complex sprawling application. In fact, it would take another book like this to detail it all. In order to fit the work into a single chapter, we'll cut down the scope of the problem to allow us to focus on the core essentials.

Order Capture

Orders will be expressed as XML documents and fed into an application called OrderLoader. (This will form part of the integrated enterprise application that we're building through the course of this book, but will be physically implemented as a .NET console application.) OrderLoader will read the XML document, and insert corresponding rows in the appropriate tables to represent the order. We'll assume that:

❑ Sub-applications our employees or business partners use squirt the order into the OrderLoader application.

❑ Web applications that our customers use for ordering squirt the order into the same OrderLoader application.

❑ We'll be able to accept the XML document over e-mail, HTTP, or FTP, and squirt the order into OrderLoader – although we won't implement such a solution in this book.

❑ As a continuation of this, we'll also be able to accept the XML document through a Web Service, again squirting into OrderLoader. (We won't be implementing this aspect of the solution, but you can find out more about Web Services in Chapter 6 if you wish to do so yourself.)

The important thing is **commonality** – we can express any order as an XML document matching a format we've defined ourselves, and we can build an application that parses these XML documents for processing.

Order Processing

Once the orders have been loaded using OrderLoader, we'll periodically run another application called OrderProcessor. (This is another part of the larger enterprise application, again implemented as a console application.) This will walk the entire list of orders looking for ones that are "open" – that is, ones that haven't been completely processed.

Our job here is to turn "orders" into "invoices". We will also deal with the back-order issue as this is a very common problem to handle – basically, if we don't have enough of a book, we need to keep the order "open".

Order Shipping

We're not going to worry too much about this. We'll assume that we have a warehouse and that when we generate an invoice, that invoice can always be satisfied – so if our records say we have 500 of a title available, we will always have exactly 500.

In a real system, we'd build a "pick list" from the invoice and transmit it to the warehouse for processing. We'd also provide mechanisms to allow the warehouse staff to change the order should the goods not be available for any reason. For simplicity however, we won't be dealing with any of these issues, and we'll just assume that when an invoice is generated, the goods are then always successfully sent to the client.

Order Reporting

This is another big area that we're not going to concern ourselves with. We'll assume that the customer has access to an extranet that allows them to check the status of their order, and that we also send the customer e-mails reporting on the status of the order.

From this point, we could also generate XML documents representing invoices for transmission to a remote system, either through a Web Service or some other means. Related to this, we could also allow customers to transmit XML documents to cancel or change an order. However, we shall ignore the ability to cancel or modify orders once loaded.

Order Loading

The first part of this problem we will address is to turn the received XML document detailing an order into a set of rows in our database ready for processing by `OrderProcessor`.

The XML document we receive will contain the following:

- ❏   The identity of the customer
- ❏   The address that the goods should be delivered to, and the shipping method that should be used
- ❏   The list of items required

Here's what a typical XML order document will look like:

```xml
<?xml version="1.0" encoding="utf-8"?>
<Order xmlns="http://tempuri.org/Template.xsd">
  <Customer>
    <Id>2</Id>
  </Customer>
  <Delivery>
    <Method>1</Method>
    <Address>
      <Fao>Alex Drew</Fao>
      <Company>My Book Distributors</Company>
      <Address1>Belvedere House</Address1>
      <Address2 />
      <City>Watford</City>
      <Region>Hertfordshire</Region>
      <PostalCode>AL2 3EN</PostalCode>
      <Country>United Kingdom</Country>
      <Phone>+44 1727 123456</Phone>
    </Address>
  </Delivery>
  <Items>
    <Item>
      <Id>54</Id>
      <Quantity>10</Quantity>
    </Item>
  </Items>
</Order>
```

In this order, the customer has identified themself by providing a customer ID of 2:

```
<Customer>
  <Id>2</Id>
</Customer>
```

We'll assume that the ID given in the document is legitimate, although in a production system we would clearly need to prevent people placing bogus orders for someone else. Using physical channels, this is relatively straightforward as the operator can confirm the identity of a caller or "faxer". Using electronic methods, we'd have to implement some form of authentication scheme, more on which is discussed in Chapter 6 and again in Chapter 10.

The delivery part of the above document indicates the chosen delivery method and address:

```
<Delivery>
  <Method>1</Method>
  <Address>
    <Fao>Alex Drew</Fao>
    <Company>My Book Distributors</Company>
    <Address1>Belvedere House</Address1>
    <Address2 />
    <City>Watford</City>
    <Region>Hertfordshire</Region>
    <PostalCode>AL2 3EN</PostalCode>
    <Country>United Kingdom</Country>
    <Phone>+44 1727 123456</Phone>
  </Address>
</Delivery>
```

We've used an ordinal to represent the delivery method, so clearly we're expecting our customers to be aware of what each ordinal means.

Finally, we can look at the items in the order itself. In this example, we've ordered 10 of item 54:

```
<Items>
  <Item>
    <Id>54</Id>
    <Quantity>10</Quantity>
  </Item>
</Items>
```

Now that you know what the XML document representing the order looks like, let's create the database tables that hold order details.

The Orders table is shown below. It has an order ID field (as you would expect), and the delivery address, the delivery method, and the time:

	Column Name	Data Type	Length	Allow Nulls
▶🔑	OrderId	int	4	
	CustomerId	int	4	
	DeliveryMethod	int	4	
	AddressFao	varchar	64	
	AddressCompany	varchar	64	✓
	AddressAddress1	varchar	48	
	AddressAddress2	varchar	48	✓
	AddressCity	varchar	32	
	AddressRegion	varchar	32	✓
	AddressCountry	varchar	32	
	Created	datetime	8	
	LastProcessed	datetime	8	
	Complete	int	4	

Next, the OrderLines table simply holds a record of which book has been ordered, together with the quantity and the price. One `OrderId` value could reference multiple `OrderLines` records. The purpose of `QuantitySent` will become apparent when we look at the application that processes the orders:

	Column Name	Data Type	Length	Allow Nulls
▶🔑	LineId	int	4	
	OrderId	int	4	
	BookId	int	4	
	Quantity	int	4	
	Price	float	8	
	QuantitySent	int	4	

Loading the XML

Visual Studio .NET and the .NET Framework are similar in functionality to the Object Builder and WEO layer when working with XML. We can give Visual Studio the XML document that we want to use, and from that template it can create objects derived from `DataSet`, `DataTable`, and `DataRow` that allow us to access that data very easily. This is substantially easier than walking through the XML document using the various classes in `System.Xml`.

This may not be immediately easy to understand, so let's look at an example to get the feel of things. We're going to create a new Class Library project called `OrderLoader` that can read the XML document, connect to the database, and create new rows in the tables that we've just looked at. Initially we'll run it from within a console application, but as a class library, it wouldn't be difficult to have it run in a Windows Service (more information in Chapter 9), or within some other part of the system.

To kick off, create a new Class Library project called **OrderLoader**. When the solution has loaded, add the **EnterpriseObject** and **BookManagerObjects** projects, and add references to these projects to the OrderLoader project:

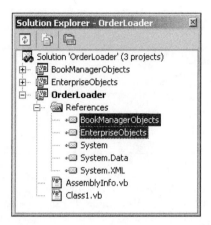

Delete the default `Class1.vb` file, and create a new class called `Loader`. We'll add methods for processing a specified XML document in a moment, but first I'd like to turn our attention to the features of Visual Studio .NET that make light of working with complex XML documents.

Using Solution Explorer, right-click **OrderLoader** and select **Add | Add New Item**. Choose **XML File** in the right-hand pane, and give it the name `Order`:

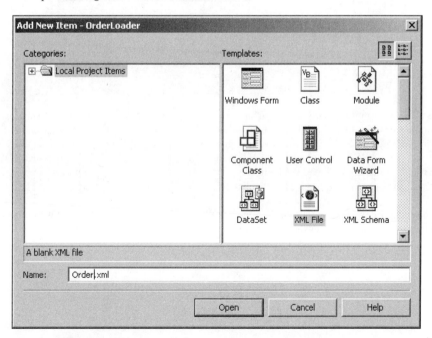

Key in the sample XML order document described towards the start of the chapter exactly as it appears (or, of course, use the version in the download package for this book):

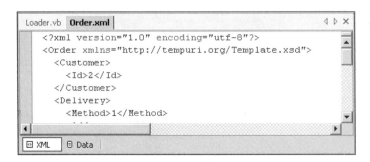

At the bottom of the editor window, you'll see a button marked Data. Click it now (or, alternatively, select View | Data from the menu). This brings up the XML document split into five tables: Customer, Delivery, Address, Items, and Item. Keep this in mind, because the DataSet that Visual Studio will build will contain five similar DataTables. If you select each table, you'll be able to see (and edit) the data described by the XML document:

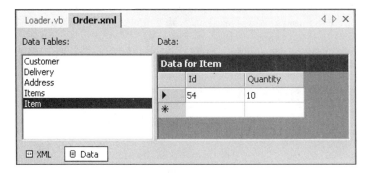

What VS.NET is attempting to do is "squash" the richly structured XML data into a form suitable for storage in a relational storage system. In order to change this XML document into a DataSet (and, interestingly, back again), we need an XML Schema. XML Schemas are a little opaque to understand, but luckily for us we don't have to. To get VS.NET to create an XML Schema file for our document, simply select XML | Create Schema from the menu (you'll need to be in the "XML" view for the menu option to be active). Order.xsd will appear in the Solution Explorer. Double-click this file to show it in Design view.

In this rather complex view, we're seeing how VS.NET looks at the XML document in terms of these five tables. There is one box per table:

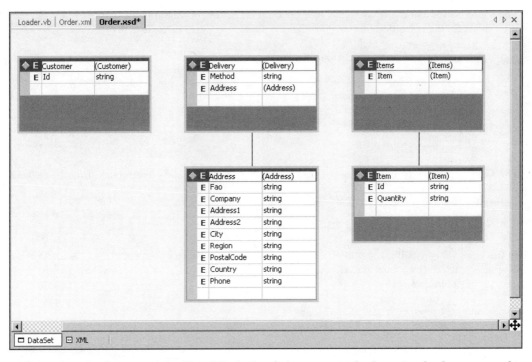

The first thing that leaps out is that Visual Studio hasn't done a great job of guessing the data types used in the document. We know, for example, that the Id element under the Customer element will always contain an integer – yet VS has flagged it as a "string". Our first job is to apply the correct data types, specifically:

- ❏   Customer.Id – change to int

- ❏   Delivery.Method – change to int

- ❏   Item.Id – change to int

- ❏   Item.Quantity – change to int

If you want, click the XML button at the bottom of the Designer to see the actual sourcecode for the schema generated by Visual Studio. Like I said, though, unless you're interested in the inner workings of schemas, this isn't something to worry about.

With the DataSet view open, select Schema | Generate Dataset from the menu. This will create a new source file containing several classes that we can see by clicking the Show All Files button on the Solution Explorer's mini-toolbar (you might need to select the OrderLoader project first). Expand Order.xsd and you'll see a .vb file and an .xsx file. We can pretty much ignore the .xsx file, as it contains extra data to serialize the Designer's UI. The .vb file, however, is important and contains a whole slew of classes for processing the XML file. You'll notice the generated code follows a similar format to WEO. For example, if you look at the top of the generated Order class that represents the entire XML document, you'll see these attributes set:

```
<Serializable(), _
System.ComponentModel.DesignerCategoryAttribute("code")>
```

147

You'll also notice that the `Order` class inherits from `DataSet`, in the same way that `EntitySet` does. We can access the collection of items through the `Items` property in `Order.vb`:

```
<System.ComponentModel.Browsable(false), _
    System.ComponentModel.DesignerSerializationVisibilityAttribute( _
    System.ComponentModel.DesignerSerializationVisibility.Content)> _
Public ReadOnly Property Items() As ItemsDataTable
    Get
        Return Me.tableItems
    End Get
End Property
```

The above method returns an object of class `ItemsDataTable`, a class that inherits from `DataTable`:

```
Public Class ItemsDataTable
    Inherits DataTable
    Implements System.Collections.IEnumerable
```

In this case, we can drill through the table until we eventually get to objects of class `ItemsRow` and then `ItemRow`, each derived from `DataRow`. `ItemRow` implements properties to access the `Id` and `Quantity` columns directly:

```
Public Property Id() As Integer
    Get
        Try
            Return CType(Me(Me.tableItem.IdColumn), Integer)
        Catch e As InvalidCastException
            Throw New StrongTypingException( _
                            "Cannot get value because it is DBNull.", e)
        End Try
    End Get
    Set
        Me(Me.tableItem.IdColumn) = value
    End Set
End Property

Public Property Quantity() As Integer
    Get
        Try
            Return CType(Me(Me.tableItem.QuantityColumn),Integer)
        Catch e As InvalidCastException
            Throw New StrongTypingException( _
                            "Cannot get value because it is DBNull.", e)
        End Try
    End Get
    Set
        Me(Me.tableItem.QuantityColumn) = value
    End Set
End Property
```

To load the data from a particular XML document, all we need to do is create a new instance of `Order`, and call the `ReadXml` method on it. We can either pass in the name of the XML file (useful for debugging), or a string representing the entire document.

For this first stage, we'll try something basic. We'll get the `DataSet` to load data from a file, and we'll output the contents of the `DataSet` to the console. Add these namespace import declarations to the `Loader` class:

```
Imports System.Data
Imports System.IO
```

To process a document, we need either a stream representing the document, or the document's filename. First, we'll create the method that takes the XML document as a `Stream`, and loads it into the `Order DataSet`. All we have to do is call `ReadXml` on a new instance of `Order`, and the base class handles the rest for us. For debugging purposes, we'll pass the new `Order` object to a method called `DebugOrder` that writes the contents of the `DataSet` to the console so we can see what's going on:

```
Public Sub Process(ByVal stream As Stream)
   ' Create the DataSet
   Dim myOrder As Order = New Order()

   ' Load in the XML document
   myOrder.ReadXml(stream, XmlReadMode.Auto)

   ' Output debug info
   DebugOrder(myOrder)

   ' Dispose of the DataSet
   myOrder.Dispose()
End Sub
```

If, on the other hand, we only have the XML document's filename, we'll open it as a `FileStream`, and pass it to the first `Process` method above for loading:

```
' Process - process the document
Public Sub Process(ByVal filename As String)
   ' Open it
   Dim stream As FileStream = New FileStream(filename, FileMode.Open)
   Process(stream)
   stream.Close()
End Sub
```

`DebugOrder` is where things start to get a little tricky. Although Visual Studio's tools build `DataSet`-derived objects just like Object Builder, in my opinion Visual Studio's objects are harder to use. In our specific case, we have to access the `Delivery` element through an indexer as if the document could contain multiple versions of the element, even though we know there may only ever be one such element. This isn't too much of a problem, but it does mean that when writing code based on these techniques, we need to be aware of how the objects have been structured within the VS-generated code file (such as `Order.vb` in this case).

Here's the code for `DebugOrder`:

```
Public Sub DebugOrder(ByVal myOrder As Order)
   ' Output the customer ID
   Console.WriteLine("Customer ID: {0}", myOrder.Customer(0).Id)
   Console.WriteLine()
```

```
      ' Handle delivery details
      Dim delivery As Order.DeliveryRow = myOrder.Delivery(0)
      Console.WriteLine("Method: {0}", delivery.Method)
      Dim address As Order.AddressRow = delivery.GetAddressRows()(0)
      Console.WriteLine("FAO: {0}", address.Fao)
      Console.WriteLine("Company: {0}", address.Company)
      Console.WriteLine("Address 1: {0}", address.Address1)
      Console.WriteLine("Address 2: {0}", address.Address2)
      Console.WriteLine("City: {0}", address.City)
      Console.WriteLine("Region: {0}", address._Region)
      Console.WriteLine("Postal code: {0}", address.PostalCode)
      Console.WriteLine("Country: {0}", address.Country)
      Console.WriteLine()

      ' Go through the items in the order
      Console.WriteLine("Items:")
      Dim itemsRow As Order.ItemsRow
      For Each itemsRow In myOrder.Items
        Dim item As Order._ItemRow
        For Each item In itemsRow.GetItemRows()
          Console.WriteLine("Item: {0} of #{1}", item.Quantity, item.Id)
        Next
      Next
   End Sub
```

You can see that we need to be careful when accessing the actual objects that contain the data. Instead of myOrder.Delivery, we have to call myOrder.Delivery(0). Instead of myOrder.Delivery(0).Address, we have to call myOrder.Delivery(0).GetAddressRows()(0). This is still easier than walking the document using XmlTextReader et al, but it can get a little tricky. In particular, note how we have to get a list of ItemsRow objects back and then separately request a set of ItemRow objects from each.

We can now try running this. To the solution, add a new console application project called OrderLoaderHost. Add a reference to the existing OrderLoader and EnterpriseObjects projects to this new project, and using Solution Explorer, right-click OrderLoaderHost and select Set as StartUp Project.

Import the EnterpriseObjects, System.IO, and System.Data namespaces into Module1.vb, and add this code to its Main method:

```
Module Module1
   Sub Main()

      ' Set database connection string
      EnterpriseApplication.Application.ConnectionString = _
               "integrated security=sspi;initial catalog=bookmanager;" _
            & "data source=chimaera"

      ' Load the order
      Dim loader As OrderLoader.Loader = New OrderLoader.Loader()
      loader.Process("c:\BookManager\OrderLoader Data\Order.xml")

      ' Wait until Enter key is pressed
```

```
        Console.ReadLine()
    End Sub
End Module
```

Before running the project, create a new folder called `c:\BookManager\OrderLoader Data`. Into this folder, copy the *same* `Order.xml` XML document from the `OrderLoader` project. Run the project and you'll see this:

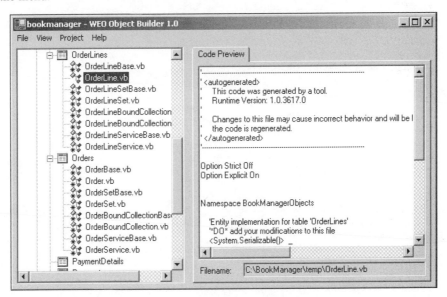

Processing the XML

OK, so we've managed to load the XML into a `DataSet`-derived object, and we've walked through this object looking for the data held in the XML file. The next step is to load the orders into the database ready for processing. We've already created the necessary tables earlier in the chapter, and now we need the Object Builder to create new classes to handle the Books, Orders, and OrderLines tables.

Fire up the Object Builder application and open the Object Builder project you've been using up to now. Include the Books, Orders, and OrderLines tables in the project, and select Project | Synchronize from the menu:

Next, open the existing `BookManagerObjects` project, and add the new files that the Object Builder created to make the **Books**, **Orders**, and **OrderLines** tables accessible through code. We're now ready to change the implementation of `Process` to write the data contained in the XML document to the **Orders** table. First, we need to insert a new row in the **Orders** table using the shared `Insert` method on `BookManagerObjects.Order`. (Note that we have to access that object using its fully-qualified name; otherwise we'd have an identifier clash between `OrderLoader.Order` and `BookManagerObjects.Order`.) `Insert` doesn't allow us to insert the null elements from the XML document, and we do this separately afterwards. Of course, this causes two hits on the server rather than one, so in a production environment you may want to optimize this.

We're going to assume that all of our customers get a 10% discount. In business-to-business commerce, customers typically get different rates for different products. To save getting into a labored discussion of how to handle this, I've taken the route of giving everyone a flat 10% off of the price shown in the **Books** table. In a production setting, it's likely we'd give certain customers a certain discount on a particular range of books, but not for others, and so on.

After determining the discount, we loop through the items listed in the order document. Here, we load a new `Book` object for each order line. We could improve performance by caching this information, although this brings with it issues related to the cache getting out of date. Add the highlighted code below to `Loader.vb` in the `OrderLoader` project:

```
Public Sub Process(ByVal stream As Stream)

  ' Create the DataSet
  Dim myOrder As Order = New Order()

  ' Load in the XML document
  myOrder.ReadXml(stream, XmlReadMode.Auto)

  ' Output debug info
  DebugOrder(myOrder)

  ' Get the order data
  Dim customer As Order.CustomerRow = myOrder.Customer(0)
  Dim delivery As Order.DeliveryRow = myOrder.Delivery(0)
  Dim address As Order.AddressRow = delivery.GetAddressRows()(0)

  ' Create the new order object
  Dim newOrder As BookManagerObjects.BookManagerObjects.Order = _
          BookManagerObjects.BookManagerObjects.Order.Insert(customer.Id, _
          delivery.Method, address.Fao, _
          address.Address1, address.City, address.Country, _
          DateTime.Now, DateTime.Now, 0)

  If address.Company <> "" Then
    newOrder.AddressCompany = address.Company
  End If

  If address.Address2 <> "" Then
    newOrder.AddressAddress2 = address.Address2
  End If

  If address._Region <> "" Then
```

```
        newOrder.AddressRegion = address._Region
    End If

    ' Save it
    newOrder.SaveChanges()

    ' Evaluate customer discount
    Dim discount As Double = 0.1F

    ' Now, loop through the items ordered
    Dim itemsRow As Order.ItemsRow
    For Each itemsRow In myOrder.Items
      Dim item As Order._ItemRow
      For Each item In itemsRow.GetItemRows()
        ' Load the book and get the price
        Dim myBook As BookManagerObjects.BookManagerObjects.Book = _
                    BookManagerObjects.BookManagerObjects.Book.GetById(item.Id)
        Dim price As Double = myBook.Price * (1 - discount)

        ' Insert the new line
        BookManagerObjects.BookManagerObjects.OrderLine.Insert(newOrder.Id, _
                                            item.Id, item.Quantity, price, 0)

      Next
    Next

    ' Output debug information
    Console.WriteLine("Order #{0} added to database", newOrder.Id)

    ' Dispose of the DataSet
    myOrder.Dispose()
End Sub
```

If you run the project now, you'll see the same debugging view as before. However, if we now open the Orders table, we can see that a new order has been added:

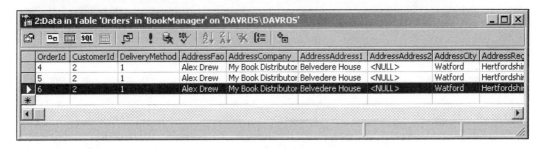

153

If we look in OrderLines, we'll see another row:

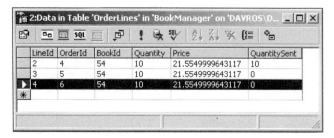

So we've read in an XML document and used that document to load an order into the database. What we have to do now is actually process the order.

Order Processing and Transactions

One aspect of these types of applications that we've neatly avoided is that of transactions. In the remainder of this chapter, we'll look at transactions and see how we can use them in the OrderProcessor application.

Transactions are critical in situations where you need absolute assurance that every part of a task has completed properly. For example, imagine we have a situation when processing a document with OrderLoader where we have successfully inserted a new row in the Orders table, but have failed to insert all of the associated rows into OrderLines for some reason. We would then have an invalid order in the system – the database representation of the order would not match the original document.

Transactions allow us to solve this problem by defining a "unit of work" that has to be either entirely complete, or not complete at all. In the OrderLoader situation, We would start a transaction at the beginning of processing an order, before we start working with the database. As we process the order, we may "abort" the transaction at any time, with the result that all tasks performed between that point and when we started the transaction are "undone". Any rows we have added will be removed from the database. Likewise, any rows we have deleted are put back, and if we've changed data, the new data is replaced by the original. This process is known as **rolling back**. If, on the other hand, we get to the end of the "unit of work" and everything is OK, we "commit" the transaction and changes to the database are made permanent.

There is an important point to note here, namely that if we add a row to a database when inside a transaction, other database users will not see that row until we commit the changes. Likewise with inserts and updates – the changes are ours and ours alone.

Suitable situations for transactions can be described using the ACID acronym:

- ❑ **Atomicity** – transactions must be single self-contained units that can either "completely complete" or not complete at all – we can "abort" a transaction and all the work done thus far can be undone ("rolled back"), or we can "commit" a transaction and all the changes are properly saved.

- ❑ **Consistency** – the database must remain in a consistent state before, during, and after the transaction – no invalid data must ever be left in the database due to a badly managed transaction or environmental problems during processing such as power loss or hardware failure.

❑ **Isolation** – transactions cannot interfere with each other – if transaction one adds a row to the database, further transactions should not be able to see that row until the transaction is committed.

❑ **Durability** – when the transaction is committed, the data must be "durable" – it must be properly saved into the underlying data store for others to use.

Let's build an `OrderProcessor` application to add support for transactions.

Building "OrderProcessor"

To build `OrderProcessor`, we need to build a pretty similar app to `OrderLoader`. Follow these steps:

1. Create a new VB.NET Class Library project called **OrderProcessor** as a new VS.NET solution

2. Delete the existing `Class1.vb`

3. Add a new class called `Processor`

4. Add a new Console Application project called **OrderProcessorHost** to the solution

5. Set **OrderProcessorHost** to be the "startup" project

6. To **OrderProcessorHost**, add a reference to the **OrderProcessor** project

7. To the solution, add the **EnterpriseObjects** and **BookManagerObjects** projects

8. To **OrderProcessor**, add references to **EnterpriseObjects** and **BookManagerObjects**

If you don't fancy doing all that, an alternative is to add the code we're about to introduce to the existing **OrderLoader** project. However, the steps we present here will assume you have a separate solution set up.

You should now have something like this:

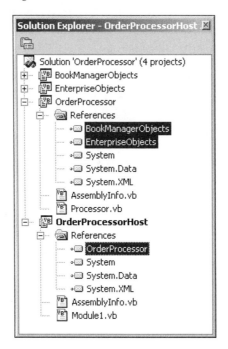

When our processor starts running, we want to walk through the orders that are open (in other words, where the Complete column is 0), and process each one in turn. The processing consists basically of allocating stock, and we can see how many of each book are in stock by looking at the StockLevel column of the **Books** table. We need to create a new invoice for each processed order by inserting a new row into the **Invoices** table, in much the same way as we did with the **Orders** table. For each order line, we create a new invoice line in the **InvoiceLines** table indicating how many were shipped and how much the customer was charged. The QuantitySent column on the relevant **OrderLines** row also has to be updated accordingly. The trick is to group all this in a single transaction, so that if anything goes wrong (and we'll determine this by listening for exceptions), we can abort the transaction and roll back the changes up to that point.

Processing the Order

The first thing we need is a stored procedure which returns the open order. We'll call it GetOpenOrders:

```
CREATE PROCEDURE GetOpenOrders
AS
  SELECT OrderId, CustomerId, DeliveryMethod, AddressFao, AddressCompany,
    AddressAddress1, AddressAddress2, AddressCity, AddressRegion,
    AddressCountry, Created, LastProcessed, Complete FROM Orders
    WHERE Complete=0
    ORDER BY Created
```

Nothing too complex there – we're just selecting out all orders that have their `Complete` column set to 0 and ordering the results from oldest to newest.

If you look in `BookManagerObjects.Sprocs`, you should find a `GetOpenOrders` method. (If you don't, make sure the above stored procedure exists in the database and re-synchronize the Object Builder project.) Copy `GetOpenOrders` over to `Processor.vb`, and change the access modifiers from `Public Shared` to `Protected`. In addition, modify the method so that it takes no parameters and always creates a `DataSet`:

```
Protected Functon GetOpenOrders() As System.Data.DataSet

    ' Create a connection
    Dim connection As System.Data.SqlClient.SqlConnection = _
        New System.Data.SqlClient.SqlConnection( _
        EnterpriseObjects.EnterpriseApplication.Application.ConnectionString)
    connection.Open()

    ' Create a SQL command object to execute the SPROC
    Dim command As System.Data.SqlClient.SqlCommand = _
        New System.Data.SqlClient.SqlCommand("GetOpenOrders", connection)
    command.CommandType = System.Data.CommandType.StoredProcedure

    ' Extract the DataSet
    Dim adapter As System.Data.SqlClient.SqlDataAdapter = _
                        new System.Data.SqlClient.SqlDataAdapter(command)
    Dim myDataset As System.Data.DataSet = New DataSet()
    adapter.Fill(myDataset)
    adapter.Dispose()

    ' Cleanup
    command.Dispose()
    connection.Close()

    ' Return dataset
    Return myDataset
End Function
```

For this to compile, you'll also need some extra namespace import declarations:

```
Imports System.Data
Imports System.Data.SqlClient
Imports System.Collections
Imports BookManagerObjects
Imports EnterpriseObjects
```

Next, to the same `Processor` class, add a method called `ProcessOpenOrders`:

```
Public Sub ProcessOpenOrders()

    ' Get a list of orders
    Dim orders As DataSet = GetOpenOrders()
    Console.WriteLine("Found {0} open orders", orders.Tables(0).Rows.Count)
```

157

```
   ' Loop through each of them
   Dim order As DataRow
   For Each order In orders.Tables(0).Rows
     ' Process each order
     ProcessOrder(order)
   Next

     ' Write debug info
   Console.WriteLine("Finished processing open orders")
End Sub
```

ProcessOrder is the crucial method in the above code, and it performs the required processing on each order passed to it. We'll turn our attention to that method in a moment.

Processing the order is going to require a number of stored procedures. However, we need to roll this stored procedure code inside the Processor class as the way that WEO works with database connections is not ideal for use with transactions. If you look at a typical method generated by WEO, you'll notice that a new connection is established and torn down within each method. For example look at the highlighted code below:

```
Public Shared Function CreateSecurityToken(ByVal userId As String, _
                                ByVal token As String, _
                                ByVal expires As System.DateTime) _
                                As Integer

   ' Create a connection...
   Dim connection As System.Data.SqlClient.SqlConnection = _
                 New System.Data.SqlClient.SqlConnection( _
        EnterpriseObjects.EnterpriseApplication.Application.ConnectionString)
   connection.Open()
   ' Create a command...
   Dim command As System.Data.SqlClient.SqlCommand = _
       New System.Data.SqlClient.SqlCommand("CreateSecurityToken", _
       connection)
   command.CommandType = System.Data.CommandType.StoredProcedure
   ' Parameters...
   Dim userIdParam As System.Data.SqlClient.SqlParameter = _
          command.Parameters.Add("@userId", _
          System.Data.SqlDbType.VarChar, 32)
   userIdParam.Value = userId
   Dim tokenParam As System.Data.SqlClient.SqlParameter = _
          command.Parameters.Add("@token", _
          System.Data.SqlDbType.VarChar, 256)
   tokenParam.Value = token
   Dim expiresParam As System.Data.SqlClient.SqlParameter = _
          command.Parameters.Add("@expires", _
          System.Data.SqlDbType.DateTime)
   expiresParam.Value = expires
   Dim returnValueParam As System.Data.SqlClient.SqlParameter = _
          command.Parameters.Add("@returnValueParam", _
          System.Data.SqlDbType.Int)
   returnValueParam.Direction = _
   System.Data.ParameterDirection.ReturnValue
```

```
  ' Execute...
  command.ExecuteNonQuery()
  ' Cleanup...
  command.Dispose()
  connection.Close()
  ' Return...
  Return CType(returnValueParam.Value, Integer)
End Function
```

To work with transactions, we need to use the same database connections across all stored procedure calls. The best way is to establish a database connection per order, tell SQL Server to start a transaction, and close the connection after we have either aborted or committed the transaction. We can use the code that Object Builder generates, but we have to tweak each method slightly to accept and use a connection string that we provide.

Let's now look at the `ProcessOrder` method. It must establish the database connection, initiate a transaction, and process the order, aborting or committing the transaction as appropriate. We're most interested in the "transaction" mechanism here, so we'll present the code that deals with that side of things first. We have emboldened the code to highlight the connection (`SqlConnection`) and transaction (`SqlTransaction`), and the `Try...Catch` block which is used to abort the transaction by calling `Rollback` should anything go wrong:

```
' Process an order
Public Sub ProcessOrder(ByVal orderData As DataRow)

    Dim connection As SqlConnection
    Dim transaction As SqlTransaction
    Try
        ' Connect
        connection = New SqlConnection( _
                        EnterpriseApplication.Application.ConnectionString)
        connection.Open()

        ' Create a new transaction
        transaction = connection.BeginTransaction()

        ' Do the order processing

        ...


        ' Commit the transaction here
        transaction.Commit()
    Catch ex As Exception
        ' Abort the transaction
        transaction.Rollback()

        ' Report the exception
        Console.WriteLine(ex.GetType().ToString() & ":" & ex.Message)
        Console.WriteLine(ex.StackTrace)
    Finally
        ' Close the connection
        connection.Close()
```

```
      End Try
   End Sub
```

Note how we have one `SqlConnection` object throughout the whole operation. We set this to create a transaction through the `BeginTransaction` method, and we can access the transaction during processing through the returned `SqlTransaction` object. Once we've set this up, any `SqlCommand` that we create must be given this `SqlConnection` and the matching `SqlTransaction` object. If anything goes wrong during processing, we catch the exception and abort the transaction by calling the `Rollback` method. Conversely, if everything goes well, the end of the `Try` block will be reached, where we commit changes with the `Commit` method.

> **In this example, if an exception is thrown, we simply display it on screen. In Chapter 12, we'll implement a system that automatically reports exceptions to system administrators.**

Building the invoice is a two-stage process. In the first stage, we have to loop through each of the order lines checking to see how many of the requested number of books we can fulfill. For example, if we have 5 of a given book in stock, and the order requires 10, we could only send 5. Likewise, if a further order then requires more of that title, we can't send any as our stock level will be at zero. As we work through each line, we'll build up a list of "invoice lines" in memory. We need to create an invoice with the relevant invoice lines *only* if we get to the end of the order lines and one or more invoice lines exist in memory.

As we're creating the invoice lines, we need to update the `QuantitySent` column of the relevant **OrderLines** row and decrement the `StockLevel` column of the relevant **Books** row. After creating all the invoice lines, we have to check if any of the lines in the order are still not satisfied. We'll be able to test for this case by comparing the `Quantity` and `QuantitySent` columns. For example, if `Quantity` is 200 and `QuantitySent` is 150, we know that the order requires us to place 50 books on back order.

During processing, we'll store the new invoice lines as a collection of `InvoiceLine` Structures. To do this, add a new class to **OrderProcessor** called `InvoiceLine` which we can then change to a `Structure`. Open the code file for the class, replace the `Class` keyword with `Structure` and give our new `Structure` the following members:

```
Public Structure InvoiceLine

   ' Members
   Public OrderLineId As Integer
   Public BookId As Integer
   Public QuantitySent As Integer
   Public Price As Double
End Structure
```

There's quite a lot going on in the `ProcessOrder` method, so I'll break it down line by line. The code we've already added for this method walks the lines that make up the order, and the code we shall add now involves actually creating the invoice.

```
Public Sub ProcessOrder(ByVal orderData As DataRow)

   ' Process the order
   Dim connection As SqlConnection
```

```
Dim transaction As SqlTransaction
Try
  ' Connect
  connection = New SqlConnection( _
                  EnterpriseApplication.Application.ConnectionString)
  connection.Open()

  ' Create a new transaction
  transaction = connection.BeginTransaction()
```

We've seen the code up to this point. After creating the transaction, we create a new `ArrayList` to hold the list of `InvoiceLine` structures:

```
  ' Create an array for the invoice lines
  Dim invoiceLines As ArrayList = New ArrayList()
```

Next, we need a list of the **OrderLines** rows that make up the order. We'll use a stored procedure, which we'll meet in a moment, called `GetOrderLinesForOrder` for this:

```
  ' Get the lines in the order
  Dim orderId As Integer = CType(orderData("orderid"), Integer)
  Dim orderLines As DataSet = GetOrderLinesForOrder(connection, _
                                              transaction, orderId)

  Dim orderLine As DataRow
  For Each orderLine In orderLines.Tables(0).Rows
```

For each order line, we find out how many are still outstanding by comparing the quantity ordered with the quantity that we've sent already:

```
    ' How many are outstanding
    Dim quantityOutstanding As Integer = _
                       CType(orderLine("quantity"), Integer) - _
                       CType(orderLine("quantitysent"), Integer)
    If quantityOutstanding > 0 Then
```

If `quantityOutstanding` is greater than zero, this order is still not yet complete. We can use the `GetById` method to get the `BookManagerObjects.Book` object with the ID given in the order line. This code needs to run outside of the transaction, as the `BookServiceBase` code creates its own connection to the database:

```
      ' Get the book of this order line
      Dim myBook As BookManagerObjects.BookManagerObjects.Book = _
              BookManagerObjects.BookManagerObjects.Book.GetById( _
              CType(orderLine("bookid"), Integer))
      If Not myBook Is Nothing Then
```

If a book is returned matching this ID, we check to make sure we have some in stock as otherwise we can't do anything. If there are some available, we work out how many of the outstanding quantity are available to send:

```
          ' is this book in stock?
        If myBook.StockLevel > 0 Then
          ' Determine how many we can send now
          Dim numberToSend As Integer = quantityOutstanding
          If numberToSend > myBook.StockLevel Then
            numberToSend = myBook.StockLevel
          End If
```

Next, we create a new `InvoiceLine` structure and populate it with the information we know so far, gleaned from the **OrderLines** and **Books** tables:

```
          ' Create a new invoice line
          Dim line As InvoiceLine = New InvoiceLine()
          line.OrderLineId = CType(orderLine("lineid"), Integer)
          line.BookId = myBook.Id
          line.QuantitySent = numberToSend
          line.Price = CType(orderLine("price"), Double)
          invoiceLines.Add(line)
        End If
      End If
```

If the book in the **OrderLines** row doesn't appear to be valid, we can throw an exception, and our exception handler will abort the transaction. However, as we haven't yet changed anything in the database, our purpose here is to report a problem rather than to roll back changes made by the transaction so far:

```
      Else
        Throw New Exception("Book #" & orderLine("bookid") & " not found")
      End If
    Next

    ' Do we have any invoice lines?
    If invoiceLines.Count > 0 Then

      ' Invoice creation goes here!

      ...

    End If

    ...

  End Sub
```

We're going to stop at this point, as we need to know about the stored procedures for creating the invoice in detail before we can write the code that calls them. Here's a summary of the stored procedures we'll be using:

Stored Procedure Name	Description
CreateInvoice	Inserts a new row into the Invoices table and returns the ID of the new row
CreateInvoiceLine	Creates a new line in the invoice
UpdateQuantitySentForOrderLine	Updates the QuantitySent column of the specified OrderLine row
DecrementStockLevel	Changes the StockLevel column in the Books table to reflect the new stock position after the invoice has been raised
CheckAndMarkOrderComplete	Examines the rows in the order to see if we have now completed the order

The SQL code for each of these is pretty straightforward, but we'll have to tweak the method of accessing the stored procedure. First off, here's the SQL for CreateInvoice:

```
CREATE PROCEDURE CreateInvoice
(
    @orderId int,
    @created datetime
)
AS
    INSERT INTO Invoices (OrderId, Created) VALUES (@orderId, @created)
    RETURN @@identity
```

We need to adapt the Sprocs.CreateInvoice method for use by the Processor class, adding support for transactions by adding two new parameters to the method: connection and transaction. We also need to delete the code that creates the connection *and* the code that closes the connection, as this will be carried out by the calling code. Also, when we create the SqlCommand object, we need to pass in the transaction object:

```
Protected Function CreateInvoice(ByVal connection As SqlConnection, _
                                 ByVal transaction As SqlTransaction, _
                                 ByVal orderId As Integer, _
                                 ByVal created as Date) As Integer

    ' Create a command...
    Dim command As System.Data.SqlClient.SqlCommand = _
            New System.Data.SqlClient.SqlCommand("CreateInvoice", _
            connection, transaction)
    command.CommandType = System.Data.CommandType.StoredProcedure
    ' Parameters...
    Dim orderIdParam As System.Data.SqlClient.SqlParameter = _
            command.Parameters.Add("@orderId", System.Data.SqlDbType.Int)
    orderIdParam.Value = orderId
    Dim createdParam As System.Data.SqlClient.SqlParameter = _
            command.Parameters.Add("@created", System.Data.SqlDbType.DateTime)
    createdParam.Value = created
```

```
    Dim returnValueParam As System.Data.SqlClient.SqlParameter = _
          command.Parameters.Add("@returnValueParam",System.Data.SqlDbType.Int)
    returnValueParam.Direction = System.Data.ParameterDirection.ReturnValue
    ' Execute...
    command.ExecuteNonQuery()
    ' Cleanup...
    command.Dispose()
    ' Return...
    Return CType(returnValueParam.Value), Integer)
End Function
```

CreateInvoiceLine is no more complex:

```
CREATE PROCEDURE CreateInvoiceLine
(
    @invoiceId int,
    @orderLineId int,
    @bookId int,
    @quantitySent int,
    @price float
)
AS
    INSERT INTO InvoiceLines (InvoiceId, OrderLineId, BookId, QuantitySent,
        Price) VALUES (@invoiceId, @orderLineId, @bookId, @quantitySent,
        @price)
    RETURN @@identity
```

Likewise, we need to make some changes to its associated method:

```
    Protected Function CreateInvoiceLine(ByVal connection As SqlConnection, _
                                ByVal transaction As SqlTransaction, _
                                ByVal invoiceId As Integer, _
                                ByVal orderLineId As Integer, _
                                ByVal bookId As Inetger, _
                                ByVal quantitySent As Integer, _
                                ByVal price As System.Double) As Integer

    ' Create a command...
    Dim command As System.Data.SqlClient.SqlCommand = _
                New System.Data.SqlClient.SqlCommand("CreateInvoiceLine", _
                connection, transaction)
    command.CommandType = System.Data.CommandType.StoredProcedure
    ' Parameters...
    ...
    ' Execute...
    command.ExecuteNonQuery()
    ' Cleanup...
    command.Dispose()
    ' Return...
    Return CType(returnValueParam.Value,Integer)
End Function
```

`DecrementStockLevel` looks like this:

```
CREATE PROCEDURE DecrementStockLevel
(
    @bookId int,
    @quantitySent int
)
AS
    UPDATE Books SET StockLevel = StockLevel - @quantitySent
        WHERE Bookid=@bookId
```

Change the method so that it supports transactions, following the same pattern that we followed when changing the others.

`UpdateQuantitySentForOrderLine` is like this:

```
CREATE PROCEDURE UpdateQuantitySentForOrderLine
(
    @lineId int,
    @quantitySent int
)
AS
    UPDATE OrderLines SET QuantitySent = QuantitySent + @quantitySent
        WHERE LineId=@lineId
```

`CheckAndMarkOrderComplete` is more complex. It selects the order lines for this order that are not complete, in other words, where `QuantitySent` does not match `Quantity`. If no rows are returned by the query, we can mark the order as complete:

```
CREATE PROCEDURE CheckAndMarkOrderComplete
(
    @orderId int
)
AS
    SELECT LineId from OrderLines
        WHERE QuantitySent <> Quantity AND OrderId=@orderId
    IF @@rowcount = 0
    BEGIN
        UPDATE Orders SET Complete=1 WHERE OrderId=@orderId
    END
```

The method to access `CheckAndMarkOrderComplete` requires more changes than the others, as the Object Builder will see the `SELECT` call, and interpret this to mean that the stored procedure returns a `DataSet`. However, it's more useful for us to execute it as a query that doesn't return any values. Here's what the method should look like:

```
Protected Sub CheckAndMarkOrderComplete(ByVal connection As SqlConnection, _
                                        ByVal transaction As SqlTransaction, _
                                        ByVal orderId As Integer)

    ' Create a command...
```

```
        Dim command As System.Data.SqlClient.SqlCommand = _
                            New System.Data.SqlClient.SqlCommand( _
                            "CheckAndMarkOrderComplete", connection, _
                            transaction)
        command.CommandType = System.Data.CommandType.StoredProcedure
        ' Parameters...
        Dim orderIdParam As System.Data.SqlClient.SqlParameter = _
                            command.Parameters.Add("@orderId", _
                            System.Data.SqlDbType.Int)
        orderIdParam.Value = orderId
        ' Extract the dataset...
        command.ExecuteNonQuery()
        ' Cleanup...
        command.Dispose()
    End Sub
```

`GetOrderLinesForOrder` is modified in a similar way:

```
    Protected Function GetOrderLinesForOrder(ByVal connection As SqlConnection, _
                            ByVal transaction As SqlTransaction, _
                            ByVal orderId As Integer)

        'create a command...
        Dim command As System.Data.SqlClient.SqlCommand = New _
                            System.Data.SqlClient.SqlCommand( _
                            "GetOrderLinesForOrder", connection, transaction)
        command.CommandType = System.Data.CommandType.StoredProcedure
        'parameters...
        Dim orderIdParam As System.Data.SqlClient.SqlParameter = _
                command.Parameters.Add("@orderId", System.Data.SqlDbType.Int)
        orderIdParam.Value = orderId
        'extract the dataset...
        Dim adapter As System.Data.SqlClient.SqlDataAdapter = New _
                            System.Data.SqlClient.SqlDataAdapter(command)
        Dim dataset As System.Data.DataSet = New DataSet()
        adapter.Fill(dataset)
        adapter.Dispose()
        'cleanup...
        command.Dispose()
        'return dataset...
        Return dataset

    End Function
```

If we now revisit the `ProcessOrder` method to add code to create the invoice, we now just have to call these stored procedures:

```
        ' Do we have any invoice lines?
        If invoiceLines.Count > 0 Then

            ' Create a new invoice
            Dim invoiceId as Integer = _
```

```
                CreateInvoice(connection, transaction, orderId, DateTime.Now)

            ' Add each line to the invoice
            Dim line As InvoiceLine
            For Each line In invoiceLines

                ' Add the line
                CreateInvoiceLine(connection, transaction, invoiceId, _
                            line.OrderLineId, line.BookId, _
                            line.QuantitySent, line.Price)

                ' Update
                UpdateQuantitySentForOrderLine(connection, transaction, _
                                        line.OrderLineId, _
                                        line.QuantitySent)

                ' Decrement the stock level
                DecrementStockLevel(connection, transaction, line.BookId, _
                            line.QuantitySent)
            Next

                ' Have we completed the order?
                CheckAndMarkOrderComplete(connection, transaction, orderId)
        End If

        ' Commit the transaction here
        transaction.Commit()

    Catch ex As Exception


        ...


    Finally
        ' Close
        connection.Close()
    End Try
End Sub
```

Testing the Processor

To test the processor, first ensure that you only have a single order in the Orders table. (Because of the relation between OrderLines and Orders, database concurrency will prevent our deleting order records unless all related rows from OrderLines are deleted first.)

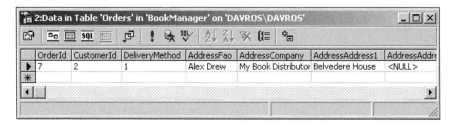

This order should have one `OrderLine`; for 10 copies of Book ID 54:

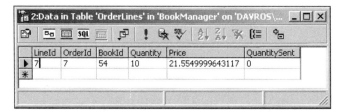

If you're wondering why the price that appears in the above table seems somewhat peculiar, remember that it has had the standard 10% discount applied. The Invoices and InvoiceLines tables should both be empty.

In addition, make sure that the Books table shows that 100 copies of book #54 are in stock:

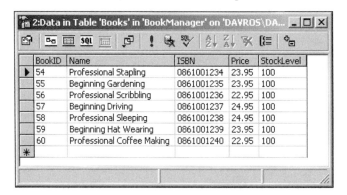

We then need to add some code into `Module1.vb` in the OrderProcessorHost project:

```
Imports EnterpriseObjects

Module Module1

    Sub Main()
```

```
' set the database connection string
EnterpriseApplication.Application.ConnectionString = _
  "integrated security=sspi;initial catalog=bookmanager;data source=localhost"
' run
Dim processor As OrderProcessor.Processor = New OrderProcessor.Processor()
processor.ProcessOpenOrders()


' Wait until Enter key is pressed
Console.ReadLine()

    End Sub

End Module
```

In the ProcessOrder method of Processor, place a breakpoint on the CreateInvoice call:

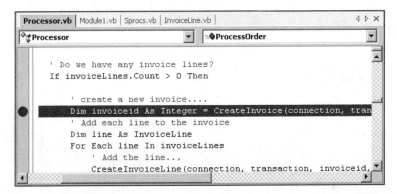

Run the project. When the breakpoint is reached, select **Debug | Step Over** from the menu. Ordinarily, you'd expect the row to be written to the **Invoices** table, but because we have an open transaction for the connection, the row will not be visible to other users, or to SQL Server's management console:

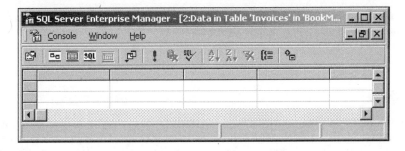

In fact, with the project in a "breakpoint" state, we don't even see the names of the columns in the table. Run the project to the end, however, and you'll see this:

When we now look in the Invoices table, we see the new invoice:

You'll also find a new invoice line in InvoiceLines:

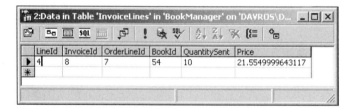

Although we won't show them here, you'll also find that only 90 copies of book #54 are now in stock, and that the Orders and OrderLines tables have been properly updated.

Testing the Rollback

To test the rollback, try throwing an exception by editing the ProcessOrder method and inserting a call to Throw New Exception just before the call to Commit. This will rollback the transaction, and any changes that you have made will be undone.

Services

Before we finish off this chapter, there's a final comment I'd like to make that you may have already picked up on. We've built console applications to handle the order processing function using class libraries, but a better route would probably be to implement a Windows Service for this purpose. Windows Services can run in the background for as long as the server is switched on (even if no-one is logged in), making them the ideal model for this part of our application. We could set up a service that monitors a certain directory for incoming XML documents that represent orders placed by our customers, and then processes them using the class library just as the console application in this chapter does. Windows Services are covered in some detail in Chapter 9.

Summary

We've now had a good look at how to build separate applications that perform essential business support functions with no human intervention. It's important not to forget that although many applications in an enterprise depend heavily on user interaction, there are equally compelling and important applications that require hardly any, and for that reason, can often go unnoticed in the day-to-day running of the company.

This is not to say of course that they are any less important – quite the contrary. It is quite essential that they work correctly and efficiently, as there will be no human around to make sure they don't do anything daft.

Following sound application design principles, we have implemented the functionality that supports these functions as separate class libraries, enabling them to be readily available to a variety of host applications. Although here we have hosted the libraries within console applications, it would be a fairly painless task, thanks to .NET, to make a Windows Service or some other type of application that draws on these same libraries.

The `OrderLoader` application was pretty straightforward and used VS.NET and .NET's ability to bind `DataSets` to XML documents. .NET makes accessing data in an XML document very simple: we just have to load it into a specially-derived class which exposes a bunch of properties and methods for manipulating XML elements and attributes. Using such a class, we took the data in an XML order document and inserted it into our relational database for processing.

`OrderProcessor` introduced the idea of working with transactions. Transactions are *very* useful in enterprise applications and, truth be told, we should really have used transactions on `OrderLoader`, but did not in order to keep the example simple. We also saw how to test that we were running inside a transactional environment, and also how to test that transactions were aborted or rolled back appropriately.

.NET Enterprise Development in VB .NET

6

Web Services

One of the most powerful features of our `BookManagerObjects` library is that it provides any client application with a simple method of accessing our data. In this chapter we'll look at exposing our data with Web Services built on this library.

This is an interesting capability, and you may be wondering why we should implement such a system when we can already access our data via the application browser we've been building up in previous chapters.

Once this has been explained we will move on to develop Web Services in the following sequence:

- ❑ A basic Web Service exposing simple `BookManagerObjects` functionality to all clients

- ❑ An authentication system for Web Services based around a centralized authentication system linked with IIS authentication and Windows user information

- ❑ An extended Web Service that accesses `BookManagerObjects` information in a secure way

To start with, though, let's examine the case for using Web Services in our enterprise application.

Why Use Web Services?

Web Services constitute a platform-independent method of exposing data from various sources over protocols such as HTTP and SOAP. The SOAP protocol, which we looked at briefly in chapter 3, is readily usable by any client since it is text based without machine dependent encoding.

The application browser is great, but it depends on the client being able to run the browser program. This may not be possible depending on the client's computing environment. A Web Service that accesses portions of our data can get round this problem, by allowing clients using Linux, MacOS, or any OS that can access the Internet via HTTP to get the data they need. Web Services can even be used by mobile clients, since they can be consumed by systems that generate (for example) WML output. We look at mobile clients in more detail in Chapter 8.

Web Services are highly configurable. Among other things, they can:

- ❑ be secured via Secure Sockets Layer (SSL) connections
- ❑ perform authorization linked to IIS authentication and Windows users and groups
- ❑ be load-balanced across multiple servers

Exposing our data in this way, then, can be an excellent way of centralizing our access channels.

Let's recap the reasons for using Web Services to access our data:

- ❑ Clients that can't use the application browser (for example if they are running a different OS or are behind a restrictive firewall) may have no other option
- ❑ Web Services can be used for simple operations that don't require the degree of interactivity inherent in the application browser interface
- ❑ Web Services, if used correctly, will put less of a load on our backend servers
- ❑ Web Services can be simple to use, as we don't have to write potentially complex remote communication code ourselves
- ❑ Web Services can be 'rolled into' a vast array of client applications, providing a fully customizable system for clients who don't wish to be restrained by the application browser structure for whatever reason

After reading the above it would be easy to turn the section title around to pose the question "Why use the application browser?" The main advantages of the application browser rather than a "pure Web Service' route (recall that Web Services also make up part of the application browser) are:

- ❑ Application browser snap-ins can be made much more interactive, and in some cases will perform complex operations that would be very difficult to implement using Web Services
- ❑ Clients that can run the application browser can access much richer functionality with less effort
- ❑ Access using the application browser will often be quicker than the Web Service equivalent, as it is less reliant on IIS and so forth

That's the case for Web Services, so let's move on to see how we can create them.

Accessing BookManager Data with Web Services

The following diagram illustrates how we can perform simple Web Service data access without user authentication:

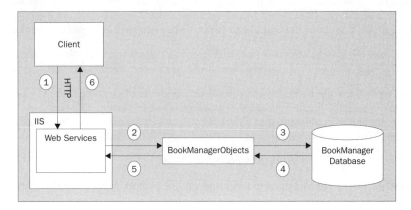

The steps involved are:

(1) The Client calls a method of the Web Service via HTTP

(2) – (5) The Web Service uses the `BookManagerObjects` library to interact with data stored in our database

(6) The Web Service returns data to the client

The Web Service can perform pretty much any operation that is possible using `BookManagerObjects`, although the techniques won't be as simple as using the library directly. The reason for this is that in order for the Web Service to be consumed by the widest audience of clients, we are restricted in the data that may be transferred via HTTP. Returning full `Author` objects, for example, may work in some situations but will make it trickier for thin clients to access the data (as it will be wrapped in more complex SOAP elements).

Instead we should return data in as simple a way as possible. One way of doing this, which is the way we will do things here, is to return data in the form of simple data structures. We'll see shortly that this results in far simpler XML. This is at the cost of performing slightly more processing on the web server, but the end result is worth it.

The same goes for operations that result in information in our database being modified or added to. We should make the syntax for this as simple as we can to allow as many clients as possible to use our Web Services.

Without further ado, it's time to build a Web Service.

A Basic "BookManager" Service

In this chapter, we shall create all our Web Services in a single Web Service project called `Services`. As with our `Coordinator` Web Service in Chapter 3, I'll assume that initial deployment and testing is to take place locally, and we can create our project on `localhost`. The full local path to the services in our project will be `http://localhost/BM/Services/Service.asmx`. Also as before, we'll set the namespace to `http://www.wrox.com/BookManager`. Our first simple service will be called `BMService1`.

If you are using the downloadable code for this chapter, don't worry about the other services in the Services project for now – we'll be covering these later in the chapter as we reach them.

Since our service will use the `BookManagerObjects` library, the first thing to do if you are building this project from scratch is to add references to `BookManagerObjects.dll` and `EnterpriseObjects.dll`. We can also delete the automatically generated `Service1` service, and add `BMService1` to the `Services` project as a new VB.NET Web Service.

`BMService1` will expose the following functionality:

- A method called `GetAuthors` that returns a list of authors as a simple data structure
- A method called `GetPaymentsByAuthorID` that returns a list of payments for a specified author
- A method called `GetAuthorSet` that also returns a list of authors, but this time in the form of an `AuthorSet` object, so that we can compare the XML exchanged with the simpler `GetAuthors` method result

Add a new VB.NET code file to the project, and name it `TransferStructs.vb`. This file will contain the structures we'll use for returning data, `AuthorDetails` and `PaymentDetails`:

```
Imports System

Namespace Services

  Public Structure AuthorDetails
    Public Id As Integer
    Public FirstName As String
    Public LastName As String
    Public Email As String
  End Structure

  Public Structure PaymentDetails
    Public Id As Integer
    Public AuthorId As Integer
    Public Total As Double
    Public PayDate As DateTime
  End Structure
End Namespace
```

As you can see, the data members of these structures correspond with the properties of our `Author` and `Payment` classes.

The Web Service code in `BMService1.asmx.vb` starts with the standard `Imports` statements and the declaration for our Web Service class, with the namespace set:

```
Imports System
Imports System.Collections
Imports System.ComponentModel
Imports System.Data
Imports System.Diagnostics
Imports System.Web
Imports System.Web.Services
Imports System.Web.Services.Protocols
Imports BookManagerObjects
Imports EnterpriseObjects

Namespace Services

  <WebService(Namespace:= "http://www.wrox.com/BookManager/")> _
  Public Class BMService1
    Inherits System.Web.Services.WebService
```

In the constructor for the Web Service, in the Web Services Designer Generated Code region, we need to configure the enterprise objects, with this now familiar code:

```
Public Sub New ()
   MyBase.New()

   ' This call is required by the Windows Form Designer
   InitializeComponent()

   ' set the connection string...
   EnterpriseApplication.Application.ConnectionString = _
     "integrated security=sspi;initial catalog=bookmanager;data " _
     & "source=localhost"

End Sub
```

After the standard autogenerated code for InitializeComponent and Dispose, which we don't need to tamper with, we come to the web methods. We'll add these in order of increasing complexity, starting with GetAuthorSet:

```
<WebMethod()> _
Public Function GetAuthorSet() As AuthorSet
  ' return the authors
  Return Author.GetAll()
End Function
```

This method simply uses the class method Author.GetAll to obtain and return an AuthorSet object, as we've seen previously.

Next we have the GetAuthors method. The code here is also simple, although a few more steps are required in order to reformat the author data into an array of AuthorDetails Structures:

```
<WebMethod()> _
Public Function GetAuthors() As AuthorDetails()
```

```
    ' get the authors
    Dim authors As AuthorSet = Author.GetAll()

    ' initialize return data array
    Dim returnData(authors.Count - 1) As AuthorDetails

    ' extract author data
    Dim index As Integer = 0
    Dim theAuthor As Author
    For Each theAuthor In authors
      returnData(index) = New AuthorDetails()
      returnData(index).Id = theAuthor.Id
      returnData(index).FirstName = theAuthor.FirstName
      returnData(index).LastName = theAuthor.LastName
      returnData(index).Email = theAuthor.Email
      index += 1
    Next
    ' return data
    Return returnData
End Function
```

Finally, we have the code for GetPaymentsByAuthorID. This method takes an int parameter representing the ID of the author to retrieve payments for, gets the info, and stashes it in an array of PaymentDetails Structures for returning.

One point to note here is that we throw an exception if an invalid author ID is supplied. This is quite safe with Web Services, as exceptions will be wrapped in instances of the SOAPException class and reformatted as SOAP faults to send to clients. If the client is a .NET application, the SOAP fault will be reconstituted as a SOAPException, and we can handle it accordingly.

```
<WebMethod()> _
Public Function GetPaymentsByAuthorID(ByVal authorID As Integer) As _
                                            PaymentDetails()

    ' Get the author
    Dim theAuthor As Author = Author.GetById(authorID)

    ' Check for valid author
    If theAuthor Is Nothing Then
      Throw New ArgumentException("No such author.")
    End If

    ' Get the payments
    Dim payments As PaymentSet = theAuthor.GetRelatedPayments()

    ' Initialize return data array
    Dim returnData(payments.Count - 1) As PaymentDetails

    ' Extract payment data
    Dim index As Integer = 0
    Dim thePayment As Payment
    For Each thePayment In payments
```

```
        returnData(index) = New PaymentDetails()
        returnData(index).Id = thePayment.Id
        returnData(index).AuthorId = thePayment.AuthorId
        returnData(index).PayDate = thePayment.DatePaid
        returnData(index).Total = thePayment.Total
        index += 1
      Next

      ' Return the payments
      Return returnData
    End Function
  End Class
End Namespace
```

This code is all that is required for this simple Web Service. We'll build an example client for this service in a moment, but before we do that we can test the service using a web browser. Make sure BMService1.asmx is set as the start page, and choose **Debug | Start**, or navigate to http://localhost/BM/Services/BMService1.asmx in a browser. You will be presented with the following screen:

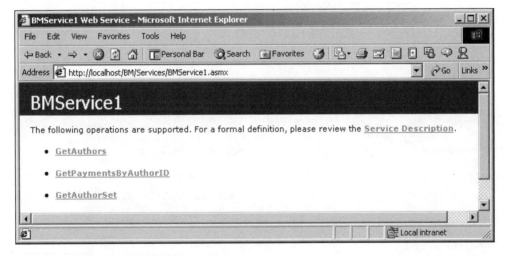

From here, we can invoke any of the methods shown, and the result will appear in the browser. Try this for GetAuthorSet, and you should see the following response XML:

```
<?xml version="1.0" encoding="utf-8"?>
<AuthorSet xmlns="http://www.wrox.com/BookManager/">
  <xsd:schema id="NewDataSet" targetNamespace="" xmlns=""
      xmlns:xsd="http://www.w3.org/2001/XMLSchema"
      xmlns:msdata="urn:schemas-microsoft-com:xml-msdata">
    <xsd:element name="NewDataSet" msdata:IsDataSet="true"
        msdata:Locale="en-GB">
     <xsd:complexType>
      <xsd:choice maxOccurs="unbounded">
       <xsd:element name="Table">
```

```
        <xsd:complexType>
          <xsd:sequence>
           <xsd:element name="AuthorId" type="xsd:int" minOccurs="0" />
           <xsd:element name="FirstName" type="xsd:string"
                 minOccurs="0" />
           <xsd:element name="LastName" type="xsd:string"
                 minOccurs="0" />
           <xsd:element name="Email" type="xsd:string" minOccurs="0" />
          </xsd:sequence>
        </xsd:complexType>
       </xsd:element>
      </xsd:choice>
    </xsd:complexType>
   </xsd:element>
 </xsd:schema>
 <diffgr:diffgram xmlns:msdata="urn:schemas-microsoft-com:xml-msdata"
          xmlns:diffgr="urn:schemas-microsoft-com:xml-diffgram-v1">
   <NewDataSet xmlns="">
    <Table diffgr:id="Table1" msdata:rowOrder="0">
     <AuthorId>2</AuthorId>
     <FirstName>Ollie</FirstName>
     <LastName>Cornes</LastName>
     <Email>ollie@pretendcompany.com</Email>
    </Table>

    <!-- Additional author entries -->

   </NewDataSet>
 </diffgr:diffgram>
</AuthorSet>
```

If we do the same for GetAuthors, the following XML will be displayed:

```
<?xml version="1.0" encoding="utf-8"?>
<ArrayOfAuthorDetails xmlns:xsi="http://www.w3.org/2001/XMLSchema-instance"
                 xmlns:xsd="http://www.w3.org/2001/XMLSchema"
                 xmlns="http://www.wrox.com/BookManager/">
  <AuthorDetails>
   <Id>2</Id>
   <FirstName>Ollie</FirstName>
   <LastName>Cornes</LastName>
   <Email>ollie@pretendcompany.com</Email>
  </AuthorDetails>

    <!-- Additional author entries -->

</ArrayOfAuthorDetails>
```

I think the simplicity here certainly justifies the use of an array of Structures rather than some more complex data type! Of course, there will be times when the additional detail might be necessary, although it would then restrict the clients that could use the service as discussed earlier.

A Client for BMService1

Before moving on to more complicated subjects, let's take a quick look at a client application for the BMService1 Web Service. Create a new VB Windows Forms application called BMService1Client, delete Form1, and add a new form called MainForm.vb with these controls on it:

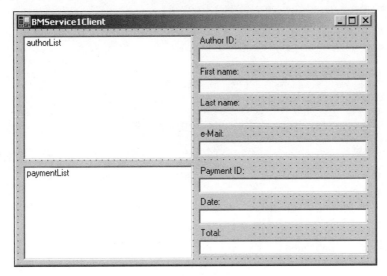

authorList and paymentList are list boxes, and the remaining seven active controls are text boxes called authorIdBox, firstNameBox, and so on. The text boxes all have their Enabled property set to False, as we'll just use them for displaying information.

To access the BMService1 Web Service, we need to add a web reference to it, as we've seen previously. We'll name this reference BMService1 and add the appropriate Imports statement to MainForm.vb:

```
Imports BMService1Client.BMService1
```

Our MainForm class will also need a few extra private members to store results and so on:

```
Namespace BMService1Client

Public Class MainForm
    Inherits System.Windows.Forms.Form

    Private service As BMService1.BMService1
    Private authorData() As BMService1.AuthorDetails
    Private paymentData() As BMService1.PaymentDetails
```

Notice how the structures defined in TransferStructs.vb are accessible here – a very handy feature!

When the form loads, we will create a service proxy to populate authorData (the private AuthorDetails array defined above), and we then use authorData to populate authorList. Double-click somewhere on the background of MainForm in the Designer, and add this code:

```
Private Sub MainForm_Load(ByVal sender As System.Object, _
                          ByVal e As System.EventArgs) _
                          Handles MainForm.Load

    ' initialize service
    service = new BMService1.BMService1()

    ' get author data
    authorData = service.GetAuthors()

    ' populate authorList list box
    If Not authorData Is Nothing Then
      Dim author As AuthorDetails
      For Each author In authorData
        authorList.Items.Add(author.FirstName & " " & _
                             author.LastName)
      Next
    End If
End Sub
```

Note that there may be a lot of authors in our production system, and a more complex UI could be required, using pagination or similar.

The text boxes will be populated by the `SelectedIndexChanged` event handlers for the two list boxes. Double-click on `authorList` in the Designer, and add this code body:

```
Private Sub authorList_SelectedIndexChanged( _
                          ByVal sender As System.Object, _
                          ByVal e As System.EventArgs) _
                          Handles authorList.SelectedIndexChanged

    ' Check if an author is selected
    If authorList.SelectedIndex = -1 Then

      ' Clear author info if no author is selected
      authorIdBox.Clear()
      firstNameBox.Clear()
      lastNameBox.Clear()
      emailBox.Clear()
      paymentList.Items.Clear()

    Else
      ' Get selected author and store author ID for payment lookup
      Dim currentAuthor As AuthorDetails = _
                          authorData(authorList.SelectedIndex)
      Dim authorId As Integer = currentAuthor.Id

      ' Populate author information text boxes
      authorIdBox.Text = authorId.ToString()
      firstNameBox.Text = currentAuthor.FirstName.ToString()
      lastNameBox.Text = currentAuthor.LastName.ToString()
      emailBox.Text = currentAuthor.Email.ToString()
```

```
        ' Get payment data for selected author
        paymentData = service.GetPaymentsByAuthorID(authorId)

        ' Clear existing payment information
        paymentList.Items.Clear()
        paymentIdBox.Clear()
        dateBox.Clear()
        totalBox.Clear()

        ' Populate paymentList list box
        If Not paymentData Is Nothing Then
          Dim payment As PaymentDetails
          For Each payment In paymentData
            paymentList.Items.Add(payment.PayDate.ToShortDateString())
          Next
        End If
      End If
    End Sub
```

Similarly for `paymentList`, which operates in a similar way:

```
Private Sub paymentList_SelectedIndexChanged( _
                        ByVal sender As System.object, _
                        ByVal e As System.EventArgs) _
                        Handles paymentList.SelectedIndexChanged
```

```
      ' Check if a payment is selected
      If paymentList.SelectedIndex = -1 Then
        ' Clear payment info if no payment is selected
        paymentIdBox.Clear()
        dateBox.Clear()
        totalBox.Clear()
      Else
        ' Get selected payment
        Dim currentPayment As PaymentDetails = _
                        PaymentData(paymentList.SelectedIndex)

        ' Populate payment information text boxes
        paymentIdBox.Text = currentPayment.Id.ToString()
        dateBox.Text = currentPayment.PayDate.ToLongDateString()
        totalBox.Text = "$" & currentPayment.Total.ToString()
      End If
    End Sub
```

The rest of `MainForm.vb` is either unchanged from the autogenerated code or relates to form layout.

We can now run this application and select some details to get a screen like this:

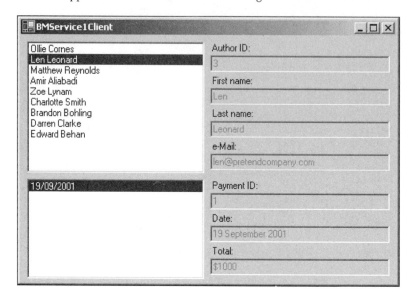

Securing BookManager Services

So far, we've seen how to expose our data via Web Services, and how to do so in such a way as to cater for the maximum number of clients. However, we need to go a bit further in order to create viable Web Services for today's enterprises. Specifically, we need to identify clients to determine what operations they are permitted to perform on our data, and a way of securing communications with these clients. Without this, we would leave ourselves wide open to assault by malicious users.

The issue of security is one we'll look at in detail in Chapter 10. For now it is enough to concentrate on the basics, to get a simple secure Web Service system up and running.

Security revolves around the following key concepts:

❑ **Authentication** – ensuring that a user is who they claim to be

❑ **Authorization** – determining what operations a client can perform

This is easy to achieve in a Windows environment using the built-in **users** and **groups** system. We can – and will – use Windows user accounts to authenticate users. In fact, there's not a huge amount to do here, as IIS is capable of doing most of this for us with its integrated security features. In an appropriately configured Web Service, we can write code that determines the current user through IIS.

In addition to the above, we also need to maintain a secure connection with our users, to prevent private information being accessible to hackers. We can do this using **Secure Sockets Layer** (**SSL**) communications over the **HTTPS** protocol. This technology involves exchanging security keys that encrypt information so that only the intended recipient can decipher it.

The system we'll use to perform this is shown in the diagram below:

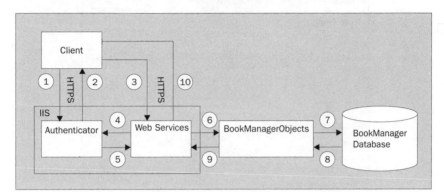

The numbered stages shown here are:

(1) & (2) The client obtains a token from an authentication service. This token will only be given to authorized users, and is transmitted over an SSL connection. The authenticator logs the token it has sent to the client along with the client's username and host information (IP address).

(3) The client sends the token they have received with any requests to Web Services in the system. These requests no longer require SSL, and use regular HTTP.

(4) & (5) The Web Services validate tokens received against the list stored in the authentication service, using client host information to further secure the user. Once the user identity is confirmed, the Web Service can determine whether the user has sufficient privileges to perform the requested operation.

(6) – (10) If the user has the required rights, the Web Service uses BookManagerObjects to interact with our database, and return the results over HTTP.

We'll build up this system in stages, discussing each issue involved as we come to it.

Authentication and Authorization

To enable our Web Services to perform authentication, we need to:

❑ Configure the secured resource (by individual file or by directory) to require authorization using the IIS manager

❑ Modify web.config to support Windows integrated authorization

❑ Change the security setting of the resource through Windows Explorer (again by individual file or by directory) to allow access only to authorized users

To start things off, we need some users and accounts to play with. We can do this using the Local Users and Groups MMC snap-in (or the equivalent active directory snap-in if this is installed). The following screenshot shows the information required to add a new user called Ivor:

Next we need a group to add our users to. We'll start with just one of these, called
BookManagerUsers, that all of our users will belong to. It is simplicity itself to add new groups later,
such as BookManagerAdministrators for instance, and add some of our users to these, but for we'll
perform authentication against the BookManagerUsers group.

The screenshot below shows the information for our BookManagerUsers group:

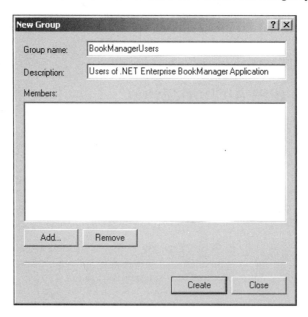

Finally, we need to add the users for this group. The screenshot below shows the users Ivor, matt, and karli added to the group:

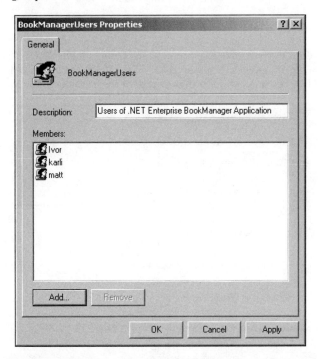

To test how we can use this group with a Web Service, we can create a Web Service for them. We'll call this first authenticating Web Service AuthenticationTest, and add it to our Services project with the following web method:

```
<WebMethod()> _
Public Function Authenticate() As Boolean

  If User.Identity.IsAuthenticated Then

    Return User.IsInRole("KARLIVAIO\BookManagerUsers")
  Else
    Return False
  End If
End Function
```

User is a property inherited from the WebService class, and gives access to the current user as authenticated by IIS in its Identity property. The IsAuthenticated property of Identity lets us know if IIS has successfully identified the user, and the IsInRole method of User allows us to check if the user is in a particular group – which must be fully qualified using the relevant domain or server name ("KARLIVAIO" is the name of the server I'm using).

At this stage, we can test the method before performing any configuration. Calling the method by navigating to the generated .asmx file in your web browser yields the following:

```
<?xml version="1.0" encoding="utf-8"?>
<boolean xmlns="http://www.wrox.com/BookManager/">false</boolean>
```

IIS isn't performing any actual authentication yet, hence `false` is returned.

So, the first thing to do is to configure IIS to deny anonymous requests and instead require authentication. Open the IIS manager snap-in (found in the **Administrative Tools** folder of **Control Panel**) and click the **File Security** tab for the properties of the `AuthenticationTest.asmx` file:

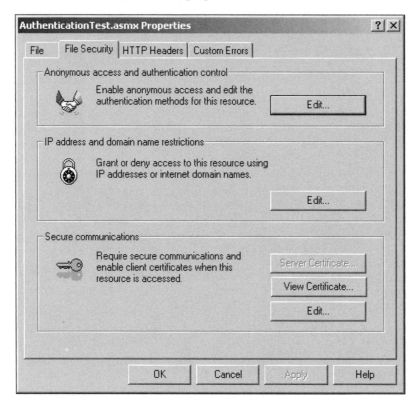

This tab contains all the settings we can apply to resources in IIS. We need to configure the first section, **Anonymous access and authentication control**. Clicking on the edit button brings up an **Authentication Methods** dialog, which needs to be set up as follows:

The changes from the default settings here are that **Anonymous access** has been disabled and **Basic authentication** enabled. Note that basic authentication is only secure over an SSL connection, but we'll come to that shortly.

Next, modify `web.config` as follows:

```
<!-- AUTHENTICATION
    This section sets the authentication policies of the application.
    Possible modes are "Windows", "Forms", "Passport" and "None"
-->
<authentication mode="Windows" />
```

The default authentication mode is None, and we change it to Windows to make use of Windows integrated authentication.

Next we need to apply security permissions to the files themselves using Windows Explorer. To do this, open the **Security** tab in the properties dialog for the file you want to set permissions for. We'll start by applying directory-wide permissions for the BM directory:

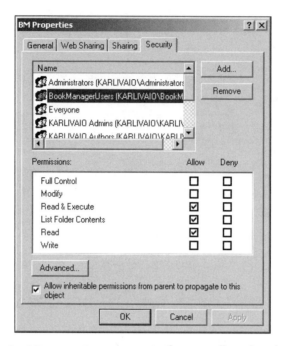

Here I have added the `BookManagerUsers` group to the users allowed, and assigned basic permissions.

Next, modify the security properties of the `AuthenticationTest.asmx` page. We disable inheritance of directory permissions, set the old inherited permissions for this file, and remove the entry for `Everyone`:

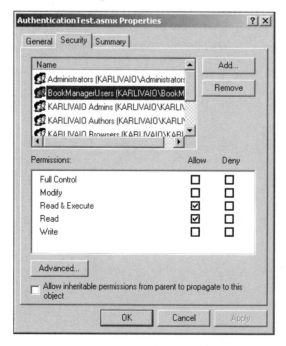

To test the service, create a very simple Windows Forms application, called AuthenticationServiceTest, with the following form layout:

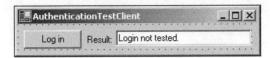

The text box, resultBox, should change to show the result of the login operation when we click on the Log in button (which is called loginButton). This is the code we need:

```
Private Sub loginButton_Click(ByVal sender As System.object, _
                              ByVal e As System.EventArgs) _
                              Handles loginButton.Click

    Dim service As AuthenticationTest.AuthenticationTest = _
                       New AuthenticationTest.AuthenticationTest()
    resultBox.Text = service.Authenticate().ToString()
End Sub
```

For this code to work, a web reference to AuthenticationTest.asmx *must be added, and given the name* AuthenticationTest. *The appropriate* Imports *statement also needs to be added to the top of the main form code.*

When we now run this project, it will fail with a System.Net.WebException exception with the message: "**The request failed with HTTP status 401: Access Denied.**". This is because we haven't supplied any actual login information to the request.

To add login information for the Web Service call, add an Imports statement for the System.Net namespace and a little extra code:

```
Private Sub loginButton_Click(ByVal sender As System.Object, _
                              ByVal e As System.EventArgs) _
                              Handles loginButton.Click

    Dim service As AuthenticationTest.AuthenticationTest = _
                   New AuthenticationTest.AuthenticationTest()
    Dim userInfo As NetworkCredential = New NetworkCredential("Ivor", _
                                            "password", _
                                            "KARLIVAIO")

    service.Credentials = userInfo
    resultBox.Text = service.Authenticate().ToString()
End Sub
```

We're creating a new instance of the NetworkCredential class and initializing it with user information – here we use the Ivor account created earlier (change "password" in the above to the password you gave this user earlier).

Now when you run the client application and click on Log in, you should see a successful login reported:

Feel free to test this using another user account that isn't already a member of the BookManagerUsers group – you should see the text False when you then click Log in.

SSL Connections

Making our Web Service work over SSL is surprisingly simple. SSL works by using a **security certificate** to enable secure communications between a client and a web server, and is (as we see shortly) enabled with a few clicks in the IIS manager MMC snap-in. The trickiest thing here is obtaining the certificate in the first place.

Security certificates are issued by certification authorities. We have two options here:

❑ Generate our own certificate

❑ Obtain a certificate from a known authority, such as Verisign (http://www.verisign.com/)

There is no real reason why we shouldn't generate our own certificates – simply install certificate server from your Win2K installation disks and you're away. Note, though, that Active Directory is required for an Enterprise-level certification authority, which is required for web server certificates. The only problem with doing this is cosmetic – receipt of a certificate from an 'unknown' source will result in a warning being shown to users in some situations, which may put some people off. There are two ways to get round this annoyance: manually register your certificate authority as a trusted authority on each client, or pay for your certificate to be shipped with Internet Explorer.

The alternative, getting a certificate from a known authority, won't have this effect, so it is definitely worth considering.

Installing a certificate on your Web Service is straightforward (you'll either get instructions from the certification authority or find them out through your own certification installation), so there's no need for details here. The important thing is that once you have one, you can open secure SSL connections to anything on your web server. What we want to do, though, is to *require* secure communications with our authentication Web Service.

Select the Edit button from the File Security tab in the properties for AuthenticationTest.asmx in IIS manager, and check the Require secure channel (SSL) box to secure access to the service:

Now try running the client again. This time, a `WebException` will be thrown with the message: "The request failed with HTTP status 403: Access Forbidden.". This is because we have added a web reference with the HTTP protocol, and we need to use the HTTPS protocol.

The required modification is simple: we just need to change the Web Reference URL property of the web reference from:

`http://localhost/bm/services/authenticationtest.asmx`

to:

`https://localhost/bm/services/authenticationtest.asmx`

and then update the web reference (right-click on it in the Solution Explorer window and select Update web reference). When we now run the client application, it should work as it did previously. You may notice it running slightly slower, as a significant chunk of data must be exchanged to set up the connection, but in our case that's a fair sacrifice to make for a secure connection.

Securing "BookManager" Service

So far we've covered all the plumbing, now we need to put things together to create the token assignment and validation system described earlier. The service we'll develop in this section, `AuthenticateService`, may be found fully formed in the code download, or if you prefer you can build it from scratch using the information here.

To get started, we need to add the new `AuthenticateService` service to our `Services` project, and configure it for SSL in the same way that we did for our last service (although we don't have to modify `web.config` again as this one file applies to the whole project). We also need a new code file to define the `UserLoginInfo` class for storing login information. Each time a user logs in, we'll create a new instance of this class, and populate it with the login user identity, the token assigned, and the client host address:

```
Imports System
Imports System.Security.Principal

Namespace Services

    Public Class UserLoginInfo

        Private _token As Guid
        Private _host As string
        Private _user As IPrincipal

        Public ReadOnly Property Token() As Guid
          Get
             Return _token
          End Get
        End Property

        Public ReadOnly Property Host() As String
          Get
             Return _host
          End Get
        End Property

        Public ReadOnly Property User() As IPrincipal
          Get
             Return _user
          End Get
        End Property

        Private Sub New ()
            '...
        End Sub

        Public Sub New(ByVal newToken As Guid,ByVal newHost As String, _
                    ByVal newUser As IPrincipal)

          _token = newToken
          _host = newHost
          _user = newUser
        End Sub
    End Class
End Namespace
```

Note that we are using Guids for tokens. Guids (Globally Unique Identifiers) are unique 128-bit numbers that are ideal for this sort of scenario. We also store the user information as an IPrincipal interface reference. IPrincipal contains the method IsInRole which we'll need for authorization in our other Web Services, and provides access to the user name and so on through the property called Identity. This interface is found in the System.Security.Principal namespace, which we therefore need to import with an Imports statement.

We also need a class to store a collection of UserLoginInfo classes. We'll call it LoginTokens, and it is a dictionary-based collection that uses Guid tokens as keys:

```
Imports System
Imports System.Collections

Namespace Services
  ' <summary>
  ' Summary description for LoginTokens.
  ' </summary>
  Public Class LoginTokens
    Inherits DictionaryBase

    Public Sub Add(ByVal newUserLoginInfo As UserLoginInfo)
      Dictionary.Add(newUserLoginInfo.Token, newUserLoginInfo)
    End Sub

    Public Sub Remove(ByVal loginToken As Guid)
      Dictionary.Remove(loginToken)
    End Sub

    Public ReadOnly Property this(ByVal loginToken As Guid) As _
                                  UserLoginInfo
      Get
        Return Dictionary(loginToken)
      End Get
    End Property

    Public Sub New ()

    End Sub

  End Class
End Namespace
```

The `AuthenticateService` class can then store current tokens in a static member of this type. This is fine for our purposes, although it might be worth storing login tokens in a database for stability (see discussion later). We also want to make this class part of the `Services` namespace:

```
Namespace Services

<WebService(Namespace: = "http://www.wrox.com/BookManager/")> _
  Public Class AuthenticateService
    Inherits System.Web.Services.WebService

    Private Shared loginTokens As LoginTokens = New LoginTokens()

End Class

End Namespace
```

`AuthenticateService`, like `AuthenticationTest`, has an `Authenticate` method, although it is a bit different:

```
    <WebMethod()> _
    Public Function Authenticate() As Guid
      If Not User.Identity.IsAuthenticated Then
```

```
        Throw New WebException("User not authenticated.")
      End If
      If Not User.IsInRole(@"KARLIVAIO\BookManagerUsers") Then
        Throw New WebException("User not part of BookManagerUsers group.")
      End If
      Dim loginToken As Guid = Guid.NewGuid()
      Dim newUserLoginInfo As UserLoginInfo = New UserLoginInfo( _
                   loginToken, Context.Request.UserHostAddress, User)
      loginTokens.Add(newUserLoginInfo)
      Return loginToken
   End Function
```

The major difference here is that exceptions are used to signify various error codes. This helps us to build clients as we can handle these errors appropriately. The following `Imports` statement is required to throw `WebException` exceptions:

```
Imports System.Net
```

In addition, note that the return value of the method is a `Guid`, not a `Boolean`. Since we'll only get a `Guid` returned if no exception is thrown, we don't need a `Boolean` to indicate success.

As well as storing tokens when we authenticate users, we also need a way to validate these tokens, so that we can permit or deny operations according to the user's privileges, as discussed earlier in the chapter. One way of doing this would be to have a validation method with the signature given below:

```
<WebMethod()> _
Public Function ValidateLoginToken(ByVal token As Guid, _
                         ByVal hostAddress As String) As Boolean
End Function
```

This method would be used by all other BookManager Web Services, which would have signatures following this pattern:

```
<WebMethod()> _
Public Function DoSomething(ByVal token As Guid, _
               ByVal doSomethingParameter As Integer) As String
End Function
```

This is all very well, but the .NET Framework provides a very neat alternative – sending information within SOAP headers.

SOAP Headers for Data Exchange

The general way we've used Web Services in our client applications so far has been as follows:

```
Dim service As ServiceType = New ServiceType()
Dim result As ResultType = service.MethodCall(parameters)
```

And to exchange token values using parameters requires the following, slightly messy, syntax:

```
Dim service As ServiceType = new ServiceType()
Dim result1 As ResultType1 = service.MethodCall1(token, parameters)
```

```
Dim result2 As ResultType2 = service.MethodCall2(token, parameters)
Dim result3 As ResultType3 = service.MethodCall3(token, parameters)
```

Using SOAP headers, we can simplify this code a little to become:

```
Dim service As ServiceType = New ServiceType()
service.TokenHeaderValue = tokenValue
Dim result1 As ResultType1 = service.MethodCall1(parameters)
Dim result2 As ResultType2 = service.MethodCall2(parameters)
Dim result3 As ResultType3 = service.MethodCall3(parameters)
```

That is, we set the token in the SOAP header *once* and it is passed automatically with every web method call. This provides a much cleaner system, as once we have set the header we can forget about it. Our method calls are also less verbose.

To set up this system with the `AuthenticateService` service, we need to:

❑   Create a class based on `System.Web.Services.Protocols.SoapHeader` to exchange (in our case) the token as a `Guid`

❑   Use this class to add a public field to the `AuthenticateService` class

❑   Add `System.Web.Services.Protocols.SoapHeaderAttribute` attributes to any web method that relies on the SOAP header

That's all we need. The required plumbing will be configured automatically, during the implicit proxy creation that VS.NET performs when we add web references for our service.

Our header class, within the `Services` project, will be like this:

```
Imports System
Imports System.Web.Services.Protocols

Namespace Services

   Public Class TokenHeader
      Inherits SoapHeader

      Public InnerToken As Guid
   End Class
End Namespace
```

This class simply stores a `Guid` as a public field. We can add this class to `AuthenticateService` as a public field as shown below:

```
<WebService(Namespace:= "http://www.wrox.com/BookManager/")> _
Public Class AuthenticateService
   Inherits System.Web.Services.WebService

   Public Token As TokenHeader
   Private Shared loginTokens As LoginTokens = New LoginTokens()
```

We also need the following `Imports` statement in `AuthenticateService.asmx.vb`:

```
Imports System.Web.Services.Protocols
```

The attribute we need to add to each web method that uses the SOAP header is then:

```
<SoapHeaderAttribute("Token", _
                     Direction := SoapHeaderDirection.In, _
                     Required := True)>
```

This tells us the name of the public field to map to the token header (and the name to use for that header), the direction of the exchange (it is also possible to send header information to clients), and the fact that the header must be included for calls to the method to which the attribute is required.

We can use this straight away to create a simple `Logout` method:

```
<WebMethod(), _
SoapHeaderAttribute("Token", _
                     Direction := SoapHeaderDirection.In, _
                     Required := True)> _
Public Sub Logout()

  loginTokens.Remove(Token.InnerToken)
End Sub
```

This method takes no parameters as it uses the SOAP header to obtain the `Guid`. Since this header is mapped to the `Token` field, we can retrieve the `Guid` using `Token.InnerToken`. Here we're simply using this as a key to remove the specified `UserLoginInfo` class from our `loginTokens` collection.

We can also use this header to validate a client login with the following code:

```
<WebMethod(), _
SoapHeaderAttribute("Token", _
                     Direction:= SoapHeaderDirection.In, _
                     Required:= True)> _
Public Sub ValidateLoginToken()
  Try
    If Context.Request.UserHostAddress <> _
                             LoginTokens(Token.InnerToken).Host

      Throw New WebException("Host mismatch.")
    End If
  Catch
    Throw New WebException("Unknown user or user not logged in.")
  End Try
End Sub
```

This could be used by a client to check that they are still logged in, which could be useful if we introduce a system where tokens expire after a given interval. We can also use this method in `Logout`:

```
<WebMethod(), _
SoapHeaderAttribute("Token", _
                    Direction:= SoapHeaderDirection.In, _
                    Required:= True)> _
Public Sub Logout()

    ValidateLoginToken()
    loginTokens.Remove(Token.InnerToken)
End Sub
```

This helps stop infiltrators from logging users off by spoofing their login token. This isn't a foolproof technique, as hosts can be spoofed too, but it will make it more difficult. Note that we don't have to do anything special to call `ValidateLoginToken` from another web method – the `Token` field will have been filled in by the SOAP header received when `Logout` is called.

We'll also add a `Friend` version of `ValidateLoginToken`, which can only be used by other services in the `Services` project:

```
Friend Sub ValidateLoginToken(ByVal token As Guid, _
                              ByVal hostInfo As String)

    Try
      If hostInfo <> loginTokens(token).Host Then
        Throw New WebException ("Host mismatch.")
      End If
    Catch
      Throw New WebException("Unknown user or user not logged in.")
    End try
End Sub
```

Since other services in the project won't be using `AuthenticateService` as a Web Service, we need this one to validate requests, and we can use standard parameter syntax here for simplicity.

Finally, we'll add a `Friend` utility method for other BookManager services, allowing access to the Windows identity of the currently logged-in user:

```
Friend Function GetUser(ByVal token As Guid) As IPrincipal
  Try
    Return loginTokens(token).User
  Catch
    Throw New WebException("Unknown user or user not logged in.")
  End Try
End Function
```

Authenticated "BookManager" Services

Now we've created `AuthenticateService`, it's time to upgrade `BMService1` to use it. We'll do this in a new Web Service, called `BMService2`. To start off, copy all the code over from `BMService1.asmx.vb`, and change the class name in the code file as appropriate.

Most of the changes to this service can be encapsulated in an abstract base class that inherits from `System.Web.Services.WebService`. When we have this, we will be able to create services that make use of `AuthenticateService` with ease.

This base class, `BMServiceBase`, will:

❑ Set up a connection to our database using the now familiar `EnterpriseApplication` class in its constructor

❑ Hold a static reference to an `AuthenticateService` instance (it makes sense to do things this way as there is no reason why all our services need separate `AuthenticateService` instances)

❑ Contain a public `Token` field, for use with SOAP header exchange as detailed in the last section

❑ Contain a protected `Authenticate` method that validates this token using the `AuthenticateService` instance

❑ Contain a protected `IPrincipal` field populated with current user information when `Authenticate` is called

❑ Contain two protected utility members, `IsInRole` and `UserName`

`IsInRole` makes use of the `IPrincipal` reference to check user group membership. This uses a protected field called `userDomain` to simplify syntax such that services inheriting from this class can use `IsInRole("Role")` rather than `currentUser.IsInRole("Domain\Role")`.

`UserName` simply returns the name of the user minus the domain name (so you'd get "Name" rather than "Domain\Name"), which may also simplify syntax.

`Authenticate` should then be called by any web method of the inheriting class, and may result in exceptions being thrown by the `AuthenticateClass` reference, which can be handled in the service or passed back to the client.

The code for this class follows:

```
Imports System
Imports System.Collections
Imports System.ComponentModel
Imports System.Data
Imports System.Diagnostics
Imports System.Web
Imports System.Web.Services
Imports System.Web.Services.Protocols
Imports System.Security.Principal
Imports BookManagerObjects
Imports EnterpriseObjects

Namespace Services

    Public MustInherit Class BMServiceBase
        Inherits System.Web.Services.WebService

        Protected Shared authenticateService As AuthenticateService = _
                                        New AuthenticateService()
        Protected currentUser As IPrincipal
        Protected userDomain As String
        Public Token As TokenHeader
```

```
      Public Sub New()
        ' set the connection string
        EnterpriseApplication.Application.ConnectionString = _
              "integrated security=sspi;initial catalog=bookmanager;data " _
              & "source=localhost"

        ' set the domain name
        userDomain = "KARLIVAIO"
      End Sub

      Protected Sub Authenticate()
        authenticateService.ValidateLoginToken(Token.InnerToken, _
                                    Context.Request.UserHostAddress)
        currentUser = authenticateService.GetUser(Token.InnerToken)
      End Sub

      Protected Function IsInRole(ByVal role As String) As Boolean
        Return currentUser.IsInRole(userDomain + "\" & role)
      End Function

      Protected ReadOnly Property UserName() As String
        Get
          Return currentUser.Identity.Name.Remove(0, userDomain.Length + 1)
        End Get
      End Property
    End Class
End Namespace
```

Using this base class is then simple. To create a Web Service, we use the following format:

```
Namespace Services

    <WebService(Namespace:= "http://www.wrox.com/BookManager/")> _
    Public Class BMServiceClass
      Inherits BMServiceBase

      '...

      <WebMethod(), _
      SoapHeaderAttribute("Token", _
                          Direction:= SoapHeaderDirection.In, _
                          Required:= True)> _
      Public Function WebMethodName() As returnType

        Authenticate()

        '...

        Return returnValue
      End Function
    End Class
End Namespace
```

Using this structure, then, the code for BMService2 differs from BMService1 as shown:

```vbnet
Imports System

...

Imports System.Security.Principal
Imports BookManagerObjects
Imports EnterpriseObjects

Namespace Services

  <WebService(Namespace:= "http://www.wrox.com/BookManager/")> _
  Public Class BMService2
    Inherits BMServiceBase

    Public Sub New ()
      MyBase.New()

      InitializeComponent()
    End Sub

    ...

    <WebMethod(), _
    SoapHeaderAttribute("Token", _
                        Direction:= SoapHeaderDirection.In, _
                        Required:= True)> _
    Public Function GetAuthors() As AuthorDetails()

      Authenticate()
      ' Get the authors
      Dim authors As AuthorSet = Author.GetAll()

      ...

      ' Return
      Return returnData
    End Function

    <WebMethod(), _
    SoapHeaderAttribute("Token", _
                        Direction:= SoapHeaderDirection.In, _
                        Required:= True)> _
    Public Function GetPaymentsByAuthorID(ByVal authorID As Integer) _
                                      As PaymentDetails()

      Authenticate()
      ' Get the author
      Dim theAuthor As Author = Author.GetById(authorID)

      ...

      ' Return payment details
      Return returnData
```

```
      End Function
    End Class
  End Namespace
```

In addition, we can remove the `GetAuthorSet` method, as it was only intended for debugging purposes.

A Client for "BMService2"

Now we have fully configured our Web Services, we ought to do something with them. We have changed the way clients must access our data, so we have a fair few modifications to make to the `BMService1Client` application to update it as `BMService2Client`.

To start with, let's look at the additional UI elements required. We need a log in/out button on the main form, and a new login form to accept the user's name and password.

The log in/out button is shown at the bottom of the screenshot below:

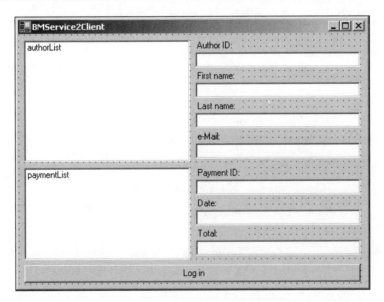

This button is called `loginButton`, and initially has the text Log in as shown.

The form for logging in, `Login`, is shown next:

The UI elements are usernameBox, passwordBox (with PasswordChar set to "*"), okButton, and cancelButton. For testing purposes, it's worth initializing the Text properties of the two text boxes to a valid login, say the user Ivor created earlier, to save having to type this information in every time you execute the application (remember to remove it before going 'live' of course!). Create a click handler for the OK button (by double-clicking on it in the Designer). This handler consists of just one line, DialogResult = DialogResult.OK. Do the same for the Cancel button. We also need to add two properties to the Login.vb code file to provide access to the username and password TextBoxes:

```vb
Public ReadOnly Property Username() As String
    Get
        Return usernameBox.Text
    End Get
End Property

Public ReadOnly Property Password() As String
    Get
        Return passwordBox.Text
    End Get
End Property
```

Before we move on to MainForm.vb, and the event handler for loginButton, let's see the other changes that need to be made to BMService2Client. First, we need to remove the web reference to BMService1 and add web references to AuthenticateService and BMService2. These should be at the following URLs:

❑   https://localhost/BM/Services/AuthenticateService.asmx

❑   http://localhost/BM/Services/BMService2.asmx

or, if the Web Services are not installed on the local machine:

❑   https://<serverName>/BM/Services/AuthenticateService.asmx

❑   http://<serverName>/BM/Services/BMService2.asmx

> When testing you *must* use either localhost for both references or <serverName> for both references. Which one you use will affect the IP address detected by the services, either 127.0.0.1 or your actual IP address respectively. If you mix these up then validation of user tokens by host address will fail.

Next we need to update our Imports statements for these two references in our main form:

```vb
Imports System
Imports System.Drawing
Imports System.Collections
Imports System.ComponentModel
Imports System.Windows.Forms
Imports System.Data
Imports System.Net
Imports BMService2Client.BMService2
Imports BMService2Client.Authenticate
```

We also need to modify our member fields to hold references to the new services, retrieved data, a `Guid` login token, and the login status:

```
Namespace BMService2Client

  Public Class MainForm
    Inherits System.Windows.Forms.Form

      Private service As Authenticate.AuthenticateService
      Private usefulService As BMService2.BMService2
      Private authorData As BMService2.AuthorDetails()
      Private paymentData As BMService2.PaymentDetails()
      Private loggedIn As Boolean = False
      Private loginToken As Guid
```

`BMService1Client` did most of its work in the `Load` event handler. Since a login is now required, we'll be doing this processing elsewhere, so the `MainForm_Load` method needs to be taken out.

Next add an event handler for the login button as follows:

```
    Private Sub loginButton_Click(ByVal sender As System.Object, _
                          ByVal e As System.EventArgs) _
                          Handles loginButton.Click

        If Not loggedIn Then
          logIn();
        Else
          logOut()
        End If

    End Sub
```

This simply redirects processing to one of two private methods, `logIn` or `logOut`, depending on the login status.

`logIn` uses our `Login` form for name and password entry, logs in (checking for exceptions), uses `BMService2` to retrieve author information, changes the text on the login button, and changes the login status to `True`:

```
    Private Sub logIn()

      ' Get login info
      Dim myLogin As Login = New Login()
      Dim loginInfoResult As DialogResult = myLogin.ShowDialog()
      If loginInfoResult = DialogResult.OK Then

        ' Log in
        service = New AuthenticateService()
        Dim userInfo As NetworkCredential = _
            new NetworkCredential(myLogin.Username, myLogin.Password, _
                        "KARLIVAIO")
```

```
      service.Credentials = userInfo

      Try
        loginToken = service.Authenticate()

        ' Log in OK if no exception thrown at this point
        loggedIn = True
        loginButton.Text = "Log out " & myLogin.Username

        ' Set token header
        service.TokenHeaderValue = New Authenticate.TokenHeader()
        service.TokenHeaderValue.InnerToken = loginToken

        ' Initialize useful service
        usefulService = New BMService2.BMService2()

        ' Set token header
        usefulService.TokenHeaderValue = New BMService2.TokenHeader()
        usefulService.TokenHeaderValue.InnerToken = loginToken

        ' Get author data
        authorData = usefulService.GetAuthors()

        ' Populate authorList list box
        If Not authorData Is Nothing Then
          Dim author As AuthorDetails
          For Each author In authorData
            authorList.Items.Add(author.FirstName & " " & _
                              author.LastName)
          Next
        End If
      Catch e As System.Net.WebException
        ' Login error
        MessageBox.Show( _
            "Please check your login details and try again. Status: " _
            & e.Message, "Authentication Error", _
            MessageBoxButtons.OK)
        Return
      End Try
    End If
  End Sub
```

logOut logs the client out and tidies up a bit:

```
  Private Sub logOut()

    ' Confirm
    Dim logoutConfirm As DialogResult = MessageBox.Show( _
            "Are you sure you want to log out?", "Confirm Request", _
            MessageBoxButtons.OKCancel)
    If logoutConfirm = DialogResult.OK Then

      ' Log out
```

```
            service.Logout()
            service.Dispose()
            service = Nothing
            loggedIn = False
            loginButton.Text = "Log in"

            ' Clear data
            authorList.Items.Clear()
            paymentList.Items.Clear()
            authorIdBox.Clear()
            firstNameBox.Clear()
            lastNameBox.Clear()
            emailBox.Clear()
            paymentIdBox.Clear()
            dateBox.Clear()
            totalBox.Clear()
        End If
    End Sub
```

And that completes our client. Functionally, there isn't a great deal that differs from
BMService1Client, except that full authentication is now implemented.

Summary

In this chapter, we've looked at expanding the reach of our application by creating Web Services that call our
BookManagerObjects classes. Because they are based on simple text and HTTP communication, Web
Services are an ideal way to create platform-agnostic interfaces to our applications.

When we start throwing open our servers to access over the Internet in this way however, we are also
throwing down the gauntlet to legions of hackers, all keen to access our private code and data. It is imperative
that an effective and maintainable security system is implemented in order to seal out unwanted users, and to
prevent genuine users accessing functionality or data to which they are not entitled.

To start with, it is a mistake to assume that the system we created above is 100% secure. Any hacker will tell
you that there is no such thing as a completely secure computer system. However, enough elements exist to
put off casual hackers, and perhaps the worst that can happen (if we assume that SSL connections are
completely secure) is that users may have session tokens stolen and sessions spoofed. Even in this worst case
scenario, we at least manage to ensure the protection of usernames and passwords.

Of particular note is the method used to store login information. AuthenticateService stores tokens
along with user identities and hostnames in a static collection. While this is fine for an example it does
raise some important issues. Most importantly, this information is likely to be lost in the case of a server
error, since rebooting the server will destroy this store. It would also be difficult to load-balance the
service with this system, as AuthenticateService instances on multiple machines may not have
access to the same collection.

A better technique, albeit more complicated, would be to store login information in a database. We
could then be more confident that the information will persist, and that it would be accessible from
multiple AuthenticateService instances on multiple servers. In addition, we could remove the
dependence of other services, such as the BMService2 service, on AuthenticateService. These
services could instead access the login information directly if needed.

.NET Enterprise Development in VB .NET

7

Internet

As the last chapter pointed out, not all our clients will be connected to our enterprise via LAN or VPN connections, so we need to add extra channels to allow such clients access to our data. Web Services are all well and good, but they require some kind of front end so we can use them effectively. When, for whatever reason, clients are unable to use the desktop applications we've covered so far, and they don't want to roll up our Web Services into their own applications, our only alternative is provide access to data over the Web.

The Active Server Pages .NET (ASP.NET) component of the .NET Framework is one way we can achieve this. The advantages of using this technology over custom HTML, whether created manually or through some other tool, include:

❑   ASP.NET is fully integrated into the .NET Framework and provides a native way for accessing existing .NET components and Web Services.

❑   ASP.NET is very good at creating dynamic web pages quickly and in such a way that later modifications are relatively simple.

❑   We can embed any .NET language in our ASP.NET pages, letting us create web applications without having to learn new notation. Naturally, we'll be using VB.NET.

❑   Due to the way that ASP.NET web content is generated by compiled code, it offers much better performance than that of interpreted scripting technologies.

In this chapter, we'll very quickly cover the basics of using ASP.NET, as I really want to concentrate on the more useful things it lets us achieve. We'll develop a "fan site" for authors in our database, where users can send them messages without getting direct access to their personal e-mail addresses.

ASP.NET – A Crash Course

A Visual Basic ASP.NET web page consists of the following:

❑ A template document (with the extension `.aspx`, also known as a web form). Contains a mix of standard HTML and ASP.NET code that defines the controls on the page.

❑ A class descended from `System.Web.UI.Page` (in a **code behind** file that has the extension `.aspx.vb`), which we can use to manipulate the contents of the web page and all the controls that it contains. This page isn't necessary if no extra code is required for the page.

To illustrate this, let's create a VB.NET ASP.NET Web Application project in Visual Studio .NET (for the purposes of this sample, I've created the project at http://localhost/BM/). We should get the following collection of files:

You can see that a default web form has been created with the name `WebForm1.aspx`. There is an associated code file called `WebForm1.aspx.vb`, but Solution Explorer doesn't show it by default. To see the code, we can right-click on the file name, and select **View Code**, which initially consists of the following:

```
Public Class WebForm1
  Inherits System.Web.UI.Page

#Region " Web Form Designer Generated Code "

  'This call is required by the Web Form Designer.
  <System.Diagnostics.DebuggerStepThrough()> Private Sub _
                                              InitializeComponent()

  End Sub

  Private Sub Page_Init(ByVal sender As System.Object, _
                    ByVal e As System.EventArgs) Handles MyBase.Init
    'CODEGEN: This method call is required by the Web Form Designer
    'Do not modify it using the code editor.
```

```
        InitializeComponent()
    End Sub

#End Region

    Private Sub Page_Load(ByVal sender As System.Object, _
                        ByVal e As System.EventArgs) Handles MyBase.Load
        'Put user code to initialize the page here
    End Sub

End Class
```

By design, the structure here is very similar to Windows Forms code. The main differences come when you are creating your form layout, which we can do by opening up the editor for WebForm1.aspx, in either Design or HTML mode by clicking the tabs at the bottom of the design pane. We can set the pageLayout property for the page to lay out our controls using either a grid layout (similar to Windows Forms), or a flow layout (a more traditional HTML concept where controls are placed sequentially one after the other). The HTML code Visual Studio .NET has generated for this page is shown here:

```
<%@ Page Language="vb" AutoEventWireup="false" Codebehind="WebForm1.aspx.vb"
        Inherits="BM.WebForm1"%>
<!DOCTYPE HTML PUBLIC "-//W3C//DTD HTML 4.0 Transitional//EN">
<HTML>
  <HEAD>
    <title>WebForm1</title>
    <meta name="GENERATOR" content="Microsoft Visual Studio.NET 7.0">
    <meta name="CODE_LANGUAGE" content="Visual Basic 7.0">
    <meta name="vs_defaultClientScript" content="JavaScript">
    <meta name="vs_targetSchema"
          content="http://schemas.microsoft.com/intellisense/ie5">
  </HEAD>
  <body MS_POSITIONING="GridLayout">
    <form id="Form1" method="post" runat="server">
    </form>
  </body>
</HTML>
```

The first two lines of code link this file to the class contained in WebForm1.aspx.vb, that is BM.WebForm1. The section of code that describes our page layout is found within that short <form> element near the bottom of the above file.

Return to Design view, and drag the following three controls from the **Toolbox** just as you would for a standard Windows Forms application:

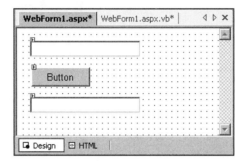

Set the following properties for these controls:

❑ The top TextBox control has an (ID) property of sourceBox

❑ The Button control has an (ID) property of reverseButton, and a Text property of Reverse

❑ The bottom TextBox has an (ID) of targetBox

Switching to HTML view, we see that VS.NET has added the following new code:

```
<form id="Form1" method="post" runat="server">
  <asp:TextBox id="sourceBox"
    style="Z-INDEX: 101; LEFT: 6px; POSITION: absolute; TOP: 5px"
    runat="server">
  </asp:TextBox>
  <asp:Button id="reverseButton"
    style="Z-INDEX: 102; LEFT: 6px; POSITION: absolute; TOP: 37px"
    runat="server" Text="Reverse">
  </asp:Button>
  <asp:TextBox id="targetBox"
    style="Z-INDEX: 103; LEFT: 6px; POSITION: absolute; TOP: 68px"
    runat="server">
  </asp:TextBox>
</form>
```

Each control that we added appears as an element within the asp namespace. Each has an id attribute specifying its name, a runat="server" attribute meaning the code for the control is to run server-side, and some control-specific attributes.

Note that all the new controls are contained within the <form> element in this code. This is essential for them to be correctly instantiated as part of our form, and if it weren't the case, the controls would be useless because they would be unable to post back to the server.

Adding these controls has also resulted in some changes to the WebForm1.aspx.vb code:

```
Public Class WebForm1
   Inherits System.Web.UI.Page
   Protected WithEvents sourceBox As System.Web.UI.WebControls.TextBox
   Protected WithEvents reverseButton As System.Web.UI.WebControls.Button
   Protected WithEvents targetBox As System.Web.UI.WebControls.TextBox
```

Note that unlike Windows Forms, we don't get a whole lot of control formatting code in other places in this code file. This is because most control configuration is specified using the attributes of the <asp> elements in WebForm1.aspx to set the control properties.

We can add events for the controls on the form in a similar fashion to Windows Form applications. For instance, double-clicking on the button while in Design view adds the following code to WebForm1.aspx.vb:

```
Private Sub reverseButton_Click(ByVal sender As System.Object, _
                      ByVal e As System.EventArgs) _
                      Handles reverseButton.Click


End Sub
```

From here we have access to the full form object model (and whatever other .NET features we want to use). Add the following code to the Button click handler:

```
Private Sub reverseButton_Click(ByVal sender As System.Object, _
                      ByVal e As System.EventArgs) _
                      Handles reverseButton.Click

   Dim sourceString As String = sourceBox.Text
   Dim reversedString As String
   Dim index As Integer
   For index = sourceString.Length - 1 To 0 Step -1
     reversedString += sourceString.Substring(index,1)
   Next
   targetBox.Text = reversedString
End Sub
```

If you now run the application by pressing the *F5* key, or by pointing your browser at http://localhost/BM/WebForm1.aspx, you'll get a form that allows you to reverse text at the press of a button:

There is far more that ASP.NET can do, as you'll find out if you work through the samples that come with the .NET Framework, or read a book such as *Professional ASP.NET* (Wrox Press, ISBN 1-861004-88-5). We'll look at ASP.NET in more detail as we work through the chapter, but this is enough to get us started.

The BookManager ASP.NET Application

Now we've covered the basics, it's time to write an ASP.NET application that uses our `BookManager` database. Before we start, we need to choose between two fundamentally different ways of accessing our data:

❑ Using the `BookManagerObjects` library directly

❑ Using Web Services

The choice here will depend a lot on where your web applications are to be deployed. If they are to be deployed on a server that has free access to your data store, then using the library directly would increase performance. However, many enterprise setups make this tricky, especially where web servers are deployed in a DMZ between firewalls, which often block access to back-end data stores. Web Services, on the other hand, may be used from anywhere with web access.

Another concern is security. Most full-scale web applications benefit from authentication of users, a problem we already addressed for Web Services in the previous chapter. We could create a new solution and access the `BookManagerObjects` library through this, but that hardly seems a sensible use of our time. Alternatively, we could ignore security and simply allow anyone access to selected data via this library (something we'll look at in more detail in the next chapter).

The web page we'll design here will be a "fan site" for book authors, where users can send e-mail to authors using a submission form, which hides the actual e-mail address of the author from the user. Since only authorized users are to be able to use this application, we'll use Web Services to provide the functionality, as that way we won't have to do too much to get users authenticated.

To build this application, we shall:

❑ Create a new stored procedure to retrieve all the authors who worked on a given book, making use of the `BookAuthors` link table

❑ Create a Web Service called `FanMail` that will return book titles along with author names and IDs (but not e-mail addresses), and provide a way to send mail to authors

❑ Create an ASP.NET Web Forms application called `AuthorFanMail` that uses this Web Service while maintaining authentication using `AuthenticateService` from the previous chapter

The first two steps are fairly straightforward, and we can cover them quickly as we have seen most of the required code already. The only new area is sending SMTP e-mail from the Web Service, which is fortunately a lot simpler than it sounds!

The web application itself is more involved. There are several areas where we'll need to invest some time in the exploration of what is and isn't possible. We need to cater for the fact that multiple users may use the web application simultaneously, and address issues such as whether every user needs a web application with a unique reference to our Web Services. Another area of concern arises because our Web Services are being used from a web application rather than from a remote client, meaning that the validation system based on host address that we created in Chapter 6 will no longer function, and we'll need to address that issue again.

The "GetAuthorsForBook" Stored Procedure

Since the relationship between the Books and Authors tables isn't a direct one (links are stored in an intermediate table called BookAuthors that links the two together in a many-to-many relationship), the query required to get the authors for a given book is slightly convoluted. To simplify matters, we'll create a stored procedure to retrieve this information. Fortunately, as we saw in Chapter 2, this is a relatively painless task.

There are several ways of adding a stored procedure (SP) to the BookManager database, including using the **Server Explorer** in Visual Studio .NET, or the **SQL Server Enterprise Manager** MMC snap-in.

The GetAuthorsForBook stored procedure code is as follows:

```
CREATE PROCEDURE GetAuthorsForBook
(
  @bookId int
)
AS
  SELECT Authors.AuthorId, FirstName, LastName, Email FROM Authors
    INNER JOIN BookAuthors ON
      Authors.AuthorId=BookAuthors.AuthorId
    WHERE BookAuthors.BookId=@bookId
GO
```

Its structure closely resembles that of the GetPaymentDetailsForAuthor SP we've seen already, except that the tables used are, of course, different.

Next we need to regenerate our BookManagerObjects project using Builder so that it generates code for executing this SP. We then can add the following code to the Book.vb file, to retrieve the authors for a book by means of this SP:

```
Imports System.Data

Namespace BookManagerObjects

  ' Entity implementation for table 'Books'
  ' *DO* add your modifications to this file
  Public Class Book
    Inherits BookBase

    Public Function GetAuthors() As AuthorSet
      Return Sprocs.GetAuthorsForBook(Id, GetType(AuthorSet))
    End Function
  End Class
End Namespace
```

This new method, GetAuthors, uses our stored procedure to return an AuthorSet object for a given book instance.

The "FanMail" Web Service

The FanMail Web Service can be created as a new Web Service (called FanMail.asmx) in the Services project, deriving it from BMServiceBase as we did for the Web Services in the last chapter. It exposes two new web methods:

- ❑ GetBooksAndAuthorNames – obtains a list of books in the database along with the names and IDs of authors that worked on the book

- ❑ SendMailToAuthor – e-mails an author, where the author ID is used to obtain their actual e-mail address from the database

The first of these methods needs some new structures for the transfer of data, which we can add to the existing TransferStructs.vb file within the Services project:

```
Imports System

Namespace Services

    ...

    Public Structure AuthorDetailsNoEMail
      Public Id As Integer
      Public Name As String
    End Structure

    Public Structure BookAuthorDetails
      Public Name As String
      Public Authors() As AuthorDetailsNoEMail
    End Structure
End Namespace
```

As you can see, each BookAuthorDetails Structure contains a book name and an array of AuthorDetailsNoEMail Structures, and each of these contains the name and ID for a single author.

The code for the FanMail service (in FanMail.asmx.vb) starts off as follows, with the standard Imports statements and the class declaration:

```
Imports System
Imports System.Collections
Imports System.ComponentModel
Imports System.Data
Imports System.Diagnostics
Imports System.Web
Imports System.Web.Services
Imports System.Web.Services.Protocols
Imports System.Web.Mail
Imports System.Security.Principal
Imports BookManagerObjects
Imports EnterpriseObjects

Namespace Services
```

```
<WebService(Namespace:= "http://www.wrox.com/BookManager/")> _
Public Class FanMail
    Inherits BMServiceBase
```

Next we have the constructor and Component Designer generated code sections, which I'll omit here for brevity.

After this, we come to `GetBooksAndAuthorNames`, which requires the standard `SoapHeaderAttribute` to work with our `AuthenticateService`, and can return an array of the `BookAuthorDetails` structs that we looked at above:

```
<WebMethod(), _
   SoapHeaderAttribute("Token", Direction:= SoapHeaderDirection.In, _
                       Required:= True)> _
Public Function GetBooksAndAuthorNames() As BookAuthorDetails

   Authenticate()
```

This code starts with the `Authenticate` call required by the Web Services according to the system developed in the last chapter.

Next we use `BookManagerObjects` to find the book information we need, and initialize the `returnData` array (which we can do as soon as we know how many books we'll be returning data for):

```
' Retrieve the books
Dim books As BookSet = Book.GetAll()

' Initialize return data array
Dim returnData(books.Count - 1) As BookAuthorDetails
```

We now need to place the book and author data into `returnData`, a fairly straightforward task as we have the `book.GetAuthors` method that quickly obtains the authors for a given book:

```
' Extract book and author data
Dim tempAuthorData As AuthorSet = New AuthorSet()
Dim bookIndex As Integer = 0
Dim authorIndex As Integer
Dim myBook As Book
For Each myBook In books
  returnData(bookIndex) = New BookAuthorDetails()
  returnData(bookIndex).Name = myBook.Name
  tempAuthorData = myBook.GetAuthors()
  Redim returnData(bookIndex).Authors(tempAuthorData.Count - 1)
  authorIndex = 0
  Dim myAuthor As Author
  For Each myAuthor In tempAuthorData
    returnData(bookIndex).Authors(authorIndex) = _
                                        New AuthorDetailsNoEMail
    returnData(bookIndex).Authors(authorIndex).Id = myAuthor.Id
    returnData(bookIndex).Authors(authorIndex).Name = myAuthor.Name
    authorIndex += 1
```

```
        Next
        bookIndex += 1
    Next
```

Finally, we return the data:

```
    ' Return data
    Return returnData

End Function
```

Moving on, we come to `SendMailToAuthor`. This method takes three parameters: the first specifies the author being mailed via an ID, a second contains the body of the message to send, and lastly we have an e-mail address for the author to reply to should they wish:

```
<WebMethod(), _
    SoapHeaderAttribute("Token", _
                        Direction: = SoapHeaderDirection.In, _
                        Required: = True)> _
    Public Sub SendMailToAuthor(ByVal authorId As Integer, _
                                ByVal body As String, ByVal from As String)

        Authenticate()
```

Next we get the full author details using `BookManagerObjects`:

```
    ' Get the author
    Dim myAuthor As Author = Author.GetById(authorId)
```

We create and send the e-mail using classes in the `System.Web.Mail` namespace, from an account with the address `administrator@pretendcompany.com` (this address could easily be configured to provide the user's own address, but that may not be ideal – autoreply e-mail could for instance be unintentionally sent straight to the user sending the fan mail, possibly revealing the author's private e-mail address):

```
    ' Create the message
    Dim message As MailMessage = New MailMessage()
    message.To = myAuthor.Email
    message.Body = "Message sent on behalf of " & from & ":" & vbCrLf & _
                   & vbCrLf & body
    message.From = "administrator@pretendCompany.com"
    message.Subject = "Fan mail from " & User.Identity.Name

    ' Send the message
    SmtpMail.Send(message)
    End Sub
  End Class
End Namespace
```

And that's all there is to sending e-mail from this service – once again the .NET classes do a great job of simplifying what might otherwise be an arduous and thankless task!

The "AuthorFanMail" Web Application

Now we've built the infrastructure, we can start on producing a web client for the Web Service. Add a new VB.NET ASP.NET Web Application project to the **Services** solution (keeping them together facilitates debugging), specifying the location `http://localhost/BM/AuthorFanMail/`. The project needs references to `AuthenticateService.asmx` (renamed to `Authenticate`) and `FanMail.asmx` (as `FanMail`), and will consist of the following four Web Forms:

❑   `Default.aspx` – the starting point for the application. For now this provides a link to the login form and can also display a status message if required (such as "login failed" if the user is returned here after an unsuccessful login attempt). Using a file with this name can streamline the user experience, and IIS will by default navigate to a file called `Default.aspx` if the directory containing this file is requested, so that users can browse to http://<server>/BM/AuthorFanMail/ rather than needing to enter http://<server>/BM/AuthorFanMail/Mail_us.aspx, or whatever. We could configure this for other filenames if we wanted, but we'll just use the default behavior for now.

❑   `Login.aspx` – a form for logging into the system using `AuthenticateService`. This form will be accessed via SSL, as this is where the client will enter a username and password, which should be transferred securely. Unsuccessful logins return the user to `Default.aspx`; successful logins to the main form.

❑   `MainForm.aspx` – displays a list of books and authors, allowing the user to click on an author name to send them mail. This form also contains a button for logging out.

❑   `MailTo.aspx` – contains a textbox for entering the body of the message to send to the selected author, and a textbox for entering a return address. The user can also hit Cancel at this stage, returning them to `MainForm.aspx`.

We can visualize the structure graphically like so:

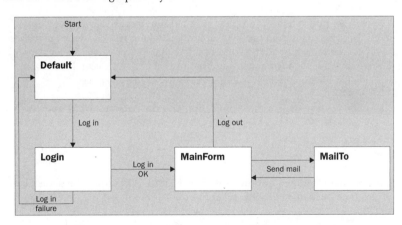

Before we start looking at these forms in detail though, there is one more issue that we need to address.

Applications, Sessions, and "Global.asax"

This section concerns the events that occur when a user browses to your web application, what happens to subsequent web requests from this user, and what happens when other users connect at the same time. To summarize:

- ❑ **Applications** – loaded by the server when the first user connects, and unloaded at some point after this (when no users have connected for a certain period of time, through intervention by the administrator, or when the web server restarts). It is possible to store 'global' data at the application level.

- ❑ **Sessions** – instantiated for each user to provide a user-specific data store. They may also be disabled for simpler web applications. By default, sessions will time out if user activity ceases for 20 minutes.

- ❑ Global.asax – a file containing specific processing instructions for events such as "Application Loading" or "Session Ending".

To streamline our application, we could store our Web Service proxy references at the Application level, so that only one reference (or perhaps a small pool of references) per service is required, easing server load. However, this raises concurrency issues when multiple users access the services simultaneously. Since each user needs to configure user information for the proxy manually (for authentication purposes), we would have to 'lock' the Application storage (see below) when it is used, effectively blocking requests from other users for significant periods of time. Instead, then, we should take the simpler route, where each user stores references to the Web Services at the Session level. This way, each web page in the application will use a given set of proxies for a given user, rather than having to make new connection each time an exchange of data is required. This is also a very scalable solution, as ASP.NET has built in support for "web farms", where several web servers can host the same web application. It is possible for session data storage to be centralized so that users can access Session data from any web server in a farm. We discuss this a little more in the next section.

We can also solve our user host validation problem with Session storage. The problem is that since every request to our Web Services comes from the web application, tokens will *always* be authorized, as every Web Service request will use the same host address (the address of the server where the web application is located). To get round this, we can store the login token and user host address in Session-level storage, and perform our own simple validation on it before forwarding requests to our Web Services.

Use the following code to store data at the Application and the Session level respectively:

```
Application("key") = value
Session("key") = value
```

Anything we place in these storage locations is stored as an Object type with an associated key string, and we need to cast data back to its original form in order to use it:

```
value = CType(Application("key"), valueType)
value = CType(Session("key"), valueType)
```

Alternatively, if we are storing simple strings we could use:

```
value = Application("key").ToString()
value = Session("key").ToString()
```

We won't use this technique here, but it is worth noting that access to Application state can be restricted. We can **lock** the data held in Application-level storage, meaning that no users other than the one using the current session can access it, but we must remember to **unlock** it when we are finished. This requires the simple syntax:

```
Application.Lock()
```

and:

```
Application.UnLock()
```

The problem here is that if we are likely to have many users, none of the others will be able to access the Application state while it's locked, possibly leading to delays and even errors. Locking in this way can only be achieved on *all* application state, not on an item-by-item basis, which would compound the problem if we were to store our Web Service references at this level, as locking state while one is used would prevent access to all of them. We could improve things slightly by implementing our own locking system code in the Global class defined in global.asax.vb. We could improve things further by accessing Web Services asynchronously, where instead of waiting for a response and tying up a thread, we release the thread querying the Web Service until an event is raised to indicate that the web method has returned a result. However, the code to do this is a bit more complex, and wouldn't necessarily offer a better solution than simply storing data in Session state, as we shall do in this application.

When a Session loads, our web application has to store references to the two Web Service proxies we are using, and dispose of them when it unloads. This requires the following modifications to Global.asax.vb for the AuthorFanMail project (you should find the method names in this file fairly self explanatory):

```
Imports System
Imports System.Collections
Imports System.ComponentModel
Imports System.Web
Imports System.Web.SessionState
Imports AuthorFanMail.Authenticate
Imports AuthorFanMail.FanMail

Namespace AuthorFanMail

   Public Class Global
      Inherits System.Web.HttpApplication

      Public Sub New()
        MyBase.New()

        InitializeComponent()
      End Sub

      ...
```

```
Protected Sub Session_Start(ByVal sender As System.Object, _
                       ByVal e As System.EventArgs)

    Session("authenticateService") = _
      New Authenticate.AuthenticateService()
    Session("fanMailService") = _
      New FanMail.FanMail()
End Sub

...

Protected Sub Session_End(ByVal sender As System.Object, _
                       ByVal e As EventArgs)

    Dim authenticateService  As Authenticate.AuthenticateService = _
                         CType(Session("authenticateService"), _
                           Authenticate.AuthenticateService)
    authenticateService.Dispose()
    Dim fanMailService As FanMail.FanMail = _
      CType(Session("fanMailService"), FanMail.FanMail)
    fanMailService.Dispose()
End Sub

...

End Class
End Namespace
```

The two references are stored in `Session("authenticateService")` and `Session("fanMailService")` ready for use when required.

In addition, we will use Application-level storage for the following simple strings:

```
Protected Sub Application_Start(ByVal sender As System.Object, _
                         ByVal e As System.EventArgs)

    Application("webServerName") = "karlixp"
    Application("authenticationServerName") = "karlixp"
End sub
```

These variables, `webServerName` and `authenticationServerName`, need to be set to the computer names you're using, as they will be used by many of our forms when we redirect users to other files or when they need a server to authenticate users. Storing this information here means that if we install the application on a different web server we only have to change the details here. We'll only ever read this information, and never write to it, so we can use it safely from all our Web Forms without having to worry about concurrency issues.

Web Farms

As mentioned in the last section, it is possible to configure ASP.NET web applications to store session state in a centralized location, so that sessions can be made available from multiple web servers in a web farm. We even have a choice of where this information is to be stored:

- ❏ In a SQL Server database

- ❏ In a Windows Service application

To configure an application to use one of these stores rather than the default "in process" storage, we need to modify the following code in web.config:

```
<!-- SESSION STATE SETTINGS
     By default ASP.NET uses cookies_to identify which requests belong
     to a particular session. If cookies are not available, a session
     can be tracked by adding a session identifier to the URL. To
     disable cookies, set sessionState cookieless="true".
-->
<sessionState mode="InProc"
        stateConnectionString="tcpip=127.0.0.1:42424"
        sqlConnectionString="data source=127.0.0.1;user id=sa;password="
        cookieless="false"
        timeout="20"
/>
```

The mode attribute of the <sessionState> element can be set to Off (no sessions will be used), InProc (the default, where sessions are stored in process), StateServer (to use a Windows Service), or SQLServer (to use SQL Server). For Windows Service or SQL Server storage we may need to edit the stateConnectionString and sqlConnectionString values respectively, changing the IP address to that of the server to use for storage.

Both of these centralized storage methods also require a little extra configuration. To use the Windows Service correctly, we need to ensure that the relevant service, **ASP.NET State**, is started on the storage machine. The screenshot overleaf shows the dialog for this service with the default settings. It is accessed through the **Services** MMC snap-in:

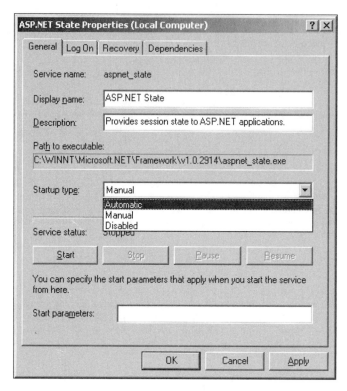

Unless you've already changed it, this service will probably be set to Manual startup, so set it to Automatic to enable this storage method by default.

In addition, some firewall configuration may be necessary for certain Enterprise setups, as TCP port 42424 needs to be open between the web server and the storage server running the service.

To configure SQL Server Session state storage (and I shall resist the temptation to refer to this as SSSSS!), we first need to configure SQL Server. ASP.NET ships with a SQL script to achieve this, found in the `<Windows>\Microsoft.NET\Framework\<version>\` directory under the filename `InstallSqlState.sql`. We can run this by any of the usual ways for script execution, remembering that we need the appropriate SQL Server administration privileges first.

"Default.aspx"

The first form we'll look at is the simplest of the four in the project: the starting point and status report form `Default.aspx`. The form layout consists of three elements laid out as shown opposite:

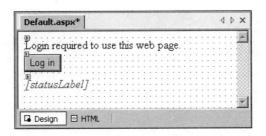

At the top and bottom are `Label` controls, and in the middle is a `Button` control. The top text is static, so we don't need to worry about assigning an ID, but the label at the bottom will show dynamic messages, so we'll call it `statusLabel` and adjust its font properties to red and italic so it stands out. The button, `loginButton`, also needs a click handler.

Now double-click on the **Log in** button, and add following code for the click handler and the `Page_Load` event. Note also that the class has been called `_Default` to avoid confusion with any similarly named keywords:

```
Namespace AuthorFanMail

  Public Class _Default
    Inherits System.Web.UI.Page

    Protected WithEvents loginButton As System.Web.UI.WebControls.Button
    Protected WithEvents statusLabel As System.Web.UI.WebControls.Label
    protected WithEvents Label1 as System.Web.UI.WebControls.Label

    Private Sub Page_Load(ByVal sender as System.Object, _
                ByVal e As System.EventArgs) Handles MyBase.Load

      statusLabel.Text = Request.Params("loginStatus")
    End Sub

    ...

    Private Sub loginButton_Click(ByVal sender as System.Object, _
                     ByVal e As System.EventArgs) _
                     Handles loginButton.Click

      Response.Redirect("https://" _
                 & Application("webServerName").ToString() _
                 & "/BM/AuthorFanMail/Login.aspx")
    End Sub
  End Class
End Namespace
```

The code in `Page_Load` assigns text to the status label based on the contents of the `loginStatus` querystring parameter contained in the URL used to access this file. Hence, if we used the URL below:

http://<server>/BM/AuthorFanMail/Default.aspx?loginStatus=OK

225

then the status text would be assigned the string OK. Note that spaces can be included in strings such as this, although they are generally replaced by the escape string %20.

The button handler simply redirects the user to the Login.aspx form, using the HTTPS protocol to obtain a secure SSL connection. The URL is built from the serverName Application variable we set in Global.asax earlier.

"Login.aspx"

Next add the form that does the logging on, Login.aspx:

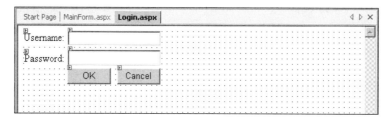

The layout here is identical to the Login.vb form we used for the Windows Forms client in the last chapter, with the dynamic elements called usernameBox, passwordBox, okButton, and cancelButton respectively. passwordBox also has its TextMode property set to Password in order to hide password input from inquisitive eyes.

The code for this form starts off with the additional Imports statements required for our AuthenticateService Web Service and the security classes it uses:

```
...
Imports System.Web.UI.HtmlControls
Imports AuthorFanMail.Authenticate
Imports System.Net
```

Next we have the member variables for our controls:

```
Namespace AuthorFanMail

  Public Class Login
    Inherits System.Web.UI.Page

    Protected WithEvents cancelButton As System.Web.UI.WebControls.Button
    Protected WithEvents okButton System.Web.UI.WebControls.Button
    Protected WithEvents passwordBox System.Web.UI.WebControls.TextBox
    Protected WithEvents usernameBox  System.Web.UI.WebControls.TextBox
    Protected WithEvents Label2 System.Web.UI.WebControls.Label
    Protected WithEvents Label1 System.Web.UI.WebControls.Label
```

This is followed by some automatically generated code, and then the code for our button click handlers. The simplest of these is for cancelButton, which merely redirects the user to Default.aspx:

```
    Private Sub cancelButton_Click(ByVal sender as System.Object, _
                        ByVal e As System.EventArgs) _
```

```
                              Handles cancelButton.Click

        Response.Redirect("http://" _
                          & Application("webServerName").ToString() _
             & "/BM/AuthorFanMail/Default.aspx?loginStatus=login cancelled.")
     End Sub
```

The handler for okButton clicks is more complicated. To start with, we get the reference to AuthenticateService:

```
        Private Sub okButton_Click(ByVal sender as System.Object, _
                             ByVal e As System.EventArgs) _
                             Handles okButton.Click

        Dim service As AuthenticateService = _
                             CType(Session("authenticateService"), _
                             Authenticate.AuthenticateService)
```

Next we need to set the security information for this proxy, in the same way we did in the last chapter:

```
        ' Create a new instance of NetworkCredential using the client
        ' credentials.
        Dim userInfo As NetworkCredential = _
          New NetworkCredential(usernameBox.Text, passwordBox.Text, _
                    Application("authenticationServerName").ToString())

        ' Add the NetworkCredential to the proxy class
        service.Credentials = userInfo
```

Next, we attempt to log in:

```
        Try

        Dim loginToken As Guid = service.Authenticate()

        ' If successful, place token and user host address in session
        ' state and redirect to main form
        Session("loginToken") = loginToken.ToString()
        Session("userHost") = Request.UserHostAddress
        Response.Redirect("http://" _
                          & Application("webServerName").ToString() _
                          & "/BM/AuthorFanMail/MainForm.aspx")
```

If we are successful, we store the information required for our Web Services at the Session level, including the host address of the current user so we can validate their requests later. Then we redirect the user to MainForm.aspx.

If there is an exception, we pass any exception details to the status display label in Default.aspx using the querystring technique described above:

```
        Catch ex As WebException
          ' If unsuccessful, return to default form with status message
          Response.Redirect("http://" _
                                & Application("webServerName").ToString() _
                    & "/BM/AuthorFanMail/Default.aspx?loginStatus=Login " _
                            & "unsuccessful. Details: " & ex.Message)
        End Try
      End Sub
```

We're now finished adding the code for the Login.aspx form.

"MainForm.aspx"

This form is the most complex in this web application, mainly because it uses data binding to display book and author data in an ASP.NET DataGrid control. This is great in the long run, as it provides a flexible display structure for our data, but can be tricky to get to grips with.

The form layout consists of a Button control called logOutButton, a (bold) Label control with a few instructions on it, and a DataGrid control called bookDataGrid. We can apply styles to the DataGrid control to produce the form layout shown here:

The main changes here are that BackColor is set to LavenderBlush (feel free to change this if you can't stand the light pink color when you see it on screen!), the font is Arial, BorderColor is Black, BorderStyle is Double, BorderWidth is 6px, CellPadding is 4, and ForeColor is Black.

However, formatting this control fully involves modifying the styles, such as HeaderStyle, used for different elements, through the properties window for the control. I do recommend you spend some time fiddling with these styles to see the effects you can achieve – not to mention the entertaining break from coding that it makes!

*Many ASP.NET controls extend this formatting system by using **templates**. Templates allow us to do all manner of interesting things when displaying data, and I recommend that you look into this subject when you have a free moment. Try a book such as Professional ASP.NET, recommended earlier in the chapter, or perhaps work through the ASP.NET Quickstart included with the .NET Framework. The results you can achieve are well worth the effort.*

Next, let's look at the code for this form. We start with the usual `Imports` and control members:

```
...
Imports System.Web.UI.HtmlControls
Imports AuthorFanMail.FanMail
Imports AuthorFanMail.Authenticate

Namespace AuthorFanMail

  ' <summary>
  ' Summary description for MainForm.
  ' </summary>

  Public Class MainForm
    Inherits System.Web.UI.Page

      Protected WithEvents bookDataGrid System.Web.UI.WebControls.DataGrid
      Protected WithEvents logOutButton System.Web.UI.WebControls.Button
      Protected WithEvents Label1 System.Web.UI.WebControls.Label
```

Next is `Page_Load`, where most of the interesting processing takes place. The first thing is to check whether a **post back** operation is in progress. When we click a button or otherwise initiate processing on a form, the server has to post back data to our forms, which is how we can maintain state and interact with the user. However, we only need to populate the `DataGrid` control once (it will then maintain state autonomously), so we only do this if a post back isn't in progress, by checking the `IsPostBack` property when the form is first loaded:

```
      Private Sub Page_Load(ByVal sender as System.Object, _
                      ByVal e As System.EventArgs) _
                      Handles MyBase.Load

          If Not IsPostBack Then
```

As long as the page is being loaded for the first time, we carry on to check to see if a user is logged in. The simplest way is to check to see if a login token has been stored in the user session:

```
          ' Check for login token
          Dim loginTokenText As String = Session("loginToken").ToString()
          If loginTokenText = "" Then
            Response.Redirect("http://" _
                          & Application("webServerName").ToString() _
                          & "/BM/AuthorFanMail/Default.aspx")
          End If
```

If a key doesn't exist, `loginTokenText` will simply be an empty string, in which case, we send the user to the default form. We need to remember this empty string checking technique when users log out later; part of logging out will be to assign a blank string to the login token.

Next we perform a little more validation, checking the client host address against that stored in the user session, as discussed earlier:

```
' Internal validation of host address
If Session("userHost").ToString() <> Request.UserHostAddress Then
  Response.Redirect("http://" _
                    & Application("webServerName").ToString() _
                    & "/BM/AuthorFanMail/Default.aspx")
End If
```

Again, a failure to validate will result in directing the user back to `Default.aspx`. If the validation succeeds, we get the data using the Web Service proxy stored in the Session:

```
' Get FanMailsevice
Application.Lock()
Dim service As FanMail.FanMail = CType(Session("fanMailService"), _
                                  FanMail.FanMail)

' Set token header
service.TokenHeaderValue = New FanMail.TokenHeader()
service.TokenHeaderValue.InnerToken = New Guid(loginTokenText)

' Get Books and Authors
Dim bookAuthorDetails() As FanMail.BookAuthorDetails = _
                              service.GetBooksAndAuthorNames()
Application.UnLock()
```

At this point, we have the data we wish to display in `bookAuthorDetails`. However, this type of data cannot be bound to the `DataGrid`; instead we need to reformat it as a `DataTable`. This involves instantiating a `DataTable`, assigning some columns, and adding a row for each entry – in our case, each book. This code also formats each author name as a hyperlink built from the URL for `MailTo.aspx` with the author ID and name stored in the querystring according to the convention described earlier:

```
' Transfer data into DataTable
Dim data As DataTable = New DataTable()
Dim newRow As DataRow
data.Columns.Add(New DataColumn("Book Title", GetType(String)))
data.Columns.Add(New DataColumn("Authors", GetType(String)))
Dim book As BookAuthorDetails
For Each book In bookAuthorDetails
  newRow = data.NewRow()
  newRow(0) = book.Name
  Dim author As AuthorDetailsNoEMail
  For Each author In book.Authors
    newRow(1) += "<A href='MailTo.aspx?AuthorId=" _
              & author.Id.ToString() & "&AuthorName=" _
              & author.Name + "'>" & author.Name & "</A><BR/>"
  Next
  data.Rows.Add(newRow)
Next
```

Finally, we bind the `DataGrid` to the `DataTable`:

```
        ' Display data
        bookDataGrid.DataSource = New DataView(data)
        bookDataGrid.DataBind()

    End If
End Sub
```

`MainForm.aspx` also contains an event handler for `logOutButton`. This carries out the now familiar validation of the host address:

```
Private Sub logOutButton_Click(ByVal sender as System.Object, _
                               ByVal e As System.EventArgs) _
                               Handles logOutButton.Click

    ' Internal validation of host address
    If (Session("userHost").ToString() <> Request.UserHostAddress)Then
      Response.Redirect("http://" _
                        & Application("webServerName").ToString() _
                        & "/BM/AuthorFanMail/Default.aspx")
    End If
```

This is followed by code to obtain the proxy for `AuthenticateService` and then use it to log out, as well as clearing any Session storage:

```
    ' Get service
    Application.Lock()
    Dim service As Authenticate.AuthenticateService = _
                            CType(Session("authenticateService"), _
                            Authenticate.AuthenticateService)

    ' Set token header
    service.TokenHeaderValue = New Authenticate.TokenHeader()
    service.TokenHeaderValue.InnerToken = _
                            New Guid(Session("loginToken").ToString())

    ' Log out
    Session("userHost") = ""
    Session("loginToken") = ""
    service.Logout()
    Application.UnLock()

    ' Redirect user
    Response.Redirect("http://horatio/BM/AuthorFanMail/Default.aspx")
  End Sub
End Class
```

We'll see how all this looks shortly, but first there's one more form in the application to cover.

"MailTo.aspx"

MailTo.aspx simply accepts text from the user and uses the FanMail Web Service to e-mail it to the selected author. The form has a couple of static labels, a third label called nameLabel to display the selected author name, a textbox called emailBox for the user to enter their e-mail address, a multiline textbox called messageBox for the message text, and two Button controls, sendButton and cancelButton:

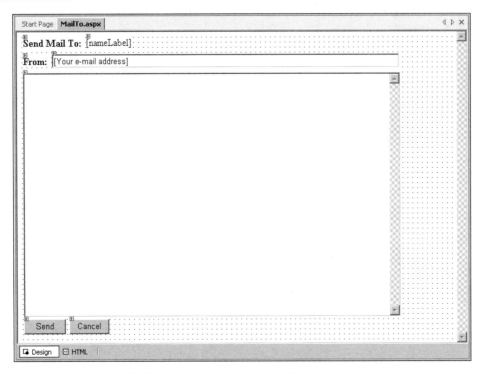

Not much new here, so we'll plough straight into the code changes:

```
...
Imports System.Web.UI.HtmlControls
Imports AuthorFanMail.FanMail

Namespace AuthorFanMail

    ' <summary>
    ' Summary description for MailTo.
    ' </summary>
    Public Class MailTo
        Inherits System.Web.UI.Page

        Private authorId As Integer
        Private authorName As String
        Protected WithEvents Label1 System.Web.UI.WebControls.Label
        Protected WithEvents nameLabel  System.Web.UI.WebControls.Label
        Protected WithEvents cancelButton  System.Web.UI.WebControls.Button
```

```
Protected WithEvents sendButton System.Web.UI.WebControls.Button
Protected WithEvents messageBox System.Web.UI.WebControls.TextBox
Protected WithEvents Label3 System.Web.UI.WebControls.Label
Protected WithEvents emailBox System.Web.UI.WebControls.TextBox
```

The two private member variables, authorId and authorName, are populated in Page_Load from Session state, after user login checks quite like those in MainForm.aspx:

```
Private Sub Page_Load(ByVal sender as System.Object, _
                      ByVal e As System.EventArgs) _
                      Handles MyBase.Load
```

```
    If Not IsPostBack Then

        ' Check for login token
        Dim loginTokenText As String = Session("loginToken").ToString()
        If loginTokenText = "" Then
          Response.Redirect("http://" _
                          & Application("webServerName").ToString() _
                          & "/BM/AuthorFanMail/Default.aspx")

        End If
        ' Internal validation of host address
        If (Session("userHost").ToString() <> Request.UserHostAddress)Then

          Response.Redirect("http://" _
                          & Application("webServerName").ToString() _
                          & "/BM/AuthorFanMail/Default.aspx")
        End If

        ' Check for author ID
        Dim authorIdText As String = Request.Params("authorId")
        If authorIdText = "" Then
          Response.Redirect("http://" _
                      & Application("webServerName").ToString() _
                      & "/BM/AuthorFanMail/MainForm.aspx?loginToken=" _
                      & loginTokenText)
        End If
        authorId = Convert.ToInt32(authorIdText)
        Session("authorId") = authorIdText

        ' Check for author name
        Dim authorNameText As String = Request.Params("authorName")
        If authorNameText = "" Then

          Response.Redirect("http://" _
                      & Application("webServerName").ToString() _
                      & "/BM/AuthorFanMail/MainForm.aspx?loginToken=" _
                      & loginTokenText)
        End If
        authorName = authorNameText
        Session("authorName") = authorNameText
        nameLabel.Text = authorName
```

The above code is only executed the very first time a user accesses the page, but we need to add some code to cater for post backs to ensure that `authorId` and `authorName` are reconstituted:

```
    Else
        authorId = Convert.ToInt32(Session("authorId").ToString())
        authorName = Session("authorName").ToString()
    End If
End Sub
```

The reason for this is that any page state we add won't persist without a little extra work on our part. This is the simplest way to do it in this case.

The handler for clicks on the `cancelButton` button is short and sweet:

```
Private Sub cancelButton_Click(ByVal sender as System.Object, _
                     ByVal e As System.EventArgs) _
                     Handles cancelButton.Click

    Response.Redirect("http://" _
                     & Application("webServerName").ToString() _
                     & "/BM/AuthorFanMail/MainForm.aspx")
End Sub
```

Finally, we have the handler for `sendButton`, which validates the host address of the user, gets the `FanMail` proxy, and sends the mail. These are tasks we've already done elsewhere in the application, and this code doesn't contain anything new:

```
Private Sub sendButton_Click(ByVal sender as System.Object, _
                     ByVal e As System.EventArgs) _
                     Handles sendButton.Click

    ' Internal validation of host address
    If (Session("userHost").ToString() <> Request.UserHostAddress) Then
        Response.Redirect("http://" _
                     & Application("webServerName").ToString() _
                     & "/BM/AuthorFanMail/Default.aspx")
    End If

    ' Initialize FanMailsevice
    Application.Lock()
    Dim service As FanMail.FanMail = CType(Session("fanMailService"), _
                                  FanMail.FanMail)

    ' Set token header
    service.TokenHeaderValue = New FanMail.TokenHeader()
    service.TokenHeaderValue.InnerToken = _
                          New Guid(Session("loginToken").ToString())

    ' Send mail
    service.SendMailToAuthor(authorId, messageBox.Text, emailBox.Text)
    Application.UnLock()
```

```
        ' Return to MainForm
        Response.Redirect("http://" _
                          & Application("webServerName").ToString() _
                          & "/BM/AuthorFanMail/MainForm.aspx")
    End Sub
  End Class
End Namespace
```

And now, we are finally ready to test the application!

The Application in Action

The best way to test the web application is to add yourself to the Authors table in the database, using an e-mail address that you can check quickly, and add yourself as the author for some of the books in the table.

When you first browse to the application, you should see the following:

Clicking the Log in button takes us to the login page (prompting you to allow a secure connection if you have your browser configured that way), where we can enter details for the user Ivor, as created in the last chapter:

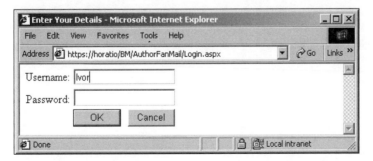

Clicking on OK will prompt you to leave the secure connection, and take you to the author selection page:

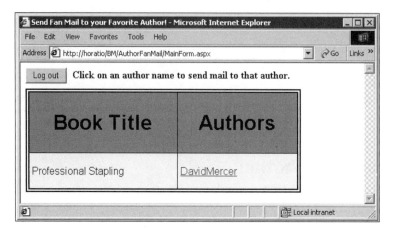

When you select an author to mail from this `DataGrid`, you will be redirected to the `MailTo.aspx` page:

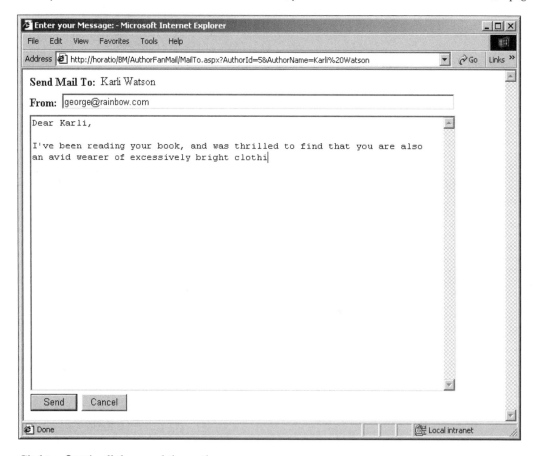

Clicking **Send** will then send the mail.

The application is a little bare as it stands because I've concentrated on the functional core that underpins any system, and it wouldn't be difficult to add more sophisticated features and controls to create a more usable and attractive interface.

Pagination

Before moving on, let's quickly consider what happens in this application when we have a large number of items to display in a `DataGrid` control. As things stand now, all items will be displayed on the one page. This may or may not be a problem, depending on whether you are happy with users scrolling through pages of data to get to the section they are interested in.

However, the `DataGrid` control has been designed with this in mind. In fact, splitting the items across several pages is quite easy. If you look at the properties of the `DataGrid` control you will see three called `AllowCustomPaging`, `AllowPaging`, and `PageSize`. The first of these can be set to `true` to give us complete control over the pagination behavior, while the second and third allow us to quickly configure the control using built-in functionality.

Set the `AllowPaging` property to **True** and the display of the `DataGrid` will change immediately to the following:

Column0	Column1	Column2
abc	abc	abc
abc	abc	abc
abc	abc	abc
abc	abc	abc
abc	abc	abc
abc	abc	abc
abc	abc	abc
abc	abc	abc
abc	abc	abc
abc	abc	abc
< ≥		

Ten rows are shown (or as many as the value of `PageSize` is set to, but ten is fine here), and navigation links (angle brackets) are added to the bottom of the control.

This sets up the UI, leaving us with the task of implementing a handler for the `PageIndexChanged` event, which is raised when one of the angle brackets is clicked on. Unfortunately, since ASP .NET works in a 'stateless' manner, we don't have access to our original data, so we need to re-run our DB query and repopulate the `DataGrid` control. However, the code is pretty simple. With `MainForm.aspx` open in Design view, double-click on the `DataGrid`, and add this code:

```
Private void bookDataGrid_PageIndexChanged(ByVal source As System.Object, _
    ByVal e As System.Web.UI.WebControls.DataGridPageChangedEventArgs) _
                        Handles bookDataGrid.PageIndexChanged

  ' Get FanMailsevice
  Dim service As FanMail.FanMail = CType(Session("fanMailService"), _
                        FanMail.FanMail)
```

```
' Set token header
Dim loginTokenText As String = Session("loginToken").ToString()
service.TokenHeaderValue = New FanMail.TokenHeader()
service.TokenHeaderValue.InnerToken = New Guid(loginTokenText)

' Get Books and Authors
Dim bookAuthorDetails() As FanMail.BookAuthorDetails = _
                                 service.GetBooksAndAuthorNames()

' Transfer data into DataTable
Dim data As DataTable = new DataTable()
Dim newRow As DataRow
data.Columns.Add(new DataColumn("Book Title", GetType(String)))
data.Columns.Add(new DataColumn("Authors", GetType(String)))
Dim book As BookAuthorDetails
For Each book In bookAuthorDetails
  newRow = data.NewRow()
  newRow(0) = book.Name
  Dim author As AuthorDetailsNoEMail
  For Each author In book.Authors

    newRow(1) += "<A href='MailTo.aspx?AuthorId=" _
               & author.Id.ToString() & "&AuthorName=" _
               & author.Name + "'>" & author.Name _
               & "</A><BR/>"
  Next
  data.Rows.Add(newRow)
Next

' Display data
bookDataGrid.DataSource = new DataView(data)
bookDataGrid.CurrentPageIndex = e.NewPageIndex
bookDataGrid.DataBind()
End Sub
```

Most of this is identical to the code in Page_Load, so it could conceivably be placed in a separate method, but I've left it here to illustrate the steps that need to be performed. As before, we get the data using the FanMail web service, format it for the table, and bind it. The only difference here (apart from not checking if a user is logged in – unnecessary if this has already been performed in Page_Load) is the following line:

```
bookDataGrid.CurrentPageIndex = e.NewPageIndex
```

This simply gets the page to display from the event arguments and sets the required property in the DataGrid control.

This system works well enough when we only have a few pages of items, but can become a little cumbersome if we have many more. This is because all the data is obtained and formatted every time, even though only small amounts are displayed at one time. We can get round this by reworking the FanMail Web Service to return smaller chunks of data per call, or by persisting the data in some other way (perhaps in Session or Application state). We might also consider the more complicated custom pagination option, although this makes more work for us.

Server Control Design

Applications such as the one presented in this chapter are very powerful and quick to produce using the tools Visual Studio .NET gives us. However, if we're likely to be doing a lot of tasks like this, we would really benefit from a more modular system where code can easily be reused. ASP.NET goes a long way to achieving this, letting us create our own server controls that we can then reuse in other applications, much like creating custom Windows Form controls.

For example, we could package up the author selection `DataGrid` as a custom control, that could perhaps be initialized with a reference to the `FanMail` Web Service proxy and a token to use for validation. We'd need to move much of the code currently in the `Page_Load` event of the `MainForm.aspx` page of our application and place it within the custom control that wraps up this functionality, but that isn't difficult, and is the only real change we'd need.

We could also package the authentication side of things as a server control, although in most situations that one might be best left as a form in its own right.

Summary

In this chapter, we have investigated how to make the functionality of applications situated on a local area network available to web browsers over the Internet. The Web Services we developed in the previous chapter already allow users access to the application in this way, but they require a client program to be specially written for each platform, and this may not be appropriate or practical for all our potential users.

Therefore, we made use of ASP.NET to dynamically create web pages – Web Forms – that expose our application's functionality to anyone with access to a standard HTML web browser. I hope that this chapter has succeeded in my intention of demonstrating the power of ASP.NET to very rapidly produce powerful, interactive sites based on live data.

We have seen how ASP.NET uses an event-driven model similar to that of standard Windows Forms applications. Many of the controls that can be placed on a page have associated events that determine their behavior when they are clicked on, initialized, and so forth. In particular, the `PageLoad` event for a page is where the lion's share of the page's processing is often contained. This event is fired when the page is accessed by the user, and is thus the ideal place for code that sets up and populates our controls.

One new concept in ASP.NET is that of server controls, which are run at the server to generate an HTML representation of their output that can then be viewed in just about any browser on just about any platform – so long as it is capable of rendering standard HTML mark-up. One such server control that we looked at is the `DataGrid` control, which provides a very handy device that we can bind to a data source such that it is populated automatically by the ASP.NET runtime.

In the next chapter, we will extend this example to support mobile browsers that use WAP, iMode, or similar, by the use of Microsoft's Mobile Internet Toolkit.

.NET Enterprise Development in VB .NET

8

Mobile Controls

Part of the justification for using Web Services in Chapter 6 was their ability to cater for disparate clients, but so far this book has only really looked at two varieties: web clients and Windows Forms clients. In this chapter, we look at how to use the mobile controls of ASP.NET to provide content to users with mobile devices. This category of devices includes the following:

❑   Wireless Application Protocol (WAP)-enabled devices (used across Europe and in some places in the US)

❑   i-Mode devices (very popular in Japan, now beginning to gain popularity in the rest of the world)

❑   HTML Personal Digital Assistant (PDA) devices (used globally)

The first two of these require significantly different markup from desktop HTML browsers, but you might be wondering at this stage why we need to look at PDA devices when their browsers are quite similar to those of PCs. We'll discuss this point, and others, during our tour of the wireless world.

One extremely effective way of providing content to all of the above is to create mobile Web Forms using the mobile controls offered by Microsoft's Mobile Internet Toolkit (MMIT). In many ways this is similar to creating standard Web Forms applications using ASP.NET, but has several significant differences that we look at in this chapter.

Once we have looked at the "Whys", we'll concentrate on the "Hows", and build a mobile web application that provides access to the BookManager data we've been using throughout the book.

The Wireless Internet

The Wireless Internet has been with us for a while now, and although it hasn't quite conquered the world with the rapidity some predicted, it remains an exciting concept with much to offer. The ability to access content from wherever our users happen to be may not have yet made land-based PC Internet connections obsolete, but it does create interesting possibilities, some of which, as we will see shortly, are not immediately obvious.

We might ask ourselves though why mobile Internet access hasn't taken off to the extent that people predicted. Well, much of this is due to an almost global misunderstanding as to what is possible. If you're expecting the same experience you can get on your PC, then you're going to be disappointed. If, on the other hand, you approach mobile Internet access from a fresh perspective, prepare yourself for a wild ride!

Let's forget for a moment about all of the enabling wireless technologies and concentrate on mobile devices themselves. They all have one thing in common, be they WAP devices, i-Mode devices, or whatever: they must be small in order to be portable. It follows that:

- ❑ They have a small display area.

- ❑ They have limited processing capabilities because there is less space available for electronics.

- ❑ User interactivity is hence potentially awkward – there are few input methods that are truly available on all devices. Generally, there's no mouse or keyboard, so users must use a combination of numeric keypad and special action buttons. Some, but not all, have a touch screen, and a select few come with basic voice recognition and activation.

Compared to PCs, the display capabilities are likely to be very limited. Most current devices use monochrome displays in order to keep costs and size down, and also to conserve battery power.

Many of the devices we're considering could be capable of accessing the Internet via a cable or infrared link connected to a PC, but we're more interested in their wireless capabilities, so we must consider these issues:

- ❑ Wireless connections currently have less bandwidth than hardwired connections, so data cannot be transferred to mobile browsers as quickly as to desktop browsers

- ❑ Wireless connections are environment-dependent (driving through a tunnel, for example, is likely to interrupt communications)

It can be argued that the bandwidth problem is a temporary one. New advances such as the much-touted third generation (3G) networks are starting to roll out. However, this is proving to be a slow and expensive process and for now it seems we're stuck with data transfer rates of around 9600 bits/second for most practical situations. In addition, most devices currently have to connect each time data transfer is required, as they have no persistent connection to the Internet. Packet networks (such as GPRS, occasionally referred to as 2.5G) are starting to appear though, which support "always on" connections. Whatever happens in the future, though, I would guess that wireless connections will always lag behind land-lines in terms of bandwidth.

If you are a follower of current wireless developments you may have noticed that I've made no mention of Bluetooth or Wi-Fi (another name for the IEEE 802.11b standard). This is because this technology is really meant for LAN type connections, and connecting a mobile device to a PC via Bluetooth is more akin to a wire between the two devices than a connection over a full wireless network as provided by mobile phone operators.

The combination of the above limitations makes standard HTML markup unsuitable, because:

❑ Mobile devices will have difficulty displaying full-blown HTML pages on their small screens with their limited display capabilities

❑ Interactive or multimedia content may not work, and would certainly slow things down over low bandwidth

❑ Using user interactivity on a web site (textboxes, buttons, etc.) that is quite acceptable for desktop browsers may make sites unusable on mobile devices because user input can be so awkward

For these reasons, WAP and i-Mode protocols both use different markup languages, the XML-based Wireless Markup Language (WML) in the case of WAP, and a variant of HTML in the case of i-Mode. These languages are tailored specifically to the devices in question, and offer capabilities such as assigning shortcut buttons from the numeric keypad to activate hyperlinks and so on. Web sites targeted at PDAs are generally simplified versions of full HTML pages.

There is an additional problem for designers of mobile-enabled internet content. Not only do we have these three new markup languages in use (in fact there are more, but these are the major players), but different devices interpret this markup in different ways. This is a similar situation to that faced by web designers when the Web first became "hip". Different browsers would render the same HTML code differently, making it hard to create consistent web sites for every user (this situation still exists today, but has improved significantly in recent years). To support WAP, however, sites often require radical revision in order to work on as many mobile browsers as possible.

The question immediately arises: how do we cope with the diversity of devices out there? Well, we have several options. Perhaps the simplest is to create different files for different browsers. However, this is also the solution that requires the most maintenance – as a minor change could quite likely require modifications to all of these files. In addition, some sort of device detection and redirection is needed so that users aren't required to remember specific URLs for particular devices. This technique can be streamlined slightly if we generate content automatically using technology such as XSLT, or hard-coding different markup into complex ASP files, but this latter technique is prone to error, and far from ideal.

The approach at the opposite end of the spectrum is to create such simple content that it can be consumed by multiple devices, using perhaps just two or three versions of each page to cater for WAP devices, HTML devices, and so on. The disadvantage here is that we lose a lot in terms of usability and interactivity, as we can't make use of more powerful features that some devices support.

The 'middle way' is to trust a third party to do the hard work for us. This is where the Mobile Internet Toolkit comes in. The Adaptive User Interfaces team at Microsoft has, in my opinion, done a tremendous job identifying differences in devices and simplifying the task of targeting a wide array of clients. By abstracting the development process and providing tools similar to those available in ASP.NET pages that target desktop browsers (indeed, the mobile pages are a part of the ASP.NET framework), our life becomes much simpler. In fact, we can get away with knowing little (or nothing) about device-specific syntax and yet still deliver compelling content.

The Mobile Internet Toolkit

At the time of writing, the Mobile Internet Toolkit is available as a separate download from Microsoft's MSDN web site. The MMIT can be found at http://msdn.microsoft.com/downloads/ by choosing Software Development Kits | Microsoft Mobile Internet Toolkit | MMIT Version 1.0 (it is a 4.11Mb download).

On installation, the MMIT integrates itself into Visual Studio .NET, making it very easy to create mobile web applications from the IDE as we see shortly. Before going any further, though, it's a good idea to install some mobile browser SDKs that let our PC simulate a mobile device for viewing pages. Directions for Microsoft browsers can be found at http://localhost/MobileQuickStart?url=doc/HowToView.aspx. This brings up the mobile Quickstart help application that was installed with the MMIT, and covers the following:

❑ Pocket PC – part of the Embedded Devices Toolkit, which in total weighs in at an enormous 300Mb download. However, this is very useful if you don't have access to an actual Pocket PC device. Make sure you install the JScript patch referred to in the quickstart guide, or else you won't be able to use it to view MMIT content.

❑ Microsoft Mobile Explorer (MME) – particularly useful due to its integration with Visual Studio .NET (you can set it up as the default browser for your MMIT projects), and is a much more reasonable 3Mb download.

The above simulators are fine as a starting point, but most mobile Internet users aren't likely to be using either of these browsers. The Nokia and Openwave browsers are currently the most popular, so we really ought to test our code out using these.

Both Openwave and Nokia have their own freely downloadable toolkits for testing. You first need to register on their respective developer sites (http://developer.openwave.com/ and http://forum.nokia.com/). The downloads are then around 20Mb each. In both cases there is some confusion as to exactly how these simulators work, that is, it is not clear whether the code used by the simulators is identical to the code embedded in real devices. However, from experience I can say that they seem to be very accurate simulations. Of course, there is no substitute for trying out your code on real devices to avoid unpleasant surprises!

I'll use all of these tools throughout this chapter, although it makes little sense to show every example on every browser, which would result in a chapter consisting mainly of screenshots.

> *One problem when developing mobile web sites is the lack of any useful i-Mode simulators. I've tried all the ones I can find on the Internet, including some Japanese language ones, and they all suffer from either being almost unusable or not giving a very accurate simulation (many just display standard HTML, which isn't really what we need).*

The beauty of the MMIT, as we will see shortly, is that it will generate markup depending on the browsing device used. If a WAP device navigates to our page, then it will automatically receive WML content. If an HTML browser is used, then it will be sent HTML content, and so on. We can even customize this behavior to generate any content we require for given browsers, but this is an advanced topic beyond the scope of this book.

Mobile Web Projects

Once everything is installed, you'll find a new project type option in Visual Studio .NET:

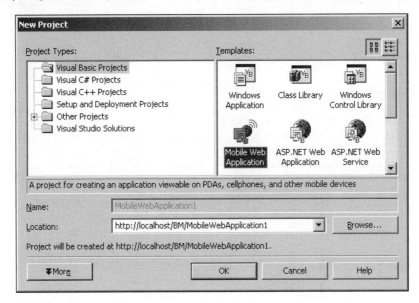

Select the default project as shown above and a project will be created consisting of pretty much the same default files as a regular ASP.NET Web Application project (mobile web applications are really ASP.NET applications with a few extra features).

The automatically generated first form, MobileWebForm1.áspx, looks a bit different from a standard Web Form:

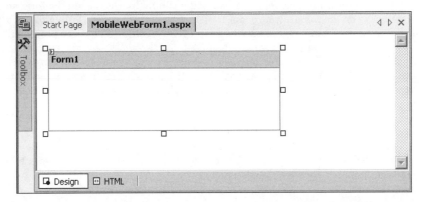

Designing the form layout requires a similar procedure to standard ASP.NET applications, however. We add controls from the toolbox, and add code to a .aspx.vb code-behind file associated with the form's .aspx page.

There is one crucial difference when designing mobile Web Form applications. A single .aspx file may contain several forms like the one shown above – we aren't limited to a single form as with ASP.NET web applications. The reason for this is that mobile browsers tend to split content up into smaller, more manageable chunks, often just a single screen of information, or at least information that won't take too long to scroll through. In WAP terminology, each of these 'screens' of information is referred to as a **card**, and files that contain several cards are called **decks**. Rather than using this language, the MMIT sticks with forms to better fit in with existing ASP.NET syntax, but (for WAP devices at least) you can visualize cards as MMIT forms and vice-versa.

Mobile Controls Example

To keep things simple, we'll implement a mobile version of the example from the last chapter, where the user enters some text into the browser and that text is then displayed in reverse (this will enable us to investigate further what I said above – that user input on mobile devices is awkward). This time, though, we'll use two forms, one for data entry and one for the result. The layout we're after is shown below:

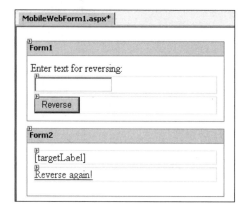

The text on the first form won't change, so we can add it simply by clicking on the form and typing, rather than having to drag a Label control out from the Toolbox. The first form also has a TextBox control called sourceBox and a Command called reverseButton with a Text property of Reverse (note that all these controls come from the System.Web.UI.MobileControls namespace). Drag a second form from the Toolbox onto the designer, and place a Label called targetLabel and a Link called backLink on it. The link also has its NavigateUrl property set to #Form1, and its Text property set to Reverse again! Note the # syntax which allows you to specify individual forms within a mobile web page, as in this example:

http://www.somewhere.com/mobilepage.aspx#MainForm.

Before moving on, let's take a quick look at the code for this layout, which can be seen by selecting the HTML tab at the bottom left corner of the designer:

```
<%@ Page Language="vb" AutoEventWireup="false" Codebehind="MobileWebForm1.aspx.vb"
Inherits="MobileWebApplication1.MobileWebForm1" %>
<%@ Register TagPrefix="mobile" Namespace="System.Web.UI.MobileControls"
Assembly="System.Web.Mobile, Version=1.0.3300.0, Culture=neutral,
PublicKeyToken=b03f5f7f11d50a3a" %>
```

```
<meta name="GENERATOR" content="Microsoft Visual Studio.NET 7.0">
<meta name="CODE_LANGUAGE" content="Visual Basic 7.0">
<meta name="vs_targetSchema" content="http://schemas.microsoft.com/Mobile/Page">
<body Xmlns:mobile="http://schemas.microsoft.com/Mobile/WebForm">
  <mobile:Form id="Form1" runat="server">
    <mobile:Label id="Label1"
           runat="server">Enter text for reversing:</mobile:Label>
    <mobile:TextBox id="sourceBox" runat="server"></mobile:TextBox>
    <mobile:Command id="reverseButton" runat="server">Reverse</mobile:Command>
  </mobile:Form>
  <mobile:Form id="Form2" runat="server">
    <mobile:Label id="targetLabel" runat="server"></mobile:Label>
    <mobile:Link id="backLink"
           runat="server"
           NavigateURL="#Form1">Reverse Again!</mobile:Link>
  </mobile:Form>
</body>
```

The code here is essentially standard ASP.NET code, mixed in with elements taken from the http://schemas.microsoft.com/Mobile/Page XML namespace. This namespace is mapped to the controls in the System.Web.UI.MobileControls .NET namespace that appears in the System.Web.Mobile assembly installed with the MMIT. This wiring up is performed by the <%@ Register ...> tag and the Xmlns attribute on the <body> element. The mobile control elements then start with the tag prefix "mobile:".

As with other ASP.NET pages, the above template file is linked to a VB code-behind file, namely MobileWebForm1.aspx.vb. We can add a handler function to the Command control in our first form by double-clicking it, which will add skeleton code to this file just as with other ASP.NET projects. Below is the code we need to add to reverse the text given in sourceBox:

```
Public Class MobileWebForm1
   Inherits System.Web.UI.MobileControls.MobilePage
   Protected WithEvents Form2 As System.Web.UI.MobileControls.Form
   Protected WithEvents reverseButton As System.Web.UI.MobileControls.Command
   Protected WithEvents sourceBox As System.Web.UI.MobileControls.TextBox
   Protected WithEvents Label1 As System.Web.UI.MobileControls.Label
   Protected WithEvents backLink As System.Web.UI.MobileControls.Link
   Protected WithEvents targetLabel As System.Web.UI.MobileControls.Label
   Protected WithEvents Form1 As System.Web.UI.MobileControls.Form

#Region " Web Form Designer Generated Code "

   'This call is required by the Web Form Designer.
   <System.Diagnostics.DebuggerStepThrough()> Private Sub InitializeComponent()

   End Sub

   Private Sub Page_Init(ByVal sender As System.Object, _
                     ByVal e As System.EventArgs) _
                     Handles MyBase.Init
      'CODEGEN: This method call is required by the Web Form Designer
      'Do not modify it using the code editor.
```

```
        InitializeComponent()
    End Sub

#End Region

    Private Sub Page_Load(ByVal sender As System.Object, _
                    ByVal e As System.EventArgs) _
                    Handles MyBase.Load
      'Put user code to initialize the page here
    End Sub

    Private Sub reverseButton_Click(ByVal sender As System.Object, _
                        ByVal e As System.EventArgs) _
                        Handles reverseButton.Click
      Dim sourceString As String = sourceBox.Text
      Dim reversedString As String = ""
      Dim index As Integer

      For index = sourceString.Length - 1 To 0 Step -1
        reversedString += sourceString.Substring(index, 1)
      Next
      targetLabel.Text = reversedString
      ActiveForm = Form2
    End Sub
End Class
```

The only new technique introduced here is use of the `ActiveForm` property:

```
        ActiveForm = Form2
```

This property determines the form that should be displayed in the client browser, so this line of code effectively changes the current form to Form2, so that we can see the reversed text appear in the second form.

It is also worth noting that controls in all the forms (and the forms themselves) are linked to member fields in the same class definition – MobileWebForm1. Code relating to each form may interact with these fields, for example the above reverseButton_Click event handler function refers to the targetLabel control directly rather than via Form2.

If you have installed the MME browser and hooked it into the Visual Studio .NET IDE, you can browse to this file very quickly (make sure you compile it first!), either by selecting the File | View in Browser menu option or by running the application:

This browser simulates a device with a touch-sensitive screen, so we can add the text and navigate by clicking on the active regions (to represent the user touching the screen with a stylus). We can also use the PC keyboard to enter text once we have selected a text entry region, although of course our real-world users won't have such a capability (design note: keep text entry to a minimum in mobile web applications!). The results are shown next:

Similarly, we can view the results in other browsers simply by navigating to the required URL. For example, here are the results we get with the Pocket PC browser emulator:

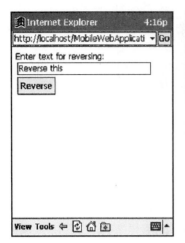

The Openwave browser renders the application like this:

While the slightly older, non-graphical Openwave browser (included as it is installed in a large number of current WAP devices) produces this output:

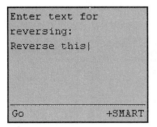
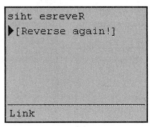

And finally the Nokia 6210 device simulator:

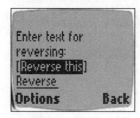

The user experience in each case is roughly the same, but notice that certain mobile controls are rendered in different ways, depending on the capabilities of the device being used. For example, the Command control renders as a button in some devices, a hyperlink in others, and will even not be rendered at all in some situations, notably in Openwave browsers where it is implemented using the built in 'Go' function of that browser. If we were to look at the code generated in each case we would see the true nature of these differences, although there is no real need to do this – it's the results that are important to us right now.

As a final, and powerful, example of the rendering differences, check out the mobile Calendar control (just start up a new mobile web project, drag the Calendar control onto the form, compile, and view). This provides a full graphical calendar interface for more powerful clients, such as Pocket PC browsers:

However, on less powerful clients, date selection is achieved quite differently, either by typing in the date manually, or by working through a series of simple selection screens:

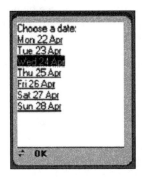

Clearly, the code generated for each case is very different, although the code in the `.aspx` and `.aspx.vb` files that are accessed *is* the same for each.

Device Capability Detection

At this point, you may be wondering exactly what is going on under the hood to achieve such flexibility. This section takes a quick look at how the MMIT determines what the client device is, how it then determines the capabilities of that device, and how we can tailor it to provide device-specific content of our own should we desire.

When the MMIT is installed, it performs some fairly major alterations to the global `machine.config` file used for ASP.NET processing. To find this file, open Windows explorer, and navigate to the `WINDOWS\Microsoft.NET\Framework\vX.X.XXXX\CONFIG` directory, replacing `vX.X.XXXX` with the number of the Framework version you have installed. Throughout this XML-format file, you will notice sections labeled by the MMIT like this:

```
<!--
BEGIN section inserted by Microsoft Mobile_Internet Toolkit installer.
Anything inserted between this and the corresponding END comment
will be lost upon uninstallation of the Mobile Internet Toolkit.
-->

    ...

<!--
END section inserted by Microsoft Mobile Internet Toolkit installer
-->
```

About a third of the way through the file, there is a section of this type that contains a vast array of device filter definitions. Basically, the HTTP_USER_AGENT HTTP header is interrogated using Regular Expressions to attempt to determine the device type, for example:

```
<filter>
  <!-- Pocket IE -->
    <case match=".*Windows CE.*">
    <filter>
      <!-- Pocket IE for Pocket PC -->
      <case match="Mozilla/.* \(compatible; MSIE 3.02; Windows CE;(?'deviceID'
\w*;)* (?'screenWidth'\d*)x(?'screenHeight'\d*)\)">
```

In the above case, the relevant header also gives additional information in the matched groups deviceID, screenWidth, and screenHeight. Other capabilities may also be extracted from other headers, such as HTTP_X_UP_DEVCAP_SCREENDEPTH for color capabilities of devices, but in most cases this won't occur. Instead, based on the known device type and painstaking testing on the part of the MMIT developers, device capabilities are assigned through values stored in the filter. Scrolling down from the code shown above, for example, yields many of these, starting with:

```
      <case match="Mozilla/.* \(compatible; MSIE 3.02; Windows CE;(?'deviceID'
\w*;)* (?'screenWidth'\d*)x(?'screenHeight'\d*)\)">
          type = "Pocket_IE"
          browser = "Pocket IE"
          platform = "WinCE"
          cookies = "true"
          backgroundsounds = "true"
          javaapplets = "false"
          javascript = "true"
          vbscript = "false"
          tables = "true"
```

One of the key capabilities defined for a device is the preferred rendering type, for example the MME filter has this assignment:

```
          preferredRenderingType_= "wml11"
```

By default this capability is set to html32 (at the start of the large area of code inserted by the MMIT, where all the default values for capabilities are set), meaning that HTML should be rendered. The above assignment to wml11 results in WML version 1.1 code being generated. i-Mode devices have this value set to chtml10.

This formula enables the mobile controls to know exactly what sort of markup may be rendered. In addition, we can make use of the device's special features in our code. There are two ways of doing this – programmatically and declaratively. The first approach involves use of the Device property in your mobile web page code, which is populated when the page is accessed. This property is an instance of the System.Web.Mobile.MobileCapabilities class, which has useful properties such as IsColor, PreferredRenderingType, SupportsBold, and more.

For example, we could add some code to the Page_Load event handler for our page to set the ImageUrl property of the Image1 image for a control according to the capabilities of the device:

```
Private Sub Page_Load(ByVal sender As System.Object, _
                      ByVal e As System.EventArgs) _
                      Handles MyBase.Load
   If Device.PreferredRenderingType = "wml11" Then
      Image1.ImageUrl = "lizard.wbmp"
   Else
      Image1.ImageUrl = "lizard.bmp"
   End If
End Sub
```

*Wireless bitmap (WBMP) images are used by WAP devices. The format of these images is a simple
two color bitmap (to save on the data taken up by these images).*

Running this on a WML and a HTML browser gives the following results:

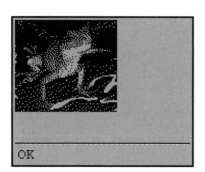

The image displayed (a picture of a friend's Chinese water dragon) will be either `lizard.wbmp` or
`lizard.bmp` depending on the browser.

The declarative method is similar, but uses the device filters provided in `web.config`:

```
<deviceFilters>
   <filter name="isHTML32" compare="PreferredRenderingType"
           argument="html32" />
   <filter name="isWML11" compare="PreferredRenderingType"
           argument="wml11" />
   <filter name="isCHTML10" compare="PreferredRenderingType"
           argument="chtml10" />
   <filter name="isGoAmerica" compare="Browser" argument="Go.Web" />
   <filter name="isMME" compare="Browser"
           argument="Microsoft Mobile Explorer" />
   <filter name="isMyPalm" compare="Browser" argument="MyPalm" />
   <filter name="isPocketIE" compare="Browser" argument="Pocket IE" />
   <filter name="isUP3x" compare="Type"
           argument="Phone.com 3.x Browser" />
```

```
    <filter name="isUP4x" compare="Type"
            argument="Phone.com 4.x Browser" />
    <filter name="isEricssonR380" compare="Type"
            argument="Ericsson R380" />
    <filter name="isNokia7110" compare="Type" argument="Nokia 7110" />
    <filter name="prefersGIF" compare="PreferredImageMIME"
            argument="image/gif" />
    <filter name="prefersWBMP" compare="PreferredImageMIME"
            argument="image/vnd.wap.wbmp" />
    <filter name="supportsColor" compare="IsColor" argument="true" />
    <filter name="supportsCookies" compare="Cookies" argument="true" />
    <filter name="supportsJavaScript" compare="Javascript"
            argument="true" />
    <filter name="supportsVoiceCalls" compare="CanInitiateVoiceCall"
            argument="true" />
  </deviceFilters>
```

Each of these default filters has a `name` attribute for us to refer to, a `compare` attribute referring to one of the capabilities defined in `machine.config`, and an `argument` attribute that specifies the text we want to match in the capability. We can add whatever filters we wish to this list, but the above default list is a pretty good starting point.

> All the filters defined by default are known as **comparison-based** filters. It is also possible to define **evaluator-delegate-based** filters, where you perform additional processing in a specified method, although I won't go into detail about these here.

We can specify controls that use these filters from within the Visual Studio .NET IDE. For example, we could get the same result as we did above by using filters, simply by editing the following two properties of an image control:

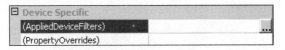

The first of these, `AppliedDeviceFilters`, allows us to choose which of the filters defined in `web.config` should be used to customize the output of the control. Clicking on the ellipsis (...) button brings up the following:

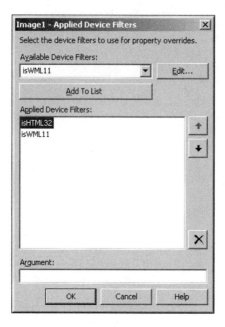

From here we can edit the filters in web.config (and create our own without manually editing this file), and select which filters to use. Here I've chosen the isHTML32 and isWML11 filters. We can override the argument attributes of these filters should we wish, but for these two, the default values are all we need right now.

Once we have configured the filters to use, we need to tell them what to do, using the PropertyOverrides property of the Image control:

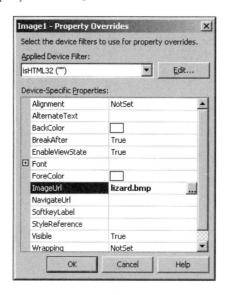

This dialog shows all the properties of the control and allows us to configure specific properties to vary depending on matched filters. In the above screenshot I've configured the `ImageUrl` property to be `lizard.bmp` for the `isHTML32` filter. By changing the filter in the dropdown to `isWML11` and the `ImageUrl` property to `lizard.wbmp`, we can achieve the same results we obtained with our previous programmatic capability check.

To make use of this, we need the following changes in the code for `MobileWebForm1.aspx`:

```
<mobile:Image id="Image1" runat="server">
  <DeviceSpecific>
    <Choice Filter="isHTML32" ImageUrl="lizard.bmp"></Choice>
    <Choice Filter="isWML11" ImageUrl="lizard.wbmp"></Choice>
  </DeviceSpecific>
</mobile:Image>
```

The `<DeviceSpecific>` element contains `<Choice>` elements for each filter defined, and overridden properties simply appear as attributes of these `<Choice>` elements.

`<Choice>` elements may also be used to define device-specific templates for controls. This enables us to make more complex controls (such as the mobile equivalents of the ASP.NET list type controls) render very differently on different devices. Full color formatting and bitmap images of lists may be used in HTML browsers, for example, while WAP devices may render the same lists as plain text. Once this behavior has been set up, we have a highly reusable way of providing content for a wide array of devices, where changes to our code and the data we use are propagated to all the devices in one go.

Note that wherever we use `<Choice>` elements we can provide one with no `Filter` attribute to use as the default. If we do this then this element will be used if none of the other `<Choice>` elements match device capabilities.

We've now covered everything we need to know to get started with the MMIT, so it's time to apply these techniques to our `BookManager` application.

Mobile BookManager Access

The first thing to ask when planning a project of this sort is what, exactly, are you trying to achieve? You could aim to expose as much functionality as is possible through other routes, but is this really sensible? Since mobile users will use 'usability-challenged' devices, it hardly makes sense to provide them with the same content as web or intranet users. The small screens and awkward input inherent in these devices would make such content virtually unusable (at least at the moment, as who knows what revolutions might be in store in terms of mobile device usability).

Instead, we need to identify what functionality would be required by users on the move. For example, a user in a bookshop may want to have a quick look at the `BookManager` database to find an ISBN number, confirm a title, or find an author name. Providing this capability via WAP or other mobile Internet services can be helpful for users who would otherwise have to get out and turn on a laptop, or rely on making notes at home before they set out.

Another important factor to consider is security. While secure connections are possible on mobile devices, we should avoid them if at all possible. The reduced bandwidth of mobile devices is not well suited to transferring certificates, which would lead to a dramatic performance drop, but perhaps more crucial is what happens at the network provider. With WAP, for example, mobile network traffic may be secured using Wireless Transport Socket Layer (WTSL) security over the connection between the device and the **gateway**. Gateways (which are usually owned by network providers) translate between WAP and HTTP protocols, so WTLS connections must be routed as SSL connections when a web server provides WAP content in addition to regular web pages. It has been pointed out many times that the gateway is therefore a prime target for hacker attack – it is where requests and responses must be repackaged using a different security protocol: in other words, they must be unencrypted and left susceptible even if for a very short period of time.

Note that the above discussion of gateways includes just one aspect of the general class of servers known as gateways. To avoid confusion it is worth noting that a gateway may do a lot more than this, or work with very different networks and protocols to provide their services. The specific type discussed here is a WAP gateway.

It is possible to implement your own WAP gateway so you can be responsible for this yourself, but this isn't very likely to turn out to be a cost-effective venture.

So, while secure connections to mobile clients are possible, it is often preferable to supply only unsecure applications to mobile clients, and that is what we will look at here. As a final point, this also means that users avoid the need to enter a username and password on a mobile keypad, which can prove tricky!

The BookList Application

The Visual Basic .NET Mobile Web Application we'll create here, called BookList, will simply provide a list of books along with associated information about those books. I created this project in the BM subdirectory that we've been using for our web projects in previous chapters, and it uses the BookManagerObjects library directly for simplicity. Add a reference to this library, and one to the EnterpriseObjects DLL also.

If we wanted, we could use the Web Services created earlier in the book by impersonating a system account for authentication (that is, using a hard-coded account rather than a genuine user created one). Using Solution Explorer, delete the existing .aspx page generated for the project and add a new mobile Web Form called default.aspx so that users can access it using the default syntax for default documents, http://localhost/BM/BookList/. Drag two forms from the Toolbox onto the default.aspx page in the designer.

Give the first the ID bookForm, and set its Title property to Book List. Place just one control, an ObjectList, on it, and call it bookList. We'll come back to this control in a moment, as setting its properties requires a little effort.

The second form, with the ID authorForm, also has a Title attribute of Book List, and contains:

- a Label called bookLabel with Font-Bold set to True
- a List with the ID authorList
- a Link called backLink with Text set to Return to book info, and NavigateUrl set to #bookForm

Lay these controls out on the forms as shown in the next screenshot:

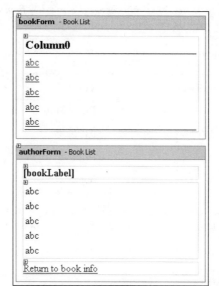

We can bind the bookList control to a BookSet instance quite easily, giving us a quick way of accessing author information (the ObjectList control is very versatile). To bind to and display the correct fields, we first need to set the AutoGenerateFields property of this control (on the bookForm form) to False, and then choose the fields to bind to with the dialog that pops up when we click the ellipsis button shown in the Fields property:

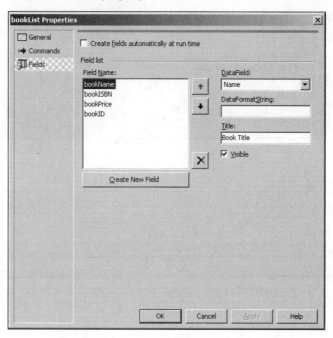

Note that the **Create fields automatically at run time** *checkbox is linked to the* `AutoGenerateFields` *property, so we can change this property from this dialog if we wish rather than through the* **Properties** *window as described above.*

The following table details the fields we need to create using this dialog:

Field Name	DataField	Title	Visible
bookName	Name	Book Title	Yes
bookISBN	ISBN	ISBN	Yes
bookPrice	Price	Price	Yes
bookID	bookID	ID	No

Note that we have to type the `DataField` data in manually rather than using the drop down, as we haven't yet set a data source to bind to (we shall do this in the code behind the form).

Next we add a command to the `Commands` collection property, through a similar pop-up dialog:

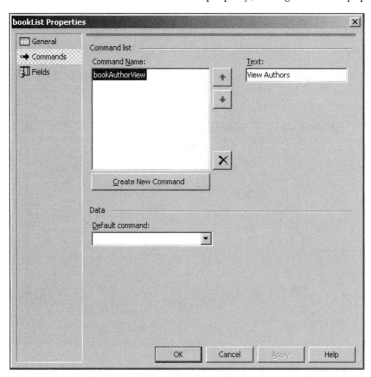

Here I've added one command, `bookAuthorView`, with the text **View Authors**. This command will, as we will see shortly, be rendered differently for different browsers, but will show the same text in all cases. It will be available from a selected item of the `ObjectList` control, and we can code for it in an `ItemCommand` event handler.

And now to the code. Most of the processing occurs in the `Page_Load` event that is fired when the page is opened by a browser. Right-click on `default.aspx` in Solution Explorer, select **View Code**, and add the highlighted code shown below:

```
...
Imports System.Web.UI.HtmlControls
Imports BookManagerObjects
Imports EnterpriseObjects

Namespace BookList
  Public Class _Default
    Inherits System.Web.UI.MobileControls.MobilePage

    Protected Shared bookForm As System.Web.UI.MobileControls.Form
    Protected Shared authorForm As System.Web.UI.MobileControls.Form
    Protected Shared authorList As System.Web.UI.MobileControls.List
    Protected Shared bookLabel As System.Web.UI.MobileControls.Label
    Protected Shared backLink As System.Web.UI.MobileControls.Link
    Protected Shared bookList As System.Web.UI.MobileControls.ObjectList
    Private Sub Page_Load(ByVal sender As System.Object, _
                    ByVal e As System.EventArgs) _
                    Handles MyBase.Load
      If IsPostBack = False Then
        ' Set the connection string
        EnterpriseApplication.Application.ConnectionString = _
 "integrated security=sspi;initial catalog=bookmanager;data source=karlivaio"

        ' Get the books
        Dim books As BookSet = Book.GetAll()

        ' Put the data in the table
        bookList.DataSource = Books
        bookList.DataBind()
      End If
    End Sub
  End Class
End Namespace
```

Don't forget to change the value of `ConnectionString` to use the name of the computer where your SQL is running. We use the `BookManagerObjects` library to retrieve all the books in the database and bind them to `bookList`. And that's pretty much it for that list as we've already configured it to handle this arrangement of data.

We also need to handle the `ItemCommand` event for `bookList` as mentioned earlier. Double-click on the `ObjectList` on `bookForm` in the designer, and add the following code:

```
Private Sub bookList_ItemCommand(ByVal sender As System.Object, _
          ByVal e As System.Web.UI.MobileControls.ObjectListCommandEventArgs)
  Dim currentBook As Book = Book.GetById(Convert.ToInt32(e.ListItem("bookID")))
  Dim authors As AuthorSet = currentBook.GetAuthors()
  Dim auth As Author
  authorList.Items.Clear()
```

```
     For Each auth In authors
        authorList.Items.Add(auth.Name)
     Next
     bookLabel.Text = "Authors of " + currentBook.Name + ":"
     ActiveForm = authorForm
  End Sub
```

This event handler is called whenever a command is triggered, and if we wish, we can interrogate the `ObjectListCommandEventArgs` instance to find out which command the user has chosen. Since there is only one command in this case, we don't need to, and we can just grab the current book details (using the ID stored in – but not displayed by – the `ObjectList`). We then use that to create an `AuthorSet` instance that we can iterate through to populate the `authorList` control of the `authorForm`. Lastly, we set the text of `bookLabel`, and navigate to `authorForm`.

This simple code is all we need to get started. Viewing the application in the older Openwave simulator gives us the following screen sequence when we select a book:

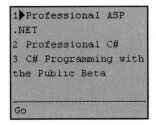 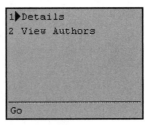

If we then select Details, we see general information for that book:

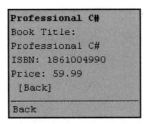

And if we select View Authors, we see the authors:

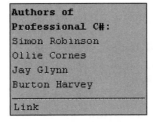

Other WAP devices work in much the same way, although they look and feel slightly different because the generated code differs. The Nokia 6210, for example, renders the first screen with no numbers:

Nokia devices require you to scroll through lists of items to make a selection, while Openwave ones let you enter the number of the option you want on the numeric keypad, allowing speedier selection. The .NET mobile controls automatically recognize that the browsers are different, and produce appropriate code as required.

In the Pocket PC, with its more powerful HTML display, we get the following:

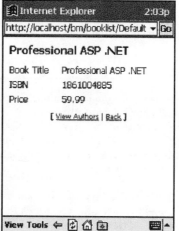

A fairly well formatted – and certainly quite usable – page.

All of the displays shown above are completely customizable. By using templates (which we unfortunately haven't got space to cover here) you can make the display look like anything you want – check out the mobile quickstart page mentioned earlier for pointers.

Pagination

The screenshots shown for the last example only show a few books. In a real-world application, however, we might have significantly more items to display, quite likely more than would fit in the limited memory of many mobile devices – and certainly more than we can see on screen at one time. One of the most useful features of the mobile controls is their ability to provide **automatic pagination**. We can turn this feature on and configure its behavior (such as how many items to display at one time) simply by modifying a few properties.

The default behavior is fine in most cases, and results in a display of seven items on most devices. This works well on the Openwave browser, which formats lists with numbers on the numeric keypad. Seven items leaves room for a Next link on button 8, and a Back link on button 9, as we will see in a moment. Of course, there are certainly lists where a different number of items per screen would be preferred, and some more powerful HTML browsers, such as the Pocket PC's, may not paginate unless this value is set, so it can be worth configuring this property anyway.

To add pagination to the last example, then, we need to make just two changes: the `Paginate` property of the `bookForm` form should be set to `True`, and the `ItemsPerPage` property of the `bookList` control on that form should be set to the number of books to display (choose a low number for illustrative purposes, such as 4). Once we have saved these changes, any browser will perform this pagination, as shown in the screenshots opposite:

When we have paginated controls like this, a number of properties become relevant, such as `Page`, which can be used to get or set the index of the current page of items being displayed.

Summary

In this chapter, we've looked at how we can expose our application functionality to mobile devices such as WAP phones and PDAs. To do this as generically as possible, we used the MMIT; a very neat product that allows us to target multiple browsers with ease.

The application developed here is a simple one, doing little more than displaying information from our database. This choice stems from the design decision to simplify access for mobile device users by removing the authentication and authorization covered in the last two chapters. Since user input can be very awkward (at least with current devices), this is sensible, and provides information specifically targeted at users on the move. Of course, should you wish to add extra functionality, the techniques covered in the last chapter apply here too – since the MMIT is based on ASP.NET and we've seen how to hook this technology into the Web Services developed for this purpose.

The MMIT is a very large and sophisticated package, with much more functionality than we've had time to cover here. However, I have attempted to illustrate some of its more powerful features (such as the pagination facility above) to give an insight into what is possible, and how easy it is to make use of these features. Quite apart from anything else, the mobile controls can be great fun to use, and if you're the sort of person who likes fiddling with new technology, exploring them will keep you occupied for days!

If you wish to find out more about this product I would strongly recommend working through the quickstart included in the MMIT referred to earlier. In addition, you might like to check out *ASP.NET Mobile Controls*, ISBN: 1-861005-22-9, also from Wrox Press.

.NET Enterprise Development in VB .NET

9

Services

So far, our n-tier development hasn't really been very "n-tier". Whenever we've needed to get data from the database, our presentation tier code and business tier code has been running in the same process. In this chapter, we're going to split the problem in two so that presentation tier code runs when data is actually presented (on the desktop for Windows Applications or via the web server for the various kinds of ASP.NET applications we've seen) and business tier code runs in a separate service process, potentially even on a different computer.

Remoting

Remoting is the core enabling technology for this separation. In essence, it allows us to have objects running on a separate server that listen to requests for methods from client code.

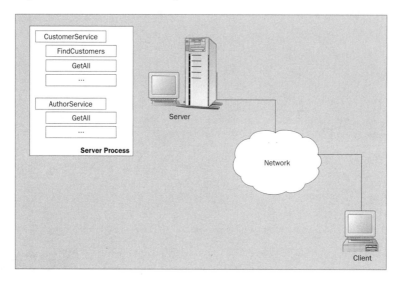

In the above figure the client is able to make calls to remote objects over a network via Remoting. Technically, there doesn't have to be a physical separation between client and server.

Some of you may be thinking that this is exactly what Web Services do. Indeed, Web Services do allow us to host objects remotely and call methods on those objects. However, Remoting is far more extensible than Web Services.

Web Services are limited to communications based on SOAP messages, typically over HTTP although other communication "channels", such as SMTP mail or MSMQ can be used. (We read all about this in Chapter 6, so you may wish to refer back.)

Remoting on the other hand is highly extensible, meaning that we can get round some of the performance problems posed by Web Services. For one thing, translating the formats that computers use to store data into XML for insertion into a SOAP message is very expensive in terms of processor time. This translation to XML is essential for platform interoperability however, we can skip it if we know that on both sides of the problem we have .NET assemblies that store data in the same way. With Web Services, how one computer stores a 32-bit integer *may* be different to how the other computer involved does, hence the need for a readily understandable format such as XML.

In our situation, we don't have to do the conversion because we have .NET on both sides, and the way that one .NET program stores a 32-bit integer is the same way any other one does. This means that rather than "formatting" the message as XML, we can transmit the message as a raw binary stream. We don't have to convert the data to text and back again, so we save a lot of processor cycles.

Another thing we don't have to necessarily deal with is the Internet. Even if we have TCP/IP running on our LAN, we don't have to use HTTP and the overhead that brings when sending messages between two machines. We could just open a raw socket to another machine and squirt data down it. Again, we save important processor cycles at the expense of interoperability. However, if we know both machines are running on the same LAN, or even if both sides of the problem are contained in separate processes on the same *computer*, there's no need to use HTTP.

Out-of-the-box, Remoting comes with two channel/formatter pairs:

❑ SOAP on HTTP – this uses the SOAP "formatter" and "HTTP" channel. It behaves very much like Web Services, and in fact, the .NET Web Service implementation shares a common code base with the SOAP on HTTP Remoting formatter-channel pair.

❑ Binary on TCP – this uses the binary "formatter" and "TCP" channel, so it's a very inexpensive communication method with very low overhead. However, it's not generally suitable for Internet use, but it is ideal for use over a LAN.

Ideally, we want to be able to configure our system so that when we have a client on the LAN that wants to talk to server-side objects hosted using Remoting on the same LAN, we use the TCP/Binary channel/formatter for optimum performance. However, if we have a client working off the LAN, such as a user at home with DSL, we might prefer the HTTP/SOAP channel/formatter. The performance won't be as good, but the communication will be more reliable.

Microsoft has made using Remoting very easy – in fact, if you found building Web Services a cakewalk you'll find this a cakewalk too. We simply have to tell Remoting which channels we want to use, what ports we want those channels to listen to and provide a list of objects that we want available over Remoting. The clients can then connect to these objects and start calling methods.

Extending Remoting

Microsoft has made Remoting fairly extensible in that we're not limited to using the two channel/formatter pairs introduced above. We can, if we want, create a new channel to handle communications over Named Pipes, Banyan Vines, or another protocol operating on our private network. Likewise, we can build our own formatters so that the Remoting messages are formatted exactly as we need. This can be useful for interoperation with legacy systems.

Token-Based Authentication

When we're inside a method call on the server, how do we know which user actually originated the call? This is one of the key precepts of an n-tier, distributed design: we have to know that the user making the call actually has the authority to do so.

In this chapter, we're not concerned with allowing or disallowing the user's activities based on who they are. These topics are covered in detail in Chapter 10. However, what we do need to do here is provide an infrastructure by which we can identify users when we're inside methods on the server.

A common way of implementing such a scheme is to use "tokens". A token is typically a long string of characters that can somehow be de-referenced into a unique user ID. To save time, we've already implemented two database tables to handle users and tokens.

The Users table is very straightforward. It consists of a UserId column and an NtlmName column:

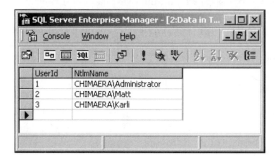

The Tokens table is a little more complicated. It has columns for a token ID, a string representation of that token (more later), the user ID that the token relates to, a created date, and an expiry date:

Again, we cover this in more detail later in the chapter.

> **IMPORTANT! You need to create new rows in the Users table to match the full names of the users that exist on your own computer, otherwise you won't be able to log into the application!**

Authenticating Users

For years now, Microsoft has suggested that applications developed by third parties should integrate their user authentication into what's now known as the Windows Security model. As you know, Windows maintains a list of users allowed access to various resources on the local computer and network computers on the domain or workgroup. What we want to do is integrate our authentication activities into Windows Security.

In Chapter 6, we did this by creating new users matt and karli in the users list for the local computer, and authenticated against these users in the Web Service. We're going to now use a similar technique in the Coordination Web Service.

When the browser starts, we'll use the login dialog to prompt for the user's username and password. This will be the same username and password that they would use if they wanted to log into the computer running the Web Service locally. (Although in most debug environments, this will actually be the same machine.)

> **For this chapter, you need to have followed the instructions set out in Chapter 6 to create the matt and karli users.**

The authentication process itself is actually handled by a combination of three things: the web server (IIS), Internet Explorer, and the various parts of Windows that deal with user authentication. Although we're calling the Web Service from within the application browser, .NET uses Internet Explorer to do this communication. IE contains code to handle the authentication between the web browser user (in this case, it's the application browser as we're dealing with app-to-app communication, not user-to-app communication as we traditionally do with a web browser) and IIS. All we need to do is give IE a username and password combination (which we capture using the login dialog) and let it and IIS work out how to actually identify the user.

We'll start by configuring IIS to handle authentication.

Configuring IIS

It's likely that VS .NET created the BookCoordinator project with permissions allowing anonymous users to log onto the site. If you run the project, you'll be presented with the Web Service test interface, even though you're actually an anonymous user. We discussed this topic in more detail in Chapter 6.

We need to configure BookCoordinator to disallow anonymous access. Open the Internet Services Manager management console and open the Properties dialog for the BookCoordinator virtual folder.

If you change to the Directory Security tab and click Edit under Anonymous access and authentication control, you'll see the dialog that we met in Chapter 6:

The important thing here is to turn off anonymous access. We'll need **Basic authentication** turned on (for when users outside of the domain need to connect – for example home users at the end of a DSL line) and either **Digest authentication** or **Integrated Windows authentication** for users on the LAN and/or domain.

Save those changes and users will have to authenticate themselves with the Web Service before they may proceed.

SSL

In this example, we've enabled **Basic authentication**, but this security scheme transmits the username and password as plain text that can easily be intercepted. We detailed SSL in Chapter 6 – so I won't repeat that here – and you're well advised to use SSL when authenticating users outside of the LAN using basic authentication.

The best technique is to make sure SSL is turned on within the call to the Authenticate method (which we're about to describe). If it isn't, we can throw an exception to force anyone consuming the Web Service to use SSL when calling the Authenticate method. You can then decide if you want to force the use of SSL for the other methods of the service.

The "Authenticate" Method

We can now turn our attention to the Authenticate method. This method is designed to examine the identity of the user and create a new token in the Tokens table for that user session, returning a string representing the token to the application browser. Objects already provided by WEO can handle most of this activity.

The System.Web.Services.WebService class implements a property called User. This returns an object that implements the System.Security.Principal.IPrincipal interface. This interface in turn implements a property called Identity that – unsurprisingly – returns an object that implements System.Security.Principal.IIdentity.

The upshot is that the User property can give us the NTLM ("NT LAN Manager") name, which usually boils down to be the name of the user. With anonymous users disallowed, the object returned by User is actually a System.Security.Principal.WindowsPrincipal object: an object representing a Windows user. The Identity property of this object returns a System.Security.Principal.WindowsIdentity instance. This object (or rather the IIdentity interface) implements a property called Name that returns the full name of the user.

The Authenticate method on Coordinator.asmx.vb should look like this:

```
<WebMethod()> Public Function Authenticate() As String
  ' Are we ntlm?
  If User.Identity.IsAuthenticated = False Then
    Throw New ApplicationException("User is not authenticated.")
  End If

  ' What user are we?
  Return AuthenticateUser(User.Identity.Name).ToString()
End Function
```

All we need to do there is look at the IIdentity-implementing object that we get from the User property, and check that IsAuthenticated is true. If it isn't, we have anonymous authentication turned on. If it is, we pass the name of the user to a separate method called AuthenticateUser, which we can build shortly.

AuthenticateUser has to look in the Users table to make sure the user exists, and if they do, a new token is created. Tokens themselves are managed through a class called EnterpriseObjects.Token. This class handles several important token management functions, which we come to in a moment.

Because AuthenticateUser has to look in the database, we need to give it a database connection string. We also need objects in EnterpriseObjects, so the first thing to do is add the EnterpriseObjects project into the BookCoordinator solution. Once that's done, add a reference to EnterpriseObjects to Coordinator.asmx.vb:

```
Imports System
Imports System.Collections
Imports System.ComponentModel
Imports System.Data
Imports System.Diagnostics
Imports System.Security.Principal
Imports System.Web
Imports System.Web.Mail
Imports System.Web.Services
Imports System.IO
Imports System.Xml
Imports System.Text
Imports EnterpriseObjects
```

We need to provide the database connection string by setting the ConnectionString property in the static EnterpriseApplication instance in much the same way as we have been doing in the application browser. However, the nature of Web Services is such that new Web Service objects are created for each incoming connection, so we need to set the string inside a Shared constructor, which will only be called the very first time a Coordinator class is instantiated:

```
Shared Sub New()
    ' Set the db string
    EnterpriseApplication.Application.ConnectionString = _
    "integrated security=sspi;initial catalog=bookmanager;data source=chimaera"
End Sub
```

> Don't forget to tweak that string to suit your own database connection parameters.

The database contains a stored procedure called GetUserForNtlmName. It looks like this:

```
CREATE PROCEDURE GetUserForNtlmName
(
  @ntlmName varchar(128)
)
  AS
    SELECT userid, ntlmname FROM users WHERE ntlmname=@ntlmname
```

When synchronizing the project, the Object Builder would have created a method called GetUserForNtlmName inside the Sprocs class of BookManagerObjects. Find that method, copy it into Coordinator.asmx.vb, and change the name to SprocGetUserForNtlmName. Also, change its qualifiers from "public static" to "protected":

```
Private Function SprocGetUserForNtlmName(ByVal ntlmName As String) As _
              System.Data.DataSet
  ' Create a connection
  Dim connection As System.Data.SqlClient.SqlConnection = New _
                System.Data.SqlClient.SqlConnection _
  (EnterpriseObjects.EnterpriseApplication.Application.ConnectionString)

  connection.Open()
  ' Create a command
  Dim command As System.Data.SqlClient.SqlCommand = New _
  System.Data.SqlClient.SqlCommand("GetUserForNtlmName", connection)

  command.CommandType = System.Data.CommandType.StoredProcedure
  ' Parameters
  Dim ntlmNameParam As System.Data.SqlClient.SqlParameter = _
  command.Parameters.Add("@ntlmName", System.Data.SqlDbType.VarChar, 128)

  ntlmNameParam.Value = ntlmName
  ' Extract the dataset
  Dim adapter As System.Data.SqlClient.SqlDataAdapter = New _
  System.Data.SqlClient.SqlDataAdapter(command)

  Dim dataset As System.Data.DataSet = New DataSet()
  adapter.Fill(dataset)
  adapter.Dispose()
  ' Clearup
  command.Dispose()
  connection.Close()
  ' Return dataset
  Return dataset
End Function
```

All the AuthenticateUser method has to do now is call this method to execute the stored procedure. If a row is returned, we have a user, so we can extract their ID and create a new Token object from it. This token is then returned to the caller, which in this case is the Authenticate method. Let's build that method now:

```
' AuthenticateUser - do the actual authentication
Private Function AuthenticateUser(ByVal ntlmName As String) As Token
  ' Get the user details
  Dim user As DataSet = Me.SprocGetUserForNtlmName(ntlmName)
  If user.Tables(0).Rows.Count = 0 Then
    Return Nothing
  End If

  ' Get user ID
  Dim userId As Integer = CType(user.Tables(0).Rows(0)("userid"), Integer)
```

```
                ' Create and save a token for the user
                Dim tkn As Token = New Token(userId)
                tkn.Save()
                Return tkn
        End Function
```

Testing Authentication

We can test authentication directly from the Web Service test interface. Run the project and invoke the Authenticate method. You should see something very similar to this:

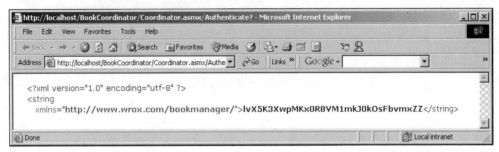

If you look in the Tokens table, you'll find that a new token has been created, and more importantly, the string contained in the SOAP message above matches the Token column:

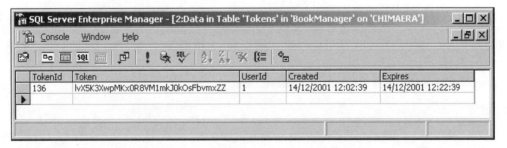

Also note that I'm logged in as user ID 1. In my Users table, this refers to CHIMAERA\Administrator, which is who I'm logged in as on my local computer.

The "Logoff" Method

When the Application Browser closes, we need a method that can be used to clear the token out. Add this method to Coordinator:

```
        <WebMethod()> Public Sub Logoff(ByVal tokenString As String)
            ' Log off
            Dim tkn As Token = Token.Load(tokenString)
            If Not tkn Is Nothing Then
                tkn.Delete()
            End If
        End Sub
```

Calling "Authenticate" From the Application Browser

We already call the `Authenticate` method whenever the **OK** button on the `Login` dialog is clicked. However, we need to provide IE with the username and password that we want to authenticate ourselves with on the Web Service before we make the call. This will mean that the username and password combination entered by the user in the `Login` form will alter the identity retrieved through the `User.Identity` call inside the Web Service's `Authenticate` method.

To do this, we need to create a `System.Net.NetworkCredential` object and give it the username and password that the user enters into the text boxes on the `Login` form.

First of all, add this property to `Login.vb` in the Application Browser project to cache an instance of `Coordination`, `Coordinator`. Don't forget to also add the private _service member:

```
Public ReadOnly Property Service() As Coordination.Coordinator
   Get
      ' Do we have one?
      If _service Is Nothing Then
         _service = New Coordination.Coordinator()
      End If

      ' Return
      Return _service
   End Get
End Property
```

The `SoapHttpClientProtocol` object that `Coordinator` is derived from exposes a property called `Credentials`. We can set this to a new instance of `NetworkCredential` once we import `System.Net` into the code file. Change `buttonOk_Click` in the same file as highlighted below:

```
Private Sub buttonOK_Click(ByVal sender As System.Object, ByVal e As _
System.EventArgs) Handles Button1.Click

   ' Authenticate
   Try
      ' Create a new credential for the service
      Service.Credentials = New _
      NetworkCredential(textUsername.Text, textPassword.Text)

      ' Call the authentication
      EnterpriseApplication.Application.SecurityToken = Service.Authenticate()

      ' run
      Run()
   Catch ex As Exception
      MessageBox.Show("You could not be authenticated: " + ex.Message)
   End Try
End Sub
```

Note the call to `Run` in the previous code snippet. This loads up the functionality catalog, and opens the main Application Browser window:

```
' Run the browser
Private Sub Run()

  ' Get the functionality catalog
  Try
    _functionality = Service.GetFunctionalityCatalog(
                          EnterpriseApplication.Application.SecurityToken)
  Catch
    MessageBox.Show("The functionality catalog could not be retrieved." &
                      "You cannot be logged in.")
  End Try

  ' Pop up main Application Browser form
  Dim myBrowser As Browser = New Browser()
  myBrowser.Show()

  ' Hide Login form
  Me.Hide()

End Sub
```

This code creates a new `NetworkCredential` object and gives it the username and password provided by the user. We then call the `Authenticate` method and set the `SecurityToken` property of the current `EnterpriseApplication` object to the returned token. If something goes wrong on the server (the user cannot be authenticated for whatever reason), an exception will be thrown.

To try this out, fire up the application browser and enter a valid username and password. A new token will be created, as we can see if we look in the `Tokens` table:

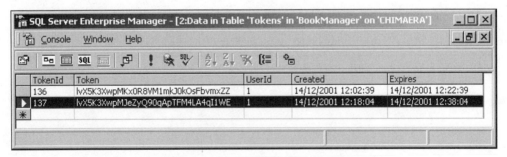

Now, close the browser and restart. Log in as a *different* user and you'll see a new `UserId`:

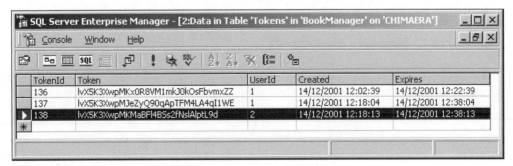

Calling "Logoff"

You'll notice that the tokens remain in the database when the application browser is closed. To fix this, we need a call to `Logoff`. Add this method to the `Login` class:

```
Protected Overrides Sub OnClosed(ByVal e As System.EventArgs)
   ' Logoff
   Try
      Service.Logoff(EnterpriseApplication.Application.SecurityToken)
   Catch
   End Try
End Sub
```

We're not too worried about exceptions that occur when we're running this method. Ideally, we need to set up a SQL Server Agent job to clean out expired tokens so they would be cleaned up eventually. However, we won't be putting that job together in this book.

Displaying the User Name

To show who is logged on, we shall write the user name in the status bar at the bottom of the Application Browser windows. We first need to add a method to the Web Service that returns the NTLM name of the user given a token string:

```
' Return NTLM name of user corresponging to tokenString
<WebMethod()> Public Function GetUserName(ByVal tokenString As String) As _
String
   Dim tkn As Token = Token.Load(tokenString)
   Return tkn.NtlmName
End Function
```

Inside `Login`, after we've been authenticated, we need to call this method and store the result in a private member, which we'll call _username. First off, add the private member:

```
Public Class Login
   Inherits System.Windows.Forms.Form

   ' Members
   Private _currentLogin As Login
   Private _username As String
```

Next, add a property to return the value of this field:

```
' Username property
Public ReadOnly Property Username() As String
   Get
      Return _username
   End Get
End Property
```

Then, make this change to `buttonOk_Click`:

```
Private Sub buttonOK_Click(ByVal sender As System.Object, _
ByVal e As System.EventArgs) Handles Button1.Click
```

```
    ' Authenticate
    Try
      ' Create a new credential for the service
      Service.Credentials = New NetworkCredential(textUsername.Text, _
      textPassword.Text)

      ' Call the authentication
      EnterpriseApplication.Application.SecurityToken = Service.Authenticate()

      ' Store the username
      _username = _
      Service.GetUserName(EnterpriseApplication.Application.SecurityToken)

      ' run
      Run()
    Catch ex As Exception
      MessageBox.Show("You could not be authenticated: " + ex.Message)
    End Try
End Sub
```

In the Browser project, make this change to OnLoad:

```
Protected Overrides Sub OnLoad(ByVal e As System.EventArgs)
    ' Set the caption
    Me.Text = ""

    ' Update the menu
    Dim functionality As AppFunctionality
    For Each functionality In Login.CurrentLogin.Functionality
      ' Create a new menu item
      Dim item As SubApplicationMenuItem = New SubApplicationMenuItem(Me, _
      functionality)

      ' Add it to the view menu
      menuView.MenuItems.Add(item)
    Next

    ' Add a sub-application
    menuView.MenuItems.Add(New SubApplicationDebugMenuItem(Me, _
    GetType(CustomerEditor.CustomerEditor)))

    ' Output the user name
    panelUser.Text = Login.CurrentLogin.Username

End Sub
```

Now run the project and authenticate yourself. You'll see the username displayed in the status bar:

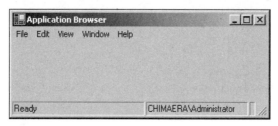

Building the Service

In the .NET world, what used to be called "Services" are now called "Windows Services". This is to differentiate them from the multitude of other types of service now available, in particular Web Services. In addition, .NET makes building services far easier than before, but there are a still a couple of points that can make developing services a little tricky.

When running a Windows Service, it's hard to attach the VS.NET debugger. In fact, you can't start a Windows Service from within VS.NET itself, as you need to use the standard management tools that start any Windows Service, such as IIS or SQL Server. The only option is to attach the debugger once it is running.

A better solution is to build the code that powers the service as a separate assembly and consume that assembly from within a console application for debugging, and move it to a Windows Service application for production. The critical code is then contained in a central library used by both console and service applications, and moving from one to the other will not entail any code changes to the library. The client, obviously, should be able to attach to either version without code changes.

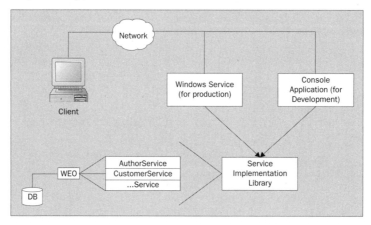

In the above figure the client doesn't care whether it's connecting to the Service or the Console App. The service implementation library is common to the Service and Console App and hosts the Service objects.

The Service Implementation Library loads the assembly containing the service objects (AuthorService, CustomerService, etc.) that contain methods that we want to expose to the client. These methods are accessed through Remoting, which by and large is handled by the .NET Remoting subsystem rather than something we have to specifically implement ourselves. As we know, these service objects use WEO to access the database.

Step 1 – The Service Implementation Library

Because the .NET Remoting subsystem does so much of the work for us with respect to making objects available to remote clients, there's very little we need to do in the Service Implementation Library.

Create a new class library called `BusinessHost`. Then follow these steps to set up the solution:

1. Add the `EnterpriseObjects` project to the solution

2. Add the `BookManagerObjects` project to the solution

3. Create a new Console Application project called `BusinessHostConsole`

4. Then, to the `BookManagerObjects` project, add a reference to the `EnterpriseObjects` project

5. To the `BusinessHost` project, add references to `BookManagerObjects` and `EnterpriseObjects`, and `System.Runtime.Remoting`

6. Set the `BusinessHostConsole` project to be the startup project

7. To the `BusinessHostConsole` project, add references to `BusinessHost`, `EnterpriseObjects`, and `BookManagerObjects`

At this stage, all of the four projects will be able to talk to the specific projects in order to get at the classes they require.

Configuring the Remoting Channels

Our first task is to create a new class inside the `BusinessHost` project that provides the actual implementation of the service. This will first register the channels and then register the classes that we want to make available over Remoting.

Create a new class called `HostService` inside `BusinessHost`. Add references to these namespaces:

```
Imports System
Imports System.Reflection
Imports System.Collections
Imports System.Runtime.Remoting
Imports System.Runtime.Remoting.Channels
Imports System.Runtime.Remoting.Channels.Tcp
Imports System.Runtime.Remoting.Channels.Http
Imports EnterpriseObjects
```

Next, add a constant to the class that will store the "application name". (More on this later.)

```
Public Class HostService
    ' Constants
    Public Const AppName As String = "BookManager"
```

As the service needs to connect to the database, create a new method called `Go` and add a call to set up the connection string. (Remember to tweak this string to suit your particular system configuration.)

```
Public Sub Go()
    ' Database string
    EnterpriseApplication.Application.ConnectionString = _
    "integrated security=sspi;data source=chimaera;initial catalog=bookmanager"

End Sub
```

As mentioned before, you can write your own channels and formatters for use with Remoting, but we're going to use the standard TCP and HTTP channels. We just create instances of them, provide a port number, and call `RegisterChannel` to register them with the `System.Runtime.Remoting.Channels.ChannelServices` class. We'll listen for TCP connections on port 8080 and HTTP on port 8081:

```
Public Sub Go()
    ' Database string
    EnterpriseApplication.Application.ConnectionString = _
    "integrated security=sspi;data source=chimaera;initial catalog=bookmanager"

    ' Create a new channel
    Dim channel As IChannel = New TcpChannel(8080)
    ChannelServices.RegisterChannel(channel)
    channel = New HttpChannel(8081)
    ChannelServices.RegisterChannel(channel)
End Sub
```

Registering the Objects

With the channels registered, we now have to register the classes. To do this, we need a `Type` object, representing the type of the object we want to make available via Remoting, and a URI – a fraction of a URL string that can identify the object. Our string is going to take this format:

/<application name>/<full name of type>`.remote`

We'll see the application name, or "appname", in more detail later.

To find the classes we want to host, we'll create a method called `LoadAssembly`. This will take a `System.Reflection.Assembly` object and walk through that assembly examining each type contained therein. Specifically, we'll be looking for classes having the `EnterpriseObjects.RemotingAttribute` attribute. Any class that has this attribute will automatically be made available through Remoting.

We'll need two versions of `LoadAssembly`. One will take any object and use the `GetType` method to find a `Type` object and from that a `System.Reflection.Assembly` object that can be scanned. The other will take the `Assembly` object. Here's the first version:

```
Public Sub LoadAssembly(ByVal useObject As Object)
    LoadAssembly(useObject.GetType().Assembly)
End Sub
```

The second version uses the `GetTypes` method of the `Assembly` object. For each `Type` object returned in the array, `GetCustomAttributes` will return the attributes of the class. We'll then walk through each attribute looking for `EnterpriseObjects.RemotingAttribute`. When we find it, we'll defer to `RegisterType`, which will do the actual work. (We'll see `RegisterType` in a moment.)

```
Public Sub LoadAssembly(ByVal useAssembly As [Assembly])
    ' Go through the types
    Dim lType As Type
    For Each lType In useAssembly.GetTypes()
        ' Go through the attributes
        Dim checkAttribute As Object
        For Each checkAttribute In lType.GetCustomAttributes(False)
            ' What do we have
            If TypeOf checkAttribute Is EnterpriseObjects.RemotingAttribute Then
                Register(lType)
            End If
        Next
    Next
End Sub
```

Below we have the `Register` method. Its job is to build the URI based on the value stored in the `AppName` constant, combine it with the full name of the type, and tack ".remote" onto the end. (This choice is arbitrary – the URI can be whatever you want it to be.) We pass this URI to `RegisterWellKnownServiceType`, and tell it to create a singleton object.

Remoting offers three main kinds of objects: singleton, single call, and client-activated:

❑ **Singleton** – these objects are the *best* for n-tier solutions. Only one instance of the object is ever created on the server, irrespective of how many clients are actually trying to use it. This is massively scalable because even if you have 100,000 clients connecting to a Remote object, you only ever need one instance on the server. The caveat is that a singleton object *cannot* have state – or rather, it should not have state in order to achieve maximum scalability.

❑ **Single Call** – such objects are less suited to n-tier environments. Whenever a method call is received, a new object is created, which services the call and is then deleted. They can have state, but as they are trashed after the call is completed, the state should be deleted along with the object itself.

❑ **Client-Activated** – these objects are instantiated on the server for each request by a client. The object remains in memory and services only a single client. It can have state, and that state is unique to the client. However, it's a scalability nightmare for n-tier, as each client has its own instance of the object on the server.

```
Public Sub Register(ByVal ltype As Type)
    Dim uri As String = "BookManager/" + ltype.FullName + ".remote"
    RemotingConfiguration.RegisterWellKnownServiceType(ltype, uri, _
    WellKnownObjectMode.Singleton)
    Console.WriteLine("Created '" + uri + "'")
End Sub
```

To register the classes, we need a call to `LoadAssembly` within the `Go` method. We can pass in an instance of any object contained by the assembly for the service objects. This doesn't have to be a service object, and in fact here we pass in an instance of an `Author` object:

```
Public Sub Go()
    ' Database string
    EnterpriseApplication.Application.ConnectionString = _
    "integrated security=sspi;data source=chimaera;initial catalog=bookmanager"

    ' Create a new channel
    Dim channel As IChannel = New TcpChannel(8080)
    ChannelServices.RegisterChannel(channel)
    channel = New HttpChannel(8081)
    ChannelServices.RegisterChannel(channel)

    ' Load the assemblies
    LoadAssembly(New BookManagerObjects.Author())
End Sub
```

That's all we need to do for the service implementation. Let's take a look at how we can run it.

Step 2 – The Console Application

To run the service, we need to write some code in the console application. You may have already guessed that all we have to do is create an instance of a `BusinessHost.HostService` object and call `Go`. Here's the entire implementation of the default class for `BusinessHostConsole`:

```
Public Sub Main(ByVal args As String())
    ' Create
    Dim service As BusinessHost.HostService = New BusinessHost.HostService()
    service.Go()

    ' wait for user to press Enter
    Console.WriteLine()
    Console.WriteLine("Press Enter to close the console.")
    Console.WriteLine()
    Console.ReadLine()
End Sub
```

If you run the console application now, you'll see this:

The debug information only displays the URI of the service, not the full URL. As my machine is called CHIMAERA, the full URLs would be:

tcp://chimaera:8080/BookManager/BookManagerObjects.CustomerService.remote
http://chimaera:8081/BookManager/BookManagerObjects.CustomerService.remote

How do we know that the objects are actually hosted? Well, we can point IE at the HTTP URL and we should get something back. Try visiting the HTTP URL, remembering to specify the port and the name of your own server in place of CHIMAERA. You should see this message under the standard IE troubleshooting blurb:

HTTP 400 - Bad Request
Internet Explorer

The Bad Request message means that Remoting is trying to do something with the object – we just haven't asked it to do anything. If you want, you can prove this by tacking ?WSDL onto the end of the URL. This will attempt to create a WSDL document for the service:

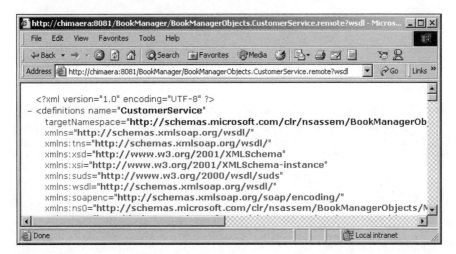

Of course, the WSDL isn't particularly useful as far as our work here is concerned, but being able to generate the WSDL does prove that *something* is found at our URL. (Refer back to Chapter 6 for a reminder about SOAP and WSDL.)

Step 3 – The Windows Service

We're not going to do this right now. Instead, we'll come back to it in the last section of the chapter. For now, we'll keep on using the Console Application to develop and debug.

Connecting to the Service

Connecting to the service is actually very easy – all we do is give `System.Activator` the URL of the remote object. However, telling the application browser where the object is can be a little trickier.

Up to this point, the application browser has always connected directly to the database. Or rather, `Service` objects like `CustomerService` have always connected directly. We want to redirect this connection away from a direct socket connection to SQL Server, and make the communication flow through the Remoting layer. Instead of creating local instances of `CustomerService`, we'll connect to remote instances, which will, in turn, connect directly to the database.

When the application browser is connecting directly – in other words it is creating instances of `CustomerService` et al inside the app domain of the browser itself – we'll call that a "Direct" connection. When it's connecting through the Remoting layer, we'll call it a "Remoting" connection.

We're currently using a fixed string inside the constructor for `Login` to provide connection information for SQL Server:

```
' Login Constructor
Public Sub New()
  ' This call is required by the Component Designer
  InitializeComponent()

  ' Save an instance of us as the current login
  _currentLogin = Me

  ' Connection string
  EnterpriseApplciation.Application.ConnectionString = _
  "integrated security=sspi;initial catalog=bookmanager;data source=chimaera"
End Sub
```

The first thing to do is delete that line from the constructor, to give this:

```
' Login Constructor
Public Sub New()
  ' This call is required by the Component Designer
  InitializeComponent()

  ' Save an instance of us as the current login
  _currentLogin = Me
End Sub
```

Notice how the property is called `ConnectionString`. What we're going to do is create an alternative type of connection string that supports Remoting connections. That string will contain these parameters:

- `Enterprise Connection Type=remoting;`
- `appname=BookManager;`
- `port=8080;`
- `protocol=tcp;`
- `servername=CHIMAERA;`

This is a proprietary format that we've constructed for the purposes of WEO. The `Enterprise Connection Type` entry indicates the type of connection being made – either `Remoting` or `Direct`. The remaining entries are specific to the connection type being made, and provide an "appname", port, protocol, and name of a host that the client can use to access the objects.

If the `Enterprise Connection Type` entry is missing, a Direct connection is assumed. In this case, the remaining entries are actually the OLE DB/ADO.NET entries needed to establish the connection.

In addition to this, we want to get our connection string from the Web Service. This has the advantage that it gives us more control over what the clients connect to. We could, should we wish, have different clients connecting to different servers. Or, we could redirect all new connections to another server very easily. Add this method to the `Coordination` class, remembering to change the name of the host from **CHIMAERA** to the name of whatever computer is hosting your remote objects:

```
<WebMethod()> Public Function _
GetConnectionString(ByVal tokenString As String) As String
   Return "Enterprise Connection Type=remoting;appname=BookManager;" & _
          "port=8080;protocol=tcp;servername=CHIMAERA"
End Function
```

You'll notice that we're returning the connection string as plain-text. This could be a security risk, especially if we return a SQL Server connection string that contains the username and password to the database. With the Remoting connection string, it doesn't matter too much as the actual authentication happens elsewhere, and with our previous SQL Server connection string examples, we have used the `Integrated Security` parameter so that we don't have to include the username and password in the string.

This method takes the token for the user which, although we're not doing so here, gives us the freedom to change the connection string depending on the user's identity.

The trick now is to call that method after the login process has completed. Open the code editor for `Login` and add this code:

```
Private Sub buttonOK_Click(ByVal sender As System.Object, ByVal e As
System.EventArgs) Handles Button1.Click

    ' Authenticate
    Try
      ' Create a new credential for the service
      Service.Credentials = New NetworkCredential(textUsername.Text, _
      textPassword.Text)

      ' Call the authentication
      EnterpriseApplication.Application.SecurityToken = Service.Authenticate()

      ' Get the connection string
      EnterpriseApplication.Application.ConnectionString = _
      Service.GetConnectionString(EnterpriseApplication.Application.SecurityToken)

      ' Store the username
      _username = _
Service.GetUserName(EnterpriseApplication.Application.SecurityToken)
```

```
    ' run
    Run()
  Catch ex As Exception
    MessageBox.Show("You could not be authenticated: " + ex.Message)
  End Try
End Sub
```

We can now move on pretty swiftly to testing that this works.

Testing the Connection

Before we try running, we'll add debug information to `CustomerService.FindCustomers`. This will prove to us that the method the Customer Editor is using is indeed running remotely. Add this code to `FindCustomers`:

```
' FindCustomers - search for customers
Public Function FindCustomers(ByVal searchFor As String) As CustomerSet
  ' Debug
  Console.WriteLine("FindCustomers called: " + searchFor)

  ' Run the sproc and return
  Return CType(Sprocs.FindCustomers(searchFor, GetType(CustomerSet)), _
                            CustomerSet)
End Function
```

Now run the BusinessHostConsole project. This will register the objects with Remoting and also create a number of end points. On my computer, called CHIMAERA, the end points for CustomerService will be:

tcp://chimaera:8080/BookManager/BookManagerObjects.CustomerService.remote
http://chimaera:8081/BookManager/BookManagerObjects.CustomerService.remote

The "appname" is BookManager, which you'll notice appears in the Remoting URLs and also in the connection string provided by the Web Service. Furthermore, the full name of the object is used, with the string ".remote" tacked onto the end.

Run the browser now and authenticate yourself. Load the Customer Editor and search for some customers. The console will show something like this:

That should show it's working as we intended. Because the server-side console application is displaying debugging information as a result of the `CustomerService.FindCustomers` call, we know that the application browser is no longer using a locally loaded copy of `CustomerService` but is in fact using the remote copy. The question remains: "How?"

How This Works

If you recall, when the **Search** button is clicked, we call the `FindCustomers` method on the `Customer` entity object. Entity objects always remain local – it's only service objects that are hosted by Remoting:

```
Private Sub buttonSearch_Click(ByVal sender As System.Object, _
ByVal e As System.EventArgs) Handles Button1.Click
  ' Get the term
  Dim term As String = textSearchFor.Text
  If term.Length >= 3 Then
    ' Get the Customers
    Me.Cursor = Cursors.WaitCursor
    Dim found As CustomerSet = Nothing
    Try
      found = Customer.FindCustomers(term)
    Catch ex As Exception
      Browser.HandleException(ex)
    End Try
    Me.Cursor = Cursors.Default

    ' What happened
    If Not found Is Nothing And found.Tables(0).Rows.Count > 0 Then
      ' Show it
      Customers = found
    Else
      Browser.Alert("No customers were found.", MessageBoxIcon.Information)
    End If
  Else
    Browser.Alert("You must enter three of more characters.")
  End If
End Sub
```

The `Customer.FindCustomers` method (running locally) defers processing to the service object:

```
' FindCustomers - search for customers
Public Function FindCustomers(ByVal searchFor As String) As CustomerSet
  Return Customer.ServiceObject.FindCustomers(searchFor)
End Function
```

The trick here is what the `ServiceObject` actually does. It's this property's job to make the decision whether an instance of `CustomerService` should be created in the local process or whether a connection to a remotely instantiated object should be made. If we look at `CustomerBase.ServiceObject`, you'll notice that it defers to `Entity.GetServiceObject`:

```
Public ReadOnly Property ServiceObject() As CustomerService
  Get
    Return CType(GetServiceObject(GetType(CustomerService)), CustomerService)
  End Get
End Property
```

The implementation of GetServiceObject is where things start to get complicated. In WEO, there is a concept of a **service object factory**. We have two factories implemented as classes which derive from ServiceObjectFactory: namely DirectServiceObjectFactory and RemotingServiceObjectFactory. As their names imply, one is designed to create service objects for direct connections, and the other for remoting connections.

ServiceObjectFactory implements a single method called Create. This method takes a System.Type object.

DirectServiceObjectFactory is the easier of the two derived classes to understand. It uses System.Activator to create a local instance of whatever type is requested in the call to Create:

```
Public Overrides Function Create(ByVal lType As Type) As Service
    Return CType(System.Activator.CreateInstance(lType), Service)
End Function
```

RemotingServiceObjectFactory is more convoluted. It has to look at the values entered into the connection string in order to form the URL for finding the remote object. This is helped somewhat by a property called ConnectionStringParts implemented in EnterpriseObjects. This property returns a System.Collections.Hashtable object, where the entries comprise the name-value pairs that were included in the connection string set using the ConnectionString property.

The RemotingServiceObjectFactory constructor goes through the parameter of the connection string and stores the values in member variables. We ignore any entry in the connection string that we don't understand, but we will throw an exception if we do not get the application name, a server name, and a port:

```
' RemotingServiceObjectFactory Constructor
Public Sub New()
    ' Go through the parts
    Dim part As String
    For Each part In _
EnterpriseApplication.Application.ConnectionStringParts.Keys
        ' Check
        Select Case part.ToLower
            Case "appname"
                RemoteAppName =
CType(EnterpriseApplication.Application.ConnectionStringParts(part), String)
                Exit Select
            Case "servername"
                RemoteServerName =
CType(EnterpriseApplication.Application.ConnectionStringParts(part), String)
                Exit Select
            Case "port"
                RemotePort =
Int32.Parse(CType(EnterpriseApplication.Application.ConnectionStringParts(part),
                    String))
                Exit Select
            Case "protocol"
                Dim protocol As String =
CType(EnterpriseApplication.Application.ConnectionStringParts(part), String)
                Select Case protocol.ToLower
                    Case "tcp"
```

```
            ChannelType = RemotingChannelType.Tcp
            Exit Select
        Case "http"
            ChannelType = RemotingChannelType.Http
            Exit Select
        Case Else
            Throw New NotSupportedException("Channel type '" + protocol + "'
                                            not supported.")
        End Select
    End Select
Next
' Did we get everything?
If RemoteAppName = "" Then
    Throw New RemotingConnectionException("You must provide a remote
                                application name")
End If
If RemoteServerName = "" Then
    Throw New RemotingConnectionException("You must provide a remote server
                                name.")
End If
If RemotePort = 0 Then
    Throw New RemotingConnectionException("You must provide a remote port")
End If
End Sub
```

When it's time to create a service object, `Create` will be called. This method calls the `GetRemotingUrl` method that we're about to meet which uses the member variables we've just configured to produce the URL. Once it has the URL, it uses `Activator.GetObject` to create a local proxy object that can connect to the remote object:

```
Public Overrides Function Create(ByVal serviceObjectType As Type) As Service
    ' Get the url
    Dim url As String = GetRemotingUrl(serviceObjectType)
    Dim serviceObject As Service = _
  CType(System.Activator.GetObject(serviceObjectType, url), Service)

    ' Return it
    Return serviceObject
End Function
```

`GetRemotingUrl` isn't remarkably complex. It uses the member variables to create the URL string:

```
Public Function GetRemotingUrl(ByVal serviceObjectType As Type) As String
    ' Create it
    Dim url As StringBuilder = New StringBuilder()
    Select Case ChannelType
        Case RemotingChannelType.Tcp
            url.Append("tcp")
            Exit Select
        Case RemotingChannelType.Http
            url.Append("http")
            Exit Select
        Case Else
```

```
      Throw New NotSupportedException("Remoting channel type '" + ChannelType
                                 + "' not supported.")
      End Select

  ' Append
  url.Append("://")
  url.Append(RemoteServerName)
  url.Append(":")
  url.Append(RemotePort.ToString())
  url.Append("/")
  url.Append(RemoteAppName)
  url.Append("/")
  url.Append(serviceObjectType.ToString())
  url.Append(".remote")

  ' return
  Return url.ToString()
End Function
```

The only question that remains at this point is how to choose whether to create a
DirectServiceObjectFactory or a RemotingServiceObjectFactory. The answer lies in
EnterpriseApplication – this class implements a property called ServiceObjectFactory that
looks in the connection string for the Enterprise Connection Type value. From this, it creates the
appropriate object:

```
' ServiceObjectFactory - create a factory
Public ReadOnly Property ServiceObjectFactory() As ServiceObjectFactory
  Get
    ' Do we have one?
    If _serviceObjectFactory Is Nothing Then
      ' Look at the string
      If ConnectionStringParts.Contains("Enterprise Connection Type") = True Then
        Dim connectionType As String = _
        ConnectionStringParts("Enterprise Connection Type").ToString().ToLower()
        Select Case connectionType
          ' Direct
          Case "direct"
            _serviceObjectFactory = New DirectServiceObjectFactory()
            Exit Select

          ' Remoting
          Case "remoting"
            _serviceObjectFactory = New RemotingServiceObjectFactory()
            Exit Select

          Case Else
            Throw New NotSupportedException("Connection Type '" + connectionType
                                       + "' not supported.")
        End Select
      End If
      ' Did we get one?  Create a default one
      If _serviceObjectFactory Is Nothing Then
        _serviceObjectFactory = New DirectServiceObjectFactory()
```

```
        End If
      End If
      ' Return it
      Return _serviceOjbectFactory
    End Get
End Property
```

So, we've covered how to choose which kind of service object factory to create, and therefore whether the new service objects are loaded locally or accessed by establishing connections to remote objects. We either get a *bone fide* instance of a `Service`-derived object, or we get a proxy that can communicate with a remote instance of a `Service`-derived object. Whichever we have, the object consuming the client (for example the `Customer` entity class) is indifferent to where the data is coming from.

Displaying the Connection Type

During testing, it could be useful to display the connection type in the status bar next to the user name. To do this, open the code editor for `Browser`, and add the highlighted code to `OnLoad`:

```
Protected Overrides Sub OnLoad(ByVal e As System.EventArgs)
  ' Set the caption
  Me.Text = ""

  ' Update the menu
  Dim functionality As AppFunctionality
  For Each functionality In Login.CurrentLogin.Functionality
    ' Create a new menu item
    Dim item As SubApplicationMenuItem = New SubApplicationMenuItem(Me, _
    functionality)

    ' Add it to the view menu
    menuView.MenuItems.Add(item)
  Next

  ' Add a sub-application
  menuView.MenuItems.Add(New SubApplicationDebugMenuItem(Me, _
  GetType(CustomerEditor.CustomerEditor)))
  menuView.MenuItems.Add(New SubApplicationDebugMenuItem(Me, _
  GetType(CustomerEditor.TestControl)))

  ' Write the connection type
  panelConnection.Text = _
              EnterpriseApplication.Application.ServiceObjectFactory.ToString()

  ' Output the user name
  panelUser.Text = Login.CurrentLogin.Username

End Sub
```

Run the project, log in and you'll see the connection type:

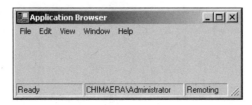

Passing Tokens

For this scheme to work, whenever a client makes a call to a method on the server, we want the token to automatically flow from client to server. In effect, this means that once inside the server-side method, we should be able to call a method to get the token string, which we can use to get an actual `Token` object. Once we have the token, of course, we'll be able to identify the user through the associated `UserId`.

In Remoting, there is the concept of a **Remoting Boundary**. When crossing a Remoting boundary, a method call is no longer a standard call through code, and is instead serialized into a message for transmission to the server, which de-serializes the message to correctly execute the required call. A Remoting boundary is typically the edge of an Application Domain, or **AppDomain**.

We haven't spoken about AppDomains in this book, but they are very similar to processes. They are software artefacts representing system 'zones' where assemblies can be loaded and code executed. Each AppDomain has its own block of memory that is isolated from other AppDomains. AppDomains differ from processes in that a single process can contain multiple AppDomains.

To call methods in a separate AppDomain, the solution recommended by Microsoft is to use Remoting. In this situation, using a channel-formatter pair of TCP-Binary is most appropriate as the app-to-app communication is all happening on the local machine. (In fact, it's happening in the same process.) In our scenario, the server's AppDomain and the client's AppDomain may be physically separated, but at the very least, they're both running in two separate processes.

An important part of this communication is the messages themselves – both the request message and the response message. In particular, we hang our own data from the message: in this case, we're going to attach the security token string. Once inside the method, we can examine the extra data to determine what string the client actually has, and from that point de-reference the actual identity of the user.

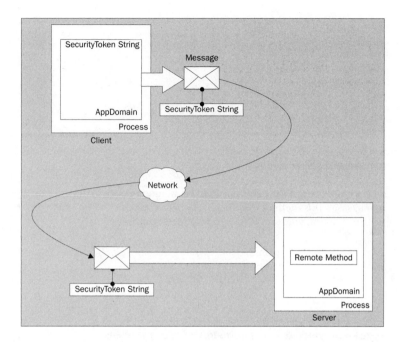

Remoting can automatically handle the transmission of extra data with the message. This is done through the "call context", which is implemented through the class called System.Runtime.Remoting.Messaging.CallContext. This class contains methods for attaching data to a *thread* using the classic key-value approach.

> **The use of the term "thread" is important here. Every time we spin up a new thread (including threads spun up using the thread pool) on our client, we have to call a method that injects the security token string into the call context for that new thread.**

As the call is made, Remoting automatically looks in the thread for information held in the call context, and packs that extra data into the message. The message is then transmitted to the server object as normal. When the message is unpacked, any extra call context information is injected into the call context for the server-side thread. The same CallContext object provides methods for getting the data back out again.

Using the Call Context

WEO automatically saves the security token in the CallContext object. If we look in EnterpriseApplication for the SecurityToken property, we'll see the call to ConfigureThread:

```
Public Property SecurityToken() As String
  Get
    Return _securityToken
  End Get
  Set(ByVal Value As String)
```

```
        ' Set the value
        _securityToken = Value

        ' Configure the thread
        ConfigureThread()
    End Set
End Property
```

What `ConfigureThread` does is store the security token in the `CallContext` object. If you spin up your own threads, you *must* call `ConfigureThread`. If you do not, the server-side code will not be passed the security token string along with the message.

The `ConfigureThread` message isn't complicated. As mentioned, `CallContext` uses the classic key-value pair approach, so all this method does is store a new `ContextToken` object (more in a moment) against the name stored in the constant `SecurityTokenSlotName`:

```
Public Sub ConfigureThread()
    ' Add it
    CallContext.SetData(SecurityTokenSlotName, New ContextToken(SecurityToken))
End Sub
```

> **SecurityTokenSlotName** is defined to be **WeoSecurityToken**.

We can store any data we like in `CallContext` objects, and any data stored there can be retrieved by any other method running in the same thread. However, if you want the data to flow over Remoting boundaries, the `CallContext` object must be marked with the `System.SerializableAttribute` attribute and it must also implement the `System.Runtime.Remoting.Messaging.ILogicalThreadAffinative` interface. The `Serializable` attribute tells .NET that the object can be transformed into a stream for transmission, and `ILogicalThreadAffinative` indicates that the object needs to be copied from the client-side thread to the supporting thread on the server side. This interface is a little odd in that it doesn't define any methods or properties.

The `ContextToken` class is marked in this way. It looks like this:

```
<Serializable()> Public Class ContextToken
    Inherits ILogicalThreadAffinative

    ' Members
    Private _token As String

    Public Sub New(ByVal token As String)
        _token = token
    End Sub

    Public Property Token() As String
        Get
            Return _token
        End Get
```

```
      Set(ByVal Value As String)
         _token = Value
      End Set
   End Property
End Class
```

In terms of what we need to do on the client, that's about it. After the security token string is set using the `Token` property, `ConfigureThread` is automatically called and a new `ContextToken` object stored inside `CallContext` for the thread. Because the `ContextToken` object implements `ILogicalThreadAffinative`, the object will be serialized and included in the message data.

Looking Server-Side

So what happens on the server? Well, roughly the same thing. `Service` implements a method called `GetSecurityToken` that looks in `CallContext` to retrieve the value stored against the string defined in `SecurityTokenSlotName`:

```
Public Function GetSecurityToken() As String
   ' Get the data from the call context
   Dim tkn As ContextToken = _
CType(CallContext.GetData(EnterpriseApplication.SecurityTokenSlotName),
   ContextToken)

   If Not tkn Is Nothing Then
     Return tkn.Token
   End If

   Return Nothing
End Function
```

Typically, when we're running a method on a server-side object, we'll be running a method on an object inherited from `EnterpriseObjects.Service`. This means that we can just call `GetSecurityToken`. If we need an actual `Token` object, we can call the `Load` method on the `Token` class to convert the string into an object.

In addition to this, there's a method on `Service` called `DebugSecurityToken`, which writes the information stored in the token out to the console. Open the `CustomerService.vb` class file, and add a call to this method inside `FindCustomers`:

```
' FindCustomers - search for customers
Public Function FindCustomers(ByVal searchFor As String) As CustomerSet
   ' Debug
   Console.WriteLine("FindCustomers called: " + searchFor)
   DebugSecurityToken(True)

   ' Run the sproc and return
   Return CType(Sprocs.FindCustomers(searchFor, GetType(CustomerSet)),
                               CustomerSet)
End Function
```

To test that the correct token is flowing across, open the code editor for `CustomerEditor`. Add this code to `buttonSearch_Click`:

```
Private Sub buttonSearch_Click(ByVal sender As System.Object, _
ByVal e As System.EventArgs) Handles Button1.Click
    ' Test
    MessageBox.Show("Local token: " + _
                    EnterpriseApplication.Application.SecurityToken)

    ' Get the term
    Dim term As String = textSearchFor.Text
    If term.Length >= 3 Then

    ...

    Else
        Browser.Alert("You must enter three of more characters.")
    End If
End Sub
```

Run the server solution and the Application Browser solution. Log on to the server as normal.

Open the Customer Editor and search for a customer. When you click the Search button, you'll see the token string displayed. (Remember, your string will be different to the one shown here.)

Click OK to dismiss the message box. Immediately after this, the call to the remote server will be made. You'll see this:

```
c:\BookManager\BusinessHostConsole\bin\Debug\BusinessHostConsole.exe                    _ |□| x|
Created 'BookManager/BookManagerObjects.CustomerService.remote'
Created 'BookManager/BookManagerObjects.SecurityChecker.remote'

Press Enter to close the console.

FindCustomers called: drew
--------------------------------------------------------------------
Security token for thread #74: 7y4YJTf/4IVlpdm7Dt3AGOjhwSp2EEfB
Token ID: 128
User ID: 1
NTLM name: CHIMAERA\Administrator
--------------------------------------------------------------------
```

You can see there that the two tokens match. That proves that the security token string is being flowed across the Remoting boundary. Also notice that we've retrieved the user ID (in this case, 1) and the name of the user.

Start another instance of the Application Browser – you can't do this from within VS.NET if you're debugging an existing instance, so you'll have to use Explorer – and log in as a different user. Do the same thing again, and you'll see this output on the server:

You can see that the second call has a different token, which is what you'd expect because the call context for the second client has its own unique token. Also, this new token is linked to a separate user (ID of 2), as we've demonstrated by displaying the NTLM name of CHIMAERA\Matt rather than CHIMAERA\Administrator.

This is all we're going to do with respect to identifying the user. In Chapter 10, we'll look further at how to use the user's identity to determine what they are allowed to do when running the application.

> Before you continue, you might want to remove the debugging message box from `buttonSearch_Click`.

The Windows Service

In theory, hosting this in a Windows Service should be a cakewalk as we've done all of the hard work already.

Before creating the service, make sure the BusinessHostConsole project is not being debugged. In the same solution, use Solution Explorer to add a new Visual Basic | Windows Service project. Call it BookManagerService:

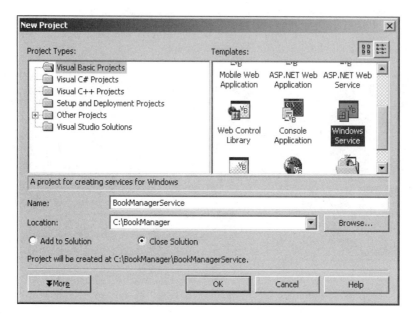

To the new service, add references to the BusinessHost, BookManagerObjects, and EnterpriseObjects projects.

Open the Designer for the new Service1.vb file, and view the Properties window. Change the ServiceName property to BookManager Service and note the Add Installer hyperlink below the property list:

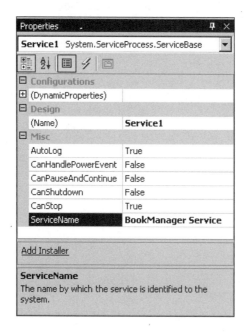

Adding the Installer

The first thing we'll do is to add the installer, so make sure you have `Service1` selected in the Designer, and click the **Add Installer** link. This will create a new file in the project called `ProjectInstaller.vb` that contains the code necessary to install the service on a computer. This is an essential step for a Windows Service, which as mentioned must be installed before we can run it.

The first of these, `serviceProcessInstaller1`, deals with integrating your service with Windows Security. If you view the properties for this component, you'll find that it has `Account`, `Password`, and `Username` properties. Change `Account` to `LocalSystem` account, so that after installation the service will run using the local system account.

The second of these, `serviceInstaller1`, allows us to provide a list of service dependencies through the `ServicesDependedOn` property (our service is not dependent on any other service, so we can leave this blank) and allows us to change the `StartType`. This defines the start type to set the service to on installation, and is `Manual` by default. The administrator is able to change this using the **Services** management console at a later time.

If we build the project at this point, it wouldn't actually do anything because we haven't yet incorporated any functionality. We need to create an instance of `BusinessHost.HostService` and call its `Go` method.

Open the code editor for `Service1`. You'll find a method stub with the name `OnStart` that – not surprisingly – gets called when the service starts. Add this code for the method body:

```
Protected Overrides Sub OnStart(ByVal args As String())
    ' Create and run the service
    Dim myService As BusinessHost.HostService = New BusinessHost.HostService()
    myService.Go()
End Sub
```

With a bit of luck, that's all we need to do to implement the class library as a Windows Service.

Installing and Running the Service

As I mentioned before, we can't run the service project within Visual Studio .NET. We have to first build the project, and then install it as a service. Build the project now.

To install the service, we use the `InstallUtil` utility that comes with .NET. Follow these steps to locate the .NET utilities:

1. Open a command prompt window.

2. Enter cd c:\winnt or cd c:\windows (the former for Windows 2000, the latter for other versions of Windows, including XP, unless of course you have installed Windows in a different folder)

3. Enter cd microsoft.net\framework

4. Enter dir

5. You'll see a list of folders named after the .NET build number they contain. If you have more than one, you'll need to know which build you're developing for, although this will usually be the latest.

6. Enter cd followed by the name of the folder.

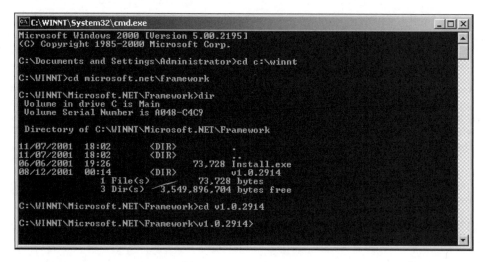

```
C:\WINNT\System32\cmd.exe                                          _ □ X

Microsoft Windows 2000 [Version 5.00.2195]
<C> Copyright 1985-2000 Microsoft Corp.

C:\Documents and Settings\Administrator>cd c:\winnt

C:\WINNT>cd microsoft.net\framework

C:\WINNT\Microsoft.NET\Framework>dir
 Volume in drive C is Main
 Volume Serial Number is A048-C4C9

 Directory of C:\WINNT\Microsoft.NET\Framework

11/07/2001  18:02    <DIR>          .
11/07/2001  18:02    <DIR>          ..
06/06/2001  19:26             73,728 Install.exe
08/12/2001  00:14    <DIR>          v1.0.2914
               1 File(s)         73,728 bytes
               3 Dir(s)   3,549,896,704 bytes free

C:\WINNT\Microsoft.NET\Framework>cd v1.0.2914

C:\WINNT\Microsoft.NET\Framework\v1.0.2914>
```

Now we can run the InstallUtil utility. This is simply a matter of providing the full path of the assembly containing the service, like this:

```
installutil c:\bookmanager\bookmanagerservice\bin\debug\bookmanagerservice.exe
```

A whole lot of debug information now appears; something like this:

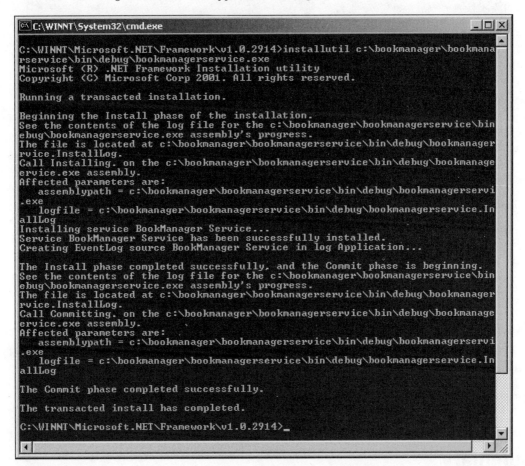

What we're looking for is the message **The Commit phase completed successfully** at the end. If you see this, installation was a success.

If we now open the **Services** management console, the **BookManager Service** will be listed and ready to start:

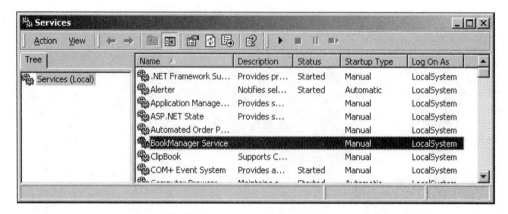

Right-click on the service and select Start. The service will start up by calling the `OnStart` method which creates a new instance of `HostService`. `Go` will be called and the objects will be made available for Remoting inside the new process.

To test the service, run the application browser, log in, and search for some customers using the Customer Editor. You'll find that the browser works as normal! We'll talk more about the Service in Chapter 11.

Continuing to Develop

At this point, we run into a minor logistical problem regarding debugging. If you need to make changes to the server-side code, you'll have to stop the Windows Service, build the changes in VS .NET and then restart the Windows Service for testing. It's for this reason that we debug our application using a console application rather than the Windows Service – it's easier to stop and start, and the VS.NET debugger is automatically attached when we run the project.

Summary

In this chapter, we started off by talking a little about the .NET Remoting subsystem and saw that it is a similar technology to Web Services, but with some important differences. We then introduced the idea of token-based authentication, a technique for identifying users as they make calls to the server-side code. We built methods on the Web Service to create these tokens, using WEO code for creating and managing such tokens.

After looking at the Web Service methods for logging on and logging off the system, we moved on to see how we could host the server-side object using Remoting. We created a separate class library containing the service implementation code, and for debugging purposes, built a console application that used the library. We then looked at how the client-side code selects between creating service objects locally for Direct connections and connecting to service objects hosted remotely.

When we were satisfied that development of the library was complete, we built a Windows Service around it ready for deployment in the production environment.

.NET Enterprise Development in VB .NET

Automated Deployment and Code Access Security

One of the nicest features of .NET is **automatic deployment**. This is one of the two things that make deploying desktop applications in .NET an order of magnitude easier than it is for traditional Windows desktop COM applications. The other is the fact that you can have multiple versions of the same assembly installed at any given moment – something we'll talk about in a moment.

Automatic deployment (sometimes referred to as "smart clients") lets you place your application's assemblies on a web server, accessible over either the Internet or the company intranet. When the application requires those assemblies, the .NET runtime automatically downloads and installs them on the local computer ready to be executed.

To understand the motivations behind this concept, let's look at it from the perspective of a large, fairly well known software house – Microsoft. Like most software today, its Office package is currently supplied as a self-contained set of programs that people must install on their local computer, an approach that leaves the door to software piracy open; a door that all software companies are very keen to seal shut. A more preferable arrangement from Microsoft's point of view would be to have a small application that is downloaded from the Internet, but contains very little functionality. As more functionality is required, the assemblies containing that functionality are automatically downloaded from a web server for use. For example, this may happen the first time the user selects Tools | Mail Merge from the menu. The application then executes the assemblies, which provide the required functionality by making calls to a Web Service that could charge a customer account accordingly. If you think about it, our Application Browser and sub-applications are already using a very similar model.

The best way for this to happen is to dump all of the assemblies on a web server and wait for .NET to sort out the downloading and installation of the components. Also, it would be great if, when a new version of the assembly becomes available, that can be downloaded to replace the cached version on disk. Automatic deployment does all this and more.

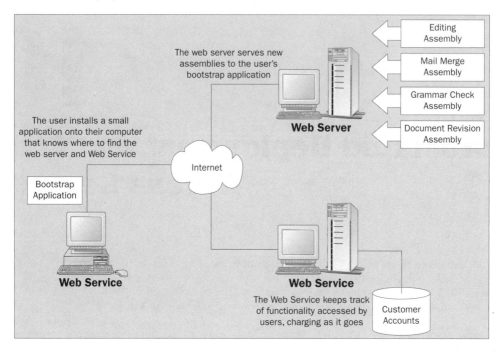

The advantage of this method is that deployment of an application like ours becomes so much easier. We need to install the Application Browser itself on the desktop, using one of these two methods:

❏ Standard desktop configuration – the IS department develops a standard desktop implementation that is rolled out to all desktops using a package such as Norton Ghost

❏ Downloadable install – the user downloads and installs the application from a package obtained locally or from a web server

In both situations, the application should be able to adjust its own configuration based on the local system settings – precisely what we've tried to achieve with our functionality catalog. When the Application Browser starts, it uses a Web Service to determine the catalog of functionality that a user may use. As we know, that catalog is basically a list of features, each associated to a given type within a given assembly.

Using automated deployment, when a functionality catalog references an assembly not already installed on the local computer, that assembly will be automatically downloaded and installed from a web server so that the browser can instantiate the types it defines, thus providing the required functionality.

Trying Automatic Deployment

To set up automated deployment, we should first take a look at what actually happens when we try to run a sub-application using one of the Debug menu options that we've been using so far.

In the ApplicationBrowser project, open the code editor for Browser. Find the SubApp property and add the code below. What we want to do is show the path of the assembly containing whatever sub-application control we want the browser to display, which we will do using a separate method called DisplayAssemblyInfo.

```
Public Property SubApp() As Control
  Get
    Return _subApp
  End Get
  Set(ByVal Value As Control)
    ' Reset
    Me.PanelApp.Controls.Clear()
    RemoveSubAppMenuItems()

    ' Do we have one?
    If Value Is Nothing Then
      ' cast it to a control
      _subApp = CType(Value, Control)

      If TypeOf (_subApp) Is ISubApplication Then
        _iSubApp = CType(_subApp, ISubApplication)
        _iSubApp.SetBrowser(Me)
      Else
        _iSubApp = Nothing
      End If

      ' Show it
      _subApp.Dock = DockStyle.Fill
      Me.panelApp.Controls.Add(_subApp)

      ' Debug
      DisplayAssemblyInfo(_subApp)

    Else
      _subApp = Nothing
      _iSubApp = Nothing
    End If
  End Set
End Property
```

DisplayAssemblyInfo takes an object and uses GetType to retrieve a Type object. From this Type object, we can get a System.Reflection.Assembly object and from that we can extract the information we need. Add this method to Browser:

```
Public Sub DisplayAssemblyInfo(ByVal theObject As Object)
    Dim theAssembly As System.Reflection.Assembly
    Dim builder As System.Text.StringBuilder = New System.Text.StringBuilder()
```

```
        ' Get the assembly
        theAssembly = theObject.GetType().Assembly

        ' Create a string builder to hold the assembly's details
        builder.Append("Type: ")
        builder.Append(theObject.GetType().ToString())
        builder.Append(vbCrLf & "Code base: ")
        builder.Append(theAssembly.CodeBase)
        builder.Append(vbCrLf & "Location: ")
        builder.Append(theAssembly.Location)
        builder.Append(vbCrLf & "Full name: ")
        builder.Append(theAssembly.FullName)

        ' Show it in an alert box
        Alert(builder.ToString(), MessageBoxIcon.Information)
    End Sub
```

Run the project, log on, and select the View | Debug: CustomerEditor.CustomerEditor menu option.
You'll see something similar to this:

The actual path isn't important – what is important is that the assembly has been loaded from
somewhere on the local computer. In fact, it's using the version of the assembly that's in the same folder
as the ApplicationBrowser.exe assembly.

Next, let's turn our attention to implementing automatic deployment.

Setting up IIS

At the moment, if we want to load a sub-application as described in the functionality catalog requested
when a user logs in, we use the static LoadFrom method of System.Reflection.Assembly. Here's
the code taken from Browser.vb:

```
Public Sub RunSubApplication(ByVal functionality As AppFunctionality)
    Dim subAppAssembly As [Assembly]
    ' Load the assembly
    Try
        subAppAssembly = _
                System.Reflection.Assembly.LoadFrom(functionality.AssemblyUrl)
```

Right now, the URL is actually a path to the file on the local computer. We need to change it from a local file to a remote file made available by a web server. I'm going to host the assemblies using IIS on another computer on my network. This remote computer does not have to have the .NET Framework installed on it. In fact, the computer I'm going to use, CORRADO, is my file server with virtually nothing installed apart from Windows 2000 Server and IIS.

To configure the assemblies, we need to create a new folder off our virtual root directory called vb\BookManagerAssemblies. We'll then have to copy all the assemblies created by the CustomerEditor project over to this new folder.

> **Aside from testing that the application works, this is pretty much all you have to do to deploy sub-applications using this technique.**

On the server, open up the IIS Management Console. Right-click on the Default Web Site entry, and select New | Virtual Directory:

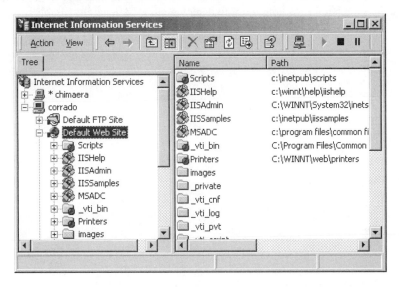

When prompted by the Wizard that now starts, enter **assemblies** in the Alias text box. Click Next to move on to a screen where we must give the local path to the physical directory we just created. When we click Next, a dialog opens showing the access types permitted for the new virtual directory. Make sure the following check boxes are set:

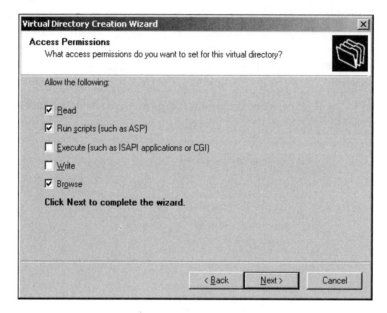

When setting up a web server in a deployment environment, we wouldn't normally turn on Browse permissions like we've done above. This feature means that if we navigate to the root of the virtual directory, IIS will show a list of folders and files that we can access. This is not usually a good idea, as it gives hackers a definitive list of files to tinker with. Here though, we need this to help us debug the server and make sure that it's working. Prior to deployment, we'd generally disable this permission.

Complete the Wizard and you should be able to navigate to the new alias of the directory on the server using a browser. You'll see something like this:

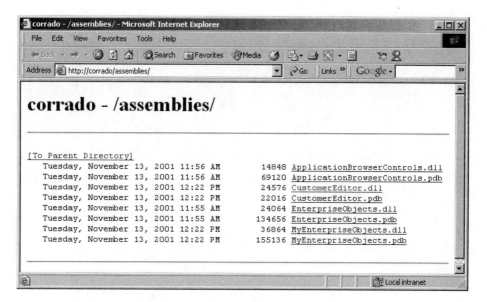

To use the new assembly, we have to change the functionality catalog returned by the Coordination Web Service to return the URL of the assembly, rather than a path on the local drive.

Open the code editor for `Coordination.asmx.vb` and make this change to `GetFunctionalityCatalog`:

```
<WebMethod()> _
Public Function GetFunctionalityCatalog(ByVal token As String) _
                                        As AppFunctionality()

  ' Create an array
  Dim functionality(0) As AppFunctionality


  ' Create it
  functionality(0) = New AppFunctionality()
  functionality(0).Name = "Customer Editor"
  functionality(0).MenuText = "Customer Editor"
  functionality(0).ToolbarIconUrl = ""
  functionality(0).TooltipText = "Allows you to edit customer information"
  functionality(0).AssemblyUrl = "http://corrado/assemblies/CustomerEditor.dll"
  functionality(0).TypeName = "CustomerEditor.CustomerEditor"

  ' Return it
  Return functionality
End Function
```

Run the project now and select View | Customer Editor from the menu. You should see this:

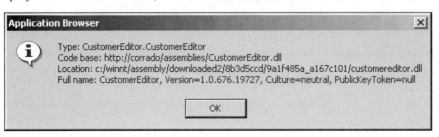

The magic happens when `Browser` calls the `LoadFrom` method on `Activator` from within `RunSubApplication`:

```
' RunSubApplication
Public Sub RunSubApplication(ByVal functionality As _
                             Coordination.AppFunctionality)
    ' Load the assembly
    Try
    Dim subAppAssembly As System.Reflection.Assembly = _
            System.Reflection.Assembly.LoadFrom(functionality.AssemblyUrl)

    ...

    Catch ex As System.IO.FileNotFoundException

    ...

    End Try
End Sub
```

`LoadFrom` looks at the URL it has been given to determine the source of the file. Web resources are downloaded and kept in the "download cache", covered in the next section.

The Global Assembly Cache

To find the download cache, open Windows Explorer and navigate to `c:\WINNT\assembly` (`c:\Windows\Assembly` if you're using Windows XP). This is the Global Assembly Cache, often known as the GAC, pronounced "gack", and it contains all the assemblies globally available to managed code on the system.

In the old COM model, when you wanted to use a component, you had to register it with Windows, adding a bunch of new entries to the Registry. Any application that starts one of these components does so through the COM subsystem, which uses the Registry to locate the DLL or EXE file containing the component.

The .NET component model works in quite a different way. For one thing, there's no Registry (well, there is one, but .NET doesn't use it). When an application needs to find an assembly, it can look in a number of places:

- ❑   In the folder containing the assembly that kicked off the process
- ❑   In the GAC
- ❑   Where it's been explicitly told to look.

The GAC is used when multiple applications wish to use the *same* assembly. If a company develops two applications and uses a common class library for both, there's a temptation to put the common classes in the GAC so that each of the two applications can access the code. However, that's a very "COM" way of seeing the problem. In COM, we were restricted by the law that only one version of a DLL could exist on a computer at any one time. With .NET, we don't have that restriction, and are free to have as many versions as we want in as many folders as we like. So, even if two applications use the same assembly, there's no absolute law that we *have* to use the GAC.

In fact, it's often better *not* to use the GAC. Imagine that we build and deploy the first application using common classes in January, and the second in July. If we were to use the GAC to locate the shared classes, both applications would be forced to use the same version of the classes – even though changes are quite likely to have occurred. It makes more sense to install the application assemblies for each of the two applications in two separate folders. This new ability partly arises from the fact that modern computers do not have the same space limitations that existed when COM was first developed. Disk space is now so cheap that it no longer need be a factor when deciding whether to follow the common libraries route.

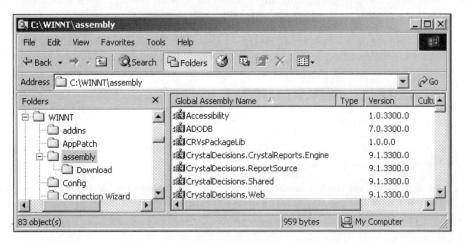

In the screenshot of the GAC above, we can see a sub-folder called `Download`: this is the download cache. .NET handles the finding, downloading, and installing of the DLL without our having to do anything other than provide a URL when we instantiate it. Open up the download cache, and you should see one or two `CustomerEditor.dll` assemblies in there. Exactly how many depends on how many times you've recompiled the assembly, as, for backwards compatibility, the download cache keeps many versions of the same DLL, automatically updating when necessary.

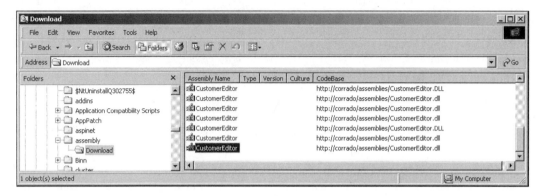

What about the other assemblies that **CustomerEditor** references? Well, this just goes to show how smart this automatic deployment functionality actually is. If .NET determines that one assembly requires another assembly that's not available locally, this too will be downloaded from the same location. There's no need to manually provide the full list of referenced assemblies – it automatically (perhaps even "automagically") works all this out by looking in the assembly's meta data to determine the DLLs it needs, automatically loading them when required by the application.

Code Access Security in .NET

That's great, but it isn't yet set up to work in our application! .NET has a sophisticated security scheme to mitigate some of the problems that viruses and worms have caused over recent years, as well as to address some of the security issues that have emerged from the many years of enterprise development on both Microsoft and other platforms.

Before you try to search for customers, close the browser. Open the code editor for `CustomerEditor` and add this code to `buttonSearch_Click` to catch and report any exceptions that occur inside the `FindCustomers` method:

```
Private Sub buttonSearch_Click(ByVal sender As System.Object, _
                               ByVal e As System.EventArgs) _
                               Handles buttonSearch.Click
   ' Get the search term from the text box
   Dim term As String = textSearchFor.Text
   If term.Length >= 3 Then
      ' Get the customers
      Me.Cursor = Cursors.WaitCursor
      Dim found As CustomerSet = Nothing
      Try
         found = Customer.FindCustomers(term)
      Catch ex As Exception
         Browser.HandleException(ex)
      End Try
      Me.Cursor = Cursors.Default

      ' What happened...
      If found.Tables(0).Rows.Count > 0 Then
         ' Show it...
         Customers = found
```

```
      Else
        Browser.Alert("No customers were found.", MessageBoxIcon.Information)

      End If
   Else
      Browser.Alert("You must enter three or more characters.")
   End If
End Sub
```

Build the project and copy the new `CustomerEditor.dll` assembly over to the **assemblies** virtual directory we made earlier.

.NET's auto-deployment mechanism will now detect that a newer version of the assembly is available on the site and automatically download and use that new version! At the same time, applications may, if necessary, request any previous version of the DLL.

Run the project, select View | Customer Editor and try searching. You'll see a huge message box, a little like this:

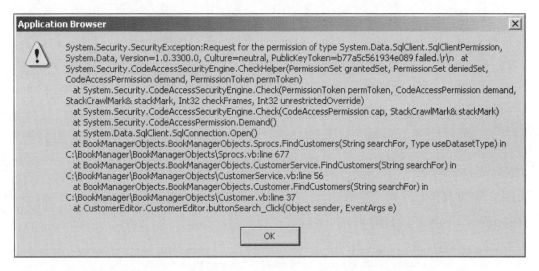

.NET's built-in "code security" functionality has looked at the assembly downloaded from http://corrado/ and determined that the code cannot be "trusted". This means that .NET cannot be certain that the assembly won't do something questionable, including such malicious activities as deleting everything on our local hard disk, or e-mailing a copy of a virus to all our Outlook contacts. To get over this, we need a way of telling .NET that the assembly is indeed from a trusted source, our own development department.

The security check itself doesn't have to happen locally. We could check the security using the service that we built in Chapter 9, thanks to a feature of .NET code access security. Whenever security is checked (in this specific case, we're trying to register a Remoting channel), .NET walks up the call stack to effectively determine the weakest link in the chain of calls. In this case, it will discover that `FindCustomers` has been called from within an assembly downloaded from the Internet and therefore treats the remote `FindCustomers` call as if that method had been downloaded from the Internet too.

317

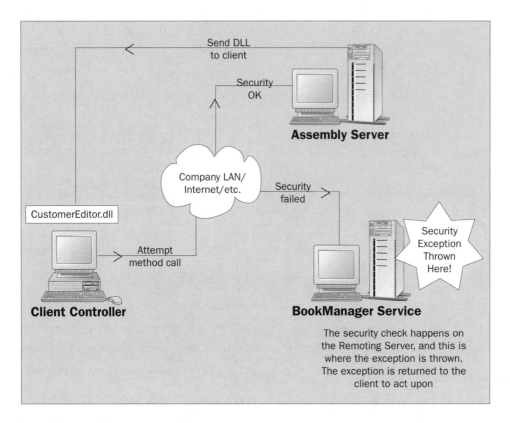

Getting Evidence

To determine what code is allowed to do, .NET uses what it calls "evidence". To get a better idea of this procedure, we'll look at the evidence attached to both the local CustomerEditor.dll assembly and the version downloaded from http://corrado/.

The evidence is actually quite long (it's a collection of XML documents), so rather than displaying it in a message box, we'll use the relatively ugly method of writing all the evidence to a separate file. In my opinion, this is a great deal less awkward than messing around with the irksome Output window in VS.NET. To retrieve the evidence, we use the Evidence property of the assembly.

To get a filename to write to, we'll use the static GetTempFileName method of System.IO.Path, and once we've written the file, we can automatically open it in Internet Explorer using the static Start method of System.Diagnostics.Process. This method opens the file passed in using the application associated with its file type, which, for .xml files, is Internet Explorer on most computers.

Find the DisplayAssemblyInfo method in Browser.vb and add this code:

```
' DisplayAssemblyInfo - show the details for the assembly
Public Sub DisplayAssemblyInfo(ByVal theObject As Object)
    Dim theAssembly As [Assembly]
    Dim builder As System.Text.StringBuilder = New System.Text.StringBuilder()
```

```
' Get the assembly
theAssembly = theObject.GetType().Assembly

' Create a string builder to hold the assembly's details
builder.Append("Type: ")
builder.Append(theObject.GetType().ToString())
builder.Append(vbCrLf & "Code base: ")
builder.Append(theAssembly.CodeBase)
builder.Append(vbCrLf & "Location: ")
builder.Append(theAssembly.Location)
builder.Append(vbCrLf & "Full name: ")
builder.Append(theAssembly.FullName)

' Prompt
builder.Append(vbCrLf & "Do you want to view the evidence for this assembly?")

' Ask the user
If Alert(builder.ToString(), MessageBoxButtons.YesNo, _
        MessageBoxIcon.Information) = DialogResult.Yes Then
   ' Write it to a file
   Dim filename As String = Path.GetTempFileName() & ".xml"
   Dim stream As FileStream = New FileStream(filename, FileMode.Create)
   Dim writer As StreamWriter = New StreamWriter(stream)
   writer.WriteLine("<Evidence>")

   ' Go through each part
   Dim evidenceObject As Object
   For Each evidenceObject In theAssembly.Evidence
      writer.WriteLine(evidenceObject.ToString())
      writer.WriteLine()
   Next

   ' Close and show
   writer.WriteLine("<Evidence>")
   writer.Flush()
   writer.Close()
   System.Diagnostics.Process.Start(filename)
End If
End Sub
```

Run the project and from the menu select View | Debug: CustomerEditor.CustomerEditor to run the local copy of the sub-application. When prompted, click Yes to display the evidence.

Of the three pieces of evidence attached to the local copy of CustomerEditor.dll, we see results from three objects: an instance of System.Security.Policy.Zone, an instance of System.Security.Policy.Url, and an instance of System.Security.Policy.Hash. The Hash doesn't do a lot for us here (it is simply a unique value that allows the assembly to be referred to unambiguously rather than using names), but the other two are worth reproducing:

```
<System.Security.Policy.Zone version="1">
  <Zone>MyComputer</Zone>
</System.Security.Policy.Zone>
```

```
<System.Security.Policy.Url version="1">
  <Url>
    file://C:/BookManager/ApplicationBrowser/bin/CustomerEditor.DLL
  </Url>
</System.Security.Policy.Url>
```

Here we see that Zone is given as MyComputer, and Url as the path to the DLL on the local disk.

> **Some will recognize MyComputer as one of the four security zones in Internet Explorer, and rightly so – the zones in .NET code access security are directly linked to the security zones of Internet Explorer.**

Now try the same thing with the downloaded copy of Customer Editor, in other words select View | Customer Editor from the menu. You'll get four pieces of evidence this time (the extra one breaks out the host name used in the URL into a separate piece of evidence) and if we again ignore Hash, we should have something like this:

```
<System.Security.Policy.Zone version="1">
    <Zone>Intranet</Zone>
</System.Security.Policy.Zone>

<System.Security.Policy.Url version="1">
    <Url>http://corrado/assemblies/CustomerEditor.dll</Url>
</System.Security.Policy.Url>

<System.Security.Policy.Site version="1">
    <Name>corrado</Name>
</System.Security.Policy.Site>
```

In this case, we can see that .NET has determined that the DLL comes from the Intranet zone. By default, Internet Explorer will treat any UNC name or any server on the same Class-C IP address as a local intranet path. For the uninitiated, a UNC (Universal Naming Convention) name is the name of the computer, in this case corrado. A Class-C IP address is the first three bytes of a full IP address. So, if our client was on 192.168.0.100 and our server was on 192.168.0.22, both would be on the same Class C because 192.168.0 appears at the start of both. In addition, you or your system administrator can add specific sites to the intranet list using the security settings for Internet Explorer.

You'll also notice that the additional piece of evidence, System.Security.Policy.Site, is listed as the name of your computer. We shall use this extra piece of information to set "security policy" in the following section.

Security Policy

In purely intellectual terms, code access and policy is quite easy. At the moment, .NET is examining the assembly with the evidence of Intranet, the URL and the server name of corrado, and determining that that evidence is not sufficient to serialize the object, based on the policy settings of the computer in tandem with the user and general settings that apply to the entire enterprise environment. We must change policy to make the evidence sufficient for full trust to be granted, hence letting us run the code as intended.

When setting policy, there are two concepts that we have to understand: Code Groups and Permissions.

Code Groups, as their name implies, group together code with similar characteristics. In most cases, the most important characteristic is the code's origin. In our example, we have one case where the assembly was installed locally and one where it was downloaded from the intranet. **Permissions** are attached to code groups and specify what the code group is allowed to do.

You can probably see where I'm going with this and realize that two options are open to us. We can either boost the permissions of the code group that the downloaded version of Customer Editor already belongs to, or we can create a new code group with enhanced permissions that the downloaded version of Customer Editor can be put into. When making policy decisions, it's best to choose the option that has the most focused effect, and also to ensure that our policy decisions don't have side effects such as crippling an already working application, or giving more permissions to assemblies that don't need them. In this case, our best option is to create a new code group.

.NET comes with seven top-level code groups in the standard installation. (Technically, there are eight as there is a master group that contains all the other seven.) We can add our own to this, but in this case there's no need. Here are the seven:

- ❑ `My_Computer_Zone` – this is the local computer. Assemblies physically installed on the local computer are in this group.

- ❑ `LocalIntranet_Zone` – these are servers on the local intranet. Our downloaded assembly is in this group.

- ❑ `Internet_Zone` – these are servers outside of the local intranet.

- ❑ `Restricted_Zone` – these are servers that have been specifically placed by a system administrator on a list of restricted sites.

- ❑ `Trusted_Zone` – these are servers that have been specifically placed by a system administrator on a list of trusted sites.

- ❑ `Microsoft_Strong_Name` – we'll cover this later, but this basically flags any assembly signed by Microsoft with full trust.

- ❑ `ECMA_Strong_Name` – similar to the `Microsoft_Strong_Name` group, except that this applies to assemblies signed as coming from ECMA.

Each code group has exactly one membership condition. In the first five cases, the condition is the zone that members belong to, in other words the zone where they were originally obtained. In the last two cases, membership is determined by whom they were signed by. We're not going to talk about code signing here, but in simple terms all it means is that before Microsoft or ECMA release the assembly, they sign it to say that it is theirs. We could do the same with our own code, but we won't in this case.

Code groups are arranged in a hierarchy, with the all-encompassing "All Code" group at the top. If we look at the first three, we have something like this:

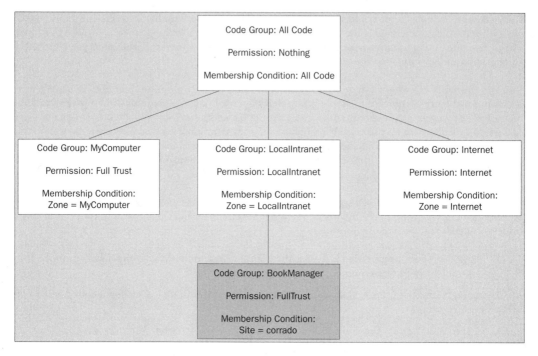

Confusingly, the code groups have two different names – one appearing to be human-readable and one appearing to be machine-readable. In the bulleted list, we've used the human-readable names, mainly because the two "strong name" groups have long hex values for their machine-readable names. The "zone" groups have textual machine-readable names, and we'll use those when we need to manipulate them.

In the diagram above, we've jumped slightly ahead of ourselves. The gray box at the bottom shows a new code group called **BookManager,** with **FullTrust** permissions set. We've also given it a membership condition of Site = corrado. This means that any assembly downloaded from the LocalIntranet zone originating from corrado will be given full trust, that is, will have the same privileges as if it were installed locally.

We can set permission in two ways. Firstly we can use a command-line utility called caspol.exe (for "code access security policy"). This is useful if we need to script security updates as part of an application deployment or system administration function. Alternatively, we can use a Microsoft Management Console snap-in that does the same thing. If you're a longtime Windows user, you're going to be more comfortable using a GUI tool for this.

Although the snap-in is installed by default, the .mmc file associated with it is not. To do this, click the **Start** button and select **Run**. Enter mmc and click OK. This will create a blank management console:

> The instructions you're about to see apply to Windows 2000. Things are a little
> different in XP, but you should be able to follow if you apply a little common sense.

From the menu, select Console | Add/Remove Snap-in. When the dialog appears, select Add. You'll see a list of available snap-ins, the first being the .NET Framework Configuration snap-in:

Select it and click Add. Then click Close and click OK. Save the management console at this point by selecting Console | Save.

Expand out the objects in the management tree until you come to Runtime Security Policy:

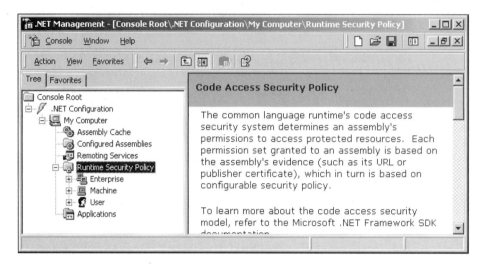

The wrinkle to security that we haven't yet been through is that of **levels**. There are three levels of security – Enterprise, Machine, and User. The All_Code group appears in all levels (which you can confirm by expanding the objects in the management tree). The Machine level contains the seven groups that we saw earlier. Security levels is a topic that we're not going to go into here, but in essence it allows us to set enterprise level policy decisions that cannot be overridden by the user. As we'd expect, it allows us to also set permissions for the current user that don't apply to the other users on the same computer, and so on.

Drill down into the objects until you get to the Machine | Code Groups | All_Code | LocalIntranet_Zone group:

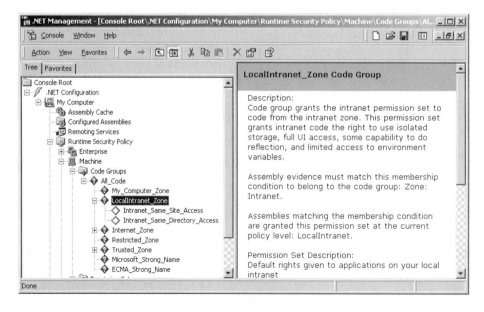

We now want to create a new code group underneath this called BookManager_Site. Right-click LocalIntranet_Zone, and select New. Enter these details into the dialog:

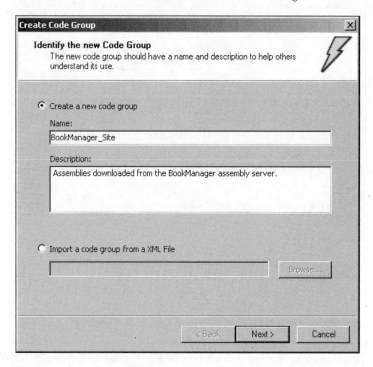

Click Next. From the condition-type drop-down, select Site and enter the name of your server in the text box underneath:

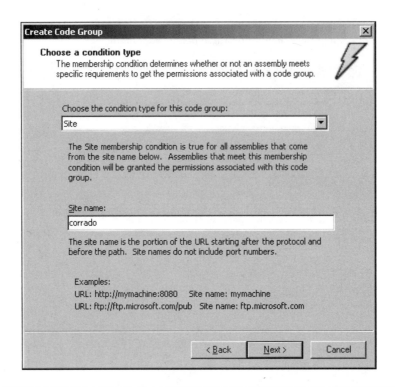

By using the **Site** option here we can set permissions for any **DLL** downloaded from the specified web server. If we wanted, we could use the **URL** option to specify a specific URL rather than an entire server.

At this point, we can create our own permission set, or we can use an existing one. Let's try to keep life simple, and use an existing permission set. Select FullTrust from the list. If we wanted, we could spend some time locking down security to eliminate as many security risks as possible. For example, we could dictate that assemblies downloaded from a site are not allowed access to files on disk, but are allowed access to printers.

When you click **Finish**, the new group will be created:

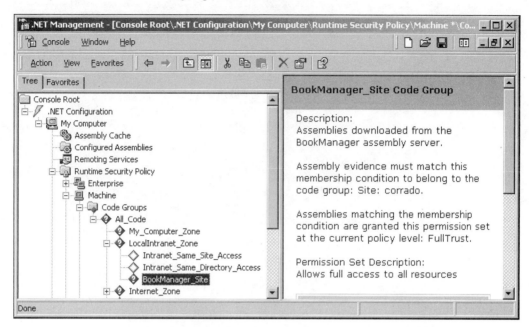

Now the acid test! If the **ApplicationBrowser** project is running, close it. Restart it, and select **View |
Customer Editor** from the menu. Try searching for something and you should get the expected results.
At this point, the code is executing with the same **FullTrust** permissions that the locally installed version
had, thus letting the search work correctly.

Evaluating Permissions

So how do we determine the permissions an assembly has? We use the same management console.
Right-click the **Runtime Security Policy** and select **Evaluate Assembly**. Enter the URL of the
downloadable assembly into the dialog. First of all, we'll take a look at the permissions the assembly
has, so make sure **View permissions granted to the assembly** is selected. If we were more deeply
involved with looking at security, we could use the **Policy level** dropdown to determine what was
happening. For now, keep **All Levels** selected and click **Next**:

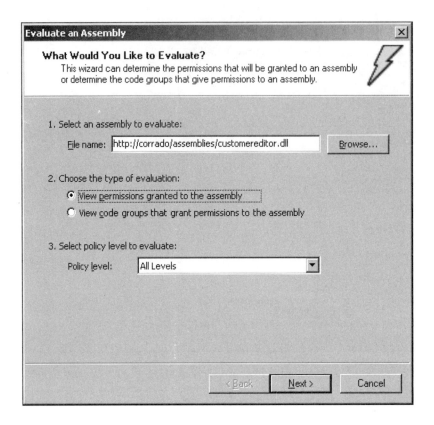

The dialog that now appears should show us that the assembly has unrestricted permissions granted to it:

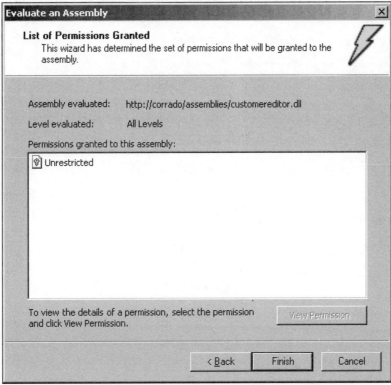

Let's compare this with what happens if the DLL is installed on another computer. Rather than actually placing the DLL on another computer though, we can provide the IP address of the server rather than its UNC name, so that the membership condition of "Site = corrado" will no longer be satisfied. Put more simply, we'll use:

```
http://192.168.0.17/assemblies/customereditor.dll
```

instead of:

```
http://corrado/assemblies/customereditor.dll
```

Although we know the two are equivalent, .NET doesn't look up the IP address of corrado (that would be woefully inefficient), so it won't fall into the same code group. This would equally be the case if we had selected the URL from the dialog earlier, rather than Site.

If you don't know the IP address of the server, open a DOS command box. Enter ping *servername* and press return. The output you'll see will include the IP address:

```
C:\WINNT\Microsoft.NET\Framework\v1.0.3617>ping corrado

Pinging corrado [192.168.0.17] with 32 bytes of data:

Reply from 192.168.0.17: bytes=32 time<10ms TTL=128
Reply from 192.168.0.17: bytes=32 time<10ms TTL=128
Reply from 192.168.0.17: bytes=32 time<10ms TTL=128
Reply from 192.168.0.17: bytes=32 time<10ms TTL=128

Ping statistics for 192.168.0.17:
    Packets: Sent = 4, Received = 4, Lost = 0 (0% loss),
Approximate round trip times in milli-seconds:
    Minimum = 0ms, Maximum =  0ms, Average =  0ms

C:\WINNT\Microsoft.NET\Framework\v1.0.3617>
```

Go through the evaluation process again, but enter the IP address of the server rather than the name.
You'll get a set of permissions, this time those granted to any assembly downloaded from a general
Internet site, like this:

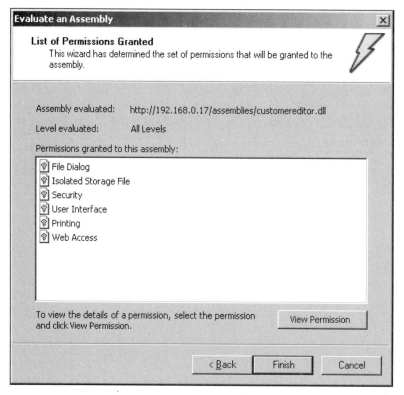

The order in which these permissions appear means that:

❑   The application is allowed to present file dialog boxes

❑   The application is allowed access to isolated storage

❑   The application is allowed to check security

❑   The application is allowed to present a user interface

❑   The application is allowed to print

❑   The application is allowed to access the Web

More About Security

Security is a huge topic, and I've already said pretty much all I want to say about it. If you want further information, you might try these Wrox books:

❑   *Professional ASP.NET ISBN 1-861004-88-5*

❑   *ASP.NET Security ISBN 1-861006-20-9 (published April 2002)*

❑   *Professional C# ISBN 1-861004-99-0*

The premise of security is that you have a flexible infrastructure that allows you to build a comprehensive, easily manageable set of rights for code. To keep things simple in our example, we've set up our security so that assemblies downloaded from our intranet share the same level of trust as if they were installed directly on the local computer. We could have created a more restrictive policy – for example, to let the assemblies read from the local disk, but not write, or to prevent the assemblies accessing the Internet, but permitting connection to SQL Server databases and so on.

Turning Security Off

During development and maintenance, you might find it best to disable security entirely. This is something that I often do when developing, but you do need to be aware that it masks many issues that may return to haunt you when you re-enable security prior to deployment. The code access security is really useful in enterprise environments, but can be restrictive. For instance, you may have already discovered that working with a project whose binaries are written to a network share causes security problems when executing.

To turn off security, you need to use the caspol utility. To find this, open a command window, and change to the c:\winnt\Microsoft.NET\Framework folder. In this folder, you'll find a sub-folder named after the Framework version. Move to this folder and run caspol with the command-line option –s off:

```
C:\WINNT\Microsoft.NET\Framework\v1.0.3617>caspol -s off
Microsoft (R) .NET Framework CasPol 1.0.3617.0
Copyright (c) Microsoft Corp 1998-2001. All rights reserved.

Success

C:\WINNT\Microsoft.NET\Framework\v1.0.3617>
```

Once this command has completed successfully, no security checking will be performed.

331

Application Security

Code access security, such as we've just looked at, is used primarily to control access to system resources, mainly to prevent code from either maliciously or accidentally doing something that could be embarrassing or disruptive. The near-constant barrage of news stories about viruses and worms like Nimda, SirCam, etc., provides an indication of the importance of this issue.

The other side of security arises from the actual users of our systems, and is concerned with controlling what people may or may not do at an application level. For example, we wish to prevent a certain user changing information in the Customer Editor, but still let them view it. Or we might decide that another user is only able to search for customers that they are the account manager for and so on.

This type of security requires a slightly different approach, so let's quickly recap where we've got so far as regards security:

❑ Chapter 3 introduced the Coordination Web Service. We pretty much ignored security at this point.

❑ Chapters 6 and 7 showed how we could build another Web Service integrated with Windows security to allow or disallow access to the application.

❑ Chapter 9 showed how we can take the same security infrastructure built in Chapters 6 and 7 and integrate it into our Remoting service.

In this chapter, we'll build on the work from Chapter 9 to selectively turn off functionality within a sub-application.

User Rights

There are a number of options we can use to record the rights of users on our system. Whatever option we choose, we need to ensure that we have a great deal of control and accountability over what users can and can't do. The best way to implement the control we need is to build a new class in `BookManagerObjects` that has the intelligence to check security for us.

The actual security scheme that's best for your application is going to vary, and for this reason the WEO layer doesn't contain classes that implement a security scheme. In the remainder of this chapter, we're going to build one. In fact, we're going to keep it pretty simple. We'll be using a database to store the data required to implement our security scheme. An alternative would be to use Active Directory or some other data management solution.

Generally, security schemes work on the principle of users, groups, and permissions:

❑ A "**permission**" determines whether or not the user can do something. "Yes, the user can create files", "No, the user cannot print", etc.

❑ A "**group**" is a collection of permissions. For example, you could create a group that prevents all file access by combining the "No, the user cannot access local files" and "No, the user cannot access network files" into a group.

❑ A "**user**" is a collection of groups. For example, an admin user will belong to groups that give them relatively free access to the system, whereas a normal user will belong to a more restrained set of groups.

Typically security schemes are implemented so that permissions take precedence according to their potential to prevent harm. For example, if the user is a member of a group that contains a permission called "Yes, allow the user to delete files" and another group called "No, stop the user from deleting files", the second one will take priority, as it is the 'safer' option. This is because the underlying principle of any security scheme is the reduction of users' rights, not their augmentation.

Securing Customer Edits

In this chapter, we're going to look at two groups – one called `CustomerEditor` and one called `CustomerViewer`, but each containing just one permission: `EditCustomers`. For the `CustomerEditor` group, this permission will be set to `True`, while for `CustomerViewer`, this permission will be set to `False`.

In our security scheme, here's how the five tables relate to each other:

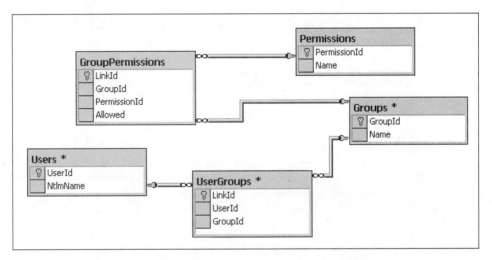

Three of these tables (`Users`, `Groups`, and `Permissions`) contain actual data. We met `Users` in Chapter 9. The `Permissions` table details the actions that each user may perform. For the purposes of this chapter, these tables only contain the minimum required to illustrate the concepts we're discussing. In fact, `Permissions` only contains one row:

This permission, `EditCustomers`, can be used to grant users the right to edit customers. The two states possible are generally known as **allow** and **disallow**.

To allow or disallow a permission, the permission has to be added to a group. For this example, we need to define two groups in the sample database:

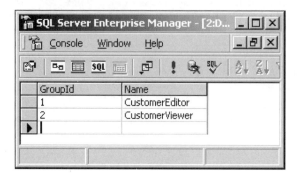

You can probably see where we're headed with this. We'll add the EditCustomers permission to both groups, setting it to "allow" for the CustomerEditor group, and to "disallow" for CustomerViewer. Here are the values in GroupPermissions:

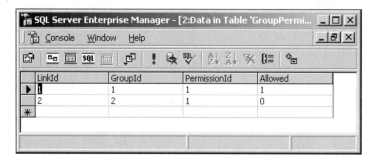

OK, so this is just a bunch of ID codes, and is not what you might call intuitive. In a while, we'll set up a view that makes understanding this easier.

In the sample database, the only user that is assigned groups is Matt. The assignment between users and groups is set up in the UserGroups table:

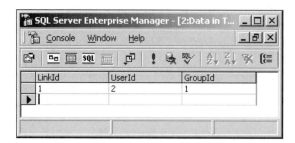

The database contains a view called vPermissions that brings all these tables together in a more logical form:

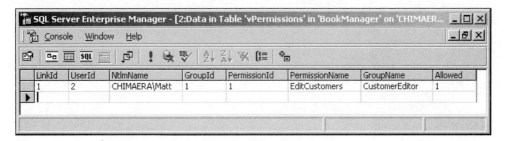

This shows us that the user with the ID of 2 (Matt) has the EditCustomers permission, as set by the CustomerEditor group. The Allowed field on the right tells us whether that permission is allowed ("1") or disallowed ("0"). All we have to do now is to apply this data to enforce security in our application.

Checking Security

To check permissions, we'll create a new class called SecurityChecker. We'll create this class in the BookManagerObjects project, inheriting from EnterpriseObjects.Service so that it will automatically work with Remoting, and to allow a service object factory to create it.

This class exposes two methods: CheckSecurity and AssertSecurity. The first, CheckSecurity, determines whether a given permission is or is not allowed for a particular user's groups. If it tells us that a user may not edit data for instance, we can then set all the TextBox controls on the Customer Editor to read-only. AssertSecurity will be used when we're deep in code and need to verify that a user is allowed to do whatever it is that they are trying to do. We'll cover this a little later.

Firstly, let's kick off and create the SecurityChecker class in the BookManagerObjects project. Set it to inherit from EnterpriseObjects.Service, as shown below. When we start the Remoting Host, this class will automatically be registered with .NET's Remoting services.

```
Public Class SecurityChecker
  Inherits EnterpriseObjects.Service

End Class
```

We'll use exceptions to report back security problems to the caller. Specifically, we'll be reporting three possible problems:

- ❑ InvalidSecurityTokenException – occurs when there is no token in the database matching the one that we've been given

- ❑ SecurityTokenExpiredException – occurs when the token has expired

- ❑ SecurityAssertionException – occurs when we're asked to assert security and security fails

Add these three inner classes to `SecurityChecker`:

```
Public Class SecurityChecker
  Inherits EnterpriseObjects.Service

    ' Exception classes
    Public Class InvalidSecurityTokenException
      Inherits System.Security.SecurityException

      Public Sub New()
        MyBase.New("Invalid security token")
      End Sub
    End Class

    Public Class SecurityTokenExpiredException
      Inherits System.Security.SecurityException

      Public Sub New()
        MyBase.New("Security token expired")
      End Sub
    End Class

    Public Class SecurityAssertionException
      Inherits System.Security.SecurityException

      Public Sub New(ByVal ntlmName As String, ByVal groupName As String, _
                ByVal permissionName As String)
        MyBase.New("Security assertion failed: " & ntlmName & ", " & _
                                      groupName & ", " & permissionName)
      End Sub
    End Class

    Public Sub New()
      ' Nothing to do...
    End Sub
  End Class
```

To create an instance of `SecurityChecker`, we'll use a shared method called `Create`. This method will use whatever `ServiceObjectFactory` is appropriate (based on whether we have a Direct or Remoting connection). You'll have to add an Imports statement for Enterprise Objects to the top of the class to use this:

```
Public Shared Function Create() As SecurityChecker
  Return CType(EnterpriseApplication.Application.ServiceObjectFactory.Create( _
                                GetType(SecurityChecker)), SecurityChecker)
End Function
```

Now let's turn our attention to the `CheckSecurity` method. We'll build two versions; one that takes a security token, and another that retrieves the security token from the `Service` class, by the `GetSecurityToken` method as in our Remoting work in Chapter 9. Here's the first version that merely passes processing to the second version:

```
Public Function CheckSecurity(ByVal groupName As String, _
                              ByVal permissionName As String) As Boolean
   Return CheckSecurity(GetSecurityToken(), groupName, permissionName)
End Function
```

For the actual security check, there are a number of things we have to do. We must load the token from the database, check to see if it has expired, update the expiry if it has not, and finally call the `CheckPermissions` stored procedure to find out whether we can or cannot do what we've been asked. We'll take a look at `CheckPermissions` in a little while, but basically this will return `null` or `0` if the permission is not available, and `1` if it is.

```
Public Function CheckSecurity(ByVal tokenString As String, _
                              ByVal groupName As String, _
                              ByVal permissionName As String) As Boolean
   ' Load the token
   Dim tkn As Token = Token.Load(tokenString)
   If tkn Is Nothing Then
      Throw New InvalidSecurityTokenException()
   End If

   ' Has it expired?
   If tkn.HasExpired() = True Then
      Throw New SecurityTokenExpiredException()
   End If

   ' Reset the expiration time
   tkn.UpdateExpiryTime()

   ' Run the stored procedure
   Dim dset As DataSet = BookManagerObjects.Sprocs.CheckPermissions(tkn.UserId, _
                              groupName, permissionName, GetType(DataSet))
   If dset.Tables.Count = 0 Then
      Return False
   End If

   ' What did we get?
   If (dset.Tables(0).Rows(0).IsNull(0) = True) Or _
                     (CType(dset.Tables(0).Rows(0)(0), Int16) = 0) Then
      Return False
   End If

   ' Return
   Return True
End Function
```

Not too complicated really, as most of the magic happens inside the stored procedure.

Let's take another look at our `vPermissions` view. It shows the single permission we have defined, for the user `CHIMAERA\Matt`, and because `Allowed` is set to `1`, the `EditCustomers` permission in the group `CustomerEditor` is granted:

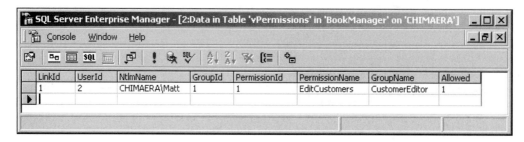

Here's the code for the `CheckPermissions` stored procedure. Following the maximum safety rule mentioned earlier, it uses the `Min` SQL Server scalar function to select the lowest possible value for `Allowed` given a particular user ID, group name, and permission name. Somewhat counter-intuitively, this value will actually be `null` if the `Allowed` column is set to 0.

```
CREATE PROCEDURE CheckPermissions
(
  @userId int,
  @groupname varchar(64),
  @permissionname varchar(64)
)
 AS
  SELECT Min(allowed) AS Allowed FROM vpermissions
    WHERE userid=@userid AND groupname=@groupname AND
      permissionname=@permissionname
```

All we have to do in our `CheckSecurity` method is examine the value returned by this stored procedure and return `True` if it is 1, or `False` if not.

Adapting the Customer Editor

To try out the security, we need to adapt the customer editor to check security when it loads. If the user is not allowed to edit data, we'll set all the `TextBox` controls to read-only, otherwise we can just leave them as read/write.

Open the code editor for `CustomerEditor`, and add this private member:

```
Public Class CustomerEditor
  Inherits System.Windows.Forms.UserControl
  Implements ISubApplication

  ' Members
  Private _browser As IBrowser
  Private _readOnly As Boolean = False
```

Next, add this code to the constructor:

```
Public Sub New()
  'This call is required by the Windows Form Designer.
  InitializeComponent()
```

```
' Check
Dim checker As BookManagerObjects.SecurityChecker = _
                          BookManagerObjects.SecurityChecker.Create()
If checker.CheckSecurity("CustomerEditor", "EditCustomers") = False Then
    _readOnly = True
End If


' Update
textFirstName.ReadOnly = _readOnly
textLastName.ReadOnly = _readOnly
textEmail.ReadOnly = _readOnly
textCompanyName.ReadOnly = _readOnly
textAddress1.ReadOnly = _readOnly
textAddress2.ReadOnly = _readOnly
textCity.ReadOnly = _readOnly
textRegion.ReadOnly = _readOnly
textPostalCode.ReadOnly = _readOnly
textCountry.ReadOnly = _readOnly
textPhone.ReadOnly = _readOnly
textFax.ReadOnly = _readOnly


' Events
If _readOnly = False Then
    AddHandler scrollerCustomers.UnderlyingDataChanged, New _
                ApplicationBrowserControls.UnderlyingDataChangedEventHandler( _
                AddressOf ScrollerCustomersUnderlyingDataChanged)
End If
End Sub
```

Run the project and log in as user Matt. As this user has permission to edit customers by default, everything should work just as it did before.

Now, using SQL Server Enterprise Manager, open the UserGroups table. Change the GroupID for the user with ID 2 from 1 to 2:

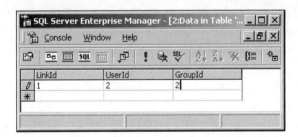

Save the changes. If we now open the vPermissions view again, we'll see that Matt now has the EditCustomers permission denied:

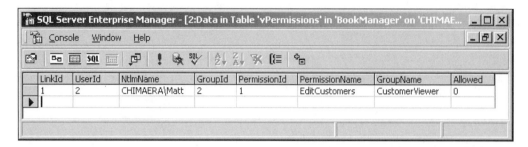

Run the browser again and log in as Matt. If you open the Customer Editor, you'll find all the text boxes are now grayed out, indicating that they cannot be modified:

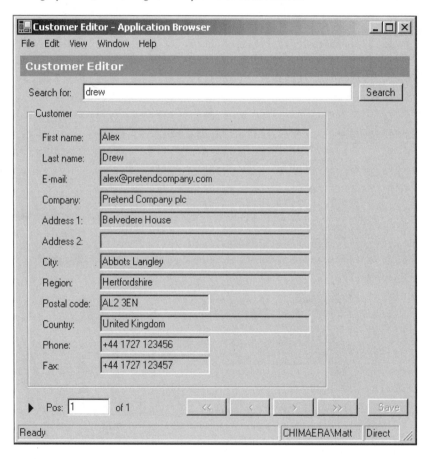

Asserting Security

We can now control which parts of the program the user may access. However, graying out the text boxes is only half the battle.

We have a relatively open system. If a user can log in and be allocated a security token, they can use that token for any calls in the system. Specifically, this means that the user is free to attempt to make calls that they may not have permission to do. Take the above example to illustrate. We've grayed out the text boxes, but what's to stop the user from calling `CustomerService.Update` directly from their own application written against the same business object tier that our Customer Editor is written against? This same problem is an issue if we have an ASP.NET application or Web Service that does the same thing. Of course, what we want to happen is nothing, and to achieve this, we need to assert that the user has sufficient rights at each critical stage of processing.

In this section, we'll look at how to control access to the `SaveChanges` method. Firstly, we'll add a new method to `SecurityChecker` called `AssertSecurity`, and secondly we'll create an overloaded `SaveChanges` method to perform the security check.

Open the code editor for `SecurityChecker`. Add these two versions of the `AssertSecurity` method:

```
Public Sub AssertSecurity(ByVal groupName As String, _
                          ByVal permissionName As String)
  AssertSecurity(GetSecurityToken(), groupName, permissionName)
End Sub

Public Sub AssertSecurity(ByVal tokenString As String, _
                          ByVal groupName As String, _
                          ByVal permissionName As String)
  ' Check the privileges
  If CheckSecurity(tokenString, groupName, permissionName) = False Then
    Throw New SecurityAssertionException(Token.Load( _
                    GetSecurityToken()).NtlmName, groupName, permissionName)
  End If
End Sub
```

All this does is call `CheckSecurity`, and throw a `SecurityAssertionException` exception if the user's security rights are insufficient.

If you recall, `Update` is implemented on `CustomerServiceBase` when the Object Builder automatically generates it. We have to provide an overridden implementation in the derived `CustomerService` to assert security, and carry on to call `Update` if no exception is thrown.

Open the code editor for `CustomerService`, and add this method:

```
' Update Method
Public Overloads Sub Update(ByVal id As Integer, _
                            ByVal firstName As String, ByVal lastName As String, _
                            ByVal email As Object, ByVal companyName As Object, _
                            ByVal address1 As String, ByVal address2 As String, _
                            ByVal city As String, ByVal region As Object, _
                            ByVal postalCode As String, ByVal country As String, _
```

```
                              ByVal phone As Object, ByVal fax As Object)
    ' Assert security
    Dim checker As SecurityChecker = SecurityChecker.Create()
    checker.AssertSecurity("CustomerEditor", "EditCustomers")

    ' Call the update method of the base class if we're still here
    ' (that is, no exception was thrown)
    MyBase.Update(id, firstName, lastName, email, companyName, _
                  address1, address2, city, region, postalCode, _
                  country, phone, fax)
End Sub
```

At this point, even if the user decides to roll out their own client application that talks directly to the Remoting layer, they will not be able to use the Update object unless their logon has sufficient privileges.

Summary

In this chapter we have investigated deployment and security issues when developing enterprise-level applications in .NET. .NET offers some amazing improvements over how applications are deployed and secured in the Windows DNA and COM world.

We started out with a look at automated deployment. This is a neat new feature in .NET that allows our applications to automatically download and install assemblies from a web server as and when they need them. It makes deployment much easier as we now only have to install a small "bootstrap" application on client machines. We can then leave that application to download and use assemblies as required, without our having to contend with the hassle of installing them manually.

After demonstrating how this works, and finding that it's really not difficult to get the feature working, we moved on to security. .NET has a comprehensive built-in security system, called code access security. Its primary goal is to control how applications may access system resources. For example, we can stop certain code accessing the local drive, network printers, and so on. .NET security is highly configurable, and to demonstrate, we took a quick look at how to designate assemblies downloaded from our intranet as having "full trust".

Then we dealt with "high-level" security – how we can control what our users are allowed to do with our applications. The scheme we put together was pretty simple, but served to illustrate the basics of building such schemes and the sort of methods we need to check security and present the proper UI to the user. Lastly, we looked at how to assert security to prevent our scheme from being circumvented.

.NET Enterprise Development in VB .NET

11

Administration

With an application like that described in this book, we will on occasion need to perform certain system administration tasks to maintain the "health" of the system. For example, we may need to change the global state of the application, alter user privileges, and such like. In this chapter, we'll look at how to put together simple administration tools to facilitate the day-to-day administration of the application. The tools we build in this chapter will all be desktop applications, although we'll construct them so that we could easily reuse a lot of the code that supports these desktop tools in web-based applications.

Building the Administration Tool

There are a number of ways that we can manage the service. In some cases, it might be appropriate to simply call methods on the `Coordination` Web Service from Chapter 3 to make changes to the database that would affect the client applications down the line. For example, we could store a list of sub-applications in the database, and add new sub-applications to the database directly, by using the Web Service. This way, we avoid having to call directly into the server process.

In some cases however, it may be useful to be able to "get inside" the service process. For example, when administering SQL Server, the SQL Server process itself supports requests from management tools such as "create table", "rebuild index", "drop stored procedure" and so on. As we'll learn later on, with our particular application there is limited need to be able to get inside the service process in this way.

To "get inside" the service process, we can use the Remoting subsystem discussed in some detail in Chapter 9. This is a two-stage process, which involves our creating classes within the service process that gather useful data for administration purposes. We can then create singleton objects that can expose this data to the admin tools.

> In the next chapter, we're going to look at performance counters and some other monitoring techniques that go hand-in-hand with the kind of tools that we're going to build here.

The following figure summarizes this arrangement. Note that the management tool running on the client can use either the admin objects running in the service process, or alternatively it can carry out administrative tasks by connecting to the Web Service:

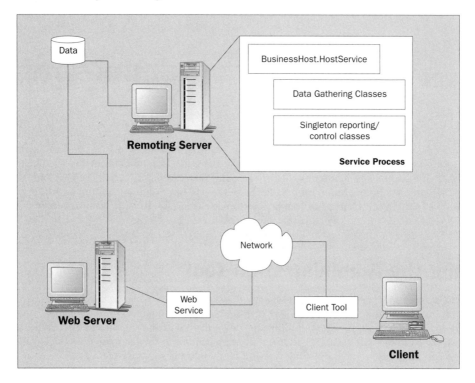

The question remains, then, what exactly are we going to do with our admin tool? In a real-world application, there would be plenty of really solid tasks that we might want it to do. In the case of our sample application, there aren't as many suitable jobs, and so we will look at building an administration tool that follows the classic "tree of objects on left, data on right" paradigm, as seen in Windows Explorer. It will be able to:

- ❑ Connect to the Web Service for some admin tasks
- ❑ Connect to the service process itself for other admin tasks
- ❑ Start and stop the service process

Building the Tool

A number of administration tools operate on the principle of "connecting to a server". Here's a snapshot of SQL Server's Management Console showing possible connections to three servers:

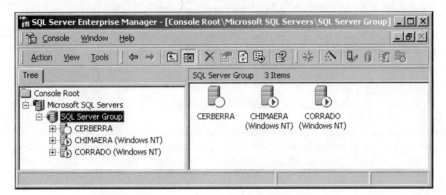

In our case, we're only envisaging a single instance of our application to be running in the enterprise, rather than having it on a per-machine basis as is common in the majority of the management consoles for Microsoft's various server products. However in order to demonstrate the technique, we'll look at how to handle this registration process. We'll have a top-level `BookManager` object and be able to register a "service instance" beneath this. The service instance will be represented by a class that will contain these properties, among others:

- ❑ A username-password combination
- ❑ The URL of the Web Service
- ❑ The URL of the client-activated service object
- ❑ The name and machine name of the Windows Service itself

The caveat here is that the service could be running in the console application rather than within a Windows Service process. We ideally want to be able to start and stop the service process from the console itself.

Creating the Project

To host the administration tools and related controls, we'll build a new class library project. This gives us a little freedom as to where to host the administration functionality, which is a topic we'll cover later in the chapter.

> **Breaking the admin functionality out into a separate library will allow us to reuse the algorithms to create web-based administration tools, should we so wish at some later date.**

Inside the class library, we'll create a user control that uses the classic "tree on left, data on right" display favored by these kinds of tools. We'll call this control AdminView, and we'll build all the administration logic into the library also.

Create a new **Visual Basic | Class Library** project now and call it AdminObjects. Once it's created, delete the default Class1 class, and add a new user control called AdminView.

For reasons that will become apparent shortly, open the code editor for AdminView and change the namespace from AdminObjects to AdminObjects.View:

```
Namespace AdminObjects.View
    Public Class AdminView
        Inherits System.Windows.Forms.UserControl
```

The combination of standard Framework controls and their resizing facilities – that Windows Forms automatically support – makes building the basic application very easy indeed. To start with, add a Panel control to AdminView and set its Dock property to Left. Also set the All sub-property of the DockPadding property to 5, and then change the Right sub-property to 0.

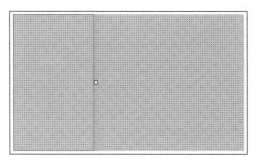

Next, drag a Splitter control onto the blank area of the form on the right. This will automatically dock to the left, and snap to the right edge of the first panel:

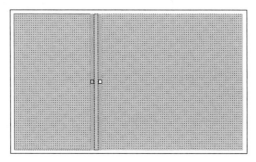

Now add another panel control to the blank area on the right. Set its Dock property to Fill (click the center button that appears when you select this property), and the All sub-property of the DockPadding property to 5. This time, change the Left sub-property to 0. Lastly, set its Name property to panelMain.

Finally, add a TreeView control to the panel on the left. Set its Name property to treeviewObjects, and its Dock property to Fill.

That's pretty much all we need to do for the basic UI of the administration view. We can test it fairly simply at this stage, by the following steps:

- ❑ Add a new **Windows Application** project to the solution called `AdminApp`
- ❑ Set `AdminApp` as the "startup" project and add a reference to the `AdminObjects` project
- ❑ Build the project to create the new `AdminView` control
- ❑ Change to the `AdmiApp` project, and draw an `AdmiView` control on th new `Form1` form
- ❑ Use the `Dock` property to make it fill the entire view

When we run this test project, we should be able to use our `Splitter` control to easily and intuitively adjust the width of the tree view:

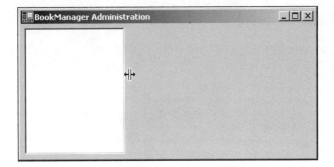

Administration Objects

There's a trap that we can fall into here if we're too short-sighted. In effect, we're about to build a library of functionality for the administration of our service, and it would be a mistake not to expose that functionality as an object library for other applications to use. To this end, we need to make sure that our `AdminView` class is just a *consumer* of this library.

So we'll build a separate `ServiceInstance` class to contain the methods required to actually administer the service. We'll then effectively build `AdminView` as a reference implementation of those classes.

First off, we'll build the `ServiceInstance` class. We already know that this will require a username and password combination, URLs for the Web Service, the singleton object that provides administration data inside the service, and the UNC name of the computer running the service along with the service name itself. The class will look like this, and should be created inside the `AdminObjects` project:

```
Namespace AdminObjects
    Public Class ServiceInstance
        ' Members
        Private _username As String
        Private _password As String
        Private _webServiceUrl As String
        Private _serviceUrl As String
        Private _uncName As String
        Private _serviceName As String
```

```vbnet
    ' Constructor

    Public Sub New(ByVal username As String, ByVal password As String, ByVal _
                 webServiceUrl As String, ByVal serviceUrl As String, ByVal _
                 uncName As String, ByVal serviceName As String)
        ' Initialize members
        _username = username
        _password = password
        _webServiceUrl = webServiceUrl
        _serviceUrl = serviceUrl
        _uncName = uncName
        _serviceName = serviceName
    End Sub


    ' Public Properties
    Public ReadOnly Property Username() As String
        Get
            Return _username
        End Get
    End Property


    Public ReadOnly Property Password() As String
        Get
            Return _password
        End Get
    End Property


    Public ReadOnly Property WebServiceUrl() As String
        Get
            Return _webServiceUrl
        End Get
    End Property


    Public ReadOnly Property ServiceUrl() As String
        Get
            Return _serviceUrl
        End Get
    End Property


    Public ReadOnly Property UncName() As String
        Get
            Return _uncName
        End Get
    End Property


    Public ReadOnly Property ServiceName() As String
        Get
            Return _serviceName
        End Get
    End Property
  End Class
End Namespace
```

We make these properties read-only because we don't want to change the registration details from within the administration tools that will access the properties.

We can now roll methods, such as `StartService`, `StopService`, and `GetServiceState`, into this class in order to control the service.

To identify the service in the console, we'll use its full name – the UNC name of the computer running the service with the name of the service itself tacked onto the end. Add the following to the `ServiceInstance.vb` file:

```
Public Overrides Function ToString() As String
    Return "\\" + UncName + "\" + ServiceName
End Function
```

To help keep objects related to admin activities separate from objects that relate to UI activities, we'll put all the UI classes in a separate namespace called `AdminObjects.View`. If you recall, we have already done this with the `AdminView` control itself.

When using the `TreeView` control, a very powerful approach is to create separate classes inherited from `System.Windows.Forms.TreeNode` for each node in the tree. So, we'd have a class called `ServiceInstanceTreeNode` to represent a service instance, an instance of `WindowsServiceTreeNode` to represent the Windows service, `FunctionalityItemTreeNode` to represent an item in the functionality catalog, and so on. In fact, we shall go one better than that and build a class called `BaseTreeNode`, which we can then inherit our other node classes from. This approach permits the node to encapsulate its own functionality, consistent with good OO design. We'll also add a `GetContextMenu` method, which we will need later. In addition, as nearly all of the nodes in the tree will need to refer back to a `ServiceInstance`, we'll add the capability to store one of these in the base class.

Add a new class called `BaseTreeNode` to `AdminObjects`. Remember to change the namespace and inherit the class from `TreeNode`, as shown:

```
Imports System
Imports System.Windows.Forms

Namespace AdminObjects.View
  Public Class BaseTreeNode
    Inherits TreeNode

    ' Members
    Private _serviceInstance As ServiceInstance

    ' Constructor

    Public Sub New()

    End Sub

    Public Sub New(ByVal servInstance As ServiceInstance)
      _serviceInstance = servInstance
    End Sub
```

```
         ' Public Property
         Public ReadOnly Property ServiceInstance() As ServiceInstance
           Get
              Return _serviceInstance
           End Get
         End Property

         Public Overridable Function GetContextMenu() As ContextMenu
           Return Nothing
         End Function
       End Class
     End Namespace
```

To make this example a little less complicated, we won't provide a UI for registering new service instances. Instead, we'll hard-code calls in AdminView that create a ServiceInstance object. In your production implementation, you'd really want to create a dialog that captures the required information from the user (probably storing it on disk to make life easier for the administrator when they open the tool again in the future). Obviously, for maximum reusability, all this UI stuff should be implemented in the AdminObjects library.

For now, create a new class derived from BaseTreeNode called ServiceInstanceTreeNode. This node will require a ServiceInstance object in its constructor and will use the ToString method of this object to set the text of the node:

```
     Namespace AdminObjects.View
       Public Class ServiceInstanceTreeNode
         Inherits BaseTreeNode

         Public Sub New(ByVal serviceInstance As ServiceInstance)
           MyBase.New(serviceInstance)
           ' Set the label for this item
           Me.Text = serviceInstance.ToString()
         End Sub
       End Class
     End Namespace
```

Most admin consoles have a "root" object. We'll create a new class called AdminRootTreeNode for this purpose. In its constructor, we'll hard-code calls to create a ServiceInstance object, which is used to create a ServiceInstanceTreeNode. We add the new node to the list of child nodes of AdminRootTreeNode itself, accessed through the Nodes property:

```
     Namespace AdminObjects.View
       Public Class AdminRootTreeNode
         Inherits BaseTreeNode

         Public Sub New()
           ' Set the text label for the root node
           Me.Text = "BookManager"

           ' Create a service instance
```

```
            Dim instance As ServiceInstance = New ServiceInstance("Matt", _
                "disraeli27", "http://chimaera/BookCoordinator/Coordinator.asmx", _
                "http://chimaera:8081/BookManager/BookManagerObjects.Admin.remote", _
                "chimaera", "BookManager Service")
            Me.Nodes.Add(New ServiceInstanceTreeNode(instance))

            ' Expand the tree to see the registered service instances
            Me.Expand()
        End Sub
    End Class
End Namespace
```

The constructor there is quite long. Here's a description of each parameter:

1. `"Matt"` – username

2. `"disraeli27"` – password

3. `"http://chimaera/BookCoordinator/Coordinator.asmx"` – Web service URL

4. `"http://chimaera:8081/BookManager/BookManagerObjects.Admin.remote"` – administration object URL

5. `"chimaera"` – service computer name

6. `"BookManager Service"` – service name

We're now all set for kick off. To get things going, we need an `AdminRootTreeNode` instance. We can create one in the `OnLoad` event handler within the `AdminView` class:

```
    Protected Overrides Sub OnLoad(ByVal e As EventArgs)
        ' Add the node
        treeviewObjects.Nodes.Add(New AdminObjects.View.AdminRootTreeNode())
    End Sub
```

Now run the project, and you should see the service instance in the tree on the left:

Starting and Stopping the Service

For our first activity, we'll add code to the admin objects to allow us to examine the state of the Windows Service, and start, stop, and pause it as required. The Framework contains classes to manage all of this within the `System.ServiceProcess` namespace, which makes our job a lot easier. To access this namespace though, the `AdminObjects` project needs a reference to the `System.ServiceProcess.dll` assembly:

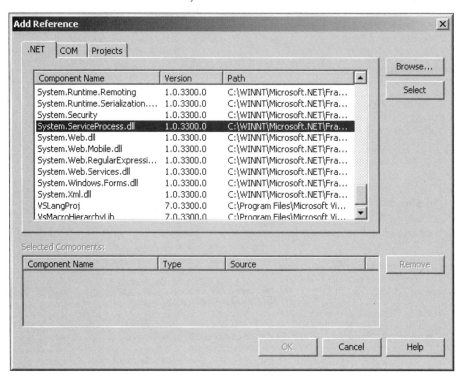

We'll represent the Windows Service as another node contained within the related `ServiceInstanceTreeNode`. Add this class to `AdminObjects`, and call it `WindowsServiceTreeNode`:

```
Imports System
Imports System.ServiceProcess
Imports System.Windows.Forms

Namespace AdminObjects.View
  Public Class WindowsServiceTreeNode
    Inherits BaseTreeNode

    Public Sub New(ByVal serviceInstance As ServiceInstance)
      MyBase.New(serviceInstance)
    End Sub
  End Class
End Namespace
```

We next create an instance of this class within the `ServiceInstanceTreeNode` constructor:

```
Public Sub New(ByVal serviceInstance As ServiceInstance)
   MyBase.New(serviceInstance)
   ' Set the label for the item
   Me.Text = serviceInstance.ToString()

   ' Add the Service as a node
   Me.Nodes.Add(New WindowsServiceTreeNode(serviceInstance))
   Me.expand()
End Sub
```

To determine the state of the service and control the service, we need to create an instance of a properly configured `System.ServiceProcess.ServiceController` class. However, all of the functionality related to managing the Windows Service would ideally be encapsulated in the `ServiceInstance` class because other applications can then enjoy its functionality.

Open the editor for `ServiceInstance.vb`, and add a reference for the `System.ServiceProcess` namespace:

```
Imports System
Imports System.ServiceProcess

namespace AdminObjects
   Public Class ServiceInstance
```

Now, add a method to return an instance of a `ServiceController` object based on the UNC name of the computer and the name of the service:

```
' GetServiceController - Returns a service controller for the service
Public Function GetServiceController() As ServiceController
   Return New ServiceController(ServiceName, UncName)
End Function
```

The `ServiceController` object returns the running state of the service through its `Status` property. A method to return the state of the service would be very useful, and we'll encapsulate this in a separate method to make life a little easier for the developer. It's important to note that `ServiceController` instances need to be cleaned up with `Dispose`:

```
' GetServiceStatus - Returns the state of the service
Public Function GetServiceStatus() As ServiceControllerStatus
   ' create and check...
   Dim service As ServiceController = GetServiceController()
   Dim status As ServiceControllerStatus = service.Status
   service.Dispose()

   ' return...
   Return status
End Function
```

When we display the service in `AdminView`, we'll want to somehow indicate the running state of the service visually. We could do this with an icon, or with text, or through a combination of both. We'll use a text-only approach to keep things simple, rather than having to ask you to download icons from the Internet or capture them yourselves from your favorite management tool.

Flip back to the code editor for `WindowsServiceTreeNode.vb`, and add this code:

```
Public Class WindowsServiceTreeNode
    Inherits BaseTreeNode


    Public Sub New(ByVal serviceInstance As ServiceInstance)
      MyBase.New(serviceInstance)

        ' Call UpdateView
        UpdateView()
      End Sub

      Public Sub UpdateView()
          ' Add a label for this node indicating the service's current state
          Me.Text = "Service (" + ServiceInstance.GetServicesStatus().ToString() _
                          + ")"
      End Sub
    End Class
```

If you run the application now, you'll see a new node for the Windows Service. This node will also tell you the running state of the service:

Most admin tools let the user select options for items in the tree view by allowing the user to right-click on them to display a context menu. We want our menu to allow the user to start, stop, or pause the service. As this is a common activity, there already is a `GetContextMenu` method on `BaseTreeNode`. We can override this method, and then create and display a new `System.Windows.Forms.ContextMenu` object, and allow the user to choose an option which we can then respond to by starting, stopping, or pausing as requested.

When we detect that the user has clicked a node on the `TreeView`, we'll call `GetContextMenu` on the node in question and assign the result returned as the new value for the `ContextMenu` property of `treeviewObjects`. This means that whenever the user right-clicks on a node, the appropriate `ContextMenu` will be ready.

First of all, add this code to the constructor of `AdminView`:

```
    ' AdminView constructor
    Public Sub New()
       ' This call is required by the Windows.Forms Form Designer
```

```
InitializeComponent()

    ' Add the treeviewObjects_Click click handler
    AddHandler treeviewObjects.Click, AddressOf(treeviewObjects_Click)
End Sub
```

Next, add a property to return the currently selected node cast as a BaseTreeNode. This allows us to call our extension methods:

```
' SelectedNode Property
Protected ReadOnly Property SelectedNode() As BaseTreeNode
  Get
     Return CType(treeviewObjects.SelectedNode, BaseTreeNode)
  End Get
End Property
```

Finally, add the click event handler:

```
Private Sub treeviewObjects_Click(ByVal sender As System.Object, _
                    ByVal e As System.EventArgs)
  ' Set the Context menu for the currently selected node
  If Not SelectedNode Is Nothing Then
    treeviewObjects.ContextMenu = SelectedNode.GetContextMenu()
  Else
    treeviewObjects.ContextMenu = Nothing
  End If
End Sub
```

Of course, we've yet to build the context menu for the WindowsServiceTreeNode class. We'll do this programmatically, but go right ahead and use the Designer if that's what you prefer. Add this code to WindowsServiceTreeNode:

```
Public Overrides Function GetContextMenu() As ContextMenu
  ' Determine the state of the service
  Dim state As ServiceControllerStatus = ServiceInstance.GetServiceStatus()

  ' Create a new blank context menu
  Dim menu As ContextMenu = New ContextMenu()

  ' Add Menu items - Start first
  Dim item As MenuItem = New MenuItem("Start")
  ' Disable the option if the service is already running
  If state = ServiceControllerStatus.StartPending Or state = _
  ServiceControllerStatus.Running Then
    item.Enabled = False
  End If

  AddHandler item.Click, AddressOf(StartServiceMenuItem_Click)
  menu.MenuItems.Add(item)

  ' Add the Pause option
```

```
      item = New MenuItem("Pause")
      ' Disable this option if the service is already paused
      If state = ServiceControllerStatus.PausePending Or state = _
      ServiceControllerStatus.Paused Then
         item.Enabled = False
      End If
      AddHandler item.Click, AddressOf(PauseServiceMenuItem_Click)
      menu.MenuItems.Add(item)

      ' Add the Stop option
      item = New MenuItem("Stop")
      ' Disable this option if the service is already stopped
      if state = ServiceControllerStatus.StopPending or state == _
      ServiceControllerStatus.Stopped
         item.Enabled = False
      End If
      AddHandler item.Click, AddressOf(StopServiceMenuItem_Click)
      menu.MenuItems.Add(item)

      ' Return the menu
      Return menu
   End Function
```

For each event handler, we need to call a method on the `ServiceInstance` class that can control the method. We'll also need a central exception handler to report on errors when controlling the service. Add the following to `WindowsServiceTreeNode.vb`:

```
   ' Menu click event handlers
   Private Sub StartServiceMenuItem_Click(ByVal sender As System.Object, _
   ByVal e As System.EventArgs)
      Try
         ServiceInstance.StartService()
      Catch ex As Exception
         HandleException(ex)
      End Try
      UpdateView()
   End Sub

   Private Sub PauseServiceMenuItem_Click(ByVal sender As System.Object, _
   ByVal e As System.EventArgs)
      Try
         ServiceInstance.PauseService()
      Catch ex As Exception
         HandleException(ex)
      End Try
      UpdateView()
   End Sub

   Private Sub StopServiceMenuItem_Click(ByVal sender As System.Object, _
   ByVal e As System.EventArgs)
      Try
         ServiceInstance.StopService()
      Catch ex As Exception
```

```
      HandleException(ex)
    End Try
    UpdateView()
End Sub

Private Sub HandleException(ByVal ex As Exception)
    MessageBox.Show("The service could not be controlled. \r\n" + _
                    ex.GetType().ToString + ":" + ex.Message)
End Sub
```

As you can see, each of these methods merely defers processing to other methods in the
`ServiceInstance` class; namely `StartService`, `StopService`, and `PauseService`. These
methods are themselves responsible for actually controlling the service, as is commensurate with the
approach we're taking of building a set of classes that do the actual work, and another set of classes that
then present the admin information.

Now, let's add the three methods to `ServiceInstance.vb`:

```
' Stop the service
Public Sub StopService()
    ControlService(ServiceControllerStatus.Stopped)
End Sub

' Pause the service
Public Sub PauseService()
    ControlService(ServiceControllerStatus.Paused)
End Sub

' Start the service
Public Sub StartService()
    ControlService(ServiceControllerStatus.Running)
End Sub
```

Each of these methods defers to another method called `ControlService`. This new method is
responsible for issuing the instruction to the service controller, which controls the service and then waits
for the service to respond. Here's the code:

```
public sub ControlService(ServiceControllerStatus requiredState)

    ' Get hold of the service controller
    Dim controller As ServiceController = GetServiceController()

    ' What new state is required?
    Select Case requiredState

      Case ServiceControllerStatus.Stopped
        controller.Stop()
        Exit Select

      Case ServiceControllerStatus.Paused
        controller.Pause()
        Exit Select
```

```
    Case ServiceControllerStatus.Running
      controller.Start()
      Exit Select

    Case Else
      Throw New ArgumentOutOfRangeException("requiredState")
  End Select

  ' Wait for the service to respond
  TimeSpan(timeout = New TimeSpan(ServiceControlTimeout * _
          TimeSpan.TicksPerMillisecond))
  controller.WaitForStatus(requiredState, timeout)

  ' Dispose of the controller
  controller.Dispose()
End Sub
```

When we call this method, we tell it what state we want the service to change to. After issuing the `Stop`, `Pause`, or `Start` command, we call `WaitForStatus` to give the service a chance to switch states. We must also define `ServiceControlTimeout` as a member of the `ServiceInstance` class. I've set it to 30 seconds here:

```
public class ServiceInstance
    ' Members
   Private _username as String
   Private _password as String
   Private _webServiceUrl as String
   Private _serviceUrl as String
   Private _uncName as String
   Private _serviceName as String
   Public ServiceControlTimeout as Integer = 30000
```

When we now run the project, we can use it to control the state of the service:

You can check to see what's happened with the service using the Service Manager:

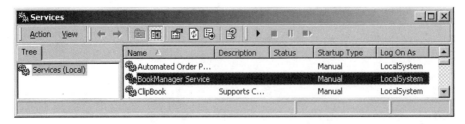

Pausing the Service

When we built the service earlier in the book, we did not code a "pause" capability, so if we select the Pause option from the menu, we will get the following exception:

In this sample, I've left adding the functionality for pausing the service as an exercise for the reader, because its won't involve anything new that we really need to know about. However, it's good for illustrating how our exception handling deals with problems encountered when controlling the service.

Controlling Remote Services

To talk to the Web Service as we've already done, or to talk to objects running directly inside the service, we can use its URL. Such a URL could be publicly accessible over the Internet, like this one:

http://someintranetsite.wrox.com/BookManager/BookManagerObjects.Admin.remote

Of course, your system administrator may restrict access to the host so that the object can only be practically reached from the local network, but at least we have the option. When working with UNC names like \\CHIMAERA or \\CORRADO we don't, because these are by their nature private. The upshot of this is that we can only control the service from inside the LAN, as we cannot address the computers that have the services installed from outside the LAN.

One way to fix this would be to add a level of indirection. Rather than connecting directly to the service, you could create another Windows Service that hosts the `AdminObjects` and makes `ServiceInstance` available over Remoting. The admin tool could then connect to this object over the Internet, solving the addressing problem.

Adding the Administration Objects to "ServiceHost"

In our sample application, there are very few clear cases where we would need to peek directly into the process hosting our service objects, that is the running instance of `BusinessHost.HostService`. Unfortunately, this is a result of attempting to explain how to build a full production-level application in a single book. However, the technique I'm going to demonstrate now is important. As mentioned before, a lot of the administrative tasks we need to perform can happen through the Web Service, which in this instance acts like a separate application providing administration support services to the main application.

> There are some instrumentation and management activities that we can undertake with the service, and these are covered in more detail in Chapter 12.

We'll set up some objects that run inside the service process and provide administration functions. We're going to gather data, which is usually more pertinent for instrumentation and management as detailed in the next chapter. These same administration objects could be used to "do" things. For example, if we had a relational database management system like SQL Server, we might have methods like CreateTable, RebuildIndex, and so on.

We're going to create a class called Admin inside of BookManagerObjects, and make it available as a singleton object. As well as this, we'll create a class called AdminData and we'll "hack" CustomerService.FindCustomers so that every call checks to see if an instance of AdminData is available and if one is, the RecordTermHit method is invoked. This method will update a Hashtable contained within AdminData that represents a log of how many times a given search term has been called, like this:

Drew	2
Pretend	3
Anything	1
Something	5

This table of data is built up *inside* the process hosting the Remoting objects, which can either be our Windows Service, or the console application used for debugging.

From our admin tool, we'll call into a method on another singleton object called Admin, which will defer to a method on the *same instance of* AdminData called GetSearchTerms. This will return the data as a DataSet for display in the admin tool. The aim is to show how we can:

- ❑ Create a remote instance of an object in the service process from the client-side admin tool
- ❑ Give that object state
- ❑ Change that state from within calls to other methods on objects accessed through Remoting
- ❑ Return that state to the client-side admin tool for processing and presentation

Hosting the Administration Object

The first thing we'll do is to build AdminData. Leave the AdminObjects solution to one side for the moment as we turn our attention to the BusinessHost solution from Chapter 9. Create a new class called AdminData inside BookManagerObjects and add these namespace import declarations:

```
Imports System
Imports System.Data
Imports System.Threading
Imports System.Collections
```

To provide state for this class, we shall use a `System.Collections.Hashtable` to record the requests that have been made through `CustomerService.FindCustomers`. We also need a `System.Threading.ReaderWriterLock` to synchronize access to this list to cater for multiple simultaneous threads. We'll also create a member that records the number of times that `GetSearchTerms` has been called and one final static member that holds a reference to the most recently created instance of `AdminData`:

```
Public Class AdminData
' Members
Private _searchTerms as Hashtable = new Hashtable()
Private _lock as ReaderWriterLock = new ReaderWriterLock()
Private _numCalls as Integer = 0
Public Shared CurrentAdminData as AdminData
```

We want a static constructor on this class that will create a physical instance of `AdminData` the first time a static member of the class is accessed. In effect, the first time we ask for the value of `CurrentAdminData`, a new instance of `AdminData` will be created and set against this field. Replace the existing constructor with the following:

```
Sub New()
   CurrentAdminData = new AdminData()
End Sub
```

This member can then be accessed from any other method in any other class and it will return the most recently created instance of `AdminData`. If no admin tool has connected to `Admin`, this will be `null`. We'll test for this case from `CustomerService.FindCustomers`. (More in a moment.)

In the `Hashtable` itself, we'll define the key to be whatever search terms were passed into `FindCustomers`. We'll increment the value held against this key every time a call is received in order to keep a count of how many times a given term has been supplied to the method. Again, it's important that we use the `ReaderWriterLock` to synchronize access to this method; otherwise we could get a situation where data is incorrectly recorded. Add this method to `AdminData`:

```
Public Sub RecordTermHit(word as String)
  ' Lock to synchronize access
  _lock.AcquireWriterLock(-1)

  ' Add word to search terms if not already there
  If _searchTerms.Contains(word) = False
    _searchTerms.Add(word, 0)
  End If
  ' Increment count for this term
  _searchTerms(word) = CType(_searchTerms(word),Integer) + 1

  ' Release lock
  _lock.ReleaseLock()
End Sub
```

In previous chapters of this book, we've seen how the `System.Data.DataSet` class can be a very useful tool for moving data around the same process and between processes. In this exercise, we're going to walk the `Hashtable` and copy its data to a `DataTable` contained within a `DataSet`. We'll then use a `DataGrid` control to present this `DataTable` to the user.

As well as providing the actual `Hashtable` contents in the `DataTable`, we'll add some debugging information. Specifically, we'll provide the hash code of the `AdminData` object itself (to show that we're using the same instance of the object each time), the hash code of the calling thread, and the number of times the `GetSearchTerms` method has been called. The `DataTable` will have two columns, `Words` and `Hits`:

```
' GetSearchTerms method
Public Function GetSearchTerms() As DataSet
    ' Create a dataset
    Dim dataset As DataSet = New DataSet()

    ' Create a table
    Dim datatable As DataTable = New DataTable("Terms")
    datatable.Columns.Add("Word", GetType(String))
    datatable.Columns.Add("Hits", GetType(Int))
    dataset.Tables.Add(datatable)

    ' Add the hash data
    Dim data(2) As Object
    data(0) = "__hashcode"
    data(1) = Me.GetHashCode()
    datatable.Rows.Add(Data)
    data(0) = "__thread"
    data(1) = Thread.CurrentThread.GetHashCode()
    datatable.Rows.Add(Data)

    ' Lock
    _lock.AcquireReaderLock(-1)

    ' Store the number of times the method has been called
    _numCalls = _numCalls + 1
    data(0) = "__numcalls"
    data(1) = _numCalls
    datatable.Rows.Add(Data)

    ' Walk the HashTable
    Dim word As String
    For Each word In _searchTerms.Keys
        data(0) = word
        data(1) = _searchTerms(word)
        datatable.Rows.Add(data)
    Next

    ' Unlock and return
    _lock.ReleaseLock()
    Return dataset
End Function
```

The final thing to do on the server-side is to "hack" `FindCustomers` so that a call to `RecordTermHit` is executed for every `FindCustomers` call, as long as an instance of `AdminData` has already been created and recorded in the static `CurrentAdmin` member. Add the highlighted code to the `Customer.vb` class file:

```
' FindCustomers - search for customers
Public Function FindCustomers(ByVal searchFor As String) As CustomerSet

    ' This method call is to track search terms
    AdminData.CurrentAdminData.RecordTermHit(searchFor)

    ' Debug info
    Console.WriteLine("FindCustomers called: " + searchFor)

    ' Run the sproc and return
    Return CType(Sprocs.FindCustomers(searchFor, GetType(CustomerSet)), _
            CustomerSet)
End Function
```

The `Admin` class itself is quite straightforward. We enable Remoting through use of the `EnterpriseObjects.RemotingAttribute` attribute and by deriving from `MarshalByRefObject`. It contains just one method, which defers to the available instance of `AdminData`:

```
<EnterpriseObjects.Remoting()> Public Class Admin
    Inherits MarshalByRefObject

    Public Sub New()

    End Sub

    Public Function GetSearchTerms() As DataSet
        Return AdminData.CurrentAdminData.GetSearchTerms()
    End Function
End Class
```

That's pretty much all we need to do for the `AdminData`, `Admin`, and `CustomerService` classes.

Calling the Remote Object

Because `Admin` is marked with the `RemotingAttribute` attribute, when we run the console application we'll see that the object is automatically available over Remoting:

We can now set the `BusinessHost` solution to one side and go back to our `AdminObjects` solution. We are going to create a property for `ServiceInstance` that establishes a connection to the singleton `Admin` object on the server side. However, to access the property, we'll need to add the `EnterpriseObjects` and `BookManagerObjects` projects to the solution and add references to them in the `AdminObjects` project itself.

Next, we need a private member capable of holding a `BookManagerObjects.Admin` instance:

```
Imports System
Imports System.ServiceProcess
Imports System.Runtime.Remoting
Imports BookManagerObjects

namespace AdminObjects
  public class ServiceInstance
    ' Members
    Private _username As String
    Private _password As String
    Private _webServiceUrl As String
    Private _serviceUrl As String
    Private _uncName As String
    Private _serviceName As String
    Public ServiceControlTimeout As Integer = 30000
    Private _admin As Admin
```

As usual, we'll create a property that performs a just-in-time activation of this object:

```
' Exposed Admin property
Public ReadOnly Property Admin()
  Get
    If _admin Is Nothing Then
      _admin = CType(Activator.GetObject(GetType(Admin), ServiceUrl), Admin)
    End If
    Return _admin
  End Get
End Property
```

The `ServiceUrl` property here retrieves the URL of the remote object, which you may remember we set up in the `ServiceInstance` constructor within the constructor for `AdminRootTreeNode`.

Presenting Data

Our next step is to present the data taken from the server. This falls nicely into the "tree of objects on left, data on right" paradigm (sometimes called an "Explorer view" because of the similarity with Windows Explorer views) that we've pretty much ignored up to now. We want to add an object to the tree as a "sibling" of (that is, at the same depth as) the `WindowsServiceTreeNode` object. We'll call this class `SearchTermsTreeNode`.

One of the great things about Windows Forms is our freedom to create and place controls on the fly. In this case, whenever we click on a `SearchTermsTreeNode` node, we want to connect to the remote service, populate a `DataSet` through a call to `GetSearchTerms`, which we can then display in a new `DataGrid` control on the right of the tree. It's common for tools like these to use a `ListView` control rather than a `DataGrid` control, but in this specific example it's easier to databind to a `DataGrid` control than to a `ListView`. It also illustrates that we are not limited to using a `ListView` control to present the data in the node.

Before looking at `SearchTermsTreeNode` though, we need to do some work with the `AfterSelect` event of the `TreeView` control. When this event is received, we want to find the node that has been clicked on, and call a method called `OnClick`, which we'll define on `BaseTreeNode`. For some reason, Microsoft chose not to include an `OnClick` method on their `System.Windows.Forms.TreeNode` implementation, so we'll add our own. During the course of this task, we'll create a new event argument class called `BaseTreeNodeEventArgs`, containing a field called `Control` that can store a `System.Windows.Forms.Control` object. As nearly all of the Windows Forms classes are derived from this (the `DataGrid` included), we can construct our own view of the data when we receive a click, and pass it back through our event argument object for the `AdminView` object itself to display.

We'll start by building the `BaseTreeNodeEventArgs` class. This class will encapsulate a `TreeViewEventArgs` class, which we'll use when the user clicks a node:

```
Public Class BaseTreeNode
    Inherits TreeNode

    ' Members
    Private _serviceInstance As ServiceInstance

    ' BaseTreeNodeEventArgs
    Public Class BaseTreeNodeEventArgs
        'Members
        Public e As TreeViewEventArgs
        Public Control As Control

        ' Constructor

        Public Sub New(ByVal eArgs As TreeViewEventArgs)
            e = eArgs
        End Sub
    End Class
End Class
```

Then, add this method to `BaseTreeNode`:

```
    Public Overridable Sub OnClick(ByVal e As BaseTreeNodeEventArgs)

    End Sub
```

The purpose of `SearchTermsTreeNode` is to connect to the service and retrieve the data as discussed. Create a new class and make the changes highlighted below:

```
Imports System
Imports System.Data
Imports System.Windows.Forms

Namespace AdminObjects.View
    Public Class SearchTermsTreeNode
        Inherits BaseTreeNode

        ' Constructor
```

```
        Public Sub New(ByVal serviceInstance As ServiceInstance)
           MyBase.New(serviceInstance)
           Text = "Search Terms"
        End Sub
     End Class
   End Namespace
```

Next, add an overridden version of OnClick that creates a new DataGrid control, connects to the singleton object on the service and retrieves a DataSet. If a DataSet is returned (meaning that everything worked OK), we data bind the DataGrid to it. The DataGrid control is then returned by setting the Control property of the supplied BaseTreeNodeEventArgs instance:

```
     Public Overrides Sub OnClick(ByVal e As BaseTreeNodeEventArgs)
        ' Create a new datagrid
        Dim grid As DataGrid = New DataGrid()

        ' Get the data from Admin
        Dim dataset As DataSet = ServiceInstance.Admin.GetSearchTerms
        If Not dataset Is Nothing Then
           grid.DataSource = dataset
           grid.DataMember = dataset.Tables(0).TableName
        End If

        ' Return the DataGrid Control
        e.Control = grid
     End Sub
```

At this point, we won't actually see an instance of a SearchTermsTreeNode object in the tree. Open the code editor for ServiceInstanceTreeNode and add this code:

```
     Public Sub New(ByVal serviceInstance As ServiceInstance)
        MyBase.New(serviceInstance)

        ' Set the label for the item
        Me.Text = serviceInstance.ToString()

        ' Add search terms node
        Me.Nodes.Add(New SearchTermsTreeNode(serviceInstance))

        ' Add the Service as a node
        Me.Nodes.Add(New WindowsServiceTreeNode(serviceInstance))
        Me.Expand(T
     End Sub
```

Next we need to add a handler for the AfterSelect event of the TreeView control. Open the Designer for AdminView and double-click on the TreeView control to create skeleton handler code. We'll add to this so that if a node is selected, a new BaseTreeNodeEventArgs object will be created and passed to the overridable OnClick method of the selected node. If we successfully get a Control returned, we'll display it in panelMain:

```
Private Sub treeviewObjects_AfterSelect(ByVal sender As Object, _
                      ByVal e As System.Windows.Forms.TreeViewEventArgs)
  If Not SelectedNode Is Nothing Then
     ' Call OnClick for the selected node
     Dim newArgs As BaseTreeNode.BaseTreeNodeEventArgs = New _
                                 BaseTreeNode.BaseTreeNodeEventArgs(e)

     ' Clear the right-hand panel
     panelMain.Controls.Clear()
     If Not newArgs.Control Is Nothing Then
       ' Set up and show
       newArgs.Control.Dock = DockStyle.Fill
       panelMain.Controls.Add(newArgs.Control)
     End If
  End If
End Sub
```

Run the service now (either the console application or the Windows Service), and start up the admin tool. If you select the Search Terms node, you'll see something like this:

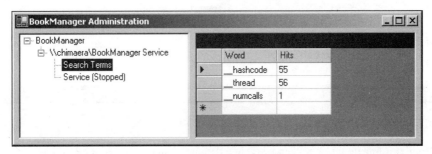

You can "refresh" the view by selecting the Service node and then selecting the Search Terms node again. Each time you do this you'll notice that __numcalls increases.

To test the code that captures the search term usage, run the application browser, open the Customer Editor, and search for customers. If you refresh the admin view, you'll see your search terms listed:

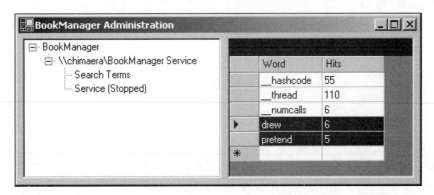

A Default View

It's fairly typical with tools like this to try to display something whenever any node is selected. A good default view for this situation is a list of the nodes contained within the current node. Here's how SQL Server does it:

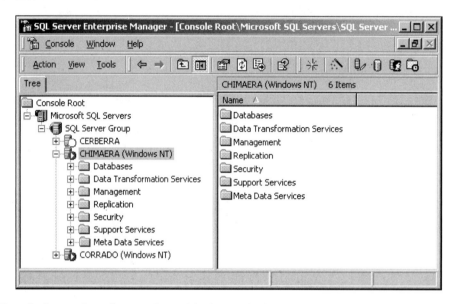

In effect, the list on the right is a subset of the list on the left.

To duplicate this functionality, we can provide a default implementation of OnClick on BaseTreeNode that configures a new ListView control to contain a list of the child node controls. As with the TreeView control, it's often easier with ListView to derive new classes from System.Windows.Forms.ListViewItem and add objects created from your derived classes to the list control. In our case, we want to hold an instance of a BaseTreeNode class inside the object for later use. Add this class definition to BaseTreeNode:

```
Public Class BaseTreeNodeListViewItem
   Inherits ListViewItem

   ' Members
   Private _node As BaseTreeNode

   ' Constructor

   Public Sub New(ByVal node As BaseTreeNode)
     _node = node
     Me.Text = _node.Text
   End Sub

   Public ReadOnly Property Node() As BaseTreeNode
     Get
```

```
        Return _node
     End Get
   End Property
End Class
```

Creating the new `ListView` object and configuring it is also pretty easy. We need to create a control, add columns to that control, and walk the list of nodes creating new `BaseTreeNodeListViewItem` instances for each node. We then pass the `ListView` control back through the event arguments for display by our existing code. Add this code to the existing, overridable `OnClick` method in `BaseTreeNode`:

```
Public Overridable Sub OnClick(ByVal e As BaseTreeNodeEventArgs)
   ' Create and configure a ListView
   Dim view As ListView = New ListView()
   view.View = System.Windows.Forms.View.Details
   view.Columns.Add("Name", 300, HorizontalAlignment.Left)

   ' Step through each node adding to the ListView
   Dim node As BaseTreeNode
   For Each node In Nodes
      view.Items.Add(New BaseTreeNodeListViewItem(node))
   Next

   ' Return the populated view
   e.Control = view
End Sub
```

If you run the project, you'll see that we have produced the desired effect:

Implementing the Double-Click

Users are used to being able to drill down into the object tree by double-clicking objects in the right-hand pane. To implement the double-click, we can create a new event handler on the `ListView` control to listen for the `DoubleClick` event. First off, add this code to `BaseTreeNode`:

```
Public Overridable Sub OnClick(ByVal e As BaseTreeNodeEventArgs)
   ' Create and configure a ListView
   Dim view As ListView = New ListView()
   view.View = System.Windows.Forms.View.Details
   view.Columns.Add("Name", 300, HorizontalAlignment.Left)

   ' Step through each node adding to the ListView
   Dim node As BaseTreeNode
```

```
For Each node In Nodes
    view.Items.Add(New BaseTreeNodeListViewItem(node))
Next

    ' Add a double-click handler
    AddHandler view.DoubleClick, AddressOf (ListViewDoubleClick)

    ' Return the populated view
    e.Control = view
End Sub
```

The double-click event handler must change the selection on the `TreeView`. Luckily for us, `TreeNode` (and therefore `BaseTreeNode`) implements a property called `TreeView`, which we can use to access the actual `TreeView` instance. Once we have that, we can set the `SelectedNode` property and change the selection on the tree:

```
Private Sub ListViewDoubleClick(ByVal sender As Object, ByVal e As EventArgs)
    ' Get the node
    Dim view As ListView = CType(sender, ListView)

    ' Check if an item is selected
    If view.SelectedItems.Count > 0 Then
        ' Change the selected item
        Dim item As BaseTreeNodeListViewItem = CType(view.SelectedItems(0), _
                                        BaseTreeNodeListViewItem)
        item.Node.TreeView.SelectedNode = item.Node
    End If
End Sub
```

Restart the project, and check that it is now possible to navigate through the object tree by double-clicking items in the right-hand pane.

The Microsoft Management Console

Since the introduction of the Microsoft Management Console (MMC.exe), Microsoft has recommended that administration tools like the one we've developed here should be written so that they may be hosted by the MMC.exe application.

The Framework of the initial Microsoft .NET release does not include support for MMC, and this is one of the reasons behind not taking this approach, as we'd have to develop a COM interop solution to create the various COM-compatible components that we could plug into the MMC environment. In addition to this, the primary advantage of using the MMC SDK is often that it makes development of these sorts of tools more straightforward. As I hope I've illustrated, the .NET Windows Forms model makes building tools that look like typical MMC applications so straightforward that this argument hardly applies.

If you'd like to learn more about integrating the application with the MMC, there are a few discussion groups that offer lively debate on the subject. You can use the ".NET 247 Discussion Search" feature to look for threads related to MMC by navigating to the following URL:

http://www.dotnet247.com/247reference/s/s.aspx?t=messages:mmc

Summary

In the first part of this chapter, we introduced the idea of a central administration library to which we can add new administration capabilities as development of our application progresses. We saw how we could roll user interface functionality into this library so that consumers of the library could call upon common UI features to make creating such applications easier and quicker.

As part of this work, we have created methods that use the Framework's `ServiceController` class to start and stop the service that we coded in Chapter 9. We moved on to build classes within the `BookManagerObjects` library that would let us monitor what was going on inside the process itself (as a precursor to topics we shall discuss in Chapter 12), and introduced this as a possible platform for creating methods that actually manipulate the application state.

.NET Enterprise Development in VB .NET

12

Management

In the final chapter of this book, we're going to take a look at some topics related to management of the enterprise application.

Specifically in this chapter we will look at the following:

- ❑ Performance counters
- ❑ Exception Reporting
- ❑ Debugging and Tracing
- ❑ Load Balancing

The kinds of management techniques we're going to meet have two distinct uses. During the development cycle (in other words before the application goes live) they can help developers understand more about the application. For example, if we design the application so that only a single instance of a given object is ever created on the server, we can actually test that this is indeed true, avoiding the nightmare situation where each client creates a distinct version of the object that would lead to a greatly increased memory footprint for the application.

Once the application is live, these management techniques can help the administrators responsible for the smooth running of the application understand exactly how the application is performing.

Let's take a look at some of these techniques now.

Performance Counters

A management capability that has been available to developers since early editions of Windows NT is "performance counters". These provide a basic way for the application to report how much of a certain resource is being used, or how often a certain feature is being requested. By monitoring the performance counters, system administrators and developers can learn more about how the application is functioning.

Introducing Performance Counters

For the sake of completeness, we'll introduce a couple of performance counters now. In a short while, we'll build our own performance counters that will report on the state of the BookManager Service.

By default, Windows is installed with a dazzling array of counters, most of which are so specialized that they are way beyond the scope of this discussion. However, there are a few that even we mere mortals can understand.

To load the Performance Monitor (also known as "PerfMon"), select Programs | Administrative Tools | Performance from the Start menu. Ignore the objects in the management tree on the left for a moment and look at the chart on the right. We can add counters to this chart to see how they change over time:

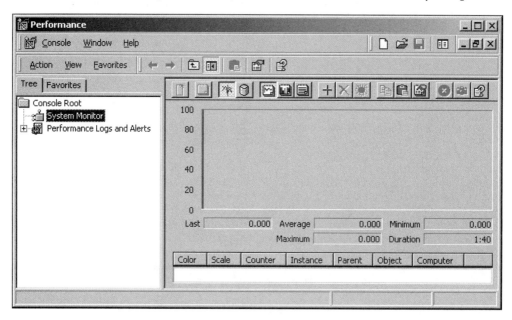

Using the toolbar on the chart, click the Add button. You'll see a dialog that allows you to choose which counters you want on the chart. Roughly speaking, counters are split into "performance objects" (the "thing" you're trying to measure) and each performance object has a number of counters hung from it. In some cases, the counter itself will have "instances". In this diagram, we're looking at the % Processor Time counter, which tells us how much work the CPUs are doing. In my case, my computer has two processors, so I get _Total (the averaged work of both), or I can individually monitor either processor. Click Add to add this counter to the chart.

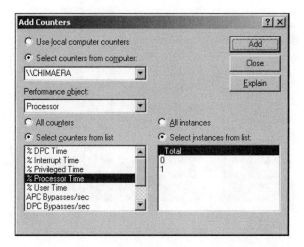

When you look at the chart, you'll see a line representing how that particular counter has changed over time. If you use your computer (for example, start up Microsoft Word, compile projects, etc.), you'll see the line respond to indicate the CPU hit:

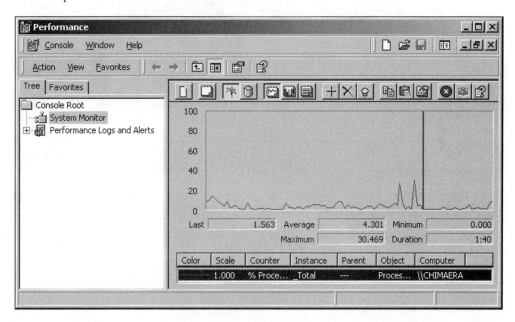

Some of you will be aware that this particular counter is the same as that used by Windows Task Manager (press *Ctrl+Alt+Del* and select **Task Manager**):

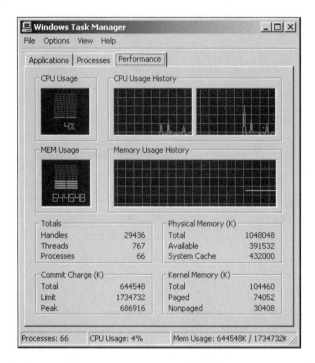

As a blanket generalization, performance counters usually fall into two camps: rate of use and actual usage. Actual usage expresses how much of a given resource is being used; for example a counter monitoring the number of open network connections is an actual usage counter. By comparison, a counter that monitors the "average number of open network connections in a second" is a rate counter, because it has an association with a measurement of time.

In reality, the types of performance counters are more involved than this, but we won't be going into this in any more detail here.

.NET Performance Counters

If you click the Add button again to bring up the Add Counter dialog, you'll find a number of .NET-specific performance objects in the drop-down list. These are installed as part of the .NET installation and allow you to measure certain aspects of the CLR as applications are running. You have the option of monitoring all managed code that is running (on a process-by-process basis), or monitoring one specific process.

Here's what the counters do:

❑   .NET CLR Exceptions – measures the number of exceptions being thrown by applications

❑   .NET CLR Interop – measures the performance of COM interop, in other words the process of using "old school" COM objects in managed code

❑   .NET CLR Jit – measures the performance of "just-in-time compilation", the process that converts the MSIL code contained within the assembly into native, processor-specific code for execution

- ❑ **.NET CLR Loading** – measures the performance of assembly and class loading
- ❑ **.NET CLR LocksAndThreads** – measures the performance of multithreading and the synchronization objects that support multithreading
- ❑ **.NET CLR Memory** – measures the usage of memory by managed code, including garbage collector performance
- ❑ **.NET CLR Remoting** – measures the performance of Remoting
- ❑ **.NET CLR Security** – measures the performance of managed code security

As tends to be the case with .NET applications, some of these are a little specific and for the most part we're not going to worry about them in this chapter. We will take a look at a couple just to prove the point.

Before we add the counters, start up the BusinessHostConsole. (If the service is running, stop it – throughout this chapter we'll be using the console application, as it's easier during the development process.) Go back to the chart and delete the Processor counter we added before, as it will make the chart a little easier to read.

With the host console running, click the Add button on PerfMon. Select .NET CLR Remoting from the Performance object list, make sure Remote Calls/sec is selected from the counters list, and select BusinessHostCon from the instance list:

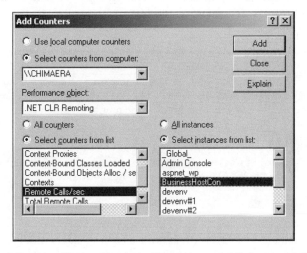

Run the browser, making sure that it will start in "Remoting mode". Log in, and start the Customer Editor sub-application. As we only have a single client running, it's going to be difficult to get the chart itself to move away from the baseline. However, we can watch the data displayed in the boxes underneath the chart. Enter a search term into the search box and click the Search button rapidly for several seconds. You'll see the values change as the Remoting calls are made:

From my values, you can see that the most Remoting calls I managed to make in a given second was 7, and that the average over the time measured was 0.273 calls per second.

Implementing Performance Counters

It's entirely our decision which performance counters are most appropriate for our application. For example, it might be useful for us to know how many service objects are currently instantiated, how many users are connected or how many times in a second a given method is called. In this section, we'll take a look at two counters. The first will record how many `CustomerService` objects are in existence. The second will record how many times `FindCustomers` is called in a second. As this method is a relatively core feature of the customer editor, and because it's potentially a long running query as far as SQL Server is concerned, it's a good candidate for analysis.

Implementing a Usage Counter

Because performance counters are an integral part of most service-based software, WEO already has capabilities to manage performance counters. We just haven't turned them on yet! WEO has a number of counters already in place to measure various system metrics, such as "number of `EntitySets` created each second", and "number of calls to `GetEntitySet`". Once we tell the service to create the counters, they will be available in PerfMon. For the most part, they're pretty trivial and self-explanatory, so there's no need to go through them here.

WEO's performance counter implementation works on the principle of asking all the classes capable of working with counters to register the counters through the `EnterpriseApplication` object. Once all the objects have registered their counters, the counters are registered with PerfMon and the objects are then told that the counters have been created. Each object then stores an instance of another object that handles the job of talking to the counter through a shared member to update the counters as required.

To see this in action, we're going to be looking at a combination of new code added to `CustomerService` and existing code inside `EnterpriseObjects`. We'll create a new counter called `NumCustomerServiceObjects`, which will record the number of open customer service objects.

Registering Counters

To mark an object as capable of working with counters, you need to implement `ICounterProvider`. This interface is already part of WEO and contains two methods:

❑   `CreateCounters` – called when WEO requires information about counters you are interested in

❑   `CountersCreated` – called after WEO registers the counters with PerfMon, giving you the opportunity to store references to the object so that you can use them

`EnterpriseObjects.Service` has already implemented this interface, because it has its own counters that it needs to register with PerfMon. We can override its implementations of `CreateCounters` and `CountersCreated` to give the derived `CustomerService` object the opportunity to register its own counters.

The best way to implement counters is to store the name of the counter as a constant within the class, and also create a shared member into which we can store the actual `System.Diagnostics.PerformanceCounter` object that we need to update. Add this code to `CustomerService`:

```
<EnterpriseObjects.Remoting()> Public Class CustomerService
  Inherits CustomerServiceBase

  ' Counters
  Protected Const NumCustomerServiceObjectsCounterName As String = _
                                       "NumCustomerServiceObjects"
  Protected Friend _numCustomerServiceObjectsCounter As _
                                 EnterpriseObjects.EnterpriseCounter
```

Registering the counter is very simple. We just need to provide its name, and its type from the `System.Diagnostics.PerformanceCounterType` enumeration. This enumeration contains a slew of counter types, but we're interested in only a couple – `NumberOfItems32` and `RateOfCountsPerSecond32`. You can find more information on the other counters at http://msdn.microsoft.com.

Add this code to register our `NumCustomerServiceObjects` counter:

```
  ' CreateCounters
  Public Overrides Sub CreateCounters(ByVal counters As _
                                 EnterpriseObjects.EnterpriseCounters)
    ' Add them
    counters.Counters.Add(New _
                   EnterpriseObjects.EnterpriseCounter( _
                   NumCustomerServiceObjectsCounterName, _
                   "Number of customer service objects in use", _
                   PerformanceCounterType.NumberOfItems32))
  End Sub
```

Notice that we *do not* call the base implementation of `CreateCounters`. When we want to register the counters, we'll use the "assembly scanning" technique that we first introduced in Chapter 10. Technically we'll create instances of `Service`, `CustomerServiceBase`, and `CustomerService` on three separate occasions as these objects are distinct, and each effectively implements `ICounterProvider` through inheritance. We don't actually need to call the base class's implementation of `CreateCounters` because what is technically the base implementation will be called separately.

When the counters have been created, we will receive a call to `CountersCreated`. At this point, we find the counter in the collection provided through the `counters` parameter and store it:

```
  ' CountersCreated
  Public Overrides Sub CountersCreated(ByVal counters As _
                                 EnterpriseObjects.EnterpriseCounters)
    ' Find them
    _numCustomerServiceObjectsCounter = _
              counters.Counters.Find(NumCustomerServiceObjectsCounterName)
  End Sub
```

What's Happening in WEO?

That's cool, but what's actually happening?

WEO contains a class called EnterpriseCounters that contains the functionality needed to talk to performance counters from a WEO application. An instance of this class is available through the Counters property of EnterpriseApplication, and you should use this instance whenever you need to work with performance counters.

EnterpriseCounters has a property called Counters that holds a collection of Counter objects. The EnterpriseCounter class itself has members for name, help text, type, and also a member that will eventually hold a System.Diagnostics.PerformanceCounter object once it has been created.

For now, all we've done is added new Counter objects to the collection. In a little while, we'll look at what WEO does with the collection.

Counting Instantiations and Finalizations

To count the number of open CustomerService objects, we have to tap into both the constructor and finalizer for the class. Find the CustomerService object and add this constructor:

```
Public Sub New()
  MyBase.New()

  ' Tell perfmon
  If _numCustomerServiceObjectsCounter Is Nothing Then
    ' Do not register instance
  Else
    _numCustomerServiceObjectsCounter.RegisterInstance(Me)
  End If
End Sub
```

Then, add this finalizer:

```
' Finalizer
Protected Overrides Sub Finalize()
  MyBase.Finalize()

  Try
    ' tell perfmon
    If _numCustomerServiceObjectsCounter Is Nothing Then
      ' Do not reregister instance
    Else
      _numCustomerServiceObjectsCounter.DeregisterInstance(Me)
    End If
  Catch
    ' do nothing
  End Try
End Sub
```

As you can see, there's nothing particular tricky about adjusting the count. We call RegisterInstance or DeregisterInstance depending on how many there are. However, the finalizer does present an issue that's worth examining.

Because we have no control over when objects are deleted in .NET thanks to the nature of the built-in garbage collector, working with finalizers can be a little tricky. In this particular instance, when the finalizer is called, we don't actually know if PerfMon is still available. We have to wrap the whole lot in a `Try...Catch` and, effectively, hope for the best. In the normal lifetime of this object, this will work A-OK. However, when we close the service itself, say when Windows itself is shutting down, we could run into all sorts of problems. This is a fairly typical issue with .NET development, but beyond the scope of this discussion.

Keeping Count of Objects

Keeping a count of a given number of objects can be a little tricky, because we're creating instances of objects in order to get the counters registered. Things can get a little out-of-sync, so if you want to keep track of the de facto number of instances from a given class loaded into memory, we can use the `RegisterInstance` and `DeregisterInstance` methods on `EnterpriseObjects.EnterpriseCounter`. The problem occurs when you try to decrement the counter from a finalizer when you didn't increment the counter in the matching constructor.

To clarify, as we're scanning the assemblies and creating objects, we're calling a constructor but we're not updating the counter, as the counter hasn't been created yet. Thanks to the non-deterministic nature of the garbage collector, we will end up in the finalizer for one of these objects. As we'll have a counter at this point, we'll be able to decrement the counter, but all that will happen effectively is that we'll decrement once more than we ever increment. This can lead to undefined results.

Below is the `RegisterInstance` method. Notice that the hash we use with the hash table is the value returned by `GetHashCode`. We do this because we don't want to keep the object in memory – if we added the entire object rather than a hash code, a reference to the object would be maintained requiring more work for the garbage collector to track its usage.

```vb
Public Sub RegisterInstance(ByVal theObject As Object)

    ' do we have this object?
    Dim hashCode As Integer = theObject.GetHashCode()
    If _instances.Contains(hashCode) = False Then
        _instances.Add(hashCode, Nothing)
        Counter.Increment()
    End If

End Sub
```

Here's the implementation of `DeregisterInstance`:

```vb
Public Sub DeregisterInstance(ByVal theObject As Object)

    ' get the hashcode...
    Dim hashCode As Integer = theObject.GetHashCode()
    If _instances.Contains(hashCode) = True Then
        _instances.Remove(hashCode)
        Counter.Decrement()
    End If

End Sub
```

Updating "HostService"

To tell the service that we want to use performance counters, we have to make two changes to
BusinessHost.HostService. In the first case, when we're given an assembly to scan for Remoting
objects, we also want to ask Counters to scan the same assembly for classes that are capable of using
performance counters. Add this code to the LoadAssembly method of HostService:

```
Public Sub LoadAssembly(ByVal useAssembly As [Assembly])
    Dim lType As Type
    Dim checkAttribute As Object

    ' Go through the types
    For Each lType In useAssembly.GetTypes()
        ' Go through the attributes
        For Each checkAttribute In lType.GetCustomAttributes(False)
            ' What do we have
            If checkAttribute Is EnterpriseObjects.RemotingAttribute Then
                Register(lType)
            End If
        Next
        ' Check this assembly for perfmon counters
        EnterpriseObjects.EnterpriseApplication.Application.Counters.ScanAssembly( _
                                                                    useAssembly)
    Next
End Sub
```

You can see that here we're using the Counters property of EnterpriseApplication. This is the
preferred method for accessing the object, as discussed before.

Next, we need to create the counters themselves. This involves providing the name of the performance
object as it will appear in PerfMon (BookManager), and also asking the Counters object to actually
tell PerfMon about the counters:

```
Public Sub Go()
    ' Security
    AppDomain.CurrentDomain.SetPrincipalPolicy(PrincipalPolicy.WindowsPrincipal)

    ' Database
    EnterpriseObjects.EnterpriseApplication.Application.ConnectionString = _
    "integrated security=sspi;data source=chimaera;initial catalog=bookmanager"

    ' Create a channel
    Dim channel As IChannel = New TcpChannel(8080)
    ChannelServices.RegisterChannel(channel)
    channel = New HttpChannel(8081)
    ChannelServices.RegisterChannel(channel)

    ' Load the assemblies
    LoadAssembly(New EnterpriseObjects.Entity())
    LoadAssembly(New BookManagerObjects.Author())
```

```
        ' create the perfmon counters...
EnterpriseObjects.EnterpriseApplication.Application.Counters.PerformanceObjectName
 _
                                                          = "BookManager"
    EnterpriseObjects.EnterpriseApplication.Application.Counters.CreateCounters( _
                                                          True)

    End Sub
```

So what actually happens when we call `CreateCounters`? Well, if you look inside the
`EnterpriseCounters` class, you'll notice that the `ScanAssembly` method looks through the types for
those that support the `ICounterProvider` interface. When it finds one, it creates an instance of the
type, calls the method and adds the instance to a private `ArrayList` called
`_counterCapableObjects`.

```
    Public Sub ScanAssembly(ByVal scanAssembly As [Assembly])

      ' go through the types...
      Dim scanType As Type
      For Each scanType In scanAssembly.GetTypes()

        ' get the attributes...
        Dim counterInterface As Type
        For Each counterInterface In scanType.GetInterfaces()

          ' do we have one?
          If counterInterface Is GetType(ICounterProvider) Then

            ' create it...
            Try

              ' call it and add it to the list...
              Dim targetObject As ICounterProvider = _
                                    Activator.CreateInstance(scanType)
              targetObject.CreateCounters(Me)
              _counterCapableObjects.Add(targetObject)

            Catch
            End Try
          End If
        Next
      Next
    End Sub
```

After all of the assemblies have been scanned, `CreateCounters` is called. One thing worth noting about
performance counters is that it's not possible to add or remove counters once PerfMon has been told about
the performance object from which the counters hang. The only modification option we have is to delete
them all and start again. In PerfMon parlance, the "performance object" is known as the "category".
Categories can be manipulated through the `System.Diagnostics.PerformanceCounterCategory`
class, or, more specifically, shared methods on that class.

For each counter, we need to create a `System.Diagnostics.CounterCreationData` instance. We then call `Create` on `PerformanceCounterCategory` and at this point PerfMon is told about the counters. After this, we create `PerformanceCounter` objects for each counter that we registered and loop through the cached objects in `_counterCapableObjects`. Here's the `CreateCounters` method on `EnterpriseCounters`:

```
Public Sub CreateCounters(ByVal force As Boolean)

    ' does the object exist?
    Dim countersExist As Boolean = _
                    PerformanceCounterCategory.Exists(PerformanceObjectName)

    ' delete the category?
    If countersExist = True And force = True Then
      PerformanceCounterCategory.Delete(PerformanceObjectName)
      countersExist = False
    End If

    ' do we need to create it?
    Dim counter As Counter
    If countersExist = False Then

        ' create a collection...
        Dim list As New CounterCreationDataCollection()

        ' go through each counter...
        For Each counter In Counters

            ' create some new data...
            Dim data As New CounterCreationData()
            data.CounterName = counter.Name
            data.CounterHelp = counter.HelpText
            data.CounterType = counter.Type

            ' add it...
            list.Add(data)

        Next

        ' create the category and all of the counters...
        PerformanceCounterCategory.Create(PerformanceObjectName, "", list)

    End If

    ' now, go back through the counters and create instances...
    For Each counter In Counters

        ' create an instance and store it...
        counter.Counter = New
        PerformanceCounter(PerformanceObjectName, counter.Name, "", False)

        ' reset the value...
        counter.Counter.RawValue = 0
```

```
Next

' ok, now tell all the objects that registered counters that they
' have been created...
Dim counterObject As ICounterProvider
For Each counterObject In _counterCapableObjects
   counterObject.CountersCreated(Me)
Next
_counterCapableObjects.Clear()

End Sub
```

One important thing to note when creating the PerformanceCounter object – make sure you create it as read/write-able so you can change it.

Testing the Counter

Start up the BusinessHostConsole project now. The counters will be created and if you open up PerfMon, you'll find that you can indeed add the counters to the chart:

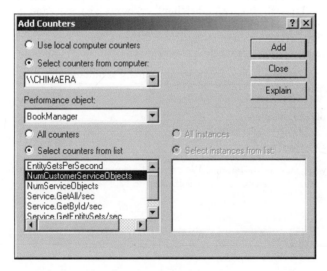

If you add a NumCustomerServiceObjects counter to the chart, you'll get a value of 0 back. That's because, although we have created instances of customer service objects, we haven't created them since the counter has been active. (We created them when scanning the assemblies when the service started.)

If you run the Application Browser, open the Customer Editor, and search for customers, you'll find that PerfMon is now reporting a single object:

Last	1.000	Average	0.120	Minimum	0.000
		Maximum	1.000	Duration	1:40

This is where things get *very* interesting. For scalability, we want the number of customer service objects to be entirely unrelated to the number of clients we have on the go. Whether we have four clients running or four thousand, we only want a single instance of `CustomerService` in memory. That's why we went to such lengths to ensure that the objects are stateless.

To test this, start up another two or three application browsers and search again. The number of `CustomerService` objects will remain constant at 1: just the effect we want.

If you close the host (press the *Enter* key in the console app, rather than stopping the debugger), you'll notice that the counter returns to 0.

Scalability Counters

Usage counters like the one we've just met are useful for confirming that our footprint-reducing efforts are actually working. We've now proven that a singleton object instance can indeed support multiple inbound Remoting connections.

By and large, this isn't the most useful type of counter for server applications. The server exists mainly to construct results and pass them back to the client, or to receive results and process them. There are two types of counters that are useful at this point:

- ❑ Rate counters – these let us see how often a given operation is running

- ❑ Concurrency counters – these let us see how many simultaneous operations are running at a given moment

Let's look at examples of these now.

Creating a Rate Counter

Rate counters are very easy to implement. We can add a counter that measures the number of calls to a method per second with the `RateOfCountsPerSecond32` counter type. Find `CustomerService` and add these members:

```
<EnterpriseObjects.Remoting()> Public Class CustomerService
    Inherits CustomerServiceBase

    ' Counters
    Protected Const NumCustomerServiceObjectsCounterName As String = _
                                        "NumCustomerServiceObjects"
    Protected Friend _numCustomerServiceObjectsCounter As EnterpriseCounter
    Protected Const FindCustomerCallsRateCounterName As String = _
                                    "CustomerService.FindCustomer/sec"
    Protected Friend _findCustomerCallsRateCounter As PerformanceCounter
```

Then, make these changes to `CreateCounters` and `CountersCreated`:

```
    ' CreateCounters
    Public Overrides Sub CreateCounters(ByVal counters As _
                                    EnterpriseObjects.EnterpriseCounters)
        ' Add them
```

```
counters.Counters.Add(New _
                        EnterpriseObjects.EnterpriseCounter( _
                        NumCustomerServiceObjectsCounterName, _
                        "Number of customer service objects in use", _
                        PerformanceCounterType.NumberOfItems32))

          counters.Counters.Add(New _
                        EnterpriseObjects.EnterpriseCounter( _
                        FindCustomerCallsRateCounterName, _
                        "Number of FindCustomer calls per second", _
                        PerformanceCounterType.RateOfCountsPerSecond32))

     End Sub

     ' CountersCreated
     Public Overrides Sub CountersCreated(ByVal counters As _
                                        EnterpriseObjects.EnterpriseCounters)
        ' Find them
        _numCustomerServiceObjectsCounter = _
                counters.Counters.Find(NumCustomerServiceObjectsCounterName)
        _findCustomerCallsRateCounter = _
                counters.Counters.Find(FindCustomerCallsRateCounterName).Counter

     End Sub
```

Now run the host and the browser. Use the Customer Editor to search for customers by clicking on the Search button like crazy. You'll be able to get between 4 and 10 calls per second.

Creating a Concurrency Counter

A concurrency counter lets us see how many simultaneous calls to a particular piece of code are being made. They are very useful in situations involving a database call. Databases are well known as being a bottleneck, so what we want is to get into the database and out again as quickly as possible. This technique lets us measure how many clients are waiting for results from a call.

Again, add these members to `CustomerService`:

```
<EnterpriseObjects.Remoting()> Public Class CustomerService
   Inherits CustomerServiceBase

   ' Counters
   Protected Const NumCustomerServiceObjectsCounterName As String = _
                                        "NumCustomerServiceObjects"
   Protected Friend _numCustomerServiceObjectsCounter As EnterpriseCounter
   Protected Const FindCustomerCallsRateCounterName As String = _
                                        "CustomerService.FindCustomer/sec"
   Protected Friend _findCustomerCallsRateCounter As PerformanceCounter
   Protected Const FindCustomerCallsConcurrentCounterName As String = _
                                "Conn. CustomerService.FindCustomer"
   Protected Friend _findCustomerCallsConcurrentCounter As PerformanceCounter
```

Then, make these changes:

```
' CreateCounters
Public Overrides Sub CreateCounters(ByVal counters As _
                                    EnterpriseObjects.EnterpriseCounters)
  ' Add them
  counters.Counters.Add(New _
                    EnterpriseObjects.EnterpriseCounter( _
                    NumCustomerServiceObjectsCounterName, _
                    "Number of customer service objects in use", _
                    PerformanceCounterType.NumberOfItems32))

  counters.Counters.Add(New _
                    EnterpriseObjects.EnterpriseCounter( _
                    FindCustomerCallsRateCounterName, _
                    "Number of FindCustomer calls per second", _
                    PerformanceCounterType.RateOfCountsPerSecond32))

  counters.Counters.Add(New _
                    EnterpriseObjects.EnterpriseCounter( _
                    FindCustomerCallsConcurrentCounterName, _
                    "Concurrent FindCustomer calls", _
                    PerformanceCounterType.NumberOfItems32))

End Sub


' CountersCreated
Public Overrides Sub CountersCreated(ByVal counters As _
                                     EnterpriseObjects.EnterpriseCounters)
  ' Find them
  _numCustomerServiceObjectsCounter = _
            counters.Counters.Find(NumCustomerServiceObjectsCounterName)
  _findCustomerCallsRateCounter = _
          counters.Counters.Find(FindCustomerCallsRateCounterName).Counter
  _findCustomerCallsConcurrentCounter = _
      counters.Counters.Find(FindCustomerCallsConcurrentCounterName).Counter

End Sub
```

Finally, make these changes to `FindCustomers`:

```
' FindCustomers - search for customers
Public Function FindCustomers(ByVal searchFor As String) As CustomerSet
  ' Flag it
  If Not _findCustomerCallsRateCounter Is Nothing Then
    _findCustomerCallsRateCounter.Increment()
  End If

  ' Run the sproc and return
  If Not _findCustomerCallsConcurrentCounter Is Nothing Then
    _findCustomerCallsConcurrentCounter.Increment()
  End If
```

```
        Dim customers As CustomerSet = CType(Sprocs.FindCustomers(searchFor, _
                                   GetType(CustomerSet)), CustomerSet)

        If Not _findCustomerCallsConcurrentCounter Is Nothing Then
          _findCustomerCallsConcurrentCounter.Decrement()
        End If

        ' Return
        Return customers
    End Function
```

Start up the projects again and you'll see the counters. It's unlikely you'll be able to make the counter move above 1 with a single client. If you want to prove this works, you could fire up a number of clients and also use `System.Threading.Thread.Sleep` before decrementing the counter to artificially load the server. This will artificially cause the database to take longer than usual to return results.

Exception Reporting

If you recall, way back when we built the application browser, we added a `HandleException` method that was called whenever an exception was caught by the browser. A neat management feature would be to report any exceptions received by the client to the administration team through a Web Service.

Microsoft is trying something similar with the "Online Crash Analysis" feature in Windows XP. If you're unfamiliar with this feature, whenever something goes wrong with an application, an error report is sent over the Internet to Microsoft so it can analyze the cause of the problem. Visual Studio .NET has a version of this feature too, which has helped a great deal during the beta development phase.

By sending exception data back to developers, the developers should be able to detect problems earlier in the maintenance cycle and have better access to performance and stability data.

Serializing Exceptions

The first step in sending the exception back to the Web Service is to serialize the exception to an XML string. This can then easily be sent over to the Web Service as a normal string parameter of a method. We'll have to serialize the exception manually using classes in the `System.Xml` namespace.

To do this, we first of all have to create a new `System.IO.MemoryStream` object, which will provide the resource that we'll serialize the exception to. We'll need instances of `System.IO.StreamWriter` and `System.Xml.XmlTextWriter` classes to write the data.

Open the code editor for `Browser.vb` and find the `HandleException` method. Add `Imports` statements for `System.IO`, `System.Text` and `System.Xml`. We'll more or less recreate `HandleException` from scratch, and we'll go through it block by block. Here's the first part:

```
    ' HandleException
    Public Sub HandleException(ByVal ex As System.Exception) _
                            Implements IBrowser.HandleException
      ' We're not too worried if this isn't 100% successful
      Dim wasReported As Boolean = False
      Try
```

First of all, we wrap everything in a `Try...Catch`. If something has gone wrong in the application, we're not going to worry about exceptions occurring in the exception reporting here. Such a facility should be considered in order to recover from situations where something really drastic has gone wrong and nothing works properly.

The first thing we do is to create the stream and the two writers. We then call a method, which we'll build in a short while, called `WriteExceptionToXml`. This will do the actual serialization. One thing to note: after calling this method we call `Flush` on the `XmlTextWriter`. This is an important step that makes sure the stream is fully populated before we read it back again:

```
' Serialize the exception
Dim strm As Stream = New MemoryStream()
Dim writer As StreamWriter = New StreamWriter(strm)
Dim xml As XmlTextWriter = New XmlTextWriter(writer)
WriteExceptionToXml(xml, ex)
xml.Flush()
```

Once we've written the XML, we need to read it back. The first step is to rewind the stream, and the second step is to create a new `System.IO.StreamReader` and get the data back:

```
' Retrieve the data
strm.Seek(0, SeekOrigin.Begin)
Dim reader As StreamReader = New StreamReader(strm)
Dim exceptionXml As String = reader.ReadToEnd()
strm.Close()
```

At this point, `exceptionXml` will contain a string of XML-formatted data representing the exception. (If you're wondering what this file looks like, we'll see an example in a little while.) Next, we pass the XML over to the Web Service using a method called `ReportException`: again, we'll write this in a moment. This method also takes the current security token:

```
' Send it to the Web Service
Login.CurrentLogin.Service.ReportException( _
                    EnterpriseApplication.Application.SecurityToken, _
                    exceptionXml)

Catch
    ' Flag it as not reported
    wasReported = False
End Try
```

Once we've done that, we have to report the exception to the user in the way we have done throughout. As we now have a little more text to present, we'll use a `System.Text.StringBuilder` object, as this is more efficient than the concatenation operator when creating a long string comprising many parts:

```
' Do something quick for now
Dim builder As StringBuilder = New StringBuilder( _
                    "An exception has occurred." & vbCrLf & vbCrLf)
builder.Append(ex.GetType().ToString())
builder.Append(":")
builder.Append(ex.Message)
```

```
    builder.Append("\r\n")
    builder.Append(ex.StackTrace)
    builder.Append("\r\n\r\n")
    If wasReported = True Then
        builder.Append("The exception was reported to the system administrator.")
    Else
        builder.Append("The exception was *not* reported to the system " _
                    & "administrator.")
    End If
    Alert(builder.ToString())

End Sub
```

Before we move on, we need to code the `WriteExceptionToXml` method. The only wrinkle to this method is that if the exception has an inner exception (that is, an exception that gets thrown remotely, but is reported locally), we have to use recursion to make sure we walk down the set.

To write the XML, we use a combination of `WriteStartElement`, `WriteEndElement`, and `WriteElementString`:

```
' WriteExceptionToXml
Private Sub WriteExceptionToXml(ByVal xml As XmlTextWriter, _
                                ByVal ex As Exception)
    ' header
    xml.WriteStartElement("Exception")

    ' data
    xml.WriteElementString("Type", ex.GetType().ToString())
    xml.WriteElementString("Message", ex.Message)
    xml.WriteElementString("Source", ex.Source)
    xml.WriteElementString("StackTrace", ex.StackTrace)
    xml.WriteElementString("HelpLink", ex.HelpLink)

    ' inner
    xml.WriteStartElement("InnerException")
    If Not ex.InnerException Is Nothing Then
        WriteExceptionToXml(xml, ex.InnerException)
    End If
    xml.WriteEndElement()

    ' footer
    xml.WriteEndElement()
End Sub
```

Now all we need to do is add the method to the Web Service.

The XML Document

Without having the Web Service in place, we can't test this. However, to help you understand what the document looks like, I'll reproduce a typical one here. What I've done is changed `CustomerService.FindCustomers` so that it always throws a `ArgumentOutOfRangeException`:

```
' FindCustomers - search for customers
Public Function FindCustomers(ByVal searchFor As String) _
                              As CustomerSet
  Throw New ArgumentOutOfRangeException()

  ' Flag it
  If Not _findCustomerCallsRateCounter Is Nothing Then
    _findCustomerCallsRateCounter.Increment()
  End If

  ' Run the sproc and return
  If Not _findCustomerCallsConcurrentCounter Is Nothing Then
    _findCustomerCallsConcurrentCounter.Increment()
  End If
  Dim customers As CustomerSet = CType(Sprocs.FindCustomers(searchFor, _
                                 GetType(CustomerSet)), CustomerSet)

  If Not _findCustomersCallsConcurrentCounter Is Nothing Then
    _findCustomersCallsConcurrentCounter.Decrement()
  End If

  ' Return
  Return customers
End Function
```

Here's the document we get if we throw that exception:

```
<Exception>
  <Type>System.ArgumentOutOfRangeException</Type>
  <Message>Specified argument was out of the range of valid values.</Message>
  <Source>MyEnterpriseObjects</Source>
  <StackTrace>
  ServerStackTrace: at BookManagerObjects.CustomerService.FindCustomers(String
searchFor)
    in c:\bookmanager\bookmanagerobjects\customerservice.vb:line 63 at
System.Runtime.Remoting.Messaging.StackBuilderSink.PrivateProcessMessage(MethodBas
e mb, Object[] args, Object server, Int32 methodPtr, Boolean fExecuteInContext,
Object[]& outArgs) at
    System.Runtime.Remoting.Messaging.StackBuilderSink.SyncProcessMessage(IMessage
msg, Int32 methodPtr, Boolean fExecuteInContext)

  Exception rethrown at [0]: at
  System.Runtime.Remoting.Proxies.RealProxy.HandleReturnMessage(IMessage reqMsg,
IMessage retMsg) at
  System.Runtime.Remoting.Proxies.RealProxy.PrivateInvoke(MessageData& msgData,
Int32 type) at BookManagerObjects.CustomerService.FindCustomers(String searchFor)
in C:\BookManager\BookManagerObjects\CustomerService.vb:line 64 at
  BookManagerObjects.Customer.FindCustomers(String searchFor) in
C:\BookManager\BookManagerObjects\Customer.vb:line 30 at
  CustomerEditor.CustomerEditor.buttonSearch_Click(Object sender, EventArgs e) in
c:\bookmanager\customereditor\customereditor.vb:line 530
```

```
  </StackTrace>
  <HelpLink />
  <InnerException />
</Exception>
```

It's a little difficult to read because the calls are so long, but you should be able to see what's happening.

The "ReportException" Web Service Method

When the Web Service receives the exception, we can do anything we particularly want to with it. One neat thing to do is if you manage to detect a problem that you have a solution for, to e-mail the user immediately with a solution. Alternatively, you could write the exception information into a database, or e-mail it directly to system administrators or developers.

At the point when we receive the exception report, we might want to add more information to the document that's used for investigation. Some obvious information to include would be the details of the user themselves. One way of doing this is to create a new document and insert the received document into it. The technique for doing this isn't vastly different from the code we've just seen, so we'll just present it as is:

```
<WebMethod()> Public Sub ReportException(ByVal tokenString As String, _
                                    ByVal exceptionData As String)
   ' Load the token
   Dim tkn As Token = Token.Load(tokenString)
   If tkn Is Nothing Then
      Throw New Exception("Invalid token supplied.")
   End If

   ' Create a new xml document
   Dim strm As Stream = New MemoryStream()
   Dim writer As StreamWriter = New StreamWriter(strm)
   Dim xml As XmlTextWriter = New XmlTextWriter(writer)

   ' add information about the token and user...
   xml.WriteStartElement("ReportedException")
   xml.WriteElementString("Token", tkn.Token)
   xml.WriteElementString("TokenId", tkn.Id.ToString())
   xml.WriteElementString("UserId", tkn.UserId.ToString())
   xml.WriteElementString("NtlmName", tkn.NtlmName)
   xml.WriteElementString( _
               "ClientIp",Context.Request.ServerVariables("remote_addr"))
   xml.WriteStartElement("Data")
   xml.WriteRaw(exceptionData)
   xml.WriteEndElement()
   xml.WriteEndElement()
   xml.Flush()

   ' get it back...
   strm.Seek(0, SeekOrigin.Begin)
   Dim reader As StreamReader = New StreamReader(strm)
   Dim body As String = reader.ReadToEnd()
   strm.Close()
   ' construct the message...
   Dim mail As MailMessage = New MailMessage()
```

```
        mail.Subject = "An exception has been reported by a client"
        mail.Body = body
        mail.To = "admin@pretendcompany.com"
        mail.From = "server@pretendcompany.com"

        ' send it...
        SmtpMail.Send(mail)

    End Sub
```

In the above code, we're creating a new XML element called `Data` and adding the required information to it.

Towards the end of the code, you'll see that we're using `System.Web.Mail.MailMessage` and `System.Web.Mail.SmtpMail` to send the report to an administrator. As I was saying before, this is just one option. If we wanted, we could write it to a database, use a knowledge base of some description to automatically determine a solution and so on.

> Remember, change the "To" address used in the code sample to your own e-mail address or you won't receive the message!

In a production system, it's unrealistic that we'd use e-mail to deliver the exceptions directly to system administrators. What's more likely is that we'd build a management application that could collate and process these management reports. E-mail is a lightweight, inexpensive mechanism (albeit primarily one-way). Alternatively, you may prefer to rig the Web Service so that the messages are dropped directly into the data store for the management application.

Testing the Exception Handler

To test the exception handler, you'll need to build the Web Service with the new `ReportException` method in place. You'll also need to update the `Coordinator` Web Service reference in the Solution Explorer of the `ApplicationBrowser` project and, obviously, build that project.

Earlier I presented a change to `CustomerService.FindCustomer` that threw an exception the instant it was called. Add this code to the method now and restart the service (I'll reproduce the code here to make life a little easier!):

```
' FindCustomers - search for customers
Public Function FindCustomers(ByVal searchFor As String) _
                            As CustomerSet
    Throw New ArgumentOutOfRangeException()

    ' Flag it
    If Not _findCustomersCallsRateCounter Is Nothing Then
      _findCustomersCallsRateCounter.Increment()
    End If

    ...

End Function
```

Run up the service and the application browser. Fire up the Customer Editor and search. An exception will be thrown and presented in the usual way. In addition however, this time an e-mail like the one below will be sent to whatever address you specified:

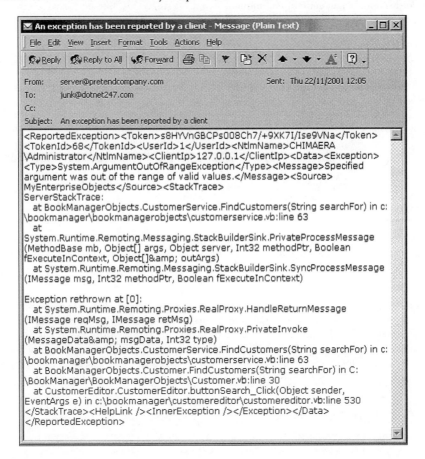

Reporting More Data

In this example, all we've sent to the server is the information contained within the exception itself. Obviously, you can send whatever data you like and you may find it useful to include more information about the application state. Some possibilities are:

- ❑ A copy of the functionality catalog, together with the versions of the assemblies that are *actually* being used
- ❑ The Windows version
- ❑ The amount of remaining disk space and memory
- ❑ A list of other processes running on the machine
- ❑ The Windows user name

Event Logging

Another "old school" management technique is event logging. This, like performance monitoring, has been around since early versions of Windows NT.

If you're not familiar with it, the event log provides a central repository into which applications can place messages. You can find it by clicking Start, and selecting Programs | Administrative Tools | Event Viewer:

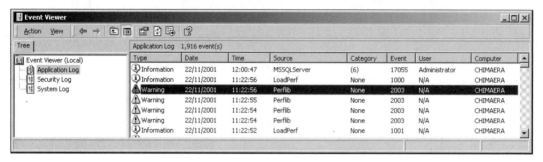

The Event Viewer typically contains three logs: Application, Security, and System. The Application log is used to report status and error information. The Security log is typically used by Windows itself to provide audit information like "such and such user logged on", or "such and such user was refused permission". The System log is used by system services to report status and error information.

The WEO objects don't have any event logging code in them, mainly because we're relying on the exception reporting functionality we discussed before to report errors to the system administrators. (In a production environment, it's unrealistic that we'd deliver the reports through e-mail. It's more likely we'd use e-mail as a messaging solution to drop the exception reports into a management application.) However, for completeness, we'll take a look at how we can write to the event log, talking a little more about the pros and cons as we go. Whether or not you choose to use this functionality is up to you.

For brevity, we'll demonstrate the event log functionality by adding an option to the Help menu of the Browser. Using the Designer, add this new option. Call it menuHelpWriteEvent:

Double-click on the option to create a new event handler. Before adding code to the handler, make sure System.Diagnostics is listed in the namespace imports:

```
Imports System
Imports System.Drawing
Imports System.Collections
Imports System.ComponentModel
Imports System.Windows.Forms
Imports System.IO
```

```
Imports System.Xml
Imports System.Text
Imports System.Data
Imports System.Reflection
Imports System.Diagnostics
Imports ApplicationBrowser.Coordination
Imports EnterpriseObjects
```

Writing an event to the log is very simple. You have to choose an arbitrary name for the event source (we're going to use `ApplicationBrowser`) and check to see if the source already exists. If it does not, you need to create it. Once that's done, you simply create a new `System.Diagnostics.EventLog` object and call its `WriteEvent` method. Here's the code:

```
Private Sub menuHelpWriteEvent_Click(ByVal sender As System.Object, _
                                     ByVal e As System.EventArgs) _
                                     Handles menuHelpWriteEvent.Click
  ' what's the source?
  Dim eventSource As String = "ApplicationBrowser"

  ' Do we need to create the source?
  If EventLog.SourceExists(eventSource) = False Then
    EventLog.CreateEventSource(eventSource, "Application")
  End If

  ' Create a new event
  Dim log As EventLog = New EventLog()
  log.Source = eventSource
  log.WriteEntry("This is an event that I have written to the log", _
              EventLogEntryType.Information, 10001)

End Sub
```

There are three types of entry log messages – Information, Warning, and Error. The one you require is supplied as the second parameter of the `WriteEntry` method. The third parameter is an arbitrary numeric code – it's value and meaning is entirely up to you.

If you run the browser now and select the menu option, the new event will be written to the **Application** log:

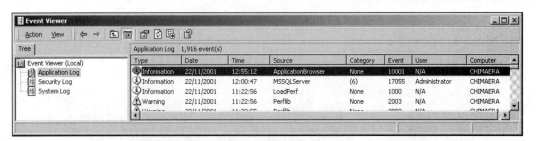

If you double-click on the entry, you'll see further details:

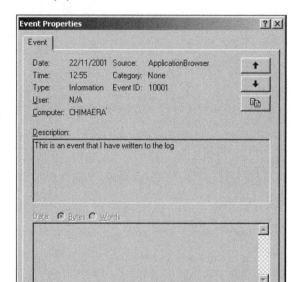

By and large, you can write whatever you like to the Event Log. However, as mentioned earlier, you may find it more manageable to create a more imaginative reporting scheme that's more centralized.

If you have the browser writing events to the event log, it's actually very hard to get hold of them if you're investigating a problem, whereas with a centralized reporting scheme the information is more readily to hand. Likewise, if you have the server writing events to the event log, you have a similar problem. It's better to have the code proactively tell you about problems rather than relying on you to hunt around for the information.

Debugging and Tracing

When writing code, it's often useful to add special code to the application that reports on its state, or details of how a certain algorithm is running. One way to do this is to render messages to the screen when a certain event occurs. For example, if we're running our service through the console application, we could render a message whenever the `FindCustomer` call was used, like this:

```
C:\BookManager\BusinessHostConsole\bin\Debug\BusinessHostConsole.exe
Created 'BookManager/BookManagerObjects.CustomerService.remote'
Created 'BookManager/BookManagerObjects.SecurityChecker.remote'

Press Enter to close the console.

FindCustomers: [drew]
1 customer(s) found
FindCustomers: [pretend]
3 customer(s) found
```

This kind of information is very useful when debugging an application, but when we put the application into production, it's crucial that we remove all of the debugging information, or in some way disable the debugging feature. In .NET, this is achieved through "tracing", which is a topic we discuss in a moment. Although, for the most part, leaving debug information in will not affect the stability of the application, it will affect the performance. In this case, we're wasting processor time preparing and presenting strings to the user that, once we're convinced the application works, would rarely need to be seen again. (And, in fact, when we're running this service as a full Windows Service, we'll never be able to see them.)

Presenting Debug Information

When compiling your assemblies, you can choose from two "build configurations", or create your own ones. Most of the projects come with two: **Debug** and **Release**. Debug is used, not surprisingly, when you are still developing your application. Release is for when you're ready to put the application into production. Ideally, when we switch from Debug to Release, we want all of the debugging code to be removed so that we're not wasting time preparing and presenting strings.

There are two ways to do this. You can either surround the code you want to miss out in conditional terminology, or you can use the System.Diagnostics.ConditionalAttribute attribute to skip calls to methods that should not be included in a given configuration.

Let's look at an example. Find the FindCustomers method and add this code:

```
' FindCustomers - search for customers
Public Function FindCustomers(ByVal searchFor As String) As CustomerSet
  ' Debug
  DebugPresentFindCustomersQuery(searchFor)

  ' Flag it
  If Not _findCustomersCallsRateCounter Is Nothing Then
    _findCustomersCallsRateCounter.Increment()
  End If

' Run the sproc and return
If Not _findCustomersCallsConcurrentCounter Is Nothing Then
  _findCustomersCallsConcurrentCounter.Increment()
End If
Dim customers As CustomerSet = CType(Sprocs.FindCustomers(searchFor, _
                                GetType(CustomerSet)), CustomerSet)

If Not _findCustomersCallsConcurrentCounter Is Nothing Then
  _findCustomersCallsConcurrentCounter.Decrement()
End If

  ' debug
  DebugPresentFindCustomersResult(customers)

  ' Return
  Return customers
End Function
```

```
' Debug methods
<System.Diagnostics.Conditional("DEBUG")> Private Sub _
                    DebugPresentFindCustomersQuery(ByVal searchFor As String)
   Console.WriteLine("FindCustomers: [" + searchFor + "]")
End Sub

<System.Diagnostics.Conditional("DEBUG")> Private Sub _
               DebugPresentFindCustomersResult(ByVal customers As CustomerSet)
   Console.WriteLine(customers.Count.ToString() + " customer(s) found")
End Sub
```

Run the project and when you search for customers, you should see the results we presented before:

OK, now we can try to turn off this code just by changing the build configuration. Using Visual Studio .NET, select Build | Configuration Manager from the menu when working on the BusinessHost solution. Change the Active Solution Configuration value to Release.

Now restart. When you search now, debug information should not appear.

What's actually happening is that the compiler is detecting that you're trying to call into a method that should be ignored from the build. In fact, the entire call is missed out. What you should be aware of is that any preparation calls would be included, which is why you want to send the optimum amount of raw information to the debugging method and let it prepare the values for presentation.

In our specific example, this would mean it was wrong to prepare the string sent to WriteLine before calling into the method. What we want to do is pass in the raw information to the method and prepare the string for presentation once we're inside. This has the implication that it prevents us from having a single, general purpose debug information presentation method that we can call from anywhere. (Well, we can do it, but it's not as efficient.)

"Debug.WriteLine"

So far, we've been using Console.WriteLine to present information to the user. We could, if we wanted, use Debug.WriteLine. This does the same thing, but it's flagged as a debugging method in the same way that we flagged DebugPresentFindCustomersQuery, and any calls to this method are automatically skipped when we flip to a release build.

As well as this method, we also have Debug.Write, Debug.WriteIf, and Debug.WriteLineIf. WriteIf and WriteLineIf can be useful if you need to render debugging information conditionally.

Trace vs. Debug

In the Framework classes, there are two very similar classes: `System.Diagnostics.Trace` and `System.Diagnostics.Debug`. If you investigate these two, you'll discover that they both have the same methods, but don't have a common base class other than `System.Object`.

Both of these classes work the same way, but have different uses. `Debug` is used for situations like those we've discussed – you're trying to get some code working and need to monitor the state of the application. Debug code is always removed before the application goes into production. `Trace`, on the other hand, is always on. The idea with trace is that if a system administrator needs to investigate a problem, they can turn tracing on without having to recompile the code. (Usually tracing is turned on by manipulating the `.config` file.)

We're not going to examine `Trace` here, but you can find lots of information about it on MSDN, or you might want to look at *Professional ASP.NET ISBN 1-861004-88-5*, also from Wrox Press.

Load Balancing

One aspect of enterprise development that was staggeringly difficult to pull off pre-.NET was load-balancing COM components. In this section, we'll take a quick look at load balancing and a couple of solutions.

What is Load Balancing?

The principle of load balancing is that rather than setting up one huge computer to serve all your users, you set up a collection of smaller computers and make them all work together to achieve the same solution. This diagram illustrates the basics of load balancing:

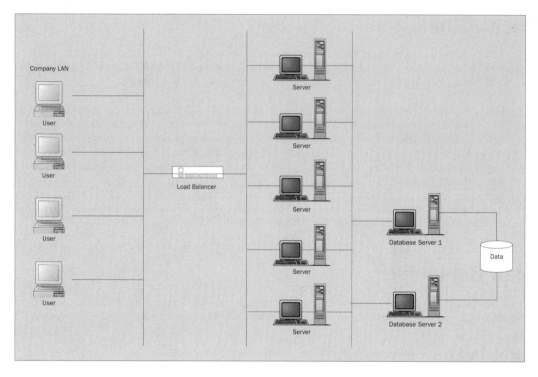

In a load balancing solution, all of the requests appear to be targeted at a single point. In the above example, we have a hardware load balancing solution: a physical device on the network responsible for distributing requests. In reality, this could be a software solution, and we'll talk about it in a moment.

All load balancing solutions work on the same principle – you have a set of computers all identically configured and all equally able at satisfying requests from users, known as a **web farm**. The "distributor" receives a request and allocates it to one of the computers in the farm.

There are a number of techniques for allocating requests, and they vary in cost depending on how reliable the solution actually is. The first solution I'll present is a "round robin" solution. In this situation, we'll assume we have three servers. The first request is issued to the first server, the second to the second, the third to the third, and the fourth goes back to the first, and so on. This is a very easy solution to implement, but it does have one major drawback.

Round Robin Load Balancing

To implement round robin load balancing, the first task is to identify the machines in the cluster. In our solution, we're going to reengineer one of the methods in the Coordination Web service. We'll then have another three machines in the farm called TUSCAN, CERBERRA, and TAMORA. As all the machines are identical, we can refer to Remoting objects using connection strings like these:

```
Enterprise Connection Type=remoting;
  appname=BookManager;servername=tuscan;port=8080
```

```
Enterprise Connection Type=remoting;
    appname=BookManager;servername=cerberra;port=8080


Enterprise Connection Type=remoting;
    appname=BookManager;servername=tamora;port=8080
```

As you know, these strings are returned by the `GetConnectionString` Web Service method, like this:

```
<WebMethod()> Public Sub GetConnectionString() as String
    return "Enterprise Connection" _
            & "Type=remoting;appname=BookManager;servername=chimaera;port=8080"
End Sub
```

All we have to do is make the method choose TUSCAN on every "first" request, CERBERRA on the "second", and TAMORA on the "third". To do this, we need to keep a count of the connections in a shared value, properly synchronized to make it thread safe. (We need to synchronize access to the counter because each inbound request to the Web Service method will run in a separate thread. To be completely purist about it, we don't want concurrent access to the same "retrieve and increment" operation that we need to undertake.) We can then use the modulus operator on this count to determine which server to use.

Before we can do that, we'll need a list of servers. For the sake of brevity, we'll add them as a shared array to the class. We'll also need a shared member to hold the index and a `System.Threading.ReaderWriterLock`:

```
<WebService(Namespace="http://www.wrox.com/bookmanager/")>
Public Class Coordinator
    Inherits System.Web.Services.WebService
    ' members...
    Protected Friend ServerNames as String()= { "TUSCAN", "CERBERRA", "TAMORA" }
    Protected Friend ConnectionIndex as Integer
    Private Friend _connectionLock as System.Threading.ReaderWriterLock = _
                                new System.Threading.ReaderWriterLock()
```

The changes that need to be made to `GetConnectionString` are very straightforward. We have to retrieve the current value for `ConnectionIndex` (remembering to lock access so that only a single thread can access it at once) and increment it. When we have the index, we need to find the server name that we want to use. We can use the modulus operator on the index together with the length of the `ServerNames` array for this purpose. Finally, we use the selected server name in the connection string:

```
<WebMethod()> Public Function GetConnectionString() As String
    ' choose a connection...

    _connectionLock.AcquireWriterLock(-1)
    Dim useIndex As Integer = ConnectionIndex
    ConnectionIndex = ConnectionIndex + 1
    _connectionLock.ReleaseWriterLock()

    ' now, select a server...
    dim serverName as String = ServerNames(useIndex % ServerNames.Length)
```

```
    ' form a string...
    Return "Enterprise Connection " _
      & "Type=remoting;appname=BookManager;port=8080;servername=" + serverName()
    End Function
```

If you make these changes, don't forget that it won't work unless you actually set up three machines on your network with identical server configurations. We can test to make sure that the service is collecting the right results, however, by invoking the method from the test pages. Run the Coordinator project and invoke the GetConnectionString method. You'll see something like this:

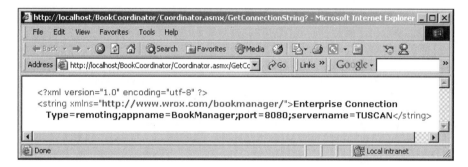

Now the clever bit! If you refresh the page, you'll see a different connection string:

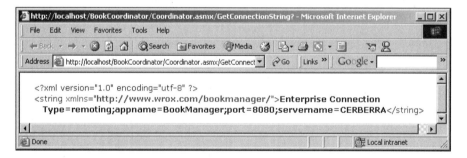

Refresh again, and you'll see the third option:

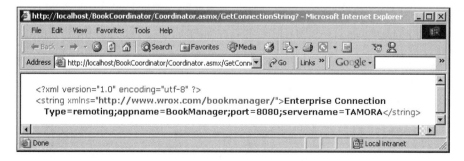

If you refresh one more time, you'll go back to the first connection string.

Who Killed Round Robin?

The problem with round robin is that it's not as resilient as some load-balancing solutions. Imagine you have a client that's been told to connect to TAMORA to get its data. If that server goes down while the client is trying to use it, the client's connection will be lost. If this happens, we ideally want to fail over to another server in the farm.

The other issue with round robin is that it pays no attention to how busy the server is. Imagine you have five clients connected to CERBERRA and CERBERRA is, due to a bug in the code or some other fault, running at nearly 100% capacity, whereas the others in the server pool are running at 20% capacity. In this situation, you want to smooth the usage out across the farm so that all servers are equally busy. Because round robin doesn't listen to the server utilization, new clients will be connected to CERBERRA, despite the fact it makes more sense to connect them to one of the others.

The real advantage of round robin is that it's very cheap and easy to set up. We've managed to implement a round robin solution in about twenty lines of code. (Of course, we've yet to buy, set up, and pay for software licenses on the servers in the farm.) However, it's important to be aware of the major shortcomings of the round robin method.

Single Point of Failure

Another aspect of load balancing worth considering is "single point of failure". Ideally, we never want to get into a position where a single thing going wrong with our system causes universal failure. For example, in our scenario, even if we have fifty servers in the farm, no one will be able to authenticate if the Web Service goes down. Likewise, if the database goes down, we would have a similar problem.

This is called "single point of failure" – something in a system that will stop everything else working properly should it fail. You'll never entirely eliminate single point of failure, but you can greatly increase reliability by redundancy. For example, if you have a hardware load-balancing device distributing requests to the servers in the farm, should that device go down, you could have another configured to take over. Likewise, the switch that connects the servers in the farm to the database cluster could also benefit from redundancy.

Microsoft Application Center 2000

A more practical, and consequentially more expensive, load-balancing solution is Microsoft Application Center 2000.

To get around the problems of round robin, you need to abstract the device you're actually talking to. With round robin, what's happening is that, per inbound connection, you're allocating a single server to work with the client for the life of that connection. This limits our ability to reallocate the client to another server as availability in the cluster changes.

Hardware load-balancing solutions like F5's BigIP or Cisco's Local Director work by presenting a single point of access. Any inbound *communications* (in our case, Remoting or Web Service method calls) come through this single point and are allocated to servers in the farm on a method-by-method basis. As there's no specific connection between the client and the target server, this gives the load-balancing solution the option of switching the client between servers dynamically.

Hardware load-balancing solutions suffer from the single point of failure issue too, and as we said one way around this is through redundancy. However, hardware load balancing is a pretty expensive proposition and when you consider you'll need at least two devices plus the expertise and other bits of kit to create the redundant set, you realize you're talking serious money.

Microsoft Application Center 2000, among other things, is a software-based load-balancing solution. It allows multiple computers to present the same IP address to create the single point of entry so clients always connect to the same IP. However, Application Center allows the servers in the farm to learn about their availability and thus dynamically share load in the same way that hardware-based solutions can.

> **We don't have space here to go into a detailed run down of Application Center. You can, of course, find out more about it at http://www.microsoft.com/applicationcenter/default.asp or you could read _Professional Application Center 2000 ISBN 1-861004-47-8_, also from Wrox Press.**

To implement our solution on a farm running Application Center, all we have to do is configure the farm and install the Remoting service and the Web Service onto the servers. (Whether or not you want to put the Web Service on the same set of servers is up to you. Remember that the Web Service has a very small footprint and is used relatively rarely. Installing it on the farm creates the reliability we need, and will probably have only a negligible impact on server performance.) We would provide the same connection string to all clients, based on the IP address presented by Application Center, unlike the round robin technique earlier.

Summary

In this chapter, we took a look at a few .NET features that can help us manage our application once it's live. We started off looking at performance counters and how they can help us learn about application behavior once users start using it.

After that, we took a look at how we could centrally report exceptions to a Web Service. Although we only saw how to do this for client-side code, this system could easily be enhanced to work for server-side code. We also took a look at how the event log could be used to keep a register of problems that occur.

Finally, we took a look at load balancing and saw how we could build a very simple round-robin system to do this, or make a larger investment and go for a hardware load balancing solution or a more sophisticated software solution like Microsoft Application Center.

.NET Enterprise Development in VB .NET

The WEO Object Builder

Throughout this book we've used the Object Builder and WEO layer to support our application. In this appendix, we're going to take a look at how the internals of the Object Builder work. This will give you the freedom to alter the Object Builder to suit your own needs. As part of the download package for this book, we've provided the source code for the Object Builder.

This appendix is going to look at two aspects of the Object Builder – the database scanner and the code generator.

The Database Scanner

The first thing the Object Builder does when it starts is present the splash screen. This is implemented in the Splash class and basically gives the user one of two options – create a new project or open an existing one. The project itself is held in a class called Project, and so we either create a new one of these or load one from disk. In terms of the database scanning functionality of this class, we're interested in the DbString, Tables and Sprocs fields.

```
<Serializable()> Public Class Project
  Implements ISerializable

  ' members...
  Private _name As String
  Public DbString As String
  Public Folder As DirectoryInfo
  Public Provider As BuilderProvider
  Public Tables As New TableCollection(Me)
  Public Sprocs As SprocsNode
```

```
Public Filename As String
Public IsDirty As Boolean = True
```

The `DbString` field holds the database connection string. The `Tables` field holds a collection of `Table` objects (we'll see more about that in a moment) and the `Sprocs` field holds a reference to the tree node that lets us view the stored procedures in the database (and again, we'll see more of that in a moment).

When the `Project` property of `Main` is set to be an instance of a `Project` class, whether loaded from disk or created from scratch, a new `ProjectNode` object is added to the tree. Those of you who have read Chapter 11 and built the administration tools will recognize the technique of deriving from `System.Windows.Forms.TreeNode` in order to add objects to the TreeView control.

```
' Project property...
Public Property Project() As Project
  Get
    Return _project
  End Get
  Set(ByVal Value As Project)

    ' set the project...
    _project = Value

    ' do the tree...
    treeviewObjects.Nodes.Clear()
    ProjectNode = New ProjectNode(_project, Me)
    treeviewObjects.Nodes.Add(ProjectNode)

    ' update the project view...
    UpdateCaption()

  End Set
End Property
```

The `ProjectNode` class creates new `TablesNode` and `SprocsNode` objects and adds them to its own collection.

```
' Constructor...
Public Sub New(ByVal project As Project, ByVal main As Main)
  MyBase.New(main, project)

  ' update...
  Text = project.Name
  ImageIndex = main.TreeIcon.Database
  SelectedImageIndex = ImageIndex

  ' add the base nodes...
  Nodes.Add(New TablesNode(Me))
  project.Sprocs = New SprocsNode(Me)
  Nodes.Add(project.Sprocs)

  ' expand...
  Expand()

End Sub
```

The `TablesNode` object is responsible for examining the tables, and we'll look at this first.

Scanning the Tables

SQL Server supports direct querying of its system tables through the `INFORMATION_SCHEMA` views. We can use the `INFORMATION_SCHEMA.TABLES` view to return a list of tables in the database. If we look in the constructor for `ProjectNode`, you'll find a call to `CreateDataSet` to execute the query. We can then walk each row checking to see if the table is already registered in the `TablesCollection` object accessible through `Project.Tables`. If it is, we have to flag whether it is a table or a view. We then create a new `TableNode` object to display the table in the TreeView. We'll look a little more at what happens in the `Table` constructor and in the `Load` method in a moment.

```
' Constructor...
Public Sub New(ByVal projectNode As ProjectNode)
  MyBase.New(projectNode)

  ' update...
  Text = "Tables"
  ImageIndex = Main.TreeIcon.Table
  SelectedImageIndex = ImageIndex

  ' get the tables...
  Dim tableSet As DataSet = Project.CreateDataSet("select table_name, " _
            & "table_type from information_schema.tables order by table_name")
  Dim row As DataRow
  For Each row In tableSet.Tables(0).Rows

    ' get it...
    Dim table As Table = Project.Tables.Find(row("table_name"))
    Dim shouldInclude As Boolean = False
    If table Is Nothing Then
      table = New Table(Project, row("table_name"))
      Project.Tables.Add(table)
    Else
      table.Load()
      shouldInclude = True
    End If
    If String.Compare("table_type", "base table", 0) = True Then
      table.Type = table.TableType.Table
    End If
    If String.Compare("table_type", "view", 0) = True Then
      table.Type = table.TableType.View
    End If

    ' create a node...
    Dim node As New TableNode(Me, table)
    Nodes.Add(node)

    ' include?
    table.IncludeInModel = shouldInclude

  Next
```

After that comes the work we have to do to discover the foreign key relationships between the tables. The query we need to run here is a little more complicated than just selecting out a list of tables, but we still use the INFORMATION_SCHEMA views. Specifically, we have to join the INFORMATION_SCHEMA.REFERENTIAL_CONSTRAINTS view with INFORMATION_SCHEMA.CONSTRAINT_COLUMN_USAGE and INFORMATION_SCHEME.KEY_COLUMN_USAGE. This gives us the information we need – in other words we get a definitive list of "this column on this table joins to that column on that table":

```
' also need the relationships...
Dim relationships As DataSet = Project.CreateDataSet("select " _
            & "a.constraint_name, b.table_name as from_table_name, " _
            & "b.column_name as from_column_name, c.table_name as " _
            & "to_table_name, c.column_name as to_column_name from " _
            & "information_schema.referential_constraints a inner join " _
            & "information_schema.constraint_column_usage b on " _
            & "a.constraint_name = b.constraint_name inner join " _
            & "information_schema.key_column_usage c on " _
            & "a.unique_constraint_name = c.constraint_name")
For Each row In relationships.Tables(0).Rows
```

After we have the dataset, we can loop the rows and establish relationships between the relevant columns:

```
' from...
Dim fromTable As Table = Project.Tables.Find(row("from_table_name"))
If Not fromTable Is Nothing Then

  ' column...
  Dim fromColumn As Column = fromTable.Columns.Find(row("from_column_name"))
  If Not fromColumn Is Nothing Then

    ' find the to table...
    Dim toTable As Table = Project.Tables.Find(row("to_table_name"))
    If Not toTable.IdColumn Is Nothing Then

      ' check...
      If String.Compare(toTable.IdColumn.Name, row("to_column_name"), _
                  True) = 0 Then

        ' right, relate these...
        fromColumn.LinksTo = toTable

      End If

    End If

  End If

End If

Next

  ' expand...
```

```
        Expand()

    End Sub
```

The `Table` class is used to hold an instance of a table in a database. It is responsible for looking in the database schema to determine the identity column and a list of the actual columns contained with a table. The `Load` method (called from within the constructor) is responsible for this.

The first thing the `Load` method does is to examine the `INFORMATION_SCHEMA.KEY_COLUMN_USAGE` view to determine which column is the primary key identity column.

```
    Public Sub Load()

        ' what's the identity column?
        Dim isSet As DataSet = Project.CreateDataSet("select column_name from " _
                    & "information_schema.key_column_usage inner join " _
                    & "information_schema.table_constraints on " _
                    & "information_schema.table_constraints.constraint_name = " _
                    & "information_schema.key_column_usage.constraint_name " _
                    & "where information_schema.key_column_usage.table_name='" _
                    & Name & "' and constraint_type='primary key'")
        Dim idColumnName As String
        If isSet.Tables.Count > 0 AndAlso isSet.Tables(0).Rows.Count > 0 Then
            idColumnName = isSet.Tables(0).Rows(0)(0)
        End If
```

Once we've found the name of this column, we then use the `INFORMATION_SCHEMA.COLUMNS` view to retrieve a list of the columns. Per column, we also assign a .NET data type based on the SQL data type of the column. For example, a SQL "int" column is assigned a data type of `System.Int32`.

```
        ' get the columns...
        Columns.Clear()
        Dim columnSet As DataSet = Project.CreateDataSet("select column_name, " _
                    & "is_nullable, data_type, character_maximum_length, " _
                    & "column_default, ordinal_position from " _
                    & " information_schema.columns where table_name='" & Name & "'")
        Dim row As DataRow
        For Each row In columnSet.Tables(0).Rows

            ' create one...
            Dim column As New Column(Me)
            column.Name = row("column_name")
            column.Ordinal = row("ordinal_position") - 1
            If row("is_nullable").ToString.ToLower = "yes" Then
                column.CanBeNull = True
            Else
                column.CanBeNull = False
            End If
            If Not row.IsNull("character_maximum_length") Then
                column.Size = row("character_maximum_length")
            End If
            If Not row.IsNull("column_default") Then
```

```
          column.DefaultValue = row("column_default")
        End If

        ' get the type...
        Select Case row("data_type").ToString.ToLower

          Case "int"
            column.SqlType = SqlDbType.Int
            column.Type = GetType(Int32)
          Case "varchar"
            column.SqlType = SqlDbType.VarChar
            column.Type = GetType(String)
          Case "datetime"
            column.SqlType = SqlDbType.DateTime
            column.Type = GetType(DateTime)
          Case "float"
            column.SqlType = SqlDbType.Float
            column.Type = GetType(Double)
          Case "nvarchar"
            column.SqlType = SqlDbType.NVarChar
            column.Type = GetType(String)
          Case "image"
            column.SqlType = SqlDbType.Image
            column.Type = GetType(SqlBinary)
          Case "smallint"
            column.SqlType = SqlDbType.SmallInt
            column.Type = GetType(Int16)
          Case "tinyint"
            column.SqlType = SqlDbType.TinyInt
            column.Type = GetType(Byte)
          Case "money"
            column.SqlType = SqlDbType.Money
            column.Type = GetType(SqlMoney)
          Case "timestamp"
            column.SqlType = SqlDbType.Timestamp
            column.Type = GetType(SqlBinary)
            column.IsTimestamp = True

          Case Else
            Throw New NotImplementedException()

        End Select

        ' id?
        If String.Compare(column.Name, idColumnName, True) = 0 Then
          column.IsId = True
          column.IdentifierName = "Id"
        End If

        ' add...
        Columns.Add(column)

    Next

End Sub
```

So at this point we have a map of the database stored as a set of objects in the database. The `Project` object contains a set of `Table` objects stored in a `TableCollection`. Each `Table` object contains a set of `Column` objects stored in a `ColumnCollection`. We can use this information to generate the various derived objects we use in our application.

Before we look at this code generation work, let's look at how we handle the stored procedures.

Scanning the Sprocs

Working with the stored procedures is slightly different. We cannot retrieve a list of the stored procedures through the `INFORMATION_SCHEMA` views. Instead, we need to use a SQL Server built-in stored procedure called `sp_stored_procedures`. This returns a list of the stored procedures, which we can walk through. This is done inside the `Refresh` method of `SprocsNode` where we create a new `SprocNode` object per stored procedure and add it to the tree. As we iterate the stored procedures, we check the name to see if it is a built-in SQL Server stored procedure as we want to ignore those. In the code shown here, I've omitted most of the case statements that check for SQL Server names.

```
Public Overrides Sub Refresh()

  Nodes.Clear()

  ' get all the sprocs...
  Dim connection As New SqlConnection(Project.DbString)
  connection.Open()

  ' run the sproc...
  Dim procs As DataSet = Callsp_stored_procedures(connection)
  Dim proc As DataRow
  For Each proc In procs.Tables(0).Rows

    ' issql...
    Dim isSqlServer As Boolean = False
    Select Case proc("procedure_name").ToString.Split(";"c)(0).ToLower
      Case "dt_addtosourcecontrol"
        isSqlServer = True
      Case "dt_addtosourcecontrol_u"
        isSqlServer = True
    ...
    End Select

    ' ignore?
    If isSqlServer = False Then

      ' add a node...
      Dim sprocNode As New SprocNode(ProjectNode, proc)
      Nodes.Add(sprocNode)

    End If

  Next

  ' close...
```

```
        connection.Close()

        ' generate...
        Code = GenerateCode()

    End Sub
```

For now, we'll ignore the `GenerateCode` call at the end, as we'll move onto generating code in a short while.

At this point, all we require is the name of the stored procedure. In fact, `sp_stored_procedures` does not return the actual code of the stored procedure itself. To get the code, we have to do a little extra work. SQL Server provides the stored procedure `sp_help_text`, which despite the odd name does not provide "help text" but rather acts as a helper function to get text blocks back from SQL Server's internal data store.

The `SprocNode` class itself implements a property called `Sql` that calls this stored procedure and obtains the relevant text. Each row in the result set contains a line of text for the stored procedure, so we use a `System.Text.StringBuilder` object to join them all together into a large block.

```
    Public ReadOnly Property Sql() As String
        Get
            If Not _sproc Is Nothing Then
                Return _sproc.Code
            End If
            If _code = "" Then

                ' exec...
                Dim connection As New SqlConnection(Project.DbString)
                connection.Open()

                ' get it...
                Dim lines As DataSet = Callsp_helptext(connection, Me.Text)
                Dim builder As New StringBuilder()
                Dim line As DataRow
                For Each line In lines.Tables(0).Rows
                    builder.Append(line(0))
                Next

                ' close...
                connection.Close()

                ' store...
                _code = builder.ToString()

            End If
            Return _code
        End Get
    End Property
```

Here's an example of a stored procedure shown in the Object Builder:

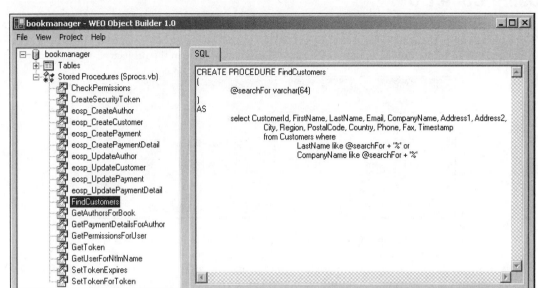

At this point we have a fairly complete set of data. We have the tables, the columns within the tables, foreign key relationships between the columns and the stored procedures. We can now look at how to generate the code itself.

The Code Generator

One of the really cool features of .NET is the work that Microsoft has done with the "Code DOM" ("Code Document Object Model"). Using the Code DOM, applications are able to generate their own code in any managed language with relative ease and simplicity. This code can then be imported into the project for compilation, or can be executed on the fly. Various .NET technologies use the Code DOM. For example, when we add a Web Service reference to our project, VS.NET creates new .cs or .vb files that are automatically included in the project. These files contain classes and methods that abstract communication between our application and the Web Service.

Some .NET technologies create and compile code using the Code DOM. System.Xml.Serialization.XmlSerializer creates assemblies on the fly containing code to serialize and de-serialize types. ASP.NET generates and compiles code to support its own activities.

As you're no doubt aware, our motivation for using Code DOM is to create the classes derived from the various WEO classes that provide our extended interaction with the database.

Using Code DOM

The best way to learn about Code DOM is to see it in action. When the project is first created, none of the tables are set to be included in the project. When we select a table, an instance of the `TableView` control is used to present the option to the user to include the table in the project.

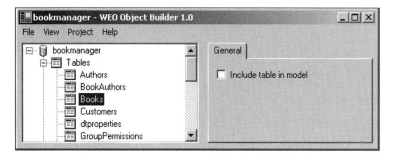

When the user selects this option, the `IncludeInModel` property for the table is set to "true". This has the side effect of calling the `IncludeInModelChanged` method of the related `TableNode` object. This in turn either adds a set of new nodes to the tree, or removes the existing nodes. Each of the new nodes represents a new class that must be generated for inclusion in the object model.

```
' IncludeInModelChanged...
Public Sub IncludeInModelChanged()

    ' are we now included?
    If Nodes.Count = 0 And Table.IncludeInModel = True Then
        Nodes.Add(New EntityBaseCodeNode(Main, Project, Table))
        Nodes.Add(New EntityCodeNode(Main, Project, Table))
        Nodes.Add(New EntitySetBaseCodeNode(Main, Project, Table))
        Nodes.Add(New EntitySetCodeNode(Main, Project, Table))
        Nodes.Add(New EntityBoundCollectionBaseCodeNode(Main, Project, Table))
        Nodes.Add(New EntityBoundCollectionCodeNode(Main, Project, Table))
        Nodes.Add(New ServiceBaseCodeNode(Main, Project, Table))
        Nodes.Add(New ServiceCodeNode(Main, Project, Table))
        Expand()
    End If
    If Nodes.Count > 0 And Table.IncludeInModel = False Then
        Nodes.Clear()
    End If

End Sub
```

Each node added as a child of the `TableNode` would be a new class generated for a specific table that we can access from our project. The naming is pretty easy to understand: `EntityBaseCodeNode` is the class derived directly from `Entity` that we do not add customizations to. `EntityCodeNode` is the class derived from whatever the `EntityBaseCodeNode` is called and is the one that we can add our customizations to.

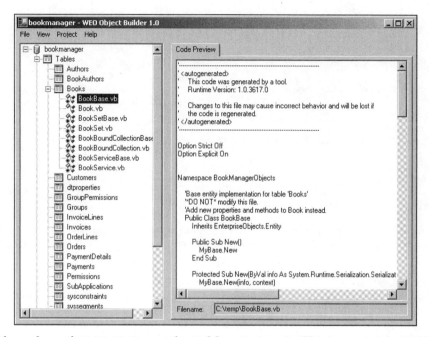

The nodes underneath `TableNode` are inherited from `CodeNode`. This in turn is inherited from `BaseTreeNode`. `CodeNode` understands how to create `CodePreviewView` controls that display the code in the right-hand pane, as shown above. `CodeNode` holds the code that should be saved to disk in a property called `Code`.

How the code actually gets generated is another matter. The `Table` object supports a bundle of methods that uses Code DOM to generate the code. These methods have names like `GenerateEntityBaseCode`, `GenerateServiceCode` and so on.

Code DOM is extremely powerful because it's not tied to a specific language. Although we'll look at specific examples in a moment, the principle is that you use methods to express the "shape" of a type in terms of the methods, properties and fields that the type supports. This is done through a "compile unit" and you can either spit out the source or compile it for execution directly through the code.

Here's the implementation for `GenerateServiceCode`, which is one of the simpler methods. All of the generation methods return a `Code` object, which among other things is able to actually generate the code and return a string containing the code. `GenerateServiceCode` creates a new `Code` object as its first action, passing in the results of the property `ServiceName` and the `Provider` property for the project. The `Provider` tells us which language we want to generate code in, which we'll see in a moment. In addition, `Code` also supports a property called `Type` that returns a `System.CodeDom.CodeTypeDeclaration` object. This object represents a type (or "class") in the Code DOM and it's into this class that we inject the members we require.

```
Public Function GenerateServiceCode() As Code

    ' create...
    Dim code As New Code(ServiceName, Project.Provider)
    Dim type As CodeTypeDeclaration = code.Type
    code.AlwaysGenerate = False
```

```
    code.Filename = Project.CreateFilename(ServiceName)

    ' create...
    type.Comments.Add(New CodeCommentStatement("Service implementation " _
                                 & "for table '" & Name & "'"))
    type.Comments.Add(New CodeCommentStatement("*DO* add your modifications " _
                                 & "to this file"))


    ' inherit...
    type.BaseTypes.Add(New CodeTypeReference(ServiceBaseName))

    ' return...
    Return code

End Function
```

We manipulate the class returned by the new `Code` object by adding comments through the `Comments` collection and we also set the class to inherit from the class whose name is returned through `ServiceBaseName`.

The issue with Code DOM is that because it's language neutral, the compromise that we have to make is that the code becomes pretty horrendous. In the above example, we cannot add the string returned by `ServiceBaseName` directly to the list of base classes. Instead, we have to create a new `System.CodeDom.CodeTypeReference` object and add that. If you look at a more complex method that generates a lot of members, like `GenerateEntityBaseCode`, you'll find that even the most trivial activity is highly complex. For example, here's some code to generate the `GetTimestamp` method on one of the `EntityBase` classes:

```
    ' add a gettimestamp method...
    Dim getTimestamp As New CodeMemberMethod()
    getTimestamp.Name = "GetTimestamp"
    getTimestamp.Attributes = MemberAttributes.Public Or MemberAttributes.Final
    getTimestamp.Statements.Add(New CodeMethodReturnStatement(New _
                               CodePropertyReferenceExpression(New _
                               CodeThisReferenceExpression(), _
                               TimestampColumn.Name)))
    getTimestamp.ReturnType = New CodeTypeReference(GetType(SqlBinary))
    type.Members.Add(getTimestamp)
```

...and here's the final code:

```
    Public Function GetTimestamp() As System.Data.SqlTypes.SqlBinary

        Return Me.Timestamp
    End Function
```

For this reason, I'm not going to attempt to present the code here as we'll end up filling an entire book just with code samples!

The resulting code above is, of course, in VB.NET. To create this, we used the `Microsoft.VisualBasic.VBCodeProvider` class. As its name implies, this provider class is used to generate VB.NET code. The Object Builder can also generate C# code by using the `Microsoft.CSharp.CSharpCodeProvider` class. Although the Builder is designed to work with just these languages, in theory it's possible to plug in alternate languages by using a different provider.

The Builder abstracts access to these classes through the `BuilderProvider` class. An instance of this class is accessible through the `Provider` property of the `Project` class, and you'll notice that in the listing for `GenerateServiceCode` above it's this that we pass as the second parameter to the constructor for `Code`. `Code` uses this provider when `Generate` is called to create the actual code listing. Before we do that, however, we need to create a compile unit. This is simply a matter of instantiating a new `System.CodeDom.CodeCompileUnit`, which is done through the `Code.CreateCompileUnit` method. Then, we call the `ICodeGenerator`'s `GenerateCodeFromCompileUnit` method to actually spit the code.

Here's the implementation for the two versions of `Code.Generate`. The first uses the provider class to create an object supporting `ICodeGenerator` and the second actually spits the code.

```
' Generate - generate some code...
Public Function Generate() As String

    ' create...
    Dim generator As ICodeGenerator = provider.provider.CreateGenerator()

    ' run...
    Dim codeString As String = Generate(generator)

    ' return...
    Return codeString

End Function

Public Function Generate(ByVal generator As ICodeGenerator) As String

    ' stream...
    Dim stream As New MemoryStream()
    Dim writer As New StreamWriter(stream)

    ' compile...
    Dim unit As CodeCompileUnit = CreateCompileUnit()

    ' run it...
    generator.GenerateCodeFromCompileUnit(unit, writer, CreateOptions())

    ' reset...
    writer.Flush()
    stream.Seek(0, SeekOrigin.Begin)
    Dim reader As New StreamReader(stream)
    Dim codeString As String = reader.ReadToEnd()
    stream.Close()

    ' return...
    Return codeString

End Function
```

By default, `CodeNode`-derived classes tell `Main` to show an instance of `CodePreviewView` to display the code. When one of these nodes is selected, the `NodeSelect` event is fired and it's at this point that a new `CodePreviewNode` is instantiated and configured with the `Code` object that the derived class created. When it's time to display the code, `CodePreviewNode` calls the `Generate` method to get a string back for presentation.

Synchronizing the Project

The Object Builder allows the user to review the code that will be generated before project synchronization. In this section we'll take a quick look at the synchronization process.

The project is synchronized through a call to `Project.Synchronize`. This creates a new `SyncProgress` form that reports back to the user on how synchronization is going. This method also uses the thread pool to spin up a new thread, and it's in this thread that the actual synchronization work is done.

The entry point for the thread, `SynchronizationEntryPoint` looks like this:

```
Private Sub SynchronizationEntryPoint(ByVal syncWindow As Object)

    ' set...
    Dim sync As SyncProgress = CType(syncWindow, SyncProgress)
    sync.AddToLog("Started")

    ' tables...
    Dim table As Table
    For Each table In Tables

        ' gen?
        If table.IncludeInModel = True Then

            ' do it...
            sync.AddToLog("Working with '" & table.Name & "'")

            ' first...
            SpitCode(table.GenerateEntityCode(), sync)
            SpitCode(table.GenerateEntityBaseCode(), sync)
            SpitCode(table.GenerateEntitySetCode(), sync)
            SpitCode(table.GenerateEntitySetBaseCode(), sync)
            SpitCode(table.GenerateBoundCollectionCode(), sync)
            SpitCode(table.GenerateBoundCollectionBaseCode(), sync)
            SpitCode(table.GenerateServiceCode(), sync)
            SpitCode(table.GenerateServiceBaseCode(), sync)

            ' do the sproc...
            If table.InsertCapable = True Then
                SpitSproc(table.GenerateCreateSproc(), sync)
            End If
            If table.UpdateCapable = True Then
                SpitSproc(table.GenerateUpdateSproc(), sync)
            End If

        End If

    Next

    ' do the sprocs...
    SpitCode(Sprocs.GenerateCode(), sync)

    ' finish...
```

```
       sync.AddToLog("Finished")

    End Sub
```

In this method we're using `SpitCode` to generate the classes and `SpitSproc` to recreate the stored procedure code. It's worth noting that the stored procedures are always deleted and re-created per synchronization. As you already know, not all of the classes are recreated per synchronization. Some are and some are not – specifically the classes that the developer can add his or her own customizations to are *never* deleted. In this case, the class is generated only if the file does not already exist. The base classes are recreated each time. Whether or not a file (as we have one class per file, we can think of them as files) is recreated is determined by the `AlwaysGenerate` member of the `Code` object.

`SpitCode` uses the `WillGenerate` property of the `Code` object to make this determination, and if the code should be generated, `Write` is called to save the code listing to disk.

```
    Private Sub SpitCode(ByVal code As Code, ByVal sync As SyncProgress)

        ' do it?
        If code.WillGenerate = True Then

            ' create the file...
            sync.AddToLog("Writing '" & code.Filename & "'")
            code.Write()

        End If

    End Sub
```

`SpitSproc` works in a very similar way. `SpitSproc` relies on a `Sproc` object being available that contains the stored procedure code. As stored procedures are always expressed in T-SQL, we don't need to get into the Code DOM here, so the `Sproc` class as returned by `Table.GenerateCreateSproc` and `Table.GenerateUpdateSproc` simply holds a block of SQL. `Sproc` also supports a method called `UpdateDb` that drops and re-creates the stored procedure itself.

```
    Private Sub SpitSproc(ByVal sproc As Sproc, ByVal sync As SyncProgress)
        sproc.UpdateDb(sync)
    End Sub
```

Here's the listing for `UpdateDb`:

```
    Public Sub UpdateDb(ByVal sync As SyncProgress)

        ' connect...
        Dim connection As New SqlConnection(Project.DbString)
        connection.Open()

        ' drop it...
        sync.AddToLog("Dropping " & Name & "...")
        Dim drop As New SqlCommand("drop procedure " & Name, connection)
        Try
            drop.ExecuteNonQuery()
```

```
        Catch
        End Try
        drop.Dispose()

        ' create...
        sync.AddToLog("Creating " & Name & "...")
        Dim create As New SqlCommand(Code, connection)
        create.ExecuteNonQuery()
        create.Dispose()

        ' connection...
        connection.Close()

    End Sub
```

Object Builder Class Reference

In this section, I'll present a run-down of the classes used by Object Builder.

"BaseTreeNode"

This class, inherited from `System.Windows.Forms.TreeNode`, is the base class from which all of the tree node display classes are inherited. In a similar method to that described in Chapter 11, this class implements a method called `OnSelect` that is called by `Main` whenever the node is selected. However, rather than inheriting directly from this, this method raises the `NodeSelect` method. Inheriting classes respond to this event.

In addition to this, the class supports `Main` and `Project` methods that allow reference back to the UI and to the `Project` object. It also supports a `Refresh` method that can be overridden by the nodes so that when the user selects the **Refresh** option, the data behind the node can be updated. This is particularly useful for the stored procedure list where the developer may add new stored procedures to the database while the project is open for editing.

"BuilderProvider"

This class encapsulates the `System.CodeDom.CodeDomProvider` object that can generate the code. The constructor of this class accepts a file type and from this file type (either ".vb" or ".cs") creates a `Microsoft.VisualBasic.VBCodeProvider` or `Microsoft.CSharp.CSharpCodeProvider` instance.

This class also controls its own serialization. When the `Project` instance is serialized to disk, the `CodeDomProvider` instance is not serialized. Instead, the relevant `Type` object is serialized and upon de-serialization, an instance of this class is created.

In addition, the class holds the name of the root namespace for the generated classes, which is first established when the project is created.

"Caser"

This class contains a single method called `ToCamel`. This method takes a string and "camel cases" it – it turns the first character into a lower-case character and preserves the Pascal casing on the remainder of the string. For example, it turns "`ThisIsAnIdentifier`" into "`thisIsAnIdentifier`".

"Code"

This class represents, in essence, a class that should be generated by the Object Builder. This class was discussed in detail in an earlier section of this appendix.

"CodeNode"

This class, derived from `BaseTreeNode`, encapsulates the action of displaying a `CodePreviewView` control for those nodes that represent classes generated during project synchronization.

It does this by defining a property called `Code` that is populated by the deriving class and creating a handler for the `NodeSelect` method. This handler creates a new instance of `CodePreviewView` and passes it back to `Main` for display.

"CodePreviewView"

This class inherited from `UserControl` presents the filename and code text of a `Code` object to the user. The two `TextBox` controls are populated when the `Code` property is set.

"Column"

This class represents a column in a table. Although it's largely a container for metrics about the column, it also contains a method called `GeneratePropertyCode`, which generates the Code DOM property code for inclusion into the relevant entity base class.

Here's a list of the properties:

- ❑   `Table Table` – holds a reference back to the containing table.
- ❑   `string Name` – holds the name of the column.
- ❑   `string Identifier` – holds the name of the variables used in code to access the column.
- ❑   `int Ordinal` – holds the position of the column in the table.
- ❑   `bool CanBeNull` – indicates whether the column can hold a null value.
- ❑   `SqlDbType SqlType` – holds the SQL data type.
- ❑   `Type Type` – holds the .NET data type.
- ❑   `int Size` – holds the size of the column.
- ❑   `string DefaultValue` – holds the default value of the column.
- ❑   `bool IsId` – indicates whether the column is the ID column.

❑   bool IsTimestamp – indicates whether the column is the timestamp column.

❑   Table LinksTo – holds a reference to the primary key that this foreign key column matches (if any).

"ColumnCollection"

This class – derived from System.Collections.CollectionBase – holds a list of Column objects.

"Connect"

This Windows Form allows the user to connect to a database but also allows the user to provide the folder name of the new project and define the namespace.

"Main"

This form contains the main UI objects for the Object Builder. This includes a TreeView control to show the database tables, generated classes and the stored procedure and a TabView control that is used by the nodes to present other UI objects to the user.

"Pane"

This class represents an instance of a Control object and a name object used by Main to add panes to the TabView control to allow the user to view the underlying data of the node and manipulate data.

"PaneCollection"

This class, inherited from CollectionBase, maintains a collection of Pane objects.

"Project"

This class contains a representation of the project, including the database map. We discuss this class in detail in an earlier section of this appendix.

"ProjectNode"

This class, inherited from BaseTreeNode, represents the project in the tree. It is also responsible for adding new instances of TablesNode and SprocsNode to the tree.

"ProvideEntityName"

This form is used to prompt the user for the name of the entity given the name of a table. It uses a pretty unsophisticated algorithm to come up with the entity name: if the table name ends in "s" or "es" it is assumed to be a plural and it's clipped from the end of the string.

"Splash"

This form is used when the application first starts to prompt whether the user wants to create a new project or load an existing one. This form is created and shown by `Main` when the application first starts.

"Sproc"

This class is similar to `Code` in that it contains a block of code. As this code is always T-SQL, there's no need to do anything with Code DOM. The code for the stored procedure is built up using the `Add` method and stored in an internal member called `_sql`.

This class can also update the database through the `UpdateDb` method. This method first drops and then re-creates the stored procedure code.

"SprocNode"

This class, inherited from `BaseTreeNode`, represents an instance of a stored procedure in the database. It uses SQL Server's `sp_helptext` stored procedure to get the T-SQL from the database and uses an instance of `SprocSqlView` to display it.

"SprocParam"

The stored procedure parser uses this class to keep track of discovered parameters in the T-SQL code.

"SprocParamCollection"

This class, inherited from `CollectionBase`, maintains a collection of `SprocParam` objects.

"SprocSqlView"

This user control is similar to `CodePreviewView`. However, this class uses the `Sproc` property to take a `SprocNode` instance and uses its `Sql` property to get the code for display.

"SyncProgress"

This form displays a simple TextBox to report the status of project synchronization. New messages are added through the `Add` method.

"Table"

This class represents an instance of a table in a database. It contains a bundle of methods for generating the actual class code – in fact, most of the Code DOM generation code appears in this class.

Here's a list of the properties:

- ❏ `Project Project` – holds a reference back to the project.
- ❏ `string Name` – holds the name of the table.
- ❏ `string EntityName` – holds the entity name for the table (for example "Book" compared to "Books").
- ❏ `TableNode Node` – holds a reference to the node on the tree that represents the table.
- ❏ `TableType Type` – indicates whether the table is a legitimate table or a view.
- ❏ `ColumnCollection Columns` – holds a list of the columns that this table has.
- ❏ `bool IncludeInModel` – indicates whether or not classes should be generated for this table, in other words whether or not it is "in the model".
- ❏ `ColumnCollection LinkedFrom` – holds a list of the columns that have a foreign key relationship to this table.

"TableCollection"

This class – inherited from `System.Collections.CollectionBase` – maintains a list of `Table` objects.

"TableNode"

This class, derived from `BaseTreeNode`, represents an instance of the table in the database. It is responsible for asking `Main` to display a `TableView` object for the table, and if the table is included in the model, it's responsible for adding the child nodes for each of the generated classes.

"TablesNode"

This class, derived from `BaseTreeNode`, is a container node that contains all of the tables known by `Project`. In fact, this node is responsible for scanning the table list as discussed earlier in this appendix.

"TableView"

This user control displays a single check box that allows the user to indicate whether the table should be included in the model or not. When the check box is selected, an instance of `ProvideEntityName` is created and used to prompt the user for an appropriate entity name.

.NET Enterprise Development in VB .NET

Index

A Guide to the Index

The index is arranged hierarchically, in alphabetical order, with symbols preceding the letter A. Most second-level entries and many third-level entries also occur as first-level entries. This is to ensure that users will find the information they require however they choose to search for it.

The ~ character is used to reduce the need to duplicate almost identical entries (e.g. AllowPaging/~CustomerPaging property means AllowPaging/AllowCustomerPaging property).

W

WriteExceptionToXML method
exception reporting, 393
WriteLine methods
debugging, 402
Wrox Enterprise Objects *see* WEO.
Wrox support, 5
WTLS (Wireless Transport Layer Security), 258

X

XML document
converting to database, 142
loading into Visual Studio, 144
typical XML order document, 142
VS.NET view, 146

WEO Object Builder utility, 151
XML Schema
Generate Dataset menu option, 147
OrderLoader application, 146
XmlSerializer class, System.Xml.Serialization
Code DOM usage, 419
XmlTextWriter class, System.Xml
serializing exceptions example, 393

Z

Zone object, System.Security.Policy
code access security example, 319

449

Notes

Notes

Notes

Notes

Notes

Notes

Notes

wrox

Programmer to Programmer™

Wrox writes books for you. Any suggestions, or ideas about how you want information given in your ideal book will be studied by our team. Your comments are always valued at Wrox.

Free phone in USA 800-USE-WROX
Fax (312) 893 8001

UK Tel.: (0121) 687 4100   Fax: (0121) 687 4101

.NET Enterprise Development in VB .NET – Registration Card

Name _____

Address _____

_____

_____

City _____ State/Region _____

Country _____ Postcode/Zip_____

E-Mail _____

Occupation _____

How did you hear about this book?

❏ Book review (name) _____

❏ Advertisement (name) _____

❏ Recommendation _____

❏ Catalog _____

❏ Other _____

Where did you buy this book?

❏ Bookstore (name) _____ City_____

❏ Computer store (name) _____

❏ Mail order_____

❏ Other _____

What influenced you in the purchase of this book?

❏ Cover Design ❏ Contents ❏ Other (please specify):

_____

How did you rate the overall content of this book?

❏ Excellent ❏ Good ❏ Average ❏ Poor

What did you find most useful about this book? _____

_____

What did you find least useful about this book? _____

_____

Please add any additional comments. _____

_____

_____

What other subjects will you buy a computer book on soon?

_____

What is the best computer book you have used this year?

_____

wrox

Programmer to Programmer™

Note: If you post the bounce back card below in the UK, please send it to:

Wrox Press Limited, Arden House, 1102 Warwick Road,
Acocks Green, Birmingham B27 6HB. UK.

Computer Book Publishers